Likkutei Dibburim

An Anthology of Talks by
Rabbi Yosef Yitzchak Schneersohn
of Lubavitch

Vol. 1

Second Edition
with Supplements and Indexes

Likkutei Dibburim

לקוטי דיבורים

•

An Anthology of Talks by
Rabbi Yosef Yitzchak Schneersohn
of Lubavitch

זצוקללה"ה נבג"מ זי"ע

Vol. 1

Second Edition
with Supplements and Indexes

•

Translated and Annotated by
Uri Kaploun

Published and Copyrighted by
"KEHOT" PUBLICATION SOCIETY
770 Eastern Parkway, Brooklyn, N.Y. 11213

5773 • 2012

LIKKUTEI DIBBURIM
Volume 1

Published and Copyrighted by
"KEHOT" PUBLICATION SOCIETY
770 Eastern Parkway, Brooklyn, N.Y. 11213
Tel. (718) 493-9250 • (718) 774-4000 • (718) 778-5436
Printed in the U.S.A.

Second Edition, with Supplements and Indexes
5773 • 2012

Library of Congress Cataloging-in-Publication Data

Schneersohn, Joseph Isaac, 1880-1950
Likkutei dibburim = [Likute diburim]
Translation of: Likute diburim.
Includes bibliographical references and indexes.
1. Hasidism. 2. Habad. 3. Fasts and feasts--Judaism--Meditations.
I. Title. II. Title: Likute diburim.
BM198.S32313   1987   296.8'33
ISBN 978-0-8266-0443-9 (set)
    978-0-8266-0444-6 (vol. 1)
LCC#87-16846

Table of Contents

Likkutei Dibburim

Publisher's Preface to the First Edition

Sixty years ago today the author of this work — the Previous Lubavitcher Rebbe, Rabbi Yosef Yitzchak Schneersohn נ"ע — was released in miraculous circumstances from incarceration, torture and capital sentence in the notorious Spalerka prison in Petersburg, today's Leningrad. (Indeed, the Rebbe's own graphic description of his imprisonment and liberation, and his reflections thereon, constitute a dominant theme of one of the later volumes in this series.) The date of that historic release was *Yud-Beis* Tammuz, 5687 (תרפ"ז; 1927).

It is therefore with a keen sense of gratitude to the Almighty that we now celebrate this date by publishing the first volume of the English translation of his *Likkutei Dibburim*. This series is an anthology of the Rebbe's talks ranging over the years 1929-1950, and first delivered in Latvia, Poland and the United States.

This unique work — by turns expository, philosophical, narrative and nostalgic, a cherished treasure-chest of the *Chabad-*chassidic heritage — was translated and annotated by Uri Kaploun, and prepared for publication by Rabbi Yonah Avtzon, director of Sichos In English. It is one of several works of the Previous Rebbe appearing in translation by various hands under the auspices of the undersigned publishing house, which itself was founded by him.

Kehot Publication Society

Yud-Beis Tammuz, 5747 (1987)

Publisher's Preface to the Present Edition of Vol. I

Eight-five years ago, on *Yud-Beis* Tammuz, 5687 (תרפ"ז; 1927), as noted above, the author of this work — the Previous Lubavitcher Rebbe, Rabbi Yosef Yitzchak Schneersohn נ"ע — was released from capital sentence in Petersburg. The present classic, *Likkutei Dibburim*, is an anthology of many of the teachings and experiences that he shared after he was finally enabled to leave Stalin's Russia.

Since this English-language series began to appear in 5747 (1987), individual volumes were repeatedly reprinted according to need, and we are now happy to publish this **Second Edition, with Supplements and Indexes,** which introduces the reader for the first time to Volume VI. Its original documents, written by the Previous Rebbe and by some of his contemporaries, appear here for the first time in English. They throw new light on the unbelievably perilous circumstances under which he and his undaunted chassidim defied pitiless brethren and a ruthless regime, and graphically describe his incarceration and liberation.

Volume VI also provides supplementary background resources (as detailed in its Table of Contents) for the entire set, including a **Biographical Index,** an **Index of Placenames** and a **Subject Index.**

Kehot Publication Society

Rosh Chodesh Kislev, 5773 (2012)

ב"ה

Translator's Introduction

The talks appearing in *Likkutei Dibburim* were delivered by the late Lubavitcher Rebbe, R. Yosef Yitzchak Schneersohn ע"נ (1880-1950), in the course of the years 1929-1950 — in Latvia, Poland and the United States. In point of fact these "Collected Talks" as published are not exactly a record of the talks as delivered. The usual procedure was that at some time after a public address the Rebbe would select and amplify certain seminal themes, clothing them meanwhile in a literary garb more suited to their appearance in print. One of the inner circle of chassidim would then prepare them for publication (usually in chronological order), put them hastily through the press, and promptly distribute them among the chassidim free of charge, for it was their voluntary contributions that had covered the cost of publication.

* * *

Our Sages teach us that "no two prophets prophesy in the same style" (Tractate *Sanhedrin* 89a). And indeed, the reader is struck at once by the very different nature of a *farbrengen* in those years. For one thing, because of the circumstances of time and place, the attendance at those gatherings was relatively small. The style of delivery is accordingly familiar, and includes answers to questions posed by elder chassidim who were present at the time.

Furthermore, the audience to which the Rebbe R. Yosef Yitzchak addressed himself was varied in the extreme. On the one hand it comprised Torah scholars of worldwide repute. Rubbing shoulders with them, in characteristically chassidic camaraderie, stood men of goodwill — nay, men of *mesirus nefesh* — who were perhaps without a great deal of book-learning. For this was a generation that under the tyranny of the Old World had been battered by accustomed adversity, and in the freedom of the New World was to be confronted by unaccustomed prosperity. Hence, perhaps on account of the very diverse composition of his audience, the style of presentation favored by the Rebbe Rayatz is often deceptively simplistic. For the most part he spurns the formality of a learned quotation couched in technical terms, preferring a homely paraphrase, a pointed parable, or a heartwarming anecdote. But

ix

whatever his message may lose thereby in the smoke of impressiveness, it gains in the fire of its impact.

The reader's imagination is overwhelmed by the sheer *range* of this work, both in subject and in atmosphere. For these talks embrace (for example) childhood memories; insightful stories; the family traditions of a family of *tzaddikim;* recollections of Stalinist dungeons and interrogations; nostalgic glimpses of faces and sounds and townlets that conjure up the mystique of a vanished world; delicately-drawn vignettes of exalted villagers and humble giants; eloquent and sometimes impassioned passages of exhortation; fascinating chronicles of the early history of the chassidic movement, treasured heirlooms that are lovingly passed on; and, of course, creative and instructive expositions of concepts crucial to the teachings of *Chassidus.* But one theme links all of these subjects like a thread of gold — the intense spiritual and personal bond with all his fellow Jews, that is of the essence of the very concept of Rebbe.

"When one hears a story of a good deed from one's Rebbe," the *Tzemach Tzedek* once said, "one becomes bound to the Rebbe's faculty of action; when one hears a Torah discussion from one's Rebbe, one becomes united with his faculty of speech; when one listens to one's Rebbe singing a *niggun,* one cleaves to his faculty of thought. The bond with one's Rebbe thus exists on the levels corresponding to each of the three names for the soul — *nefesh, ruach, neshamah.*"

And this is the sensation experienced by the reader who follows *Likkutei Dibburim* along all the manifold paths mapped out above.

Not that the journey is always smoothly predictable. From time to time the reader will discover that the Rebbe has unexpectedly forsaken the beaten road and is suddenly leading us along some charming but seemingly irrelevant byway, as if unable to resist the claims of a mere digression. A moment's patience — and after a paragraph or two we find ourselves with equal suddenness back on the familiar highway. Yet another moment — and in a flash of illumination the relevance of the detour finally becomes apparent: we now have a refreshingly new frame of reference, a new lamp to light up the road before us.

In this, the technique of the Rebbe Rayatz echoes the manner in which his illustrious forebear, the Alter Rebbe, once provided solutions for all the scholarly problems bothering the rabbinic academicians of Shklov. Instead of confronting his listeners with exposition and argumentation, the Alter Rebbe *lent them perception:* he sang a sublime melody — and thereby elevated them to a spiritual perspective from which all their seeming contradictions vanished.

In harmony with this teaching technique, the literary style and arrangement of the present work are quite unlike the ordered, logical, expository style to which the chassidim of another generation are more accustomed. Indeed, the style of *Likkutei Dibburim* is typically that of an Impressionist artist, luminous and evocative — except that the beauty portrayed here is not the mere prettiness of color and light that bewitches the physical eye, but the exalted beauty of spiritual perception that enraptures the eye of the soul.

* * *

This distinctive texture of course makes translation a daring and delicate task — the more so, since the author of these talks, finding the existing linguistic resources inadequate for his purpose, on occasion even coins words, exploiting the delicious versatility of Yiddish to the utmost. For the original text is written in a unique blend of the Holy Tongue and Yiddish. Within one resonant paragraph, even within one and the same sentence, the two languages either alternate solo, or sing in unison, or harmonize with each other.

Tackling a work of this nature, and of this stature, the translator is repeatedly reminded of the parable that a gifted teacher once told the local *chazzan* on the eve of the Days of Awe.

"As you stand at your lectern," he said, "the envoy of your congregation, charged with the weighty responsibility of ushering their New Year's supplications to their heavenly destination, consider yourself to be a muleteer. Men to whom you are answerable have entrusted you with the task of transporting a cargo of the most precious and fragile crystalware over a treacherous mountain path. Any slip on your part can be calamitous."

Embarking on his anxious way, the undersigned muleteer was fortunately able to depend on the services of an expert navigator — the director of Sichos In English, Rabbi Yonah Avtzon, whose familiarity with the pitfalls and byways of publishing helped guide the cherished manuscript along the tortuous path leading to its ultimate destination.

* * *

The translation throughout has gained in precision from the numerous explanations and definitions suggested by my learned brother-in-law, R. Yitzchak Ginsburgh (author of סוד ה' ליראיו), of Kfar Chabad. Moreover, the translator's footnotes have been enriched by the incorporation of his insightful cross references. In addition, the translation benefited inconspicuously from the wide-ranging expertise of a number of willing consultants — including (alphabetically) R. Tuvia Blau, R. Chanoch Glitzenstein, R. Shmuel Greisman, R. Yehoshua Mondshine, R. Avraham Baruch Pevsner, R. Nota Pinski, R. Yonah Slapochnik, and R. Joseph Wineberg; likewise, conspicuously, from the pioneering labors of the translators of the respective parts of *Tanya* — R. Nissan Mindel, R. Nissen Mangel, R. Zalman I. Posner and R. Jacob I. Schochet; and so too, from the historical erudition of R. Shalom Ber Levin, librarian of the Rebbe שליט"א, and editor of *Igros Kodesh,* the annotated letters of the Lubavitcher Rebbes of the respective generations. Finally, in ascertaining all manner of details, the translator is indebted to numerous elderly chassidim שי' who grew up in the midst of the very people, places and incidents that figure in this work.

Certain passages from *Likkutei Dibburim* were borrowed by HaRav Zevin ז"ל in his *Sippurei Chassidim: Moadim,* a classic which appeared, in slightly adapted form, in my English translation under the title, *A Treasury of Chassidic Stories on the Festivals,* published by Mesorah Publications of New York and Hillel Press of Jerusalem.

*   *   *

The Rebbe R. Yosef Yitzchak נ"ע, the author of these talks, is present with us here and now. On *Yud-Beis* Tammuz 5745 (תשמ"ה; 1985) the Rebbe שליט"א spoke of this, pointing out that the very *farbrengen* he was then addressing was attended by numerous chassidim who in their active involvement today in Torah and *mitzvos* are the direct fruits — or the fruits of the fruits — of the self-sacrifice of the Rebbe R. Yosef Yitzchak. For this was a *tzaddik* who in the teeth of Stalinist persecution devoted his life and risked his life for the teaching of Torah to even very small children.

The Rebbe R. Yosef Yitzchak, said the Rebbe שליט"א, inspired his disciples to the point of *mesirus nefesh,* literal self-sacrifice: "He lived in their midst, and he gave them life." And since in the language of the Torah "sons" often signifies "disciples" (see *Rashi* on *Devarim* 6:7), one may well apply to the Rebbe R. Yosef Yitzchak and to his disciples the statement of our Sages (concerning Yaakov Avinu):

מַה זַרְעוֹ בַּחַיִּים אַף הוּא בַּחַיִּים — "Just as his offspring are alive, so is he too alive" (Tractate *Taanis* 5b). The Rebbe שליט״א explained: "When one sees that 'his offspring are alive,' this is certain proof that 'he too is alive' — *for he is the life-force of his offspring.*"

* * *

Since their arrival in Australia in 1948-1949, one select band of these offspring have been so much alive that they have breathed life into the farflung Jewish communities of an entire continent. They themselves had barely caught their breath in postwar Displaced Persons camps, after having been hounded all their lives by the NKVD in Moscow and Leningrad. Now, however, when lesser men might understandably think it was time for a well-deserved retirement, they asked the Rebbe R. Yosef Yitzchak for their marching orders, and promptly set out for an obscure Australian outback township called Shepparton. This tiny community, with its miniscule weatherboard *shul,* was the cradle of today's vast and multifaceted *Chabad*-Lubavitch educational network in Australia, for it was the home of my revered grandfather, Reb Moishe Zalman Feiglin ע״ה. For many years this solitary, noble chassid had been urged by the warm and visionary letters of the Rebbe R. Yosef Yitzchak to bring these families from the other end of the world, in order to patiently and lovingly change the face of Australian Jewry. And this they have certainly done (even literally...). Over the years, moreover, the dynamic emissaries of the Rebbe שליט״א have refuelled and buttressed the mighty lighthouse raised by the founding fathers.

Out of respect and gratitude, this translation is dedicated to that original stalwart band of emissaries[1] to Shepparton, and later to Melbourne —

R. Bezalel Wilschansky and his Rebbitzin
R. Shmuel Althaus and his Rebbitzin
R. Nachum Zalman Gurewicz and his Rebbitzin
R. Issar Kluwgant and his Rebbitzin
R. Abba Pliskin and his Rebbitzin
R. Zalman Serebryanski and his Rebbitzin

— for in their private and public lives, these men and women furnished living models of the ideal that was envisaged by the

Rebbe R. Yosef Yitzchak, the author of the present work, when he
spoke of what constitutes an authentically *chassidisher Yid.*

Uri Kaploun

Jerusalem, ‏עיר הקודש ת״ו‎
9 Adar[2] 5747 (‏תשמ״ז‎; 1987)

1. In order of arrival.

2. By a visible stroke of Providence (‏מִגַּלְגְּלִין זְכוּת לְיוֹם זַכַּאי‎), this translation of the first
volume of the message of the Rebbe R. Yosef Yitzchak into the language of the New
World was completed on 9 Adar — the anniversary of the very day on which its
saintly author ‏ז״יע‎ landed in New York in 1940.

Prefatory Notes

1. *Supplementary Material:* Each English volume in this series carries its own footnotes, sources and glossary. The miscellaneous talks and letters that were appended to the original Hebrew/Yiddish volumes all appear, chronologically, in Volume V. A number of unique documents, which were written by the Rebbe Rayatz and by other contemporary hands but did not appear in the Hebrew/Yiddish volumes as originally published, now appear in English, for the first time, in Volume VI.

That volume also provides supplementary background resources for the entire set, including: a **Biographical Index,** an **Index of Placenames** and a **Subject Index;** a map; a biographical outline of the author; a partial family tree of the author's forebears; and a chronological listing of all the talks and letters that appear in all six volumes, with page references.

2. *Sources:* As a rule, quotations and paraphrases have been traced for the *Tanach, Talmud, Midrash, Rambam,* and various other classical primary sources. References to the literature of *Chassidus,* however, except for a few major and readily-accessible sources, have not been given: they would be virtually endless.

3. *Brief Titles:* For the sake of convenience, several frequently recurring titles have been given short forms of reference, as follows:

HaTamim: Kovetz HaTamim (Kehot, Kfar Chabad, 1971)

Igros Kodesh: Volumes of letters of the respective Rebbes, edited and annotated by R. Shalom Ber Levin (Kehot, N.Y.)

Kehot: Kehot Publication Society (770 Eastern Parkway, Brooklyn, N.Y., 11213)

Machzor for Rosh HaShanah: The prayer book, translated by R. Nissen Mangel (Merkos, N.Y., 1983)

Machzor for Yom Kippur: Ibid.

Merkos: Merkos L'Inyonei Chinuch; publishing house (770 Eastern Parkway, Brooklyn, N.Y., 11213)

Siddur: Siddur Tehillat HaShem with English Translation, Annotated Edition: the prayer book, translated by R. Nissen Mangel (Merkos, N.Y., 2002)

Siddur of the Alter Rebbe: *Seder Tefillos MiKol HaShanah* (Kehot, N.Y.)

Tanya: Bi-lingual edition of *Likkutei-Amarim–Tanya* (Kehot, London, 1973); or *Lessons In Tanya* by R. Yosef Wineberg (Kehot, N.Y.)

4. *Punctuation:* In keeping with the traditions of rabbinic literature, the text in the original employs a minimal system of punctuation far less formal than what the English reader is accustomed to. This of course increases the possibility of differing interpretations.

5. *Indented Passages:* Descriptive and connecting passages interpolated by the editor of these talks when they were first published appear here indented. Additions or summaries by the translator are indicated by square brackets [].

6. *Footnotes:* The translations of the footnotes added in the original text are asterisked. Below them appear the sources and notes added by the translator; these are keyed by catchphrases.

7. *"Chapter":* This term corresponds to *Likkut* in the original; i.e., one of the scores of booklets published in different times and places that together constitute *Likkutei Dibburim.*

8. *Crossreferences:* In the present **Second Edition, with Supplements and Indexes,** the internal crossreferences throughout all the volumes have been streamlined.

9. *The Title "R.":* This may be pronounced casually as "Reb," or more formally as "Rabbi" (i.e., *HaRav*), as appropriate.

U.K.

Chapter 1

At Evening Seudah of Shemini Atzeres 5693 (תרצ״ג; 1932)
In the Sukkah
[Riga]

1.

"Thinking is potent." Not only is thought the first and innermost of the three garments or *levushim* of the soul, and united with it: thinking produces results that extend into the realm of action. Concentrating on a good thought concerning another is in itself an act — though it is an act only in the context of the world of thought. It still needs to pass through the succeeding stages of speech and practical action.

At this point the subject turned to the members of the chassidic brotherhood who were then in Russia, and some of the past and present *yeshivah* students *(temimim)* and older chassidim *(Anash)* were mentioned by name.

The Rebbe proceeded: "Thought knows no bounds; no partition can stand in its way; at all times it reaches its required destination."

One of those present, who had recently reached Riga from Russia, then asked: "But what benefit does the other party have from that?"

"He benefits in rich measure," replied the Rebbe.

Riga: After his release from imprisonment and capital sentence in Leningrad on *Yud-Beis* Tammuz 5687 (תרפ״ז; 1927), the Rebbe Rayatz had settled in Riga, then the capital of Latvia ("Lettland"), on Isru Chag HaSukkos 5688 (תרפ״ח; 1927). There he lived for almost six years. Most of his chassidim, however, were still in Russia.

Thinking is potent: In the original, מַחֲשָׁבָה מוֹעֶלֶת (Tractate *Sanhedrin* 26b) — though there the phrase is used in a negative sense.

The Rebbe: I.e., the Rebbe Rayatz.

One of those present: R. Mordechai Dov Teleshevsky.

1

After a long pause the Rebbe turned to the questioner: "And where were *you* last Sukkos...?"

On Simchas Torah Evening

2.

It is known and certain that thinking bears fruit. As everyone knows from his own experience, thinking is a starting-point for action, which comes into being after a certain progression from one spiritual level to the next.

Our Sages teach us that "the measure in which blessing is given is greater than the measure of punishment." The word for measure — *middah* — also signifies garment, as in the verse which says, "And Aharon shall put on his garment of linen," or: "And Shaul clothed David in his garments." The "measure of punishment" *(middas purannus)* thus means "garments that bring punishment." This refers to evil thoughts and imaginings [since thought, as mentioned above, is the first of the three *levushim* or "garments" of the soul]. For these not only diminish the divine image in man, but undermine and even (G-d forbid) destroy one's physical health.

But "the measure in which blessing is given is greater than the measure of punishment." This "measure of goodness" *(middah tovah)* refers to those "garments" of the soul that elicit good; in general, these are thoughts of Torah, and of divine service — meditation in prayer. In regard to Torah thoughts, this does not mean merely thinking about Torah subjects, but the kind of profound contemplation that arouses one to practical action.

In relation to one's fellow, thinking is likewise potent.

And where were *you:* It was the custom of the Rebbe of each generation to bring each of his chassidim to mind at certain times. (See *HaYom Yom,* entry for 14 Shevat.)

The measure in which blessing: In the original, מִדָּה טוֹבָה מְרוּבָּה מִמִּדַּת פּוּרְעָנוּת (Tractate *Sotah* 11a).

And Aharon shall put on: *Lev.* 6:3.

And Shaul clothed David: *I Sam.* 17:38.

With a thought one can help another — especially since a concentrated thought is a basis for action.

3.

In a letter to R. Dov Ber, the Maggid of Mezritch, dated *erev* Sukkos 5521 (תקכ״א; 1760), R. Pinchas of Korets writes: "Many thanks for having called me to mind on Yom Kippur. You should know that at the very moment I was privileged to be thus remembered, I felt it here."

Now this incident needs to be understood at its innermost level, for if viewed superficially it involves no remarkable spiritual achievement at all.

Love is manifested at many levels, and the modes of conduct which are the "vessels" through which the light of love is revealed are patterned in harmony with the various levels of this light.

The first level among the "vessels" or vehicles of love is extending one's hand in offering or receiving the greeting of *Shalom*. This is only an external mannerism, to be sure; for around the whole world whenever people meet they shake hands as a mark of recognition which need not imply any feeling of love whatever. In truth, however, this very superficiality has been brought about by today's worldly coolness.

In days gone by the ordinary *Shalom Aleichem* was different: it was true, and pure. Things used to be different: truth used to be sound currency. Coins too come in various denominations — you have a *tzveier*, a *pitak*, a ruble and so on — but a true little *tzveier* was worth its true value.

Because people themselves were true, their everyday *Shalom Aleichem* and *Aleichem Shalom* were true; because people themselves were warm, their ordinary midweek *Shalom Aleichem* and *Aleichem Shalom* were warm; and when two Jews met, their *Shalom Aleichem* and *Aleichem Shalom* sprang from the life within.

The current acceptance of worldly notions has indeed introduced a certain order into the conduct of people's lives — but with it a certain frigidity, a certain absence of truth, and occasionally a lie. In today's ordinary greeting of *Shalom Alei-*

chem one can sometimes, or even often, detect a "Go in good health." But the Torah-inspired *Shalom Aleichem* — the *Shalom Aleichem* of bygone days — is a vehicle for the light of love.

When two friends meet and kiss each other one sees the manifestation of a greater light of love than that expressed in a handshake. A yet higher manifestation may be observed in the long conversation in which good friends love to tell each other of all their experiences.

Beyond this there is a kind of love so intense that words are too dry to express it: two friends in this state can simply stand and gaze at each other without uttering a word.

These, then, are various ways in which friends express their love, the bond which brings them to oneness.

But there is also an inward bond, a bond of thought, through which one friend senses the other. Just as a person sees his friend who stands facing him near at hand, so it is with thought, which is not limited by distance. Through thought alone one man is aware of this friend, just as the friends of Iyov (Job) felt his plight despite their distance from him. Speaking in terms of the various levels in the soul of man, their sensitivity belongs to the realm of *middos* — feelings, and attributes of character — for they were men of refined character; it cannot be placed in the realm of intellect.

True indeed, this sensitivity indicates beauty of *middos* — attributes of the kind which characterize the level of man. But they are after all *middos,* and *middos* exist as well in the animal kingdom; it thus follows that even the beauty of *middos* does not yet represent the ultimate standard of perfection of the spiritual level which is the exclusive province of man. A magnate, by way of analogy, might build his animals a magnificent stable — but it is still a stable; so too *middos,* be they ever so beautiful, do not yet represent the ultimate perfection of man's exalted state.

Friends of Iyov: *Job* 2:11. The *Gemara* (Tractate *Bava Basra* 16b) cites two opinions as to how they all knew of his plight despite their great distance from him and each other.

If, therefore, we take the incident superficially, there is nothing wondrous about the fact that despite the physical distance between them, R. Pinchas of Korets was aware of the moment at which the Maggid of Mezritch had called him to mind. It must be obvious that my intention here is not (G-d forbid) to belittle the value of the incident. Quite the contrary: because our limited minds cannot plumb the depths of the holy words of these *tzaddikim*, we are obligated to endeavor to comprehend each word in an orderly manner. And by approaching the story by this means we can learn that this point marks the revelation of the path which the Alter Rebbe was later to pave and follow — namely, the teaching that through thought a person should be with his friend wherever he may be. This is the meaning of the above statement that a concentrated thought is a starting-point for action, that with a thought one can help a distant friend materially and spiritually.

And this is the point of R. Pinchas's letter. What is remarkable is not that R. Pinchas was aware of the Maggid's thought: what is remarkable is that by calling him to mind the Maggid accomplished an actual deed — for with a thought one can indeed help a distant friend reach a higher state of being, both materially and spiritually.

4.

From every letter of Torah and prayer a good angel is created. During the Days of Awe — Rosh HaShanah and Yom Kippur — some 17 million Jews pray, read *Tehillim*, study Torah, and do good deeds, and from all these activities angels are created. This sets up a tumult in heaven, as vast hosts of angels arrive there — a troop of angels from each country, where they were created from the prayers of ardent worshipers as they cried out קָדוֹשׁ אַתָּה — 'Holy are You ...''; — וּבְכֵן תֵּן פַּחְדְּךָ "Instill fear of You upon all that You have made ...''; וְתִמְלוֹךְ —

Holy are You (and succeeding phrases): From the *Amidah* of Rosh Ha-Shanah and Yom Kippur. (See *Siddur*, p. 270ff.)

"You will reign..."; מְלוֹךְ עַל הָעוֹלָם כֻּלּוֹ — "Reign over the entire world..."; וּנְתַנֶּה תּוֹקֶף — "We shall express the might..."; and so on, throughout the prayers of the Days of Awe.

Now these exclamations of "Holy are You" and "You will reign" vary from country to country, according to the state of affairs in each region. Those proceeding from Russia cause a great stir, for they are an outcry of physical suffering and spiritual anguish.

But then comes the time of the joyful angels of Simchas Torah, the angels created by the exultant verses of *Atah hareisa* — and now the angels from Russia occupy pride of place. For now, forlorn in his dark house, sits a hungry Jew; his wife and children are famished and broken in spirit; his heart weeps for his lot and for theirs; he almost despairs (G-d forbid) that things could ever improve. But suddenly he remembers that today is Simchas Torah. A gleaming ray of rollicking memories strikes his whole being like a lightning bolt. His spirits are raised. He runs off to the local *beis midrash* for *Hakkafos* and leaps into the circle of dancers. *"Elokei haruchos, hoshiah na,"* he cries out, "G-d of all spirits, deliver us; examiner of hearts, grant us success; mighty Redeemer, answer us on the day we call!" And he grasps the wooden handle of a nearby *Sefer* Torah and sings at the top of his voice: *"Sisu vesimchu beSimchas Torah* — Rejoice and exult on Simchas Torah!"

Men of this kind are envied not only by all the angels of heaven, but even by the loftiest souls — the souls of *tzaddikim,* souls connected with all their brethren, souls whose abode is the supernal World of *Atzilus;* they too envy this self-sacrificing *mesirus nefesh,* the pure innocence of this simple faith. Such a *mesirus-nefesh* Jew is cherished and held sacred in all the Worlds. Together with such Jews we should now proceed to *Hakkafos* — and it is clear and certain that "thought is potent."

Atah hareisa: Biblical readings introducing the *Hakkafos.* (Ibid., p. 335.)

Elokei haruchos: From the readings which accompany the *Hakkafos.*

Sisu vesimchu: From the liturgy of Simchas Torah. (Ibid., p. 338.)

May the Almighty accept everyone's requests, and the prayers which seek to arouse His compassion; may He soon free those people (and us as well) from suffering, so that they will be able to observe the Torah and the *mitzvos* at their heart's ease. And if the exile as ordained requires that things should be (G-d forbid) as they have been until now, let the Almighty send down angels. Then we will see what benefit we will have from them — just as they have shown in other days when they have come down to This World.

5.

On Rosh HaShanah 5650 (תר"ן; 1889) my father delivered the chassidic discourse which begins with the words הַיּוֹם הֲרַת עוֹלָם ("Today the world was born"), and which appears in the course of the *maamar* beginning *Tik'u* of that year. On that occasion, [alluding to the similarity between *haras* and *reses*, meaning trembling,] my father expounded the above phrase to mean "Today the world trembles." He resumed this theme a few weeks later, after *Kiddush* on Simchas Torah. *Kiddush* used to be recited at the home of my grandmother — *Rebbitzin* Rivkah, the wife of the Rebbe Maharash — and this would be the occasion for a *farbrengen*. He now added: "On the eve of Rosh HaShanah the world is like someone who feels faint,

---

Send down angels: Evidently an allusion to the fallen angels of *Gen.* 6:4; they descended to This World, and succumbed to temptation. (See *Targum Yonasan* there, and *Rashi* on Tractate *Yoma* 67b, *s.v.* עוּזָא וַעֲזָאֵל. See also *Farbrengen* of *Parshas Ki Seitzei*, 14 Elul, תשמ"ה; 5745).

My father: I.e., the Rebbe Rashab.

Hayom haras olam: From the prayer following the sounding of the *shofar* on Rosh HaShanah. (See *Machzor*, p. 152.)

Expounded...to mean...trembles: Based on the interpretation of ראב"ן (a *Rishon*), as quoted in *Maaseh Oreg*, a commentary in the *Me'or Einayim* edition of the *Machzor*.

The world...shudders...calms down: This recalls the discussion of the *Gemara* (Tractate *Shabbos* 88a) on the verse, מִשָּׁמַיִם הִשְׁמַעְתָּ דִּין אֶרֶץ יָרְאָה וְשָׁקָטָה — "You caused judgment (i.e., the Torah) to be heard from heaven; the earth feared, and was still" *(Ps. 76:9).*

and who shudders in anxiety while waiting for his life-force to be restored to him. On Simchas Torah, when the blessing *Shehecheyanu* is recited over the renewed reading of the Torah, the world calms down."

6.

In the year 5648 (תרמ"ח; 1888) my father was elected *gabbai* of the *chevrah kaddisha* in Lubavitch, and according to the custom of the time he was conducted to the synagogue with a canopy spread out overhead. Arriving there he stood at the lectern and delivered a *maamar* which opened with the Talmudic phrase, אֵין הַקָּדוֹשׁ בָּרוּךְ הוּא בָּא בִּטְרוּנְיָא — "The Almighty does not confront His creatures with unfair demands." A central theme in this discourse is the contrast between intellectuals (*baalei mochin*) and men of simple faith (*anashim peshutim*) with regard to divine service. Whenever there is a call to duty in the Torah-observant community the unsophisticated believer is ready to act, without spiritual preparations and introductions. If, for example, a new Torah school is needed, it is he who contributes the first *tzveier:* devotedness to the point of self-sacrifice is no difficult thing for him. An intellectual by contrast thinks, then thinks again — and in the end intellect does not grant its consent to the superrational, self-sacrificing demands of *mesirus nefesh*.

A relative of ours once lived in Lubavitch, a grandson and namesake of my grandfather's great-uncle R. Chaim Avraham, the son of the Alter Rebbe. For a time he lived in Moscow for business reasons, so he was known as Avraham Moskver. He was a man of sound understanding, a *bar daas,*

Shehecheyanu...of the Torah: The blessing pronounced the previous evening in honor of the festival refers also to the renewed reading of the Torah. (See *Siddur*, p. 251.)

Elected *gabbai*: The Rebbe Rashab was then 27 years of age.

The Almighty does not confront: Tractate *Avodah Zarah* 3a.

Contributes the first *tzveier:* See *Rashi* on *Deut.* 33:18.

but a *maskil* — one whose approach to divine service has intellectualization as its starting point. His observance of the *mitzvos* in practice was impeccable: it was only that he had a certain way of thinking things over, and occupied his mind with philosophical speculation, *chakirah.*

My father once said to him: "Avraham, repent! And do your *teshuvah* like a man of simple faith, like an *ish pashut,* without the artful antics of the speculative mind."

My father then explained to him at length the subject of the above-mentioned *maamar,* and went on as follows: "If, G-d forbid, you don't, then whether in a year's time I do not know, but in two years' time he will be in the World of Truth."

My father did not say "he": he addressed him directly in the second person; but I do not want to say such things in the second person.

My father continued: "Whether where you will be situated will be a World of Truth,* I do not know."

One of those present asked the Rebbe what came of this encounter. The Rebbe replied: "R. Avraham confirmed by a handshake that he would do as he was instructed. It seems however that he did not fulfill his undertaking, for within the next two years he traveled to America, and immediately after his arrival his wife was left widowed and his children fatherless. News of this reached home, and my father was most grieved."

7.

The Rebbe resumed a topic on which he had spoken

---

* This refers [only] to the period of judgment, *before* the time of reward [which everyone ultimately reaches].

A *maskil*: Some hold that the definition offered in the above text (i.e., as in chassidic usage) is too charitable, and that the term here bluntly signifies an adherent of the Haskalah, the so-called "Enlightenment" movement.

A certain way of thinking things over: In the understated Heb. original, הָיָה חוֹשֵׁב מַחֲשָׁבוֹת. Some hold likewise that this phrase means that the person in question entertained thoughts alien to a Torah worldview.

Without the artful antics...mind: In the Heb./Yid. original, *on chakirah-chochmes.*

the previous day, Shemini Atzeres, in the *maamar**
beginning with the words, בְּיוֹם הַשְּׁמִינִי שְׁלַח. In the course of
that discourse he had elaborated on the words from *Shir
HaShirim*, שְׁלָחַיִךְ פַּרְדֵּס רִמּוֹנִים. In their literal meaning, according to *Rashi*, these words mean, "Your arid areas (hence,
'the least worthy among you') are an orchard of pomegranates." In this verse the Rebbe perceived an
instruction.

We Jews are obliged to make an "orchard" out of these
"pomegranates". The rind of a pomegranate, its *kelippah*, is
tough; what is of value is its inner content, its *toch*. It is in this
sense that the pomegranate figures in the Talmudic metaphor depicting the attitude of R. Meir to his teacher who had
strayed from the path: תּוֹכוֹ אָכַל קְלִפָּתוֹ זָרַק — "Its inner content he
ate, its rind he discarded." And just as the pomegranate has its
pnimiyus and *chitzoniyus*, its inner content and its outward
aspect, so too do we find this duality at all spiritual levels,
even in the realm of the black silk frockcoat of the most pious
of folk. The same duality is to be found at lower levels likewise. And from all of these one is obliged to make a *pardess*.

In order to illustrate the bitter regret of the Egyptians
after the Exodus, the *Midrash* presents the parable of a man
who owned a stretch of wasteland which was marred by a
mound of stones, and sold it. The purchaser cleared the
rubble, dug a well, and planted trees — olive trees and grape-
vines; and they were irrigated by the waters of the well until
his plot was transformed into a lush grove. Passing by one day
the-former owner wailed: "Woe unto me, for this is what I
sold!"

This, then, is our task: out of these very pomegranates to

---

* *Sefer HaMaamarim (Kuntreisim)*, Vol. I, Kuntreis 21, p. 507-8.

Bayom hashemini shilach: 1 Kings 8:66.
Shlachayich pardess rimonim: Song of Songs 4:13.
Its inner content: Tractate *Chagigah* 15b.
Parable of a man: *Shemos Rabbah* 20:5.

make a lush orchard — to speak to a fellow Jew and to persuade him to put on *tefillin*, to wear *tzitzis*. And even though on the next day he may perhaps not perform these *mitzvos*, today's *mitzvah* is nevertheless a thing of value. Take even the case of a well-to-do family who keep up the customs of their father for appearance' sake. The local *rav* sends them an *esrog* as a gift; then since there is now an *esrog* at hand, the house-holder will take it up together with a *lulav* and give it a shake. And this too is of value.

In whatever direction one can involve a fellow Jew in a positive activity, to reinvigorate his *inner* essence, in that direction should one exert oneself. This should be done only through *kiruv*, bringing him close to the *mitzvos* in a spirit of friendliness. One must however keep in mind that this *kiruv* requires caution: such friendship must be kept within limits. For just as one man exerts an influence on his friend, so in turn does his friend exert an influence on him. This is a process that passes through various stages. At first one feels compassion for the other. This gives rise to a *limud zechus:* one seeks ways of justifying the other's conduct. And this is as it should be: one should indeed seek such ways. The person who is the object of this thought, however, must not know of it. The place where this *limud zechus* belongs is within oneself, when with tears from the heart one reads a passage of *Tehillim* for another's sake, through its words requesting the Almighty to have pity on him. *This* is *ahavas Yisrael,* the love of a fellow Jew, which each Jew should practice toward his good friend — in the meantime being wary of excessive companionship, until with the Almighty's help the friend is properly set up in an upright manner so that one may and should seek his companionship.

In the Torah we read: לֹא תִשְׂנָא אֶת אָחִיךָ בִּלְבָבֶךָ, הוֹכֵחַ תּוֹכִיחַ אֶת עֲמִיתֶךָ וְלֹא תִשָּׂא עָלָיו חֵטְא —"You shall not hate your brother in your heart; you shall repeatedly rebuke your friend, and not bear sin because of him." On the one hand, then, there is the

---

You shall not hate: *Lev.* 19:17.

requirement of the verse, תַּכְלִית שִׂנְאָה שְׂנֵאתִים — "I hate them (the heretics) with the utmost hatred." *At the same time*, however, we are commanded, "You shall not hate your brother in your heart." (The meaning of this verse will be understood by reference to the commentary of *Ramban*.) And this is how one should speak to a fellow Jew about putting on *tefillin* in the morning, or saying the afternoon *Minchah* prayer. For there are those who draw distinctions between the morning prayer of *Shacharis*, and *Minchah*. Such a person needs to have it explained to him that in the ten minutes that *Minchah* takes he will not forfeit his livelihood. And if he does not understand this now, he will understand it in his 121st year... Then he will be grateful that someone persuaded him to *daven*, and the like; *then* he will be happy that he took notice.

8.

In the writings of the Mitteler Rebbe, R. Dov Ber, one occasionally finds the expression, וּבְדֶרֶךְ צָחוּת יֵשׁ לוֹמַר — "In lighter vein one might interpret as follows..." In our subject too, one might expound the verse שְׁלָחַיִךְ פַּרְדֵס רִמּוֹנִים in this spirit, for שְׁלָחַיִךְ reading שְׁלוּחַיִךְ, "your emissaries" — the emissaries of the House of Israel in the various communal institutions, whose duty it is to make an "orchard" out of "pomegranates", through the strengthening of Torah study and of the observance of Judaism. And may the Almighty grant them His help.

9.

The *Mishnah* uses the expression, הַתּוֹרָה נִקְנֵית — "The Torah

---

I hate...with the utmost hatred: *Ps.* 139:22.

At the same time: See the discussion of this paradox in *Tanya*, end of Ch. 32. This discussion is in turn explained by the Rebbe שליט״א in: Rabbi Yehoshua Korf, *Likkutei Biurim BeSefer HaTanya* (N.Y., 1968), p. 160.

Commentary of *Ramban:* Candid remonstration with one's friend over his apparent misconduct averts such concealed hatred.

In his 121st year: The traditional lifespan being 120 years (cf. *Gen.* 6:3).

is acquired." That is to say, the Torah must become an acquisition within the soul, a *kinyan banefesh.*

R. Yehoshua Zeitlin* once asked the Alter Rebbe: "What
is the situation in your camp with regard to Torah study?"

The Alter Rebbe replied that the working men, who were
not professional scholars, all had fixed times for the study of
the Torah.

"But the same is true of us!" protested the learned opponent of the new movement. "So what have you innovated
with the path of *Chassidus?*"

"I have already shown you a great deal of what has been
innovated through the path of *Chassidus,*" replied the Alter
Rebbe, "and more I will yet show you. As to the present
question, the innovation is that whereas with your people the
study of the Torah is *fixed in time,* the teachings of *Chassidus*
require in addition that the study of the Torah be *fixed in one's
soul.*"

10.

In earlier days the *maamarim* discussed matters of *avodah,*
divine service, with explanations given according to *haskalah,*
the theoretical dimension of chassidic teaching. With my
father — who "rose and took the measure of the earth" until
the coming of *Mashiach,* with regard to the divine light which
is to be drawn down into This World — the *maamarim* were all
on the plane of *haskalah,* while questions of *avodah* he discussed
with individuals, at *yechidus.* Now, however, explanations concerning *avodah* need to be given in public.

---

* One of the *geonim* of Shklov, and one of the three outstanding Torah
scholars chosen by the *misnagdim* to debate the path of Chassidism with the
Alter Rebbe.

The Torah is acquired: Tractate *Avos* 6:6. In fact the whole chapter
  is called קִנְיַן תּוֹרָה — "the acquisition of the Torah."
Fixed in time: In the original, קְבִיעוּת בִּזְמַן; cf. Tractate *Avos* 1:15.
Fixed in one's soul: In the original, קְבִיעוּת בַּנֶּפֶשׁ.
Rose and took: Cf. *Hab.* 3:6.

11.

In the *maamarim* of my father one often encounters the expression, לְהַרְגִּישׁ עִנְיָן הָאֱלֹקִי — "to experience a divine insight"; or, לְהַרְגִּישׁ עֶצֶם עִנְיָן הָאֱלֹקִי — "to experience the essence of a divine insight." It is exactly this that one takes the liberty of demanding in others, and of aspiring to.

12.

Thought has a drawback: removing oneself from a thought requires activity. Thus R. Zeira, for example, undertook one hundred fasts in order to forget the Babylonian *Talmud,* to which the Sages apply the verse, בַּמַחֲשַׁכִּים הוֹשִׁיבַנִי — "He caused me to dwell in dark places." This R. Zeira did even though he was yet to return to his study of it — but in order to reach the spiritual level of the *Talmud Yerushalmi* he was obliged to undertake a hundred fasts.

13.

My father used to say that fulfilling the commandment, וְאָהַבְתָּ לְרֵעֲךָ כָּמוֹךָ — "Love your neighbor as yourself," is a vessel or a means to fulfilling the commandment, וְאָהַבְתָּ אֵת ה' אֱלֹקֶיךָ — "Love the L-rd your G-d."

Every Jew needs to constantly arouse himself to the performance of this *mitzvah* of *ahavas Yisrael* — to love a fellow Jew, which is indeed to love the Almighty. This means having

---

Thus R. Zeira: When leaving Babylonia for *Eretz Yisrael,* in preparation for the less argumentative mode of study favored by the *Talmud Yerushalmi;* cf. Tractate *Bava Metzia* 85a.

He caused me to dwell: *Lam.* 3:6.

Love your neighbor: *Lev.* 19:18.

A vessel or a means: In the original, כְּלִי.

Love the L-rd: *Deut.* 6:5.

Love your neighbor...Love the L-rd: This saying of the Rebbe Rashab is based on a teaching of the Baal Shem Tov — that "Love your neighbor as yourself" is an elucidation of "Love the L-rd your G-d," for by loving the innermost essence of a fellow Jew, viz., the divine spark within him (see *Tanya,* Ch. 2), one automatically loves G-d, the Source of that soul. (See *HaYom Yom,* entry for 12 Menachem Av.)

good friends, and exerting oneself for them both physically and spiritually — not fulfilling one's obligations in a general way, as if one could discharge one's duty by merely meditating on the subject of *ahavas Yisrael*. Rather, the *mitzvah* requires doing tangible deeds, having numerous friends and acquaintances, keeping oneself close to the Torah and to *avodah,* and bringing them likewise close to the Torah and to *avodah,* each according to his capacity.

At this point the Rebbe said: "We will proceed with *Hakkafos* together with the *mesirus-nefesh* Jews, and together with Jews the world over."

He then rose and gave his blessing for children, health and sustenance, in the following words: "Jews everywhere should have children. As to those whose hearts have not yet been made happy, may the Almighty gladden their hearts this year. Jews everywhere should be healthy. As to those who need to be healed, may the Almighty grant them a recovery this year. Jews everywhere need a livelihood. As to those for whom this is still lacking, may the Almighty this year give them sustenance."

The Rebbe and all those assembled then began *Hakkafos.*

14.

In the course of the announcement of the verses of *Atah hareisa* which the Rebbe was soon to be honored with reciting,* one of the chassidim who participated in

---

* [It is customary before *Hakkafos* for congregants to "buy" the verses comprising *Atah hareisa* as they are "auctioned" one by one, i.e., to bid for the privilege of reciting a particular verse aloud, in exchange for the promise of a contribution to a charitable cause.] The custom of Lubavitch is to extend this "auction" to include as well, by means of written proxy, those chassidim who are absent or overseas; the Rebbe is then honored with the reading of all the verses. The contributions are forwarded in due course to the Tomchei Temimim Yeshivah which is under his auspices.

Children, health and sustenance: In the original Aram., בְּנֵי חַיֵּי וּמְזוֹנֵי; cf. Tractate *Moed Katan* 28a.

the bidding was a respected householder known for his active support of the Yeshivah in Riga. The verse he "bought" was, וִיהִי נָא אֲמָרֵינוּ לְרָצוֹן לִפְנֵי אֲדוֹן כֹּל — "May our words find favor before the Master of all things."

Before reciting this verse, the Rebbe said: "There are various verses in the Torah which have two versions, a *kri* and a *ksiv* — the way they are to be pronounced, and the way they are written.

"Today is Simchas Torah, the Rejoicing of the Torah. *Today the Torah rejoices.*

"The sentence as written says, אֲמָרֵינוּ — 'our words.' That is the *ksiv*. But the practical consequence of the verse should accord with its inner intention, which is, וִיהִי נָא פְּעוּלוֹתֵינוּ לְרָצוֹן — 'May our *deeds* find favor.'

"The dissemination of Torah is a matter of actual deeds, things which need to be done. Not merely talked about, but done. May the Almighty grant that the students should grow up to be G-d-fearing men — chassidim, and that those who work in this field be blessed both materially and spiritually."

15.

At the beginning of the evening meal of Simchas Torah the Rebbe took the piece of bread over which he had pronounced the blessing *HaMotzi* and dipped it in salt. There was also honey on the table, according to the custom. After he had eaten the piece of bread the Rebbe said: "On Shemini Atzeres and Simchas Torah honey is not needed, because all things (i.e., the heavenly blessings) are already prepared above. But if there is honey on the table, one can dip the *HaMotzi* in honey."

16.

The order of the passages in the Torah is also Torah, and a guide to *avodah* as well.

May our words: Strictly speaking, this is not a verse; in fact it is the only one of the readings comprising *Atah hareisa* that is not of Scriptural origin.

In *Parshas Pinchas,* a passage in which all the festivals appear, the last-mentioned *Yom-Tov* is Shemini Atzeres. As to the concluding verse, ...וַיֹּאמֶר מֹשֶׁה אֶל בְּנֵי יִשְׂרָאֵל — "And Moshe told the Children of Israel according to all that G-d had commanded Moshe," it could be said that this refers to Simchas Torah. The passage on the festivals is followed by the passage on *nedarim,* vows, and this in turn is followed by the episode of the battle with Midian.

After Shemini Atzeres the stage of *avodah* next required is that represented by *nedarim.* In this context the Torah uses the expression אִישׁ כִּי יִדֹּר נֶדֶר — "If a man (*ish*) should make a vow." Unlike the laws of *negaim,* diseases, where the word used for "man" is *adam,* the word used here is *ish;* this refers to the level of *middos,* character attributes or emotions, for *nedarim* in general have to do with *middos.*

In the paths of *avodah* everything should find its place in an organized fashion. Now every kind of order demands time. But even before any such plan gets into motion, one should see to it that in the most dispensable of material things, *No* should take precedence over *Yes.* This is a general principle in *avodah* — that in all material things one should wherever possible refrain.

After this stage of *avodah* with one's *middos* comes the battle of Midian. This name is etymologically connected with *medanim,* which means disputing or contending — in this case, contending in the cause of holiness. That is to say that even *middos* of holiness need to have bounds. How does one come

---

Last-mentioned *Yom-Tov: Num.* 29:35-38.

And Moshe told: *Num.* 30:1.

This refers to Simchas Torah: I.e., the additional day observed only in the Diaspora.

Passage on *nedarim: Num.* 30:2-17.

Episode of the battle: *Num.* 31:1-54.

If a man: *Num.* 30:3.

Laws of *negaim: Lev.* 13:2.

Midian...disputing: See the series of *maamarim* by the Rebbe Rashab entitled הֶחָלְצוּ, Ch. 5.

out of this battle victorious? Through אֶלֶף לַמַּטֶּה. For "elef lamateh" — the thousand (elef) from each tribe (mateh) conscripted by Moshe Rabbeinu to do battle with Midian — read "alef lamateh." Alef, the first letter of the alphabet, represents the primary intellectual faculty of chochmah; the word mateh stands for middos. The phrase alef lamateh thus stands for hamshachas mochin bamiddos — the task of drawing down alef, the intellectual level of the soul, lamateh, into the level of the middos, in order that it should influence them.

In general terms, then, the order of the stages in avodah is as follows. Shemini Atzeres is the time of klitah — literally "absorption", hence "conceiving". In order that this "conception" should give rise to a sound "pregnancy" and an easy "birth", Shemini Atzeres is followed by Simchas Torah, the time when the recipient rejoices. The next stage, as mentioned above, is the avodah which corresponds to the next passage in the Torah, that which sets out the laws of nedarim; and this labor of controlling and refining the middos is followed in turn by the stage of avodah represented by the battle of Midian, namely, the avodah of bringing intellectual guidance to bear on the middos.

As for a thorough comprehension of this subject, this can only be secured by studying the lengthy expositions to be found in the teachings of Chassidus.

17.

Simchas Torah, and the concluding Ne'ilah service of Yom Kippur, are times which are equal for all. True, they vary according to the essence of each person — but they are nonetheless equal. Simchas Torah and Ne'ilah are times of the revelation of the innermost level of the soul, the yechidah

---

Elef lamateh: Num. 31:4.
Alef...represents...chochmah: In fact the very name of the letter alef stems from the verb meaning "to teach," which appears together with the word chochmah in the phrase, וַאֲאַלֶּפְךָ חָכְמָה — "And I shall teach you wisdom" (Job 33:33).

shebanefesh; the *yechidah* is then in a state of arousal. On Simchas Torah *all* Jews have an *aliyah* to the Torah — all Jews *ascend* to the Torah.

At the Kiddush and Daytime Seudah of Simchas Torah

18.

Yesterday I promised to tell a story (and don't ask me for details about it because I will only tell what I have been allowed to). And my intention in recounting this story is that something of essential value should result from it.

The celebrated chassid by the name of R. Shmuel Ber of Borisov spent the festival of Simchas Torah in the year 5614 (תרי"ד; 1853) in Lubavitch. Now the house of the Rebbe at the time, the *Tzemach Tzedek,* stood on the spot later occupied by the large study hall of the Tomchei Temimim Yeshivah, and in the same courtyard there stood another house in which lived his son, [later to be known as] the Rebbe Maharash. One day this chassid fell asleep in the *minyan* that was held next to the study of the Rebbe, the *Tzemach Tzedek.* He woke up suddenly and heard the Rebbe going to the house of his son R. Shmuel and telling him to accompany him, because his grandfather [R. Shneur Zalman of Liadi, the Alter Rebbe, who had passed away some forty years before] had promised him that he would teach him a *mishnah* from Tractate *Sukkah* just as it is studied in the Lower Garden of Eden. The father and son entered the room of the *Tzemach Tzedek,* and the chassid in the next room overheard the beginning of the *mishnah* together with its explanation — and fell asleep.

The next day the *Tzemach Tzedek* said to him: "If one overhears what one shouldn't one is liable to get a flick — children who grow up to be ignoramuses."

Throughout his life R. Shmuel Ber revealed nothing of

Get a flick: Metaphor borrowed from the reprimand once given by a
teacher to bring his wayward pupil to task.

this incident, until he felt his end drawing near, and then he recounted it to my father.

19.

A person entered while the Rebbe was speaking, upon which the Rebbe said that his entry was a revelation of his thought.

"Today," said the Rebbe, "I thought of you a great deal" — and mentioned the person's name and the name of his mother.

20.

A *niggun* was sung, but hurriedly, and on this the Rebbe commented.

A situation like this arose on *Yud-Tes* Kislev 5663 (תרס"ג; 1902). At the time my father said: "When one is involved in one matter and hastens to another, this is a case of 'one thing in the mouth and another in the heart' (this being the classic Hebrew idiom for hypocrisy). *And who permitted that?"*

21.

The Rebbe resumed the subject of thought — one of its distinctive merits being that in thought one can be in two places at once; and another being that in thought, souls *(neshamos)* can serve as emissaries for salvation. For in general, all missions which are related to the material world are carried out by angels, while missions carried out by souls involve only the clarification of matters of Torah study and of *avodah,* the service of the Creator. (Eliyahu the Prophet alone is assigned to both kinds of mission, in that he is also an angel, as is known.) But a mission of salvation through the means of *thought* can be carried out by a soul as well.

22.

In *Shir HaShirim* there appear the words, וְנֹזְלִים מִן לְבָנוֹן — "And running waters from Lebanon." The Hebrew word לְבָנוֹן

And running waters: *Song of Songs* 4:15.

comprises two clusters of letters: ל"ב— נו"ן. The numerical value of the letters ל"ב totals 32, in reference to the Thirty-two Paths of *Chochmah* (Wisdom); the value of the letter *nun* is 50, in reference to the Fifty Gates of *Binah* (Understanding). The verse thus intimates that from *chochmah* and *binah* which are in *etzem haneshamah*, the essential being of the soul which remains Above, there is a constant flow into the *he'aras haneshamah*, the reflection of the soul which is clothed in the body.

For this we have two abstract explanations. The first is *ko'ach hamaskil*, the superconscious source of the intellect, which is in a state of constant cognition. This source does not exist only when perception reaches a state of conscious revelation: it is constantly in a state of revelation in itself, and only when a person exerts his intellectual powers does it become conscious in them as revealed intellect. This insight then becomes refined and organized through the intellectual faculties of *Chabad* (acronym for *chochmah*, *binah* and *daas*), and especially through *hisbonenus*, profound contemplation, which is *iyun*, study.

The second explanation, or analogy, is the power of growth latent in the earth, which is constantly in readiness to function, waiting for the seed from a particular kernel to be sown.

23.

The Baal Shem Tov revealed — and his disciples, our Rebbes, explained and amplified his teaching — that it is within the reach of every single Jew, through cleaving *(dveikus)* to the letters of the Torah and of prayer, to transform צָרָה into צֹהַר.

The Thirty-two Paths of *Chochmah*: In the original, ל"ב נְתִיבוֹת הַחָכְמָה.

The Fifty Gates of *Binah*: In the original נ' שַׁעֲרֵי בִּינָה.

Hisbonenus...which is *iyun*: Compare the definition of *hisbonenus* of the Mitteler Rebbe at the beginning of his *Kuntreis HaHisbonenus* (or *Shaar HaYichud*).

To transform: The same three letters which spell צָרָה, meaning tribulation, when transposed produce צֹהַר, a window admitting illumination.

24.

The Rebbe asked that a *niggun* be sung, and
instructed one of those present to conduct the singing
"like a *melamed* who points the place with his finger." He
then proceeded to explain to him what kind of person a
chassidisher melamed should be.

The function of a *chassidisher melamed* is to bring light into a
household, to make the household luminous, without a great
deal of ingenious philosophizing *(chakiros un chochmos)*. Your
distinctive contribution is not your ability to teach the
alphabet — *kometz alef: oh*. For it was to the *temimim* — to all of
you here who are alumni of the Tomchei Temimim Yeshivah
which he founded — that my father applied the prophet's
expression of affection and esteem, עַל כַּפַּיִם חַקֹּתִיךְ — "I have
engraved you on the palms of my hands." And as a teacher
you have (may no *ayin hara* harm you) a powerful ability to
illuminate your fellow Jews with the light of the Torah and
the *mitzvos*.

You come from Nevel. It is a familiar story that once the
Mitteler Rebbe was visited in Lubavitch by twenty-odd chassidim from Nevel — young men who were supported during
their years of study after marriage by their fathers or fathers-
in-law. While in Lubavitch they continued their accustomed
practices — *davenen* at length, their prayer being accompanied
by earnest meditation on relevant teachings of *Chassidus*, and
studying Torah assiduously — as is described in a certain
letter. Observing this, the Mitteler Rebbe quoted two words
from *Tehillim*, הַלְלוּהוּ בְּנֵבֶל ("Praise Him with the harp"), and
then echoed them: הַלְלוּהוּ בנעוועל ("Praise Him in Nevel...").

A *chassidisher melamed:* It was once common for families to hire a res-
    ident tutor, or *melamed,* to teach their children. The adjective *chassid-*
    isher means more than simply "chassidic": it embraces all the positive
    qualities of character that distinguish a person imbued with the
    teachings of *Chassidus.*
I have engraved you: *Isa.* 49:16.
Twenty-odd: In the original, "some two *minyanim.*"
Praise Him: *Ps.* 150:3.

And my father once said: "I cherish more a butcher from Nevel than a scholarly *maskil* from Kremenchug."

25.

One of those present asked whether it is preferable to study Torah at home or in a group, and the Rebbe gave his answer.

Without a doubt Torah should be studied in a group — in *shul,* or wherever people gather. It is true that Torah study at home has a great advantage insofar as the tone of the household is concerned. For the respect shown at home to a husband and father should not derive only from the fact that he is the breadwinner who provides for the family's needs. It should derive from loftier things, from spiritual considerations. One's family should know that one studies and that one's mind is occupied with topics of Torah and the fear of heaven — and then at home one finds favor in a very special way. And this is the genuine domestic harmony, *shalom bayis,* which the Torah treasures. (In the matter of domestic harmony, by the way, there are a number of misconceptions current which call for correction.)

Nevertheless, Torah should be studied with a group. As for the benefits which the household could gain, it is advised that when the father of the family comes home he should explain some topic taken from his study — some apt quotation from the *Gemara,* for example.

26.

The Rebbe said *LeChaim* over a sip of strong drink — *mashke,* in the vernacular.

A scholarly *maskil:* In the chassidic usage of the term (except in etymology quite unconnected with the Haskalah movement), this signifies a person more occupied with the comprehension of the philosophy of *Chassidus* than with the demands of *avodah* — the labor of self-refinement through structured meditation, as in the mode of prayer (*"davenen* with *avodah")* exemplified by the young men from Nevel.

LeChaim! May the Almighty grant that the *mashke* should go the right way, and that you all likewise go the right way.

Any word may be interpreted in various directions. There is a right way in a straightforward sense, and there is a right way at ever higher levels, one ascent following the other, materially and spiritually.

27.

One of the chassidim present asked how the Rebbe's frequent emphasis on the need for *avodah shebalev* applied to working people who were not fulltime scholars. According to the Rebbe's published statements on the subject it would seem that this "service of the heart" — prayer prolonged by the disciplined contemplation of relevant themes in the teachings of *Chassidus* — belonged more to the realm of the scholars. For such "dwellers in the tents" *(yoshvei ohel)* are able to devote the time demanded by such *avodah*, while working people are occupied throughout the day with their business or profession. What, concluded the questioner, should their situation be?

The Alter Rebbe has been quoted above on the subject of *kviyus banefesh:* one's Torah study should be fixed in one's soul.

A chassid who works for his livelihood should be like a son-in-law supported by his father-in-law — *an eidim oif kest.* So long as one is in this situation one has no worries. When, however, one's father-in-law begins to drop hints that conditions are such that a certain degree of help is called for in his business, one begins to become involved, and helps out a little. Nevertheless, such a young man is still *oif kest.* So first he eats his breakfast, and drinks his fill, and only then does he set out for his father-in-law's place of business.

Exactly so should a *chassidisher* working man be. And everyone here knows what is represented in the teachings of

---

Quoted above...fixed in one's soul: See above, p. 13.

Chassidus by eating and drinking — Torah and the *avodah* of prayer, respectively.

May the Almighty grant a comfortable livelihood to all of *Anash* together with all of our brethren of the House of Israel, so that they will be in a position to occupy themselves with Torah and *avodah*.

Chapter 2a

The Eve of Yud-Tes Kislev 5

Riga

1.

Year after year my great-greatuncle R. Nachum, the son of the Mitteler Rebbe and the grandson of the Alter Rebbe, used to narrate the story of *Yud-Tes* Kislev from beginning to end. He used to begin as follows.

"For ten years my grandfather was a disciple of R. Dov Ber, the Maggid of Mezritch, and for five years the leader of the holy brotherhood of the Maggid's disciples — until he became renowned as the preacher of Liozna. For twenty years he toiled in a number of tasks. The first of these was the establishment and consolidation of the three celebrated *chadarim* for outstanding scholars. His other tasks in this period included the guidance of his chassidim, and disseminating and explaining the doctrines of his teachers, the Baal Shem Tov and the Maggid of Mezritch. When the various regions were allocated to the disciples of the Maggid for this purpose, my grandfather undertook the most difficult, for this area was

---

The story of *Yud-Tes* Kislev: On 19-20 Kislev 5559 (חקנ״ט; 1798) the Alter Rebbe was freed from capital sentence and imprisonment in Petersburg, after being slandered to the czarist authorities by his opponents, the *misnagdim*. See: Rabbi A.C. Glitzenstein, *The Arrest and Liberation of Rabbi Shneur Zalman of Liadi* (trans. Rabbi J.I. Schochet; Kehot, N.Y., 1964); Rabbi Nissan Mindel, *Rabbi Schneur Zalman of Liadi* (Kehot N.Y., 1971).

Chadarim (pl. of *cheder*): Generally signifies children's Torah schools. The entrance requirements of these *chadarim*, however, founded between 1778 and 1782, included expertise in the entire *Talmud, Midrash* and *Zohar*.

Most difficult... nearest to Lithuania: This was the stronghold of the *misnagdim*.

nearest to Lithuania. When *Tanya** first appeared — and by that time there were already (thank G-d) many thousands of chassidim, including a great number of scholars and halachic authorities who followed his legal decisions (as in the construction of the *mikveh*, the insistence on honed slaughtering-knives for *shechitah*, and so on) — that was when the libelous accusation took place."

At this point R. Nachum would proceed to describe in detail the accusation which the *misnagdim* brought to the czarist authorities, and the exultation in their camp when the Rebbe was taken to Petersburg. For example, when on Sunday, the twenty-seventh of Tishrei 5559 (תקנ״ט; 1798), horse-borne couriers arrived in Vilna, Minsk and Shklov with the news that he had been taken off to Petersburg in the infamous black wagon,** guarded by mounted gendarmes with swords drawn, it was announced publicly that on the next day, Monday, all the synagogues and *batei midrash* should introduce the thanksgiving Psalms of the *Hallel* into the morning service and the townsmen should conduct a festive meal to mark the occasion. This announcement encountered opposition from some of the older sages in the *misnagdish* camp, for in each of these three towns there were scholars who had had the opportunity of getting to know the Alter Rebbe, and they exerted whatever influence they could to

---

* The word in fact used by R. Nachum for *Tanya* is *Kuntreisim*. Before *Tanya* was first published as a book in 1796, its subject matter was disseminated among the chassidim in the form of single handwritten chapters and even half-chapters, which were called *Kuntreisim* ("leaflets"). For this reason, the older chassidim who remembered those days continued to use this name for the work even after it was printed as a book with a title.

** This wagon was reserved by the czarist regime for rebels and others who were under capital sentence. Covered on all sides with heavy black panels of iron, and with mere slits for air, it was designed to cast dread on all those who saw it.

Tanya: The Alter Rebbe's basic exposition of *Chabad Chassidus.* "*Tanya*" is the initial word of the book, which is also called *Likkutei Amarim* ("Collected Discourses") and *Sefer shel Beinonim* ("The Book of the Intermediates").

restrain these expressions of vindictiveness. Thus it was that in the majority of *shuls* in these three towns the announcements encouraging merrymaking were ignored. May their memory be blessed!

From this R. Nachum would move on to describe the Alter Rebbe's stay in prison, the details of his liberation, the way in which the glad tidings spread among both the chassidim and the *misnagdim*, and his itinerary from Petersburg. For as he made his way toward his hometown thousands of people accompanied him, until on Tuesday the second day of Chanukah he arrived in Vitebsk, where thousands of townsmen came out to greet him, and where he remained for the whole of Chanukah.

All this was recounted clearly and succinctly. When he recalled the arrest his voice would drop unawares, as if he were weeping; when he reached the liberation, his voice would rise with the joy of remembered triumph. He adopted the rule which obtains with the reading of the *Megillah* on Purim — once at night, and a full repetition by day. Moreover, if one of the dignified elder chassidim would join the gathering after he had begun, — why, he would go back to the very beginning and start all over again.

2.

Late in life, for some particular reason, R. Nachum more or less settled for several years in Haditch, the burial place of his grandfather, the Alter Rebbe. In earlier times no one had any explanation for this. Previously, when he had moved permanently from Lubavitch to Niezhin (the burial place of his father, the Mitteler Rebbe), he used to have a fixed time every year when he would travel to Haditch. There he would remain for a long time, two months or more. Generally he took up residence in the *beis midrash* which was near the burial

---

Haditch, the burial place: The resting place of a *tzaddik* is an auspicious place for prayer, in part because it evokes a contrite frame of mind. For further reasons see the Mitteler Rebbe's *Kuntreis HaHishtatchus*. In Eng. translation: *Praying at the Gravesite of a Tzaddik* (SIE, N.Y., 5769/2009).

place; he also had a room in the house of the *shammes* who took care of the *ohel*, and at times he used to stay there. The town itself he visited only rarely.

When he reached his seventies his yearly visits to Haditch grew longer. At first he used to leave Niezhin before *Shabbos Mevarchim* Elul and remain in Haditch for some four months until after Chanukah. On later visits he would set out earlier in the year, in time for *Shabbos Nachamu,* and stay in Haditch for seven months until just before Purim; and at a yet later stage he would stay until after Purim.

In 5624 (תרכ״ד; 1864) he was in Lubavitch on a visit to his brother-in-law, my great-grandfather the *Tzemach Tzedek.* After a few months there he traveled directly to Haditch, where he remained for three years, interrupted only by brief visits to his home in Niezhin. So it was that at the time when the *Tzemach Tzedek* passed away on 13 Nissan 5626 (תרכ״ו; 1866), R. Nachum was in Haditch. From that time on, he settled there more or less permanently for several years. As he would put it, "I'm a guest at my grandfather's."

3.

The chassidim of the time found his stay in Haditch puzzling, because when he had lived in Niezhin they used to come from all around those parts to visit him periodically. Though he did not regularly deliver chassidic discourses, they would enjoy being in his presence even when he expounded mere snippets of chassidic teaching. Above all, they valued the opportunity of ennobling their own characters by observation and emulation.

On this subject he was accustomed to saying: "My grandfather had literal *mesirus nefesh* in order to implant in chassidim *avodas halev* — divine service stemming from the heart, and finding expression in the refinement of the *middos.*"

He would often repeat those *maamarim* which he had heard from chassidim who had themselves had the 'good fortune to hear them from the mouth of his grandfather during his early years as Rebbe — 5538-5540 (תקל״ח-תק״מ; 1778-1780). On those occasions he would take care to repeat the discourses in the very same voice and tone in which he had first heard them — and as is known, the chassidim of the Alter Rebbe were punctilious in passing on to their listeners the exact intonation and singsong of their mentor's teachings.

Here is one of those *derushim* which I heard from my great-greatuncle, who heard it from one of the Alter Rebbe's earliest disciples.

The *Talmud* teaches: כָּל הַכּוֹעֵס, כָּל מִינֵי גֵיהִנֹּם שׁוֹלְטִין בּוֹ — "Whoever is angry, all manner of *gehinnom* rule him." The commentary of *Rosh* explains that through anger a man is brought to sin, and hence causes himself to come under the dominion of purgatory. The Alter Rebbe further expounded this topic which appears in Tractate *Nedarim*, relating it to the stages by which a person can (G-d forbid) fall from his accustomed spiritual standards. When a man's heart is arrogant from birth, as it is written, כִּי יֵצֶר לֵב הָאָדָם רַע מִנְּעֻרָיו — "For the inclination of man's heart is evil from his youth," and when he does not occupy himself with *Chassidus* in order to refine the *middos* of his character, and hence remains in the state in which his inborn nature makes it possible for him to grow angry, *then* it comes about that he sins. The Hebrew word for trangression, עֲבֵרָה, derives from the root עבר, meaning to transfer, to go across — from the domain of sanctity to the unholy domain of the *sitra achra*, "the other side." Moreover, as the above quotation from the *Talmud* continues, תַּחְתּוֹנִיּוֹת שׁוֹלְטוֹת בּוֹ. Though in its literal sense this means that he is affected by a physical ailment, the first word if vocalized differently may be understood as an abstract noun, תַּחְתּוֹנִיּוּת — lowliness. That is to say, one who succumbs to anger becomes a materialistic person who is preoccupied with the תַּחְתּוֹנִיּוּת שֶׁבָּאָדָם, the lowliest aspects of man. For man comprises elements from both the *elyonim* and *tachtonim*, from both the

---

Whoever is angry: Tractate *Nedarim* 22a.
The commentary of *Rosh: Ibid.*
For the inclination: *Gen.* 8:21.
The above quotation... continues: Tractate *Nedarim* 22a.

heavenly levels of creation and the lowly strata of creation.
His soul is loftier than the *ne'etzalim harishonim*, the beings
created in the highest of the spiritual worlds; his body is
lowlier than the humblest of creatures. [The Alter Rebbe
here goes on to explain how the various consequences of
anger as listed by the *Talmud* are in fact connected in a sequen-
tial order.] And when (G-d forbid) materiality rules a man,
then (heaven forfend) even the Divine Presence is of no
estimation in his eyes — אֲפִילוּ שְׁכִינָה אֵינָה חֲשׁוּבָה כְּנֶגְדוֹ. When this
happens, he forgets the Torah which he was taught before his
birth — מְשַׁכֵּחַ תַּלְמוּדוֹ. And when he propounds novel expositions of the Torah according to his own understanding, he
merely increases in foolishness — מוֹסִיף טִפְּשׁוּת. In his original
interpretations he even reaches a stage at which עֲוֹנוֹתָיו מְרוּבִּין
מִזְכִוּיוֹתָיו [literally, "his sins outnumber his merits," but here
expounded on the level of *derush* as follows]: the wrong-
headedness (from the root עוה) outweighs the clarity (from
the noun זַכּוּת).

For the root of *avodah* is the refinement of character
traits, *middos*.

*   *   *

With this discourse my forebear the Alter Rebbe gave
Jews a new heart, introducing thousands to the service of
HaShem; and many of them ultimately became chassidim.

The Alter Rebbe, as my great-greatuncle R. Nachum
used to say, literally had *mesirus nefesh* in order to implant in
chassidim *avodas halev*, divine service stemming from the
heart; my father had *mesirus nefesh* in order to implant in
chassidim *avodas hamo'ach*, divine service rooted in the brain.
His disciples used to discuss among themselves the profoundest concepts in the subject of *achdus*, the Unity of *HaShem*,

---

Even the Divine Presence: Tractate *Nedarim* 22b.
He forgets the Torah: *Ibid.*
Taught before his birth: Cf. Tractate *Niddah* 30b.
Increases in foolishness: Tractate *Nedarim* 22b.
His sins... his merits: *Ibid.*

basing themselves on foundations of truth.

* * *

When my great-greatuncle stayed on in Haditch few chassidim made the journey to Niezhin, and their number increased only when my greatuncle R. Yisrael No'ach moved there. As to R. Nachum's prolonged residence in Haditch, this left the chassidim baffled.

4.

In the year 5572 (הקע״ב; 1812), at the height of the Napoleonic War, the Alter Rebbe fled from Liadi together with his entire household and a large following of chassidim. The convoy numbered 60 wagons in all, as well as many people who accompanied them on foot. The date was *erev Shabbos Parshas Re'eh*, 29 Menachem Av, *erev* Rosh Chodesh Elul. Though he was advised by the Russian generals to flee by way of Bayev, the Alter Rebbe directed his party instead via Krasna, and urged them to cross the Dnieper with the utmost haste.

When they were about two viorsts out of Liadi he gave the order to cross the river. He then instructed his followers to ask the Russian gendarmes who had been assigned as his escort for the duration of his journey to provide him with a light carriage drawn by two good horses, and two armed coachmen. Accompanied as well by two of his chassidim he set out in the carriage at a brisk pace and headed for Liadi. Hastening to his house, he told his men to check thoroughly lest any item of his household effects had remained. In the attic they found a worn-out pair of slippers of his, some rolling pins, and a sieve. He instructed his men to take these with them, and to set the house on fire. And before leaving in haste, he gave his farewell blessing to his townsmen.

Barely had the Alter Rebbe left the town by the road leading to the Dnieper when the first courier of Napoleon's army arrived from the opposite direction. Within a short time, surrounded by a retinue of generals mounted on mighty horses, Napoleon himself arrived on the scene. He imme-

diately made his way to where the Alter Rebbe's home had
stood, but found the house and all its environs blazing fur-
iously. He gave the command that the fire be extinguished,
but all approach was barred by the flames and smoke. He then
had it announced throughout the town and its neighboring
villages that any man or woman who would bring him any
object or vessel which had belonged to the Alter Rebbe, or
even a coin which he had received from his hand, would be
paid in gold rubles. His troops searched throughout the town,
but in vain.

By this time the Alter Rebbe had crossed the Dnieper by
ferry. He made haste to reach the convoy, and proceeded to
journey on with the party until they arrived at a village half
an hour before sunset. After spending *Shabbos* there they
traveled all night until on Sunday, the second day of Rosh
Chodesh Elul, they reached Krasna, and rested there.

On Friday, *erev Shabbos Parshas Shoftim*, the sixth of Elul,
they were forced to resume their flight. At this point the
carriage in which the Alter Rebbe sat was third in line, while
the first wagon was occupied by my great-greatuncle and the
two gendarmes. Whenever they came upon a crossroads they
would alight and ask the Alter Rebbe which road to take.

The Alter Rebbe would usually alight from the wagon,
approach the crossroads, and lean on his stick in deep contemplation; then he would direct which road to take. Sometimes
he would indicate the direction while remaining seated.

It so happened that at one such intersection my great-
greatuncle mistook the instruction which he had been given.
After some ten viorsts the Alter Rebbe asked when they
would arrive at a certain village. Realizing his error, R.
Nachum wept bitterly in his distress. The Alter Rebbe sighed
deeply and said:"How good is it when a grandson follows in
the path of his grandfather — and the opposite is true when a
grandfather has to follow the path in which his grandson
leads him." And he gave the order for them to continue.

All of the chassidim in the party knew of the prayer
which the Alter Rebbe had uttered as they had fled from
Liadi: "May the Almighty have mercy, so that we will arrive

within the borders of the province of Poltava before Rosh
HaShanah." The mistake at the crossroads caused all kinds of
troublesome detours, and soon after the Alter Rebbe passed
away in Piena. Thereafter, to the end of his days, R. Nachum
was grieved, blaming himself for whatever had come about in
the wake of his mistaken direction.

And that is why there were chassidim who assumed that
they knew why R. Nachum tarried so long in Haditch.

5.

It once happened that a goodly number of the surviving
elder chassidim of the Alter Rebbe and of the Mitteler Rebbe
were gathered together in Haditch and sharing memories of
the chassidic brotherhood in days gone by. On this occasion
one of them mustered the daring to pose the question to
R.Nachum: Why had he moved to Haditch? Would it not have
been far better, especially in his old age, to live at home in
Niezhin within the circle of his family?

It was then that he told them the story of the silk coat as
follows.

"This is how it all came about. Among the clothes that
were tailored for my wedding was a *kotinke,* a silk coat. My
grandfather the Alter Rebbe called for me and said: 'Nachum,
would you agree that the *kotinke* should have a patch?' I answered: 'Not only don't I agree, but I really don't want it to be
that way.' So my grandfather said: 'And what would you like
in order that you *should* agree that the silk coat should have a
patch?' 'I don't want a coat with a patch,' I said; 'I want a whole
garment.' My grandfather then said that he would promise to
study with me — but I still refused. Then he said: 'If you will
do this thing, I promise you that you will be אַתְּ עִמִּי בִּמְחִיצָתִי —
that in the World to Come you will be with me, in my abode.'
This struck a deep chord within me, so I said: 'Very well.' But I
went on and asked: 'Do I have to want this truthfully, or will it
suffice to want the patch only out of a sense of duty, out of

---

With me, in my abode: Tractate *Berachos* 12b.

kabbalas ol?' My grandfather replied: 'Truthfully, of course — and with the truth of the innermost level of the soul, with the truth of *yechidah.'* Hearing this reply I fell silent, and that was that."

Now R. Nachum's silk coat was made with a long collar, a sort of cape of sable or fox or some other fur. When he entered his grandfather's study in order to receive his blessing before the *chuppah,* the Alter Rebbe tore off one little piece of fur from the collar, and in exchange for this promised him long life.

And in order to set aright this matter of the *kotinke,* my great-greatuncle R. Nachum spent several years near the resting-place of the Alter Rebbe in Haditch. This went on until about a year-and-a-half or two years before his passing, when he had to go to Niezhin, saying that his grandfather had given him a message to be given to his father. And then, for one reason and another, he could no longer return to Haditch.

6.

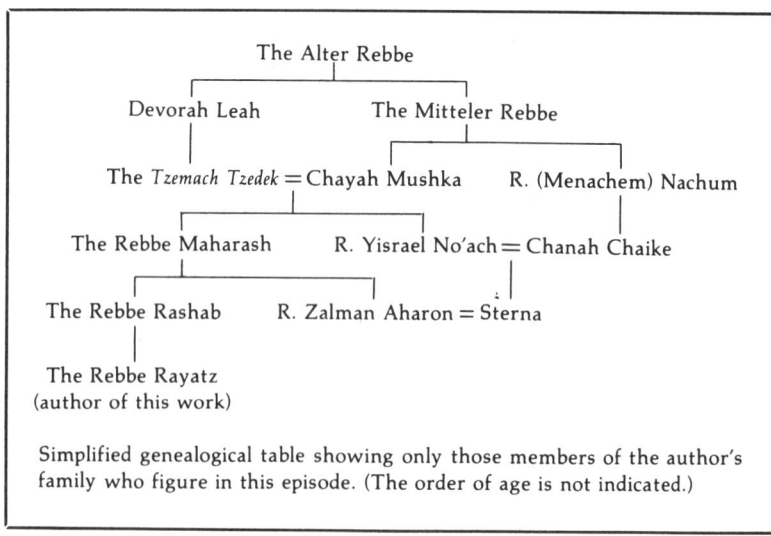

Simplified genealogical table showing only those members of the author's family who figure in this episode. (The order of age is not indicated.)

My greatuncle R. Yisrael No'ach was the son-in-law of his uncle, my great-greatuncle, R. Nachum, having married his daughter, Chanah Chaike. Their daughter, Sterna, married the son of R. Yisrael No'ach's brother, R. Shmuel (the Rebbe Maharash) — R. Zalman Aharon, the brother of my father (the Rebbe Rashab). The wedding was celebrated in the month of MarCheshvan 5634 (תרל״ד; 1873) in Lubavitch. R. Yisrael No'ach lived at the time in Niezhin, and in the summer of 5634 (תרל״ד; 1874), after the festival of Shavuos, my uncle, R. Zalman Aharon, visited his father-in-law there and remained with him for over two months until the beginning of Elul.

R. Nachum, who also lived in Niezhin, showed great affection for my uncle R. Zalman Aharon, and my uncle for his part was fond of visiting him at every opportunity in order to hear stories from his mouth.

Regarding R. Nachum, my uncle told me that by nature he was a man of cheerful temperament and friendly countenance. In addition, though his hair and beard and eyebrows were white, he was so light on his feet that no one would ever believe that he was already eighty. And when he recounted a story or episode it was transmitted with every minute detail, down to the name of every single personage mentioned in it, and the precise order of events by month and day. In brief, when you heard him tell a story the events would spring to life before your eyes.

My uncle R. Zalman Aharon reminisced: "Whenever I would go to visit my greatuncle — my wife's grandfather R. Nachum — I would imagine that I was about to open a book of chronicles covering seventy years. It was a rare delight to hear his conversation and his stories — not to speak of the chassidic expositions that were always at hand. For the most part these were maamarim of the Alter Rebbe's early years, and R. Nachum would recall the full name of the chassid from whom he had heard every such discourse."

R. Nachum was older than my greatgrandfather the Tzemach Tzedek by two years or perhaps three. Throughout his entire life he knew neither illness nor ailment, and on this he used to comment: "All our family are healthy — except for the Rebbes, whose health is undermined by the suffering which Jewry undergoes. My grandfather (the Alter Rebbe) was as strong as iron. If not for his hard labor, and the persecution and suffering resulting from his communal activity, he would have lived for 120 years. My father (the Mitteler Rebbe) too was a sturdy man. If not for the grinding poverty of his brethren, and the decrees which recall the Seleucid monarchs, he would have lived with the same degree of vigor with which any *chassidisher* young man grasps the difference between *daas elyon* and *daas tachton*. But he took all that poverty and all those decrees to heart — until he persuaded my grandfather to take him to his abode. And who would ever have believed about your grandfather (the *Tzemach Tzedek*) — a man so hardy that he would fast for entire weeks at a time, day after day, and then break his fast with a bit of bread and chicory; a man who would sleep three hours out of twenty-four; — who would ever have believed that for five years he would be so ill, and suffer so much pain."

It was from R. Nachum that my uncle R. Zalman Aharon heard all the details of how the Alter Rebbe was libeled and eventually liberated; particulars of his flight from Liadi, and the subsequent wanderings; his passing away, and how he was brought to Haditch for burial. All this my uncle recorded faithfully in his lucid and concise style. And when in the summer of 5666 (תרס"ו; 1906) he stayed with our family at a country resort — Chorne Rutze, some four kilometers from Liozna — he showed these manuscript pages, together with records of various other events and notes of discourses he had heard, to my father (the Rebbe Rashab), who perused them with great pleasure.

7.

R. Nachum began the story of the Alter Rebbe's arrest with the news that reached him late on Wednesday night, *Motzaei* Simchas Torah, 5559 (תקנ"ט; 1798), that police agents dispatched especially for the purpose had arrived in Liozna with orders to arrest him and escort him to Petersburg. The whole chassidic brotherhood was thrown into turmoil. On Thursday evening the Alter Rebbe was apprehended. He was granted permission to pray the evening *Maariv* service in his home, and then he was hauled off in a black-plated wagon guarded by armed militiamen. A deathly terror descended upon the entire family.

That same night a group of chassidim met to deliberate possible courses of action. The participants were the Alter Rebbe's students in the first, second and third *"cheder"*, who by this time had already established a reputation in the chassidic community for their assiduity in studying and disseminating the teachings of Chassidism. First of all it was agreed that all those present, as well as other chassidim who were named, were to free themselves from all their business and domestic affairs, and devote themselves — physically, spiritually, and materially — to the rescue of the Rebbe and the salvation of Chassidism.

The meeting elected a committee which was charged with coordinating all the efforts aimed at saving the Rebbe, maintaining all the activities which he had organized, and strengthening the morale of his chassidim wherever they were scattered. It was further decided that all of *Anash* (an acronym for *anshei shlomeinu* — "the men of our brotherhood"), old and young alike, were obliged to take their orders from this committee without question, on pain of exclusion from the chassidic fraternity.

The committee's first act was to issue a signed protocol, to be binding on *Chabad* chassidim everywhere so long as the Rebbe would remain imprisoned: (1) all the chassidim were to maintain a communal fast every Monday and Thursday, unless prevented by physical disability as defined in the *Halachah;* (2) on weekdays they were to eat only bread and drink hot water, and on *Shabbos* only one cooked dish was to be eaten at each meal; (3) no engagements and weddings were to be fixed for this period; weddings which had already been arranged would be solemnized without musical instruments and with one meatless meal for ten people only; (4) every *melamed* was to recite *Psalms* with his pupils every day, and before this he was to explain to them the episode of the libelous accusations leading to the arrest, for the *tzaddik* of a generation is brought to account for the sins of his generation; (5) each chassid was to tell his wife and young children and any other member of his household of the whole story, pointing out the extent of the Rebbe's suffering, the villainy of his libelers, and the praiseworthiness of those who share in the anguish of a sage and *tzaddik;* (6) each chassid was to be punctilious in paying his regular *maamad* for the upkeep of the Rebbe's household, as well as his other contributions for the maintenance of the brethren who had moved to *Eretz Yisrael;* (7) each man was to list all the silver and gold vessels and jewelry that he owned; (8) each community of chassidim was to choose one trustee who would superintend the fulfillment of all the above orders, and would collect funds [as in (6) above] and lists [as in (7) above]; (9) if, G-d forbid, one of *Anash* were to pass away during this period, all the men of that community were to assemble and immerse themselves in a *mikveh.* After the deceased had been prepared by *taharah* and clothed for burial, his soul was to be solemnly adjured to ascend as an emissary of the community to the abode in heaven of the Baal Shem Tov and the Maggid of Mezritch, and to tell them that the Rebbe was incarcerated and the teachings of Chassidism were under threat. Three times were they to administer this oath — after the deceased was clothed, on arrival at the place of burial, and before the grave was closed. On that day, moreover, all were to fast.

The committee then set up three groups of activists: (a) those entrusted with rescuing the Rebbe; (b) those committed to raising the funds needed for this (such as traveling expenses), as well as for the maintenance of the Rebbe's household, and for the members of the fraternity in the Holy Land through the Rabbi Meir Baal HaNess Fund; (c) those charged with protecting the survival of the teachings and customs of Chassidism, and with sustaining the morale of the chassidic communities.

The *tzaddik* of a generation: Cf. Tractate *Shabbos* 33b.

The first group, whose members were named and directed by the committee, was subdivided into three cells: one based in Petersburg in order to assemble intelligence and to take action according to their findings; one based secretly in Vilna in order to be apprised of developments mooted among the *misnagdim;* a third cell in Shklov with the same task. These three cells were to communicate only through their own appointed liaison agents, never through the mail, and all their activities were to be kept utterly secret.

The second group raised its funds according to assessments made by the trustee and two elder chassidim of each locality. They examined the lists of all the silver and gold vessels, jewelry and valuables, in the possession of each household, and secured documents of sale from their owners, who were notified that if after a certain period the Rebbe was still (G-d forbid) in prison, they would all be obliged to transfer these objects into the safekeeping of the trustee, so that if funds were needed there would be no delay. While these lists were being made, accounts were also drawn up of all deposits of dowry money. Here, too, the owners furnished the local trustee with documents entitling him to use them on demand. Exact copies of all these lists and documents were forwarded to the committee.

The third group undertook its task of defending and spreading the teachings of Chassidism by traveling through cities, villages and rural settlements, explaining the Rebbe's* philosophy and the way of life upheld by the movement to the masses among whom they moved. In the course of their teaching new chassidim joined their ranks.

At the same meeting the various regions had been apportioned to groups of two or three emissaries, one of them to remain longer where appropriate, and their itineraries were to include the places known to be strongholds of the *misnagdim.*

---

* By this time he was already known as the Rebbe (instead of the Maggid) of Liozna; in Poland the title "Maggid" was still used.

8.

I read R. Zalman Aharon's chronicles extensively, and almost persuaded him to allow me to copy them, when all of a sudden some urgent public need demanded that I travel on a certain mission abroad. (As is well known, that was the year — 5666 (תרס״ו; 1905) — in which the notorious Black Hundreds involved Jewry in grave problems in the highest government circles, and pogroms [G-d forbid] were feared daily.) So it was that I managed to write down only a few brief texts, as well as the notes I made of what I had heard from my uncle.

A few days before his passing, in the month of Mar-Cheshvan 5669 (תרס״ט; 1908), my uncle burned all of his manuscript records together with a great number of bundles of papers and notes. He collected the ash and placed it in a purse of white material, and summoned R. Meir Mordechai, a chassid who was a family friend, and the aged R. Levi Yitz-chak (the brother of the learned R. Shneur Zalman of Lublin). He told them that this was the ash of the papers which he had written in the course of over thirty years, and asked them to do him a favor of truth by promising to bury it with him without anyone's knowing about it.

*　*　*

We left Lubavitch on Sunday the sixteenth of Mar-Cheshvan 5676 (תרע״ו; 1915) and after three days' journey arrived at Orol on Wednesday the nineteenth of MarChesh-van at six in the evening. As we were sitting in our second-

---

Black Hundreds: Virulently anti-Semitic terrorist squads newly recruited by the right-wing Union of the Russian People, supported by Czar Nicholas II and active in the pogroms of that period.

R. Meir Mordechai: Borisover; see pp. 267-268 below.

A favor of truth: In the original, *chessed shel emes.* "A favor done to the deceased is a favor of truth" (i.e., with no expectation of reward); *Bereishis Rabbah* 96:5, quoted by *Rashi* on *Gen.* 47:29.

class railway carriage my father said: "For 102 years our family has lived in Lubavitch — 102 years to the month. The Mitteler Rebbe settled there in MarCheshvan 5574 (תקע"ד; 1813), and now in MarCheshvan 5676 (תרע"ו; 1915) we are leaving Lubavitch."

My father went on to explain how sometimes a bigger number can be regarded as superior, while at other times a smaller number can be regarded as superior — depending on whether one is speaking in terms of *Oros* or *Kelim*.

My father then expounded at length the Talmudic dictum, "He who reviews his studies 100 times cannot be compared to him who reviews his studies 101 times" (אֵינוֹ דּוֹמֶה שׁוֹנֶה פִּרְקוֹ מֵאָה פְּעָמִים לְשׁוֹנֶה פִּרְקוֹ מֵאָה וְאֶחָד). He concluded by pointing out that the number ק"ב (102) is greater than ק"א (101) out of all proportion to the addition of one unit, for the numerical value of the letters ק"ב is equivalent to the numerical value of the letters of the word יְסוֹד (meaning "foundation") when combined with כ"ב, representing the 22 letters of the Hebrew alphabet. "In the course of these 102 years," he explained, "Lubavitch has with G-d's help made a יְסוֹד מוּסָד — a firmly-based foundation — out of the 22 letters [of which the Torah is written]." There were also many other teachings on that occasion, which were duly recorded.

The above discussion led my father to mention that R. Nachum of Niezhin had passed away 102 years after the birth

---

The Mitteler Rebbe: For a brief chronology of this period, see the author's footnote to Chapter 5a, Section 4, below. The author's *Sefer HaSichos* of Summer 5700 (ש"ת; 1940) records in detail how the Interior Ministry of Czar Alexander I ordered the provincial governors of Poltava, Minsk and Mohilev to arrange "fine carriages, hostelries and escorts for the Rabbin Schneuri and his family" all the way from Kremenchug to Lubavitch. There the Mitteler Rebbe arrived on *Chai* Elul, though he did not settle there permanently until MarCheshvan, as recorded above.

Oros or Kelim: See Rabbi J.I. Schochet, *Mystical Concepts in Chassidism*, Ch. V; in *Tanya*, p. 860-862.

He who reviews: Tractate *Chagigah* 9b.

of the Mitteler Rebbe. This observation in turn brought to mind the stories that he had read in the records kept by my uncle R. Zalman Aharon. When he learned that I had bought all of my uncle's books he asked me about these papers, so I told him that before his passing my uncle had burned them all. He replied: "*Nu*, very well . . . . If it wasn't wanted, then it's better that way."

9.

In the course of the time that the Alter Rebbe was in prison a great furor rocked all the lands which the alarming tidings reached. As is well known, the Alter Rebbe's colleagues — the disciples of the Maggid of Mezritch — together with all the chassidim of the various trends shared in the anguish of the *Chabad* chassidim. This reinforced the endeavors of the above-mentioned groups of chassidim who were traveling around the towns and villages, with the result that on all sides the movement was joined by new chassidim and supporters of their cause — for the lies and slanders that had been fabricated by the instigators of strife became known. Moreover, some of the leading *misnagdim* realized that they had become involved in an error and withdrew from the fray. The outcome of all the above was that the justice of the Alter Rebbe's cause became known in the world.

On his way home after his release the Alter Rebbe stayed in Vitebsk for several days. By the time he reached Liozna many hundreds of chassidim from the nearby towns had converged there, and travelers reported that all along the road they had seen throngs of people from faraway communities who were meeting and coming to welcome him home.

There were chassidim who wanted to write a *Megillah* of *Yud-Tes* Kislev telling of the Rebbe's deliverance, and to have it read annually like the *Megillah* of Esther. In fact a select number of elder chassidim had already prepared drafts for such a chronicle, and after secret consultation had decided to arrive in Liozna as a delegation between Pessach and Shavuos in order to request the Rebbe's approval of their project.

When they approached the Rebbe on this question he did

not agree to it, and answered as follows: (*First Version:**) "This day will be fixed as an everlasting festival for Israel, a day on which the great Name of G-d will be exalted and hallowed. The hearts of thousands of Jews will be aroused in repentance and the service of the heart (i.e., prayer), for this episode is engraved in the heart of the Israel of the World Above, and inscribed in the heart of Israel in This World." (*Second Version:***) "This day will be fixed as an everlasting festival for Israel, a day on which the great Name of G-d will be exalted and hallowed. The hearts of thousands of Jews will be aroused in repentance and the service of the heart (i.e., prayer), for when this episode will be engraved in the heart of *Yisrael Sava,**** it will be inscribed in the heart of Israel in This World."

10.

To the Alter Rebbe, Jews in general and chassidim in particular were like the apple of his eye. Moreover, what with his towering scholarship on the one hand, and his divine inspiration on the other, every word he spoke was measured. Not only was every act vigilantly checked against the requirements of the *Halachah* as interpreted in its richest and most stringent manner, but every word before being spoken was likewise carefully considered, so that no unworthy attribute of character could ever derive any nourishment from his speech.

---

* From R. Abba Persohn, quoting his grandfather, R. Ze'ev Vilenker.

** From R. David Zvi Chein, quoting his father R. Peretz Chein and other elder chassidim.

*** The Alter Rebbe was accustomed to using the word *Sava* (סָבָא; lit., an elder, or sage) to describe *baalei mochin,* those whose soul-root is such that the perception they attain through their divine service is ignited by intellectual endeavor, and *baalei de'ah,* those who have developed the definitive world-view outlined by *Chassidus.* This use of the word recalls the expression, [in the *Zohar, Parshas Naso,* 128b, סָבָא דְעַתוּי סָתִים וּמוֹחֵיה סָתִים וְשָׂכִיךְ, paraphrased by the author as] סָבָא דְעַתֵיה סָתִים וּמִיוּשָׁב.

Israel of the World Above [...] *Yisrael Sava:* These phrases (in the original, יִשְׂרָאֵל דְלְעֵילָא and סָבָא יִשְׂרָאֵל, respectively) are Kabbalistic terms for certain *partzufim.*

If one's *middos*, the attributes of a man's character, are the product of his *avodah*, his labor of self-cultivation, they may be called good *middos*. And if moreover these *middos* are sparked and guided by *seichel*, by intellectual endeavor, then surely we are speaking of beautiful *middos*. Nevertheless, even in such a case, there still exists the possibility of a leakage of nourishment, as it were, to an unworthy attribute.

When my father taught me *Tanya* and *Iggeres HaKodesh*, we came to the second epistle in the latter work, the one beginning "*Katonti*...", in which the Alter Rebbe [on his release from Petersburg in 1798] writes to his chassidim: "Let not your hearts grow haughty in relation to your brethren [i.e., the *misnagdim* who had brought about his near-calamitous incarceration], and the like; nor are you to speak defiantly against them, nor whistle at them, Heaven forfend. An awesome warning: hold your peace!" On this passage my father gave me profound explanations, pointing out its application to *avodah* — as to how a lad brought up in the way of Chassidism should rework his heart. In this connection he clarified for me what is meant by the verse, וַיִּגְבַּהּ לִבּוֹ בְּדַרְכֵי ה׳ — "His heart was lifted up in the ways of G-d." The animal soul, my father explained, argues that the lifting up of one's heart is in fact prompted by positive *middos* stemming from a source of holiness. My father proceeded to demonstrate how through this one can (G-d forbid) become deluded, and ultimately stumble from one failure to the next —without even sensing that one is falling, and becoming ever more grossly materialistic.

My father turned to me: "This phrase of the Alter Rebbe, '*nor whistle at them, Heaven forfend*,' — observe it minutely; steep your mind in it. The verb the Alter Rebbe uses (לִשְׁרוֹק) means to whistle, for it is a whistle [of scorn] that lies at the root of the ejaculation *Aha!* [even when it is] prompted by the force of holiness. And it is on this that the Alter Rebbe says, 'Heaven

---

A leakage of nourishment...: In the original, יְנִיקָה לְמִדָּה רָעָה.

His heart was lifted up: II *Chron.* 17:6, with reference to Yehoshafat, king of Yehudah.

The animal soul: In the original, נֶפֶשׁ הַבַּהֲמִית.

forfend.' And as if that did not suffice he adds, 'An awesome warning: hold your peace!'

"How much *ahavas Yisrael* lies in those words!" my father continued. "What holiness and *yiras Shamayim* lie in this guidance! Recall the circumstances. After the Alter Rebbe had endured an ocean of suffering — one should not recount, nay, one *may* not recount, (though one should nevertheless understand and sense) how much bodily suffering and spiritual anguish the Alter Rebbe and his chassidim endured, — after all of that he issues 'an awesome warning': 'Let not your hearts grow haughty in relation to your brethren.'"

Enlarging on the subject of caution regarding one's *middos*, my father explained to me on that occasion that the *middos* of *kedushah* require scrupulous vigilance, for "in the open-ended alley of holiness there is also the possibility (G-d forbid) of nourishment for the Philistines."

*   *   *

This, then, is the point of my father's above-quoted comment — upon the fact that the full story of the liberation of *Yud-Tes* Kislev was not recorded, and on my uncle R. Zalman Aharon's destruction of his historical jottings: "*Nu*, very well.... If it wasn't wanted, then it's better that way."

The open-ended alley... for the Philistines: The term "open-ended alley" (*mavoi mefulash*) is borrowed from the laws of *eruvin* (Tractate *Eruvin* 9:4), which in the context of the prohibitions of *Shabbos* discuss the possibility of establishing joint partnership of alleys of certain dimensions. The adjective here translated "open-ended" is מְפֻלָּשׁ, whose three root-letters are identical with those of פְּלִשְׁתִּים, the Hebrew word for Philistines. In the *Talmud* the Philistines are represented as scoffers (see Tractate *Avodah Zarah* 19a on *Ps.* 1:1). In chassidic literature, the "open-endedness" of the Philistines represents lack of restraint — either (a), when stemming from *kedushah*, in the rapturous expression of holy joy, or (b), when stemming from *kelippah*, in the uninhibited utterances of the riotous scoffer. (See the Alter Rebbe's *Torah Or*, last section of the first *maamar* on *Parshas Beshalach*, p. 122, where some of the very terms of the author's above-quoted warning to his chassidim in "*Katonti*..." — e.g., לֹא לְהַרְחִיב עֲלֵיהֶם פֶּה — are echoed.)

It's better that way: For otherwise the consequent *Aha!* of chassidim over the centuries would have unwittingly provided the unholy side of Creation with an insidious leakage of nourishment.

11.

According to the account that has been handed down, a great number of chassidim — including many who had formerly been *misnagdim* — foregathered in Liozna on *Yud-Tes* Kislev 5560 (ס″קת; 1799), the first anniversary of the Alter Rebbe's release from Petersburg. On that occasion he delivered the *maamar* which opens with the words, בָּרוּךְ שֶׁעָשָׂה נִסִּים לַאֲבוֹתֵינוּ — "Blessed be He Who wrought miracles for our forefathers [in those days, at this time]." (There is a reliable tradition that the Alter Rebbe introduced this discourse with the following words: "'Blessed be He Who wrought miracles for our forefathers' — this refers to the Baal Shem Tov and our Teacher, the Maggid [of Mezritch]; 'in those days' — this refers to Purim and Chanukah; 'at this time' — this refers to *Yud-Tes* Kislev.") In this *maamar* the Alter Rebbe exalts *avodas hamochin*, divine service which is intellectually based, and disparages *avodas halev behispaalus*, the ecstatic service of the heart. This was only a directive dictated by the needs of the time, for throughout that year the chassidim had been in a state of extreme excitement and ecstasy on account of the act of open lovingkindness which G-d had wrought for them and for their Rebbe, by saving both him and the teachings of the Baal Shem Tov.

The above *maamar* beginning *Baruch she'asah nissim* takes up the theme of the *maamar* of 25 Kislev, which the Alter Rebbe delivered in Vitebsk on Chanukah 5559 (ט″נקת; 1798) on his way home from Petersburg.*

---

* In 5563 (ג″סקת; 1803) the Alter Rebbe repeated this *maamar* for my greatgrandfather the *Tzemach Tzedek*, whose written record of it as he heard it has been preserved. This same version is also extant with long annotations which my greatgrandfather added in 5571 or 5572 (ב″עקת—א″עקת; 1811-1812). It comprises fifteen long chapters as well as summaries, and occupies more than nine folio sheets of medium-sized handwriting. Its kernel, as the *Tzemach Tzedek* received it from the Alter Rebbe, is not a long *maamar*: some five pages in all, but it is significant in that these teachings are among the first discourses delivered after the Alter Rebbe's release from Petersburg.

Who wrought miracles: From the blessing of thanksgiving pronounced before the reading of the Scroll of *Esther* on Purim and before the kindling of lights on Chanukah.

Elsewhere I have told of a note which appears in a manuscript of my grandfather the Rebbe Maharash explaining why these discourses were delivered. However, since there the subject is mentioned so briefly that it is unclear in its context, I will explain it now.

The *maamar* of 25 Kislev is extant in a copied manuscript, while the *maamar* beginning "Blessed be He Who wrought miracles" is preserved in a manuscript written by my grandfather the Rebbe Maharash, to which he added the following note: "I have heard from my father (the *Tzemach Tzedek*) that the intention of my greatgrandfather the Alter Rebbe in delivering this discourse was to distance his chassidim from an excess of emotional enthusiasm [in prayer], and from externally visible modes of behavior — for they used to leave the city for the countryside and there cry out loudly in prayer. This is why he delivered this discourse which exalts the virtues of *Chabad* — i.e., the ecstasy of the *intellect*. This was indeed a timely directive for which there was a need."

The note proceeds to explain other subjects which are of key importance for an understanding of *avodah* and guidance.

When my father entered his father's study for *yechidus,* the Rebbe Maharash explained him that the emotional enthusiasm of those chassidim was so intense that they would suspend themselves between heaven and earth, and through these *maamarim* the Alter Rebbe showed them how to internalize their experiences soberly.

12.

The *maamarim* delivered after the imprisonment at Petersburg show an entirely new approach. It is true that they are also different from those of yet earlier and of long before — for from time to time the Alter Rebbe revised the manner in which he chose to reveal his teachings in Torah, as has been explained elsewhere at length. But the contrast between before and after Petersburg is a striking one.

A certain incident took place early in the year 5567 (תקס״ז; 1806) surrounding a serious question which involved both

our uncle the Maharil (the brother of the Alter Rebbe) and my
greatgrandfather the *Tzemach Tzedek*. Because on that occasion
the *Tzemach Tzedek* acted with forebearance* he was granted
the privilege of having the Alter Rebbe set aside fixed hours
during which he studied with him both the revealed levels of
Torah, and *Chassidus,* including the manuscripts and teachings
which he had received from the Baal Shem Tov and the
Maggid of Mezritch. The Alter Rebbe repeated especially
those teachings and *maamarim* which he had expounded on
earlier occasions in public or in private, when the *Tzemach
Tzedek* had still been very young. He used to say: "I will repeat
for you those teachings and discourses which you heard with
your *neshamah,* though not with your intellect."** And most of
these were culled from the *maamarim* predating Petersburg.

13.

One of those present asked: "Would it not appear,
then, that the difference between before and after
Petersburg was that before Petersburg there was *gilui or*
[lit., "the revelation of light"; i.e., the Alter Rebbe's earlier teachings gave his chassidim a direct perception of
spiritual truth], while afterwards began the stage of
haskalah [lit., "intellectualization"; i.e., he now guided his
chassidim in their meditative quest for the comprehension
of spiritual truth through a more scholarly exposition of
the teachings of *Chassidus*]?"

---

* This was a private matter involving the *Tzemach Tzedek* and his *rebbitzin,*
our greatgrandmother, who had shown his manuscripts to the Alter Rebbe
without her husband's knowledge. [They were both the grandchildren of the
Alter Rebbe. See *Sefer HaToldos Admur HaMaharash,* pp. 9-11.]
** The story involving the venerable chassid R. Aizik of Homil is well
known — as to how on Shavuos 5590 (תק"ץ; 1830) the *Tzemach Tzedek*
repeated the first of the *maamarim* which begin with the words, "On three
things the world stands," which he had heard from the mouth of the Alter
Rebbe in the year 5553 or 5554. [I.e., תקנ"ג—תקנ"ד; 1793-1794, when the
Tzemach Tzedek was three or four years old. See Rabbi A.C. Glitzenstein,
Rabbeinu HaTzemach Tzedek, pp. 73-76.]

Our uncle the Maharil: R. Yehudah Leib.

The Rebbe answered as follows.

How can one say "the stage of *haskalah* began"? For according to this conception *or* and *haskalah* are two separate entities, there having been first a period of *or*, following which there began a period of *haskalah* — as if to say: "Thus far extends the realm of *or*; from this point on begins the realm of *haskalah*." This is simply not the case. Heaven forfend that we should draw such a distinction between (on the one hand) *or*, light, and between (on the other hand) the *seichel* of *Chassidus*, its intellectual dimension, for the latter is a divine order of intellect. The truth is that not only can *haskalah* without *or* not be called *haskalah* (this being axiomatic); but moreover, *or* which is bereft of *haskalah* is not light from the World of *Tikkun* [lit., "Order"]: it is light from the World of *Tohu vaVohu* [lit., "Chaos"].

Haskalah and *or* are as one — body and soul. Or, on a deeper level, they correspond to *Naran* (*nefesh, ruach, neshamah*) and *Chai* (*chayah, yechidah*). This is the rule: *or* without *haskalah* is not *or*, and *haskalah* without *or* is not *haskalah*. Rather, once a person's mind has been illumined by the *haskalah* with which it has been occupied, then that person — if he is one who discerns things in truth through the *avodah* of prayer — can perceive that he has before him (on the one hand) the *body* of the matter, that is, its *haskalah* (or, on a more inward level, the *Naran* of the matter), and (on the other hand) its *soul*, that is, its *or* (or, on a more inward level, the *chayah* and *yechidah* of the matter).

That which is today known as *haskalah* is in fact a veil. Concerning Moshe Rabbeinu it is written: "And behold the

---

World of *Tikkun...Tohu:* For an exposition of these terms, see Rabbi
    J. I. Schochet, *Mystical Concepts in Chassidism*, Ch. IX; in *Tanya*, p. 876.
Haskalah and *or* are as one: In the original, *"Or* and *haskalah* are as
    one"; here reversed for ready comprehension of the paragraph.
Naran...Chai: Acronyms for the five levels of the soul; cf. *Bereishis Rabbah* 14:9.
A veil: In the original, מַסְוֶה (*Ex.* 34:33).
"And behold...": *Ex.* 34:30.

skin of his face was luminous, and they (the Children of Israel) were afraid to approach him." Moshe Rabbeinu himself, however, did not know that his face glowed, for as far as the revelation of divine light that illumined him is concerned, the beginning and end were the same. That is to say: before it became known to him that his face was luminous there was a revelation of light, and after it became known to him there was likewise a revelation of light. It was only by means of the veil that the distinction came into being between (on the one hand) the time during which he either spoke with the Holy One, Blessed be He, or taught the Torah to the Children of Israel, these times being without the veil, and (on the other hand) all other times, when there was a veil. It was thus by means of the veil that he too learned that the skin of his face was radiant.

Now this veil is, in general terms, today's *haskalah,* and it is a source of nourishment for those self-styled *maskilim* — those who study *Chassidus* but do not occupy themselves with the service of the heart, nor with refining their character attributes, nor do they conduct themselves according to *Chassidus* — who think that *haskalah* and *or* are two separate entities. This is a veritable heartache.

But today is *Yom-Tov,* so we should really be speaking only of things that cause delight.

14.

As far as the essential being of the Alter Rebbe is concerned, there was no difference between before and after Petersburg. The experience of Petersburg of course effected and drew upon him a noteworthy elevation, analogous to the elevation experienced by a soul when it descends to This World to be clothed in a body. For the soul this descent is exile and captivity — but if it brings to realization the divine

---

The service of the heart: In the original, עֲבוֹדָה שֶׁבַּלֵב; i.e., prayer as a form of divine service (cf. Tractate *Taanis* 2a).

But today is *Yom-Tov:* This talk was delivered on *Yud-Tes* Kislev, which to this day is celebrated as the *Chabad* chassidic festival *par excellence.*

intention underlying its descent, this realization elevates the essential being of the soul to an exceedingly lofty degree. At such a degree of elevation was the Alter Rebbe after Petersburg. But as far as his revelation of light to others was concerned — that is, in relation to his disciples and chassidim — the situation before and after Petersburg may respectively be compared to the situation of Moshe Rabbeinu before he was obliged to wear the veil and after he was obliged to wear the veil.

The veil was worn by Moshe Rabbeinu so that the people should not be nourished by the rays of glory except when he was teaching them Torah — for he *removed* the veil from his face when speaking with G-d, and likewise when he taught the Torah to Aharon, his sons, the elders, and all of Israel (in the order set out in Tractate *Eruvin* and cited by *Rashi* on the *Chumash*). If so, what did the veil accomplish?

Its function may be understood by comparison with the function of *tzimtzum* in the familiar analogy of a *rav* teaching his pupil, where it is through *tzimtzum* that the teaching can be transmitted. So too in our case. The very existence of a veil, and the knowledge that one needs a veil, — *this* is the difference between before Petersburg and after Petersburg.

A query from one of the listeners: "If so, then the fact that Moshe Rabbeinu did not know that the skin of his face was radiant is in itself a virtue."

The Rebbe's reply follows.

Not knowing and not feeling the loftiness of one's own level is without a doubt a wonderful virtue. This is the *bittul* of *Tikkun* in all its superiority to the *bittul* of *Tohu*. The latter is also a wonderful degree of self-effacement, but this is a *bittul* which may be perceived by another: one's fellow is able to see just how self-effacing one is. True, a person in this situation does not sense his existence *(metzius)* as such: he is an *atzmi* [one who is absolutely true to his true self, or *etzem*], and his *etzem*

Should not be nourished: *Rashi* on *Ex.* 34:33.
Set out in Tractate *Eruvin:* Page 54b.
Cited by *Rashi:* On *Ex.* 34:32.

effaces itself before the light of the Infinite One, Blessed be He, with a great intensity, as only an *atzmi* can be self-effacing. But this very intensity of self-effacement is itself visible and recognizable as a *metzius,* as an empirical state of existence. Here, then, lies the superiority of the *bittul* of *Tikkun,* for this is a self-effacement of one's very existence, *bittul bimetzius,* a state in which one's own existence is not felt *at all.*

This will enable us to understand why in the case of Moshe Rabbeinu before he needed the veil and in the case of the Alter Rebbe before Petersburg, there was a virtue in their not knowing that the skin of their holy faces was radiant. There is indeed a virtue in such a situation, but this is true only of an individual. For with every virtue or rise in stature, if it changes or if it is absent this becomes a defect; that is, in the case of an individual, since the change was brought about by a personal or individual reason. But Moshe Rabbeinu and the Alter Rebbe are souls from the World of *Atzilus,* all-embracing souls, leaders of Israel. In each of them, for we are not dealing here with an individual, the reason for a change is a comprehensive one [embracing all of Israel].

15.

In the case of Moshe Rabbeinu and the Alter Rebbe, their essential being in its entirety was the love of G-d, the love of Torah, and the love of their fellow Jews. Moreover, the entire aim of their self-sacrificing divine service was to bind these three together. In every kind of Jew they saw the soul within, and invested it with the strength to prevail over the claims of corporeality. This is clearly apparent from their conduct.

When the Children of Israel grow discontented — and how much more so when there is strife — Moshe Rabbeinu pleads with them in gentle terms. Not only does he show forebearance by forgiving all those who raise vulgar and

---

Souls from the World of *Atzilus...* leaders of Israel: In the original, נְשָׁמוֹת דַּאֲצִילוּת, נְשָׁמוֹת כְּלָלִיּוֹת, פַּרְנְסֵי יִשְׂרָאֵל.

lowly suspicions against him: he exerts himself and intercedes with heaven in order to restore peace.

So too does the Alter Rebbe plead with his opponents,
writing long conciliatory letters aimed at removing all the
suspicions which have been raised against the teachings of
Chassidus, explaining the various paths taken by the chassidim
in the service of G-d, and in addition undertaking journeys
which involve self-sacrifice — all for the sake of peace.

The reason: To a leader of Israel every Jew is as dear as
the apple of his eye — as indeed this should be, according to
the Torah. It follows that Moshe Rabbeinu's becoming aware
of the need for a veil, and so too the change in the Alter Rebbe
after Petersburg, does not involve their own essential being:
it relates to all Israel, for it was the material and spiritual good
of Israel that occupied all their essential being. And with the
fiery intensity of an *avodah* based on the concept of "The
Almighty and Torah and Israel are all one," they led the
community of Israel.

16.

One of the chassidim present asked: "Would this not
mean that the difference between before and after
Petersburg was that before Petersburg there was a revelation of *light,* while afterwards the Alter Rebbe's teachings resembled the *Torah?* — For with the study of the
Torah, even if a person has not attained a spiritual pitch
which is attuned to the level of his study, it is still
Torah."

The Rebbe gave this reply.

Superficially, this describes the situation in a general
way. However, closer scrutiny aimed at ascertaining the
truth of the matter shows that these two terms — "light" (*or*)

They led the community: In the original, *mefarnes givehn;* lit., "nourished"; Heb./Yid. verb derived from the noun *parnas,* "communal
   leader," but also (and more usually) connected with the noun *par-
   nasah,* "nourishment" or "livelihood".

and "Torah" — do not comprise the whole subject in all its truth.

To explain in brief. Before the need for a veil — that is, before Petersburg — there was a revelation of the luminary (*maor*), a revelation which was for everyone;* after the veil of Petersburg the luminary became fused with the Torah and presented itself in the garments of comprehension which belong to the world of nature. That is to say, before Petersburg there was a revelation of light without such garments of comprehension; after Petersburg the luminary became fused with the Torah in order that it should bring about a refinement of the garments of comprehension.

It is true that even if one is [intellectually] not at the level of the Torah one is studying — that is, the person reading the letters of the Torah does not grasp what he is saying — this is still Torah. This is also the case with the teachings of *Chassidus*, that if one reads without understanding this is still Torah; and if a person goes along to hear chassidic discourses, even if he understands little, nevertheless a word or idea remains with him, and in its wake can bring (and indeed does bring) all manner of good — surely a positive thing.

But the real truth is that if we are speaking of *Chassidus*, then if a person is not at the level [of self-refinement] demanded by the subject under discussion, *this is not Chassidus*. For *Chassidus* makes a chassid, and such a study of *Chassidus* that does not cause a person to become a chassid — or at least

---

* One illustration of this is the well-known story of the Alter Rebbe's *tefillin* transmitted by the learned chassid R. Dov Ze'ev [of Yekaterinoslav], who heard it from the elder chassidim R. Avraham and R. Koppel (a scholar who heard many discourses from the mouth of the Alter Rebbe), both of Baturin, in the Chernigov region. They in turn heard it from the gentile squire of one of the estates near their town, who was one of the guards who [in 1798] had ferried the Alter Rebbe across the Neva River to the Peter-Paul Fortress.

The garments of comprehension: i.e., the medium, or vehicle, of comprehension.

This is still Torah: This statement refers to the Written Law, Torah *Shebichsav*.

to acquire a perception of the character attributes ˙which *Chassidus* leads to — is not what *Chassidus* is all about. It may be called knowledge, understanding, wisdom — but none of these constitutes *Chassidus*. The study of *Chassidus* should cause one to become a chassid with the personal attributes that characterize *Chassidus*; if not, this is not *Chassidus*.

The same questioner commented: "But there are lofty levels [of spiritual achievement] that one cannot live at."

To this the Rebbe replied.

If one cannot live at such a level, then one cannot. *Chassidus* is inwardness; a chassid is a man of inner integrity (a *pnimi*). And such a person does not delude himself. He knows that there are various levels, and not all of them are appropriate to him. There are levels which he is at; there are levels which he is not yet at; and there are levels which he is unable to attain. But one has to understand what is meant by saying that one is unable to attain them.

17.

It is written, וְדָבָר בְּעִתּוֹ מַה טּוֹב — "A word in due season, how good it is!" On this *Rashi* comments: "One studies the laws of Pesach and of Sukkos in their season."

Every subject should be studied at its proper time, as opposed (for example) to studying the *maamarim* of Pesach during the winter or the *maamarim* of Rosh HaShanah at an inappropriate time of year. And in this one should distinguish between study for the sake of knowledge or familiarity with the material, such study being equally in order at all times, and study connected with the *avodah* on a particular theme which a person is presently working on.

This must be clear to all: that (as explained earlier) the

Inwardness: In the original, *pnimiyus*.
"A word in due season...": *Prov.* 15:23.

study of *Chassidus* isolated from *avodah* and deeds is not *Chassidus*. The effect of one's study of *Chassidus* must be felt in practical *avodah*. It is true that in order that this should happen there needs to be — in each man according to his measure — a knowledge and an understanding of the area of *avodah* being dealt with, and this takes a great deal of time in advance. But then when the season of Pesach comes around, and once again the person studies in brief the themes underlying Pesach, and with these concepts occupying his mind he prays, and experiences his Pesach; or studies in advance the subjects appropriate to Rosh HaShanah and then exercises himself accordingly in the acceptance of the yoke of heaven; — *then* his study has realized its function. True enough, even there distinctions may be drawn — as to whether or not the person involved is in fact living at the level of his spiritual exercise; and if so, to what extent. But without a doubt something meaningful has resulted from his study, even if he is one of those whose aspirations are undefined.

This may be understood by means of a physical analogy. Playing a musical instrument is a profound art: there is much to be learned as to how to produce each individual sound; or a variety of harmonizing sounds from the same instrument; or a composition combining a range of instruments, all of which need to be tuned according to the laws of musical theory. Now one who is expert in this discipline knows that if his finger touches a certain string of the violin a certain note will result, and if his finger strikes a certain drum a particular sound will result; and so too with an ensemble of instruments which combined in harmony can produce sweet music to arouse and delight the soul. It is true that when one who is

---

He prays, and experiences his Pesach: In the original, דאװינט ער און פּסח׳ט. The last word is a charming and original verb created from the noun "Pesach"; roughly translatable as: "He does his Pesach thing."

Exercises himself accordingly in the acceptance of the yoke of heaven: In the succinct Yiddish original, און קבלת עול׳ט; an original verb, as above, from the noun *kabbalas ol*, "the acceptance of the yoke [of heaven]."

unschooled in musical theory touches the string or strikes the drum a sound is likewise produced, according to all the laws of musical theory. But he is ignorant of them.

The lesson from this analogy can be understood by all. The soul has five names, whose acronym is *Naran Chai [nefesh, ruach, neshamah, chayah* and *yechidah]*. They are, as it were, ground floor, second floor, third floor, fourth floor and fifth floor. These levels of the soul correspond to all of the Four Worlds — *Atzilus, Beriah, Yetzirah* and *Asiyah* — as well as the infinite worlds above *Atzilus,* for these are all represented in the faculties *(kochos)* of the soul. This is known from the familiar statement that the faculties of the soul derive from the Ten *Sefiros* of *Atzilus,* and *re'usa deliba* [the soul's innate yearning for G-d] and *mesirus nefesh* [self-sacrifice] derive from the infinite worlds above *Atzilus.* Through the teachings of *Chassidus,* the path of *re'usa deliba* and *mesirus nefesh* in the divine service of the Reading of *Shema* has, thank G-d, become a highway open to all. In other words, the ground floor thus has a connection with the fifth floor.

So when a Jew down here on the ground floor is called up to the Torah, and says, בָּרְכוּ אֶת ה' הַמְבֹרָךְ — "Bless G-d Who is blessed," then even though he does not know what [kabbalistic] *kavanos* to have in mind, nevertheless these words of his are echoed in all the Four Worlds. Just as the *nefesh* says them here in the World of *Asiyah,* so too do his *ruach* and *neshamah* and *chayah* say them in the respective Worlds of *Yetzirah, Beriah* and *Atzilus.* And these words are all sensed by the *yechidah* of his soul in the manner in which they appear in the infinite worlds above *Atzilus.* Here too one may distinguish between a person who has mastered all the intricacies of the mystical *kavanos,* and one who understands these concepts in general terms only, and one who does not even have a general percep-

---

Naran Chai: The five levels are listed in ascending order.

The Four Worlds — *Atzilus, Beriah, Yetzirah* and *Asiyah:* Here listed in descending order; their acronym is אבי"ע. The Four Worlds represent the main stages in the creative process resulting from *tzimtzum.* See Schochet, *op. cit.,* p. 852ff.

tion of what is involved. Nevertheless his words do set up reverberations in all the lofty worlds, just as in the analogy of the violin string. But he, poor fellow, knows nothing of all that.

This not knowing, however, refers only to the lowest level, the "ground floor"; at the higher levels these things are known, sure enough, and concerning this it is written, וְצִדְקָתוֹ עֹמֶדֶת לָעַד — "And his righteousness endures forever." For the worshiper described above has capital deposited in the Higher Worlds: *he* will know in due course.

Through this we will understand something puzzling. *(May the Almighty grant all Israel length of days, and good and radiant years, materially and spiritually, and may we be privileged to witness the coming of the Righteous Redeemer!)* In the Garden of Eden — both in the Lower Garden of Eden (a level which is no mean attainment), and most certainly in the Upper Garden of Eden — when a *tzaddik* sits in a heavenly palace surrounded by *tzaddikim,* chassidim, *geonim* and Torah scholars, as well as by plain householders and artisans, a query presents itself. There is no difficulty in understanding why the chassidim and *geonim* and Torah scholars are to be found in the palace of the *tzaddik.* But what of the plain unsophisticated Jews, those who recite *Psalms* and who listen in to someone explaining *Ein Yaakov,* just simple ordinary Jews who drop in on a comradely *chassidisher farbrengen,* — how did *they* find their way there?

The answer is, that when an ordinary fellow wearing market boots goes along to his local *beis midrash* to join in communal prayers, and is called up to the Torah, and recites

---

Poor fellow: In the original, *nebbich.*

"And his righteousness...": *Ps.* 112:3.

May the Almighty: Before turning to speak of the life awaiting mortal man in the World to Come, the Rebbe pauses to wish his listeners long life in *This* World.

The plain unsophisticated Jews: In the original, *di poshute Yidn.*

A comradely *chassidisher farbrengen:* Here, not an audience addressed by a Rebbe, but an informal gathering of chassidim for mutual edification and brotherly criticism.

Tehillim, listens in to the reading of *Ein Yaakov,* helps Torah scholars, and listens to the study and public exposition of *Chassidus,* then even though he may not understand everything he hears, *the benefit accrues,* and the account comes at the end. And that explains why after this life men whose learning is scant occupy their due place in the heavenly palaces of *tzaddikim.*

From the foregoing one may understand that there is a difference between the revealed levels of the Torah and the inner levels of the Torah. For in the revealed levels, the various topics may be classified according to the degree of understanding appropriate to each, and the student's *avodah* is geared to increasing his grasp and knowledge of his subject; for in addition to the observance of the laws which have practical application, knowledge too is required. With the inner levels of the Torah, however, the main thrust of a person's *avodah* is preparing himself for the acceptance of the yoke of heaven — observing even that which transcends his comprehension, in a manner that bespeaks his utter devotion to *Chassidus.* Thus it is that with an unscholarly person too, the effects of this *avodah* are in truth tangible.

18.

Now we will be able to understand the difference in approach between before and after Petersburg.

The manner of the Alter Rebbe's teaching before Petersburg could be described as the revelation of the luminary *(gilui hamaor).* The luminary was in a state of self-revelation, but as to the brotherhood of chassidim, their divine service was not yet set out in orderly fashion, working upward step by step. This is illustrated in the well-known story of the chassid R. Yekusiel of Liepli. On his first visit to Liozna he clambered up to the window of the attic where the Alter Rebbe had his study, sat himself on the sill, and said: "Rebbe, chop off my

---

The revealed levels...the inner levels: In the original, *galia sheba-Torah...pnimiyus haTorah.*

left side!" — referring to the left side of the heart, where the Evil Inclination dwells. The Rebbe, who was sitting at his table, wearing his *tefillin* of Rabbeinu Tam, motioned him to step down from the window sill, and then leaned his hand on his head and said: "Master of the Universe! Is it not written, 'And You give life to them all...' (וְאַתָּה מְחַיֶּה אֶת כֻּלָּם)? And from that time on, R. Yekusiel was charged with *chiyus,* vitality. (Ultimately this vitality gave rise to a command of the profoundest of subjects, though this took some years, being attained in the time of the Mitteler Rebbe.) The vitality with which he was immediately endowed manifested itself as a revelation of light: he would be utterly lit up by a flash of light.

When this light flared up within him he would become quite a different man, and would sing away, "Time to dance, it's time to dance!" And whomever he happened to encounter had no choice but to join him in his little dance — especially since a refusal might soon make the stranger feel the persuasive weight of his cane. One day R. Yekusiel was suddenly bestirred to sing his jolly ditty while walking down a street in Borisov, so his partner for that day's dance was — the local postman. In the words of my grandfather the Rebbe Maharash, "When the revelation came, he would be utterly lit up by a flaring light."

R. Yekusiel had been in fact no outstanding scholar. He used to conduct his business with integrity.* In time his comprehension of *Chassidus* grew so exceedingly that my grandfather the Rebbe Maharash once said that R. Yekusiel

---

* When a certain gentile customer once made a mistake involving a few kopeks while buying salt in his shop, R. Yekusiel investigated on all sides until he traced which village he came from, and then walked several miles there so that he could return the difference to him. Hearing of this the Alter Rebbe commented: "For such a sanctification of the Divine Name *(Kiddush HaShem)* one is blessed with extremely wealthy grandchildren." And in fact the banker Solovey was his grandson.

Where the Evil Inclination dwells: Cf. *Tanya,* Ch. 9.
"And You give life...": *Neh.* 9:6.

had clarified for him a certain abstruse subject in *Imrei Binah.* *

My grandfather the Rebbe Maharash told my father that each of the books which my great-greatgrandfather the Mitteler Rebbe wrote was intended for a particular category of chassidim; *Imrei Binah* was written for R. Yekusiel of Liepli. Furthermore, as has been mentioned above, his grasp of *Chassidus* grew in the course of a number of years, but even after this time it came in the manner of a revelation from above. In fact, my greatgrandfather the *Tzemach Tzedek* wanted to clothe this revelation [in the garments of steady intellectual endeavor], and instructed him to study *Kav HaYashar,* and *Chumash* with the commentary of *Rashi* — though the instruction was not so readily accepted.

I heard from my father that R. Shmuel Ber of Borisov had told him that R. Yekusiel used to call on him with his heavy fur coat, lay his cane on the table, and say: "Shmuel Ber, tell me what is the question that's bothering me!"

Now R. Yekusiel was not the kind of man you could trifle with. In fact one had to watch one's every word. A man once made some remark to him in jest, and R. Yekusiel reacted sternly: "He is jesting?! I myself heard from the [Alter] Rebbe that when one jests one gets involved with demons. Let the

---

* The subject referred to is to be found in *Imrei Binah, Shaar HaKriyas Shema,* from Chapter 12 onwards, and discusses the philosophic concepts of *etzem* and *hispashtus, he'elem* and *gilui.* My father (the Rebbe Rashab) studied this subject when he was in Yalta in the winter of 5645 (תרמ"ה; 1884-1885), and his brief notes on it are extant. At a later date he explained it at length in the discourse beginning *BeShaah SheHikdimu,* 5672 (תרע"ב; 1912), in the context of a discussion which distinguishes between four related pairs of concepts: *ko'ach* and *po'al, he'elem* and *gilui, etzem* and *hispashtus, yesh* and *ayin.*

Imrei Binah: Philosophic treatise by the Mitteler Rebbe.

Manner of a revelation: In *Sefer HaSichos* of Summer 5700 (ת"ש; 1940), while amplifying this discussion, the author remarks that "chassidim did not hold R. Yekusiel in especially high esteem, because he attained his spiritual level through the gift of the Rebbe's blessing — rather than through the labors of his own *avodah.*"

Kav HaYashar: A collection of 102 (ק"ב) ethical discourses by R. Zvi Hirsch Kaidonover.

demons get hold of that man!" And that man (heaven forfend) went out of his mind. Neither the remedies of the physicians nor the *segulos* that were tried were able to help in the slightest.

At any rate, when R. Yekusiel visited him and made his demand, R. Shmuel Ber would suggest all manner of topics which are discussed in the philosophical literature of *Chassidus* until he would light upon the subject on which his visitor had sought instruction. R. Yekusiel would then reply excitedly: "Yes, yes! You've found it exactly! Now go ahead and explain it to me!"

R. Shmuel Ber remarked that his visitor's questions were sharp, and related to the profoundest concepts in chassidic literature.

* * *

This, then, was the style of teaching before Petersburg; the luminary was revealed for everyone. True, the Alter Rebbe had initiated an order of inward *avodah* as reflected in the graded course of study in the three *chadarim* which he had founded. In a sense this was the making of vessels for the light, but in the main the luminary was revealed for all; and when a luminary is in a state of revelation, then that which is not a vessel also illuminates. After Petersburg, however, the light of *Chassidus* was revealed only in an orderly and gradated fashion, in the appropriate [intellectual] vessels, and with ample verbal explanation.

19.

The path of *Chassidus* is a paved road; it is (thank G-d) a broad, sealed, sturdy, clear road. But for various reasons involving certain young chassidim who study *Chassidus* by their own approaches, a few weeds (G-d forbid) begin to appear on that paved road. This means that one's own "I" — the "I" that has grasped something, the "I" that forces away the very Divine Presence — makes *Chassidus* cease being *Chassidus*. As has been said earlier, the study of *Chassidus* unaccompanied by practical *avodah* in the refinement of one's character traits is not *Chassidus.* (But of course we are not dealing with fools. No doubt this kind of study does not exist — this being the difference between the wisdom of the holy side of creation and wisdom stemming from the Other Side — except in isolated cases. This needs to be rectified, and the Almighty will grant his help.)

My greatuncle R. Yehudah Leib once sat at a *farbrengen* of his father the *Tzemach Tzedek.* (R. Yehudah Leib was a man of varied states of mind. There were times when he was in high spirits, in the sense of the verse, 'וַיִּגְבַּהּ לִבּוֹ בְּדַרְכֵי ה — "His heart was lifted up in the ways of G-d," and his gladness of heart found characteristic expression in the singing which accompanied his prayers. At other times, he was anxious and melancholy.) At that *farbrengen* he gave vent to his distress: "Where is *Chassidus?* Where does one find people practicing *avodah?* Where does one find people steeped in *haskalah?*"

And his father the *Tzemach Tzedek* replied: "What do you think my grandfather the [Alter] Rebbe expected from chassidim and *Chassidus?* He wanted to do away with the state of affairs described in the holy *Zohar:* 'Hearts are stopped up, eyes are closed, people see and know not what they see.' So (thank G-d) with his self-sacrifice he brought it about that *Chassidus* should accomplish the opposite: hearts that are open, and eyes that are open, and know what they see."

There were times when *Chassidus* meant *avodah,* and one began with oneself. Nowadays there are those for whom *Chassidus* becomes a cause for haughtiness — plain ego — and for whom *avodah* begins by dispraising one's fellow, which is of course the exact antithesis of what *Chassidus* demands. But despite all of this, one should not become despondent. Each person should be bound to *Chassidus,* for when one is bound one does not fall.

All in all, it's about time to arrive at the truth.

R. Yehudah Leib: Of Kopust; elder brother of the Rebbe Maharash; not to be confused with the. brother of the Alter Rebbe.
"His heart was lifted up...": *II Chron.* 17:6, with reference to Yehoshafat, king of Yehudah.

20.

The Alter Rebbe's liberation took place at the time of the afternoon *Minchah* prayer. During the three prayers of that last day he had with him the Baal Shem Tov and the Maggid of Mezritch. As is well known, the three hours [immediately following his release] which he spent in the home of one of the *misnagdim* caused him more distress than his entire imprisonment. For once he had vindicated his cause — since his imprisonment was a spiritual matter, in that it hinged on spiritual considerations — his bodily needs were of no interest to him. What with being in the company of the Maggid, and hearing the Baal Shem Tov, one can well imagine that the Alter Rebbe would not have minded remaining in prison for another three hours or even another whole day. So it was that when he was brought the news that he was now free, he had no desire to leave.

21.

Many years after the events of 5559 (תקנ"ט; 1798), R. Levi Yitzchak of Berditchev challenged the Alter Rebbe with the following question: "Why did you burden your shoulders with so much, more even than the Rebbe (the Maggid of Mezritch) intended? For there was so much suffering for Jewry in general, and so much anguish On High, as well as your own spiritual and physical distress. The same ends could have been achieved through *makkifim*" [lit., "encompassing lights," i.e., supernatural means].

The Alter Rebbe replied: "'The Almighty desired to have an abode below' [i.e., in this lowest of all worlds]. *Atzmus* desired to have an abode below. On the plane of *makkifim* a thing may be either so or otherwise. On the plane of *pnimiyus*

He had with him... Mezritch: I.e., spiritually, since this event of course took place after their passing.

The three hours... the *misnagdim:* See Rabbi Nissan Mindel, *Rabbi Schneur Zalman of Liadi,* pp. 182-183.

'The Almighty desired...': *Midrash Tanchuma, Parshas Bechukosai,* sec. 3.

[lit., "indwelling lights"] — the middle line, the attribute of Yaakov, which is the level of truth — there is no such thing as imaginary truth: truth is exactly so and not otherwise."

22.

In *Cheder Alef,* which the Alter Rebbe founded in 5538 (תקל״ח; 1778), there were fifteen students, whose entrance requirements included a thorough knowledge of the *Talmud, Midrash,* the *Ikkarim* and the *Kuzari,* and a familiarity with the *Zohar.* For five years the Alter Rebbe taught them as if he were locked in there (apart from essential journeys; as is known, this was a period during which some of his journeys were undertaken secretly).

Cheder Beis was founded in 5540 (תק״מ; 1780), and *Cheder Gimmel* in 5542 (תקמ״ב; 1782); the period of study at these levels was three years. From this time onward, the Alter Rebbe's disciples spread out widely and began to disseminate the teachings of *Chassidus* and its path in divine service — with the result that chassidim and men of good deeds abounded.

The Alter Rebbe's activities in the spreading of *Chassidus* were remarkably well organized. Some of his emissaries were sent out secretly to arouse in their listeners the desire to find their way to the path of *Chassidus;* some were dispatched to remote regions. He sent his disciple R. Moshe Vilenker, for example, to Bessarabia, with the instruction that he should not return to him until he had completed his task. This took

---

The middle line...Yaakov...level of truth: The connection between these concepts is explained in chassidic literature; see, for example, the end of Epistle 2 in *Iggeres HaKodesh,* in *Tanya,* p. 395, and note 26 there.

In *Cheder Alef:* The first class in the academy which the Alter Rebbe founded in Liozna for advanced students.

Founded in 5538 (תקל״ח; 1778): The dates given here (1778, 1780, 1782) are at variance with the genealogy appearing in *HaYom Yom,* viz., 5533-5538 (תקל״ג-תקל״ח; 1773-1778). See also p. 173 below.

Ikkarim: Sefer HaIkkarim, a classic exposition of the principles of the faith by R. Yosef Albo (15th cent.).

Kuzari: Sefer HaKuzari, as above, by R. Yehudah Halevi (1075-1141).

him in fact fifteen months, and the fruits of his stay included
the well-known chassid R. Yitzchak of Jassy and the chassidim of Kalarash.

23.

When the *Tzemach Tzedek* was slandered to the authorities
for the fifth time in 5619 (תרי״ט; 1859), and was undergoing
considerable suffering, he told his son, the Rebbe Maharash:
"When I was a child I was brought up in the home of my
grandfather (the Alter Rebbe, for he had lost his mother).
During the Blowing of the *Shofar* and during the Blessing of
the *Kohanim* he would take me under his *tallis* — for *tekios* until
the age of nine, and for the Priestly Blessing until my marriage. When it came to the Blowing of the *Shofar* on Rosh
HaShanah 5559 (תקנ״ט; 1798) I saw that during the forthcoming year my grandfather would undergo great distress. The
salvation I did not see — evidently because it was not a
complete deliverance."

24.

This year, 5693 (תרצ״ג; 1932-1933), marks the centenary
of two important and connected events in Lubavitch history:
it will be a century since my greatgrandfather the *Tzemach
Tzedek* bought the site on which he was to build his house, and
a century since the birth of my grandfather, the Rebbe
Maharash.

25.

In the days when the Maggid of Mezritch was still alive,
the Alter Rebbe was once about to leave Mezritch for home.
As the Maggid's son R. Avraham the Malach ("the Angel")

Rosh Hashanah 5559 (תקנ״ט; 1798): The *Tzemach Tzedek* was then exactly
    nine years old.
Would undergo great distress: In fact the Alter Rebbe was ar-
    rested three weeks later.
Not a complete deliverance: Two years later, in late 1800, the Alter
    Rebbe was again imprisoned.

was seeing him off, he said to the wagon-driver: "One has to whip the horses until they stop being horses." (Or, according to another version, "... until they *know* that they are horses.")

Hearing this the Alter Rebbe reacted by saying that he had now learned a new path in divine service. He therefore deferred his departure and stayed on for some time in Mezritch.

In 5533 [תקל״ג; 1773, the year following the passing of the Maggid] the Alter Rebbe spent over two months visiting R. Avraham the Malach, whom he called רבי ברבי, and after his passing he visited R. Menachem Mendel of Vitebsk several times.

26.

In 5658 (תרנ״ח; 1897) my father (the Rebbe Rashab) sent seventeen students to Zhebin to study under the tutelage of R. Shmuel Gronem [Esterman]. I have my father's manuscript list with his comments on the talents, character attributes, and level of ethical achievement of each of these young men, as well as a comprehensive evaluation of where each of them stood. That was in the beginning of 5658 (תרנ״ח; 1897) — the Tomchei Temimim Yeshivah had been founded on 15 Elul 5657 (תרנ״ז; 1897) — and at the end of 5658 (late 1898) these students returned to Lubavitch. During the *Hakkafos* of Simchas Torah my father began reading aloud: *"Tomech temimim, hoshiah na!"* ("Supporter of the sincere ones, help us, we beseech You!") At this point he broke off and said: "What kind of a question is there as to what the *yeshivah* should be called? Why, it is written explicitly (and this he read in the traditional

---

Visiting...visited: In chassidic usage, this kind of visiting signifies spending time at the "court" of a *tzaddik* whom one recognizes as one's Rebbe, in quest of instruction in Torah and guidance in one's divine service.

Whom he called רבי ברבי: The first word simply signifies that he now regarded him as his Rebbe; the second word, vocalized either בְּרַבִּי or בְּרִבִּי, is a Talmudic title reserved for certain eminent scholars.

Tomech temimim: From the prayers which accompany *Hakkafos.*

chant of Simchas Torah): '*Tomchei temimim, hoshiah na; takif laad, hatzlichah na; tamim bemaasav, aneinu beyom koreinu!*'" ('Supporters of the sincere ones, help us; eternally invincible One, grant success; He Who is perfect in His ways, answer us on the day we call!') He then announced loudly: "The *yeshivah* is called 'Tomchei Temimim,' and I ask of everyone, those who are present and those who are not, *Hoshiah na!* ('Help us, I beseech you!') And in exchange I promise [the blessings of] *Hatzlichah na* ('Grant success')."

Chapter 2b

The Eve of 20 Kislev 5693 (תרצ״ג; 1932)
At the Evening Meal
[Riga]

1.

Someone remarked that the Baal Shem Tov was born near the time of Jewish martyrdom in the wake of the [Chmielnicki] massacres of 1648-49. The Rebbe's comment follows.

From these events until the birth of the Baal Shem Tov a long, long time elapsed — some 40 or 50 years. For the Baal Shem Tov was born on the 18th of Elul *(Chai* Elul) in the year תנ״ח (5458/1698), and these letters when transposed comprise the word נַחַת ("peacefullness, a sense of fulfillment").

Among the letters known collectively as the Kherson

Massacres of 1648-49: The massacre of tens if not hundreds of thousands of Jews in the course of the Cossack and peasant uprising against Polish rule in the Ukraine led by Bogdan Chmielnicki. A wealth of contemporary sources document the martyrdom that great numbers of Jews chose when confronted with the option of apostatizing to Christianity. In Hebrew this holocaust is known as גְּזֵרוֹת תַּ״ח וְתַ״ט, lit., "the edicts of the years (5)408-409." (The prefix ה׳ representing the implied millenial — 5000 — is commonly omitted from dates.)

The actual relationship between these events and the birth of the Baal Shem Tov is alluded to on pp. 82-83 below.

Chai Elul: The letters whose numerical value totals 18 are י״ח, which, when inverted, are pronounceable as the word חַי ("alive").

Kherson Archive: A package of documents' confiscated by the Russian authorities from the *tzaddik* R. Yisrael of Ruzhin (greatgrandson of the Maggid of Mezritch) in 1838-40, deposited in the government archives in Kiev, and found in Kherson in 1919; contains copies of a

Archive there is a letter written by the Baal Shem Tov to R.
Yaakov Yosef HaKohen [of Polonnoye], the author of *Toldos
Yaakov Yosef,* and dated Tuesday of the week of *Parshas Miketz*
5513 (תקי״ג; 1752). In this letter the Baal Shem Tov fulfills his
longstanding promise to let his correspondent know the day
and the year in which his mentor Achiyah HaShiloni revealed
himself to him. These are his words: "On the day on which I
turned 26 years of age, on the 18th day of Elul in the year
5484 (תפ״ד; 1724), in the town of Okup, at about midnight, he
revealed himself to me.[...] The first subject we studied was
Parshas Bereishis, and when we completed the Torah up to
'before the eyes of all *Israel'* I was 36 years of age, and I became
revealed."

Accordingly, since the Baal Shem Tov turned 26 on the
18th of Elul 5484 (תפ״ד; 1724), he was born on the 18th of Elul
in the year 5458 (תנ״ח; 1698), and became known on the 18th
of Elul 5494 (תצ״ד; 1734). This latter date is likewise clear from
all the letters that are extant. It is true of the letters from R.
Adam Baal Shem to the Baal Shem Tov covering the years
5491-93 (תצ״א — תצ״ג; 1731-33). These contain expositions of
the Torah and of excerpts from the *Zohar* and the *Tikkunim,*
and rebuke him for his refusal to reveal himself, informing

---

few hundred letters, mostly on parchment, written by the Baal Shem Tov
   and his circle. See *HaTamim,* p. 851.
In this letter: *HaTamim,* p. 348, Letter No. 89.
Achiyah HaShiloni: I.e., Achiyah of Shiloh, a prophet first appearing in the
   Tanach early in the First Temple period (*I Kings,* chs. 11 and 14); and see
   Tractate *Bava Basra* 121b. See also pp. 177-178 below.
Completed the Torah: I.e., the *Chumash,* the Five Books of Moses.
Before the eyes of all *Israel:* The last phrase of the *Chumash (Deut.* 34:12).
   In the letter, the word יִשְׂרָאֵל is written thus: יִשְׂרָאֵ״ל, indicating an
   additional connotation — an allusion to the author's name.
I became revealed: Remaining no longer a hidden *tzaddik.*
Letters from R. Adam Baal Shem: See summaries of them in *HaTamim,* pp. 116-
   117.
Rebuke: In the printed text, the word תּוֹכָחָה ("rebuke") appears in error as תּוֹרָה;
   cf. *HaTamim,* loc. cit.

him that the entire brotherhood had decided that he ought to do so. The same date — 5494 (תצ"ד; 1734) — is also evident from a letter addressed by the Baal Shem Tov to his brother-in-law R. Gershon [of Kitov].

Certain aged chassidim passed on the following tradition that they had received from the chassidim of R. Menachem Mendel of Vitebsk, who had heard it from the mouth of their Rebbe. The year in which the Baal Shem Tov was born was תנ"ח (ה') — (5)458. When rearranged, the letters that constitute this date comprise the words נַחַת (nachas — "peacefullness, sense of fulfillment") and חָתָן (chasan — "bridegroom"). That is to say: חַד מִשְּׁמֵי שְׁמַיָּא נָחַת — "There was one who descended (נָחַת) from the highest heavens; this is also the meaning of חָתָן, from the root נחת, as in the Talmudic dictum, נְחִית דַּרְגָּא וּנְסִיב אִתְּתָא — 'Descend a rung and marry a wife'; and his descent brought about peacefullness and a sense of fulfillment below (נַחַת רוּחַ לְמַטָּה), that is, in this mortal world, for a new spirit descended into This World (שֶׁנָּחַת רוּחַ חֲדָשָׁה בְּעוֹלָם זֶה). That is to say, he taught a way of divine service which showed how one should bring about a state of satisfaction or contentment to the One Above."

* * *

I once heard from the well-known chassid R. Chanoch Hendel — who heard from R. Zisskind Kurnitzer, who in turn quoted R. Zalman Zezmer — that the Baal Shem Tov was born and was revealed in a land that was saturated with the blood of Jewish martyrdom.

* * *

When my father read the above-mentioned letter from the Baal Shem Tov to R. Yaakov Yosef of Polonnoye he said to

---

The entire brotherhood: This phrase, referring to the fellowship of the hidden *tzaddikim* of the time, is implied by the word כּוּלָם in the original.

To his brother-in-law: See *HaTamim*, p. 118, Letter No. 30.

There was one who descended: Paraphrase of *Daniel* 4:10: עִיר וְקַדִּישׁ מִן שְׁמַיָּא נָחַת — "A wakeful and holy one descended from heaven."

Descend a rung: *Talmud*, Tractate *Yevamos* 63a; and see *Rashi* there.

Martyrdom: In the original, *mesirus nefesh*.

When my father: The Rebbe Rashab.

me: "How would this correlate with the tradition handed down from one Rebbe to the next that the years of the Baal Shem Tov's life in This World numbered 72 (ע"ב)? But it is not known whether this number is intended to represent the years as they are revealed, or as they were filled."*

* * *

My father strongly disapproved of the inaccurate transmission of stories, the more so if the story in question told of something wondrous. On this subject he used to say: "The Torah was given at Mt. Sinai in *space* and *time*. The divine intention in so doing was that through one's *avodah* there should be a perception *within the confines of time and space* of the reality which transcends time and space. The power to thus perceive is what is meant by the Gates of Light that were opened up during the Revelation at Mt. Sinai. This too is the meaning of the Torah and the *mitzvos*. They themselves are expressed in time and space — except that *in* them and *through* them there can be perceived within time and space that which is beyond the limitations of time and space. The commandment of *tefillin*, for example, is to be fulfilled only in specified categories of time and space — but the *tefillin* are a means [כֵּלִים — lit., "vessels"] of drawing down into This World that which transcends time and space.

One of those present remarked that there is a tradition current amongst the chassidim of Volhynia that the Baal Shem Tov passed away on a Wednesday; a mnemonic of this is to be found in the phrase [referring to the fourth day of Creation as] יוֹם שֶׁנִּתְלוּ הַמְּאוֹרוֹת — "the day

---

* [In the original, שְׁנוֹת הַגָּלוּי אוֹ הַמְּלוּי.] This refers to the days of doubled content — the ten years of study.

Correlate: The year of the Baal Shem Tov's passing is undisputed; the years 5458-5520 (1698-1760) total [almost] 62. See Vol. IV, p. 48.

Gates of Light: Cf. אוֹרָה זוֹ תוֹרָה — "'Light' refers to the Torah" (Tractate *Megillah* 16b).

Volhynia: Former name of a certain region in N.W. Ukraine.

The fourth day of Creation: See *Rashi's* first comment on the phrase *yehi meoros* ("Let there be luminaries"; *Gen.* 1:14), and its source in Tractate *Chagigah* 12a (וְלֹא נִתְלוּ עַד יוֹם רְבִיעִי).

on which the luminaries were suspended [in the heavens]." According to this tradition it is clear that the Baal Shem Tov passed away on the first day of Shavuos.*

To this the Rebbe replied.

Now I understand the meaning of the words which the Alter Rebbe said on Wednesday, the day following his liberation from imprisonment: "On the fourth day the luminaries were *taken away* (בַּיּוֹם הָרְבִיעִי נִטְלוּ הַמְּאוֹרוֹת) — but on the same day the luminaries were *suspended* (נִתְלוּ הַמְּאוֹרוֹת)."**

2.

On Wednesday of the week of *Parshas Ki Savo* 5657 (תרנ"ז; 1897), during the seven days of celebration following my wedding, I was honored by a visit from a group of venerable chassidim — including R. David Zvi Chein [of Chernigov], R. Dov Ze'ev [of Yekaterinoslav], R. Yaakov Mordechai Bespalov, R. Leib Hoffman, R. Shalom-R. Hillel's,*** R. Asher [Grossman, of Nikolayev], R. Monye [Menachem Manes] Monensohn, and R. Yaakov Kuli Bass. Since my room was small we retired to the table and benches in the garden behind our house, and there my guests exchanged thoughts on the teachings of *Chassidus* and the customs of chassidim.

R. Monye Monensohn recalled: "When I was little I heard this from my teacher R. Gedaliah. (R. Gedaliah was an extremely old man who still remembered the Alter Rebbe's first visit to Shklov. He also remembered the first person in Shklov to become a chassid, who recounted how he had

---

* In the year 5520 (תק"ך; 1760) Shavuos fell on Wednesday and Thursday.

** See below, Section 13.

*** He acquired this nickname through being the constant travelling companion of R. Hillel [of Paritch].

Taken away... suspended: The sole difference in Hebrew is between the letters ט and ת, which are pronounced similarly, and are phonetically interchangeable within the group of five letters formed by the tongue — דטלנ"ת.

First visit to Shklov: In 5531 (תקל"א; 1771).

The first... to become a chassid: Shklov, like Vilna, was a bastion of the *misnagdim*.

visited Mezritch and with his own eyes had seen the Maggid; and this chassid was an outstanding scholar and a G-d-fearing man. What the emissaries from Vilna tell about the Maggid and his disciples is a lie.) This R. Gedaliah told me that long, long ago, the 18th of Elul (*Chai* Elul) used to be observed as a *Yom-Tov:* the Baal Shem Tov was born on the 18th of Elul."

R. Shalom-R. Hillel's then told the gathering that R. Hillel once recounted that he had heard from the *guter Yid* R. Mottele of Chernobyl, that *his* father (the *tzaddik* R. Nachum of Chernobyl) had said: "The Baal Shem Tov was born on *Chai* Elul — in body, in *nefesh,* and in *ruach.* 'In body' (בְּגוּפוֹ) — simply, on that date he was born physically; 'in *nefesh*' (בְּנַפְשׁוֹ) refers to the revelation of his mentor on *Chai* Elul; 'in *ruach*' (בְּרוּחוֹ) refers to his own revelation on *Chai* Elul. All these events took place on *Chai* Elul."

R. Shalom proceeded to pass on R. Hillel's own comment: "I would have liked to establish *Chai* Elul as a day of feasting and rejoicing — except that the setting up of a *Yom-Tov* should be left to a Rebbe. And why in fact was it not established as a *Yom-Tov?* The reason, it seems to me, is that *Keser* is not enumerated with the [other] *Sefiros.*"

3.

R. Dov Ze'ev told us that on one of the seven days of festivities following the wedding of my father in Elul 5635 (תרל"ה; 1875), my grandfather explained: "The three days before *Shabbos* are a preparation for *Shabbos.* The *Zohar* says about *Shabbos* that 'from it all the days are blessed.' 'All the days' refers to the six days of the week on which G-d con-

---

To establish *Chai* Elul: On *Chai* Elul 5703 (תש"ג; 1943) the author made it publicly known that exactly fifty years earlier, on *Chai* Elul 5653 (תרנ"ג; 1893), his father (the Rebbe Rashab) had received him with the festive greeting of *Gut Yom-Tov!* and had revealed to him that this date had long been privately celebrated by the respective Rebbes in each generation. It is now of course a major date in the chassidic calendar. See *Kuntreis Chai Elul, Taf-Shin-Gimmel* (Kehot, N. Y., 1955), p. 5-6.

My grandfather: The Rebbe Maharash.

The three days... a preparation: Cf. Tractate *Pesachim* 106a.

From it all days are blessed: In the Aramaic original, מִינֵיהּ מִתְבָּרְכִין כֻּלְהוּ יוֹמִין.

ferred a general blessing — 'G-d will bless you in all you do.'
Now the blessing of *Shabbos* extends both to the days preceding it and to the days following it. The preparations for *Shabbos*
begin on Wednesday, and are heralded by the brief *Lechu
neranenah* of three verses."

*   *   *

"On this occasion," recalled R. Dov Ze'ev, "the Rebbe
was in an exceedingly joyful and outgoing frame of mind. The
seudah took place in the garden, and a great number of people
had come to participate. His countenance was strikingly
handsome at all times, but now in his joy it was literally
luminous: the Divine Presence rested on his holy face. Radiating joy he now said," — and here R. Dov Ze'ev resumed his
account of the words of the Rebbe Maharash: "The ultimate
truth of what these three verses signify should be apprehended — and it is in fact apprehended — in a general way in
the course of one's study of *Chassidus;* and as to the particular
ways in which this affects each person according to the
nature of his soul and his tasks in *avodah,* this should be
explained individually. But now is a time of joy in the World
Above for our grandfathers and their Rebbes, and, yet
higher, it is a time of joy for the Holy One, Blessed be He, and
His Divine Presence, as well as a time of joy in This World
below. So I will explain these three verses as they apply to a
middle path, in a manner meaningful to all men.

"On Wednesday we begin thinking: 'What will we have
for *Shabbos?'* This is a concern in the literal sense, and spiritu-

---

G-d will bless you: *Deut.* 15:18.
Brief *Lechu neranenah:* The first three verses of *Ps.* 95 appended to *Ps.*
        94, the Psalm for Wednesday. They correspond respectively to the
        three days — Wednesday, Thursday and Friday — leading up to
        Shabbos, and also constitute (as the beginning of *Lechu neranenah* proper,
        Ps. 95) the opening of the Friday evening service for the inauguration
        of *Shabbos.*
Our grandfathers: A non-literal reference to the successive Rebbes
        of the preceding generations, counting from the Alter Rebbe.
Their Rebbes: The Baal Shem Tov and the Maggid of Mezritch.

ally as well:' How can we live a real *Shabbos?* After all, every Jew is quite different on *Shabbos* than on a weekday. So we become a little despondent. The solution to this is: *Lechu neranenah* ('Come, let us sing [to G-d]') — trust in Him. Comes Thursday, it is now closer to *Shabbos,* and we are still emptyhanded. It doesn't seem to *neranenah* so easily; we realize we must do something. But when we settle down on Thursday night to study *Chassidus,* then by Friday we sense that 'The L-rd is a great G-d and a great King....' And with this a Jew can live his *Shabbos.*"

* * *

"This coming *Shabbos,*" the Rebbe Maharash had gone on to say, "will be *Shabbos HaGadol* — a great *Shabbos:* the day on which the Baal Shem Tov was born. My father told me that the chassidim who hailed from Horodok used to relate a wealth of stories that they had heard from R. Menachem Mendel [of Horodok]: stories that had been passed on to him — about the Baal Shem Tov before his revelation, the manner of his revelation, the brotherhood of his disciples, and the trials and tribulations which he encountered."

R. Dov Ze'ev continued to describe the events of that memorable occasion: "When the Rebbe concluded his words

---

How can we live a real *Shabbos?:* In the Yiddish original, מיט וואָס וועט מען שבת'ן. The last word, here translated "live a real *Shabbos,*" is an original verb created from the noun *Shabbos.* (A third-person form of the same hypothetical verb is likewise used to close this paragraph: "And with this a Jew can live his *Shabbos.*" In the untranslatable original, און מיט דעם שבת'ט א איד.)

Every Jew is quite different: Cf. *Talmud Yerushalmi,* Tractate *Demai* 4:1: "[Even one so unlettered that he normally cannot be depended upon to tithe his produce] stands in awe of *Shabbos,* and tells the truth" (אֵימַת שַׁבָּת עָלָיו וְהוּא אוֹמֵר אֱמֶת); and *Bereishis Rabbah* 11:2: "The light of a man's face on weekdays is not the same as it is on *Shabbos*" (לֹא דוֹמֶה אוֹר פָּנָיו שֶׁל אָדָם כָּל יְמוֹת הַשַּׁבָּת כְּמוֹ שֶׁהוּא דוֹמֶה בְּשַׁבָּת).

It doesn't seem to *neranenah* so easily: Another instance of poetic licence. In the original, נְרַנְנָה'ט זעך ניט.

By Friday... 'The Lord... a great King': *Ps.* 95:3; the third of the above-mentioned three verses.

My father told me: The *Tzemach Tzedek.*

R. Menachem Mendel [of Horodok]: Same as R. Menachem Mendel of Vitebsk.

he had it announced that whoever could sing should join in the *niggun* which he indicated. The melody was to be sung three times over, and in measured tones, all singing together. In order to make this possible he instructed R. Eliyahu (Virabaitchik) of Obel and R. Tzadok (Nechamkin) of Homil to stand in a high spot and lead the singing. When the singing drew to a close the Rebbe delivered the *maamar* which opens with the words, כִּי עַל כָּל כָּבוֹד חֻפָּה — lit., 'For over each [kind of] honor there will be a canopy.' He explained that *kavod* and *chuppah* are both *makkifim* [lit., 'encompassing lights'], an immediate and a distant *makkif*, respectively. In the course of his teaching he said in a singsong: 'The immediate *makkif* — this refers to our predecessors; the distant *makkif* — this refers to the Maggid and the Baal Shem Tov.'

"The joy that we chassidim then experienced is indescribable," continued R. Dov Ze'ev. "Immediately after delivering the *maamar* the Rebbe left the table to dance for a short while, and then went up the steps which led from the garden to the porch.* There he sat by the window watching us, the chassidim, as we danced in the garden in dozens of circles. Next to him stood his son R. Zalman Aharon, and my uncle R. Moshe Aryeh Ginsburg, from Vitebsk, the Rebbe's son-in-law. They later said that the Rebbe had remarked to them: 'See, my children, how chassidim are glad in the joy of a *mitzvah*. This is how Jews will dance in the streets when *Mashiach* comes!'

"That *Shabbos*, which was *Chai* Elul, was a cloudy day, so the *Kiddush* took place in the large hall.** In the course of the

---

* The garden behind the Rebbe's home was some 25 by 9 klafter, and the steps led up to the porch adjoining his study.

** On the site of the home of his father, the *Tzemach Tzedek*, and according to his will, my grandfather the Rebbe Maharash built a large room ten klafter [=18 meters] square which was known as the large hall (*der groisser zal*). In due course this served as the main study hall of the Tomchei Temimim

The Rebbe delivered: The Rebbe Maharash.

A canopy: *Isa.* 4:5.

An immediate and a distant *makkif*: In the original, מַקִּיף הַקָּרוֹב וּמַקִּיף הָרָחוֹק.

Our predecessors: In the original, *di zeides*: lit., "our grandfathers."

Kiddush the Rebbe said: 'The Baal Shem Tov was born on *Chai Elul.* Through the teachings of *Chassidus* the Baal Shem Tov introduced vitality into the mode of *avodah* [of *teshuvah* through love, initiated by the worshiper] which is represented by the words, אֲנִי לְדוֹדִי וְדוֹדִי לִי — lit., "I am my Beloved's, and my Beloved is mine."' The Rebbe then delivered a *maamar* opening with these four words, whose initial letters (אלו״ל) constitute the name of the month [which is the classic season for this mode of *teshuvah*], and whose final letters are four times *yud* [whose numerical equivalent is ten], totalling 40, and representing the 40 days which Moshe Rabbeinu spent on Mt. Sinai receiving the Torah.

"After the *maamar* those assembled sang together, and following this the Rebbe said: 'Dancing in a circle, the way chassidim do, is a custom renewed in the days of the Baal Shem Tov. A circle represents that which is *makkif.* The first stage of revelation [of divine light] must be in a mode of *makkif* [lit., "encompassing the recipient from without"]. It does not allow itself to be brought down at all in "vessels" *(kelim),* and certainly not in a mode of *pnimiyus* [that is, capable of perception by conscious and intellectual means]. My greatgrandfather the Alter Rebbe, through his self-sacrifice for the teachings of *Chassidus* and for chassidim drew down the encompassing (*makkif*) lights into the [internalized] mode of *pnimiyus;* he constructed "vessels" [of intellectual perception] for the *pnimiyus.* Now, when chassidim dance in a circle, this

---

Yeshivah. [For a plan of the layout of the Rebbe's household, and a map of Lubavitch, see Rabbi Raphael Nachman Kahn, *Lubavitch VeChayaleha* (Kfar Chabad, 1983; Heb.), p. 15 and 22.]

Vitality: In the original, *chiyus.*

I am my Beloved's: *Song of Songs* 6:3.

The 40 days: Viz., the month of Elul and the Ten Days of Penitence culminating in Yom Kippur. The reference is to Moshe Rabbeinu's third stay of 40 days, and to the giving of the Second Tablets. See *Rashi* on *Ex.* 33:11.

Oros, kelim, pnimiyus: See Rabbi J. I. Schochet, *Mystical Concepts in Chassidism,* Chs. V and VI; in *Tanya,* p. 860-864.

represents a state of *oros bekelim*, lights contained within vessels; a light which is *makkif* rests upon them; and this *makkif* has its effect on the [lesser, indwelling] light which is *pnimi.*'

"The Rebbe retired to his study, while the chassidim went out to the courtyard and danced in dozens of circles.

"At the *Shabbos* meal which followed, the Rebbe said: 'The Baal Shem Tov opened the gates of the inner realms of the Torah *(pnimiyus haTorah)*, and the Alter Rebbe opened the gates of *Chabad*. Accordingly, the meaning of *Chai* Elul nowadays is that *Elul itself has come to life* [lit., "Elul lives" — as if written thus:חַי אֱלוּל]. In days gone by, when the month of Elul drew near, everyone became enshrouded by melancholy, each person ensconced in his own cloud. The Alter Rebbe however brought vitality down into a state of inwardness, making it intrinsic to the worshiper. That is, he drove out the extrinsic melancholy, and in its stead introduced a *merirus* [lit., "bitterness"; i.e., a constructive and contrite anguish] which is generated from within.'"

R. Dov Ze'ev continued his account of what he had heard on that occasion from my grandfather the Rebbe Maharash.

"The Alter Rebbe opens his *Tanya* with a discussion of the *tzaddik* and the *rasha*, the righteous man and the wicked; he raises queries concerning the status of the *rasha*, quoting the *Mishnah*, 'And do not be a *rasha* in your own estimation,' and proceeds to ask, 'Furthermore, if a man considers himself to be wicked,' and so on. Now one might have expected that he should have discussed instead the level of the *tzaddik*.

"But the matter can be understood thus. It is characteristic of *baalei makkifim* [i.e., those whose mental attitude toward reality is subject to the powerful overt impressions of *makkifim*, "encompassing lights" (or: intuited potential states of being), these impressions not being integrated into their inner character] that they are *baalei ketzavos* [lit., 'men of

---

Opened the gates of *Chabad: Chabad* here signifies the apprehension of
    divinity through intellectually-generated means. See also Glossary.
Melancholy... *merirus:* Cf. *Tanya*, Ch. 26.
And do not be a *rasha:* Mishnah, Tractate *Avos* 2:13.

extremes']. From their perspective, one may waver between two opposite positions. On the one hand the speaker may consider himself at times to be a *tzaddik*, while at other times he may describe himself as being (G-d forbid) a *rasha*. The reason: such a person's perceptions are not settled (*behisyashvus*). However, in the realm of *pnimi* [that is, in the realm of perceptions that have been intellectually digested, integrated, and internalized], the confusion of extremes is inconceivable. That which is *pnimi* is by definition organized. It follows that in bygone times, when Elul approached and people felt that it was time to become more pious, they were beset by melancholy. For in order to rouse himself a person would refer to himself as (G-d forbid) a *rasha*, so that a heavy despondence set in, and throughout the month of Elul everyone was weighted down by a cloud. Came the Baal Shem Tov and injected a vitality into the service of G-d. The Alter Rebbe then illuminated the path of the Baal Shem Tov. He dispelled the murky melancholy and dolefulness, and in addition brought people to realize that a *tzaddik* too has to do *teshuvah*. The *Chassidus* which the Alter Rebbe and his successors gave us is a revelation of *Mashiach*." And the Rebbe Maharash went on to expound the statement in the *Zohar* that "*Mashiach* comes in order to cause the *tzaddikim* to return in *teshuvah*."

He then delivered the *maamar* which begins with the words, אָז תִּשְׂמַח בְּתוּלָה בְּמָחוֹל — "Then will the virgin rejoice in the dance."

4.

R. David Zvi Chein now recounted something that he had heard from his father R. Peretz Chein, who in turn had heard it from the aged chassid R. Yaakov of Horodok, who had received it from the mouth of his Rebbe, R. Menachem Mendel of Horodok, as follows: "The Baal Shem Tov was born on *Chai* Elul in the year (ה'תנ"ח) — (5)458 (1698). These

---

Mashiach comes... in *teshuvah:* In the original, מָשִׁיחַ אָתָא לְאַתָבָא צַדִּיקַיָּא בְּתִיוּבְתָּא.
Rejoice in the dance: *Jer.* 31:12.

three Hebrew letters when rearranged comprise the words נַחַת and חָתָן [as explained in Section 1 above]. The year that the Baal Shem Tov was born saw the second printing of *Shnei Luchos HaBris,* the *Shlah HaKadosh,* in Amsterdam. At this time a stern edict was mooted in the Heavenly Court against the Jewry of Poland, exactly as had been the case when this work was first published. (While the printing was then still in progress, readers bought the work section by section. The hearts of many Jews were ignited, and an Evil Eye took effect; and soon after came the massacres of 1648-49.) The year of the second printing, however, the year in which the Baal Shem Tov was born, was (thank G-d) a year of repose. For the first 26 years of his life he had the outward appearance of an ordinary individual; for ten years his holy mentor taught him; he then became revealed, and for 26 years he was a leader of his brethren."

R. David Zvi Chein further told of another statement of R. Menachem Mendel of Horodok which had likewise been passed down by the latter's close disciple, R. Yaakov of Horodok.

It once happened that during the festive meal of Shavuos, R. Menachem Mendel was rapt in the ecstatic state of *dveikus.* In due course he quoted a verse from *Psalms* — יוֹדֵעַ ה' יְמֵי תְמִימִם ("G-d knows the days of the perfect ones") — and began to expound its component phrases homiletically, as follows: "יוֹדֵעַ ה' — *The Name of G-d can be known* through יְמֵי תְמִימִם, *the days of the perfect ones,* who draw G-dliness down into This World and connect it with G-dliness; for through this activity one renders the world complete, and realizes the Divine Will. The Rebbe, the Baal Shem Tov, lived twice 26 years and once ten years. The first 26 years correspond to the numerical value of the letters compris-

---

Shnei Luchos HaBris: Monumental work on law and ethics by R. Yeshayahu Halevi Horowitz (d. 1630).
First published: In 1649.
G-d knows: *Ps.* 37:18.
Through... *the days:* Day signifies the advent of light.

ing the Hidden Name of G-d, which explains why during those years he was a hidden *tzaddik;* the later 26 years correspond to the numerical value of the letters comprising the Revealed Name of G-d, and this is why at this stage in his life he was revealed. But in order that it should be possible for him to be revealed, he had to pass through the series of Ten *Sefiros.* This corresponds to the middle ten years of his life. The above verse in *Tehillim* concludes: וְנַחֲלָתָם לְעוֹלָם תִּהְיֶה — 'Their heritage shall be forever.' And indeed, with the teachings of the Baal Shem Tov we will come to our Holy Land." With this R. Menachem Mendel rose, and broke out in a joyful dance.

5.

[At this point the Rebbe cited an exposition of the above teaching on the Hidden and Revealed Names of G-d, propounded by a chassid named R. Leib Hoffman, and couched in part in the learned terminology of the Kabbalah. The Rebbe then proceeded to quote an episode recounted by R. Leib.]

"Once when I was in the presence of the Rebbe [Maharash] at *yechidus,*" R. Leib Hoffman recalled, "I had asked for clarification on various points encountered in my studies, and had made a mental note of certain further queries. However, since I had been in the Rebbe's study longer than the time allowed me by the *gabbai* — R. Leivik *Meshares,* who determined the order of entry — even though the Rebbe spoke to me in a cheerful manner, answering all my queries clearly and at length, I made a move towards the door, because R. Leivik had by now opened it twice.* The Rebbe then gave me his

---

* This was his sign that it was time to leave. The chassidim all stood in dread of him, knowing that he might refuse them entry at their next request.

The Hidden Name: In the original, שֵׁם הֲוָיָ׳ הַנֶּעְלָם.

The Revealed Name: In the original, שֵׁם הֲוָיָ׳ הַגָּלוּי.

Ten *Sefiros:* Divine emanations or manifestations: see Schochet, *op. cit.,* p. 826ff.

blessing, and looking at me at length he said: 'Leibe, you are thinking about the Baal Shem Tov. What do you want to ask? Ask!'

"So I said: 'I have a notion that the Baal Shem Tov, the Mezritcher Maggid and the Alter Rebbe represent the *Keser, chochmah* and *binah* of *Chassidus.*'

"A change overcame the Rebbe's face. Elated, he stood up from his chair, and said: 'This is the case only in the general manner of the revelation Above; that is, it is true of the sequence in which the teachings of *Chassidus* were progressively revealed from the higher levels to the lower. From our perspective, the Baal Shem Tov, the Mezritcher Maggid and the Alter Rebbe are the *Keser, chochmah* and *binah* of *Chassidus.* And in practice this is what is apparent to the observer. The manner of the revelation of the Baal Shem Tov parallels the manner of the revelation of *Keser* — first being concealed, then revealing itself; and in its revelation encompassing (like a crown from above) all levels equally, from the loftiest to the nethermost. So too was the manner of the revelation of the Baal Shem Tov — being at first concealed, and then revealing himself; and in his revelation adopting the mode of a *makkif klali* — an all-encompassing mode of revelation which transcended in equal measure the loftiest levels and the nethermost, so that from this perspective there was no distinction of degree between the occasions when his soul would ascend to the realms Above, and the occasions when he would reveal himself in a miraculous incident in this world.

"The Baal Shem Tov won the Maggid as a disciple neither through working miracles nor through *makkifim* [lit., "encompassing lights"; i.e., superrational revelations]. The Maggid was seeking *haskalah*, intellectual awareness; he was seeking *nekudas hachochmah*, the initial and quintessential point in the

---

The *Keser, chochmah* and *binah* of *Chassidus:* In the original, abbreviated as בַּחַ״ב.

Like a crown: The literal meaning of *Keser*.

Working miracles: In the original, *mofsim*.

intellectual perception of G-dliness; and when he found this in the Baal Shem Tov he became his disciple.

"As to the Alter Rebbe, what made its mark on him was not *haskalah:* he sought *havanah,* the fully integrated understanding afforded by *binah.* My father [the *Tzemach Tzedek*] once told me that his grandfather, the Alter Rebbe, had told him the following: 'When I had with the help of G-d established myself in the knowledge of the Torah, I sought *havanah,* understanding. In those days two places were talked about — Vilna and Mezritch; in Vilna one learned how to study, and in Mezritch one learned how to pray. I was in search of the understanding which resides in the heart — in the words of *Pasach Eliyahu,* בִּינָה: לְבָּא; through a miracle I reached Mezritch and there, thank G-d, I found what I was seeking, and in generous measure.'

"All the above, however," the Rebbe Maharash continued his reply to R. Leib Hoffman, "is true of what goes on Above, in relation to the workings of Divine Providence *vis-à-vis* the created universe as it is gradated in various levels. But when viewed from the perspective of the divine service of the individual, the Baal Shem Tov, the Mezritcher Maggid and the Alter Rebbe correspond to *Chabad* — *chochmah, binah* and *daas.*"

The Rebbe Maharash concluded his words by quoting two verses from *Mishlei:* ה' בְּחָכְמָה יָסַד אָרֶץ כּוֹנֵן שָׁמַיִם בִּתְבוּנָה. בְּדַעְתּוֹ תְּהוֹמוֹת נִבְקָעוּ וּשְׁחָקִים יִרְעֲפוּ טָל. [Literally translated, these verses mean: "G-d founded the earth with wisdom; he established the heavens with understanding. With this knowledge the depths burst open, and the highest heavens drip with dew." The Rebbe Maharash however expounded them phrase by phrase according to the teachings of *Chassidus,* on the non-literal level of *derush,* as follows:]

"הַוָיָ: In order that the essential and transcendent *Name of G-d* should be perceived in This World in a mode of internalized understanding,

---

Pasach Eliyahu: Tikkunei Zohar, Introduction II.
Two verses from *Mishlei: Prov.* 3:19-20.

"בְּחָכְמָה יָסַד אָרֶץ: G-d founded the earth with chochmah — this corresponds to the Baal Shem Tov;

"כּוֹנֵן שָׁמַיִם בִּתְבוּנָה: He established the heavens with understanding (tevunah/binah) — this corresponds to the Mezritcher Maggid;

"בְּדַעְתּוֹ: with His daas (i.e., with the daas of the revealed levels of the Torah and Chassidus together with the avodah of the heart to the extent of literal self-sacrifice),

"תְּהוֹמוֹת נִבְקָעוּ: the depths of the abyss were burst open — this corresponds to the Alter Rebbe; and in consequence,

"וּשְׁחָקִים: the highest heavens (referring to all of the Rebbes, through whose avodah and guidance even stony hearts are crushed [שחק — "to grind"] and replaced by hearts of flesh) —

"יִרְעֲפוּ טָל: will drip with dew [signifying the gift of life-giving divine inspiration], until the coming of Mashiach."

6.

In the course of that same visit by the delegation of elder chassidim to my home soon after my marriage, R. Yaakov Mordechai Bespalov recounted that once while at yechidus he had asked the Rebbe [Maharash] to elaborate on certain points that had been raised during the maamar of the preceding Shabbos, concerning the definition of the term Adam Kadmon. In reply the Rebbe had told him to study the discourse in Likkutei Torah which opens with the words לַמְנַצֵּחַ עַל הַשְּׁמִינִית, and had then said: "Ask my son [i.e., the Rebbe Rashab] for the unpublished explanation of this maamar."

[Here is recorded a brief but involved exchange between the Rebbe Maharash and his chassid R. Yaakov Mordechai, which connects the definition of the term

---

Internalized understanding: In the original, havanah u'kelitah.

וּשְׁחָקִים... heavens... [שחק — "to grind"]: This interpretation, connecting this word for "heavens" with the avodah of tzaddikim, is foreshadowed in the Talmudic derush (Tractate Chagigah 12b) on the verses in Tehillim (Ps. 78:23-24) which speak of the שְׁחָקִים giving manna.

Discourse in Likkutei Torah: Expounds this verse (Ps. 12:1); appears under Parshas Tazria.

under discussion with the path in *avodah* taught by the
Alter Rebbe.]

R. Yaakov Mordechai concluded his account of that *yechidus* by quoting the words with which the Rebbe Maharash
closed his discussion of the Alter Rebbe: "And he was the
Rebbe — and when there is a Rebbe there are chassidim!"

With these words R. Yaakov Mordechai broke down in
such bitter tears that all those present were amazed. They
tried to calm him from his sobbing, but to no avail — until R.
Leib Hoffman said: "Come now, this is a time of threefold joy
— it is the birthday of the Baal Shem Tov; it is the day on
which the Baal Shem Tov was revealed; and our Rebbe is
celebrating the marriage of his only son. Is this a time to cry?!
Rav of Poltava, it's time to do *teshuvah!*"

And with this he began to sing a *niggun* — he had a
wonderful voice — and all of his companions joined in. R.
David Zvi Chein, R. Shalom-R. Hillel's and R. Asher Grossman then rose from the table and began to dance. They were
soon joined by all the others — all, that is, except for R.
Yaakov Mordechai, who sat with his head in his hands, still
weeping. The other elder chassidim returned to the table and
filled glasses for *LeChaim!* — and while they were so occupied
his crying ceased, but he said in a tearful voice: "The Rebbe
told me then, 'When there is a Rebbe there are *chassidim!'*"

R. Yaakov Mordechai then resumed his account of the
words with which the Rebbe Maharash had concluded that
yechidus: "That is, chassidim who are active in *avodah*. But if one
is a chassid who is not a chassid, this causes the Rebbe to cease
being a Rebbe. The Alter Rebbe was a Rebbe, so he made
chassidim. And the chassidim, through being chassidim and
men of deeds in the realm of divine service that stems from
the heart, gave strength to the Rebbe."

7.

Yesterday I recounted that the three hours which the

Yesterday I recounted: See p. 66 above.

Alter Rebbe inadvertently came to spend in the home of one of his opponents immediately after his release caused him more anguish than his entire imprisonment. I said too that when he was brought the tidings of his impending release he did not want to leave the fortress.

The whole episode of the imprisonment came about with the consent of the Alter Rebbe. And indeed not only the Alter Rebbe, but every *tzaddik* likewise rules over all material matters. What the Torah has to say about the created universe is decisive: all temporal matters are subject to the dominion of the Torah. It follows that whatever is due to befall a *tzaddik* takes place only with his consent. And this of course includes the imprisonment of the Alter Rebbe.

Had the Alter Rebbe not been agreeable he would not have been arrested — as witness his journey to Petersburg. On Friday the black wagon remained stationary, and harnessing four horses to it did not help in the slightest. The wagon did not budge because the Alter Rebbe did not want it to.

Six hours before candle-lighting time the Alter Rebbe did not want to travel any further, so the wagon stopped in its tracks. When the general and his gendarmes understood that this was no simple matter — first an axle had suddenly broken; and when it was repaired one of the horses collapsed; and when fresh horses were brought they were unable to drag the wagon an inch — they asked the Alter Rebbe's permission to travel on as far as a nearby village. When he declined, they asked him to allow them to move the wagon to a field at the roadside. To this he agreed, and that is where they spent *Shabbos*. This spot is two or three viorsts from

---

An axle had suddenly broken: [Footnote in the original:] On this the Alter Rebbe remarked: צְוָחִין אַף עֲקָתִין בְּטֵלִין וּשְׁבִיתִין.

The quotation is from *Azamer BiShvachin,* one of the *Shabbos* table hymns *(zemiros)* composed by the *Arizal,* and means: "[The forces of evil] cry out, yea, and despair, yet they are made null and void." The third Aramaic word *(aksin)* is a pun on the Yiddish word for "axle", as if to say: "Even the axles cry out; they are made null and void."

Saliba Rudnia, which is near the town of Nevel. The chassid known as "the aged R. Michael" used to relate that he knew chassidim who were able to point out the exact spot at which the Alter Rebbe had spent that *Shabbos*. In fact he had gone there himself to see it with his own eyes. All the way there he had seen drooping old trees on both sides of the road, but near that spot where the wagon had stopped for *Shabbos* stood a tall tree with luxuriant foliage. And whenever R. Michael used to recall that moment, and would describe the site in detail, his soul would light up with a noble awakening of pious awe. Indeed, the recollection of the tree did more to arouse his soul than the study of a whole moral tract in *Chassidus* does to certain chassidim today...

8.

I would like to mention something parenthetically. It does not directly concern the present narrative, but it *is* relevant to the whole make-up of chassidim. It is something that affects oneself, one's wife and one's children (*May they be blessed with good health!*).

It is said that everything depends on the heart, and the heart depends on the purse. Now the root and source of the *avodah* of chassidim has always been — rubbing shoulders with elder chassidim. Everyone knows that if you want your house to be warm you have to heat the stove. If one yearns for the ardor of holiness, zeal in the performance of a *mitzvah*, and

---

Everything depends on the heart: Paraphrase of a statement in the *Talmud Yerushalmi* (Tractate *Terumos,* end of Ch. 8): כָּל הָאֵיבָרִים תְּלוּיִין בַּלֵּב וְהַלֵּב תָּלוּי בַּכִּיס —"All the organs depend on the heart, and the heart depends on the purse."

The *avodah* of chassidim: In the original, "... of *chassidishe yungelait.*" The Yiddish adjective means more than simply "chassidic": it embraces all the positive qualities of character that distinguish a person imbued with the teachings of *Chassidus.* The noun *yungelait* (*yungerman* in the singular) literally means "young folk," but in chassidic parlance signifies adult members of the brotherhood of any age whatever — on the confident assumption that in spirit, chassidim remain forever young.

a relish in the study of the Torah, then one must heat the stove, that is to say, arouse one's heart. And this can be accomplished only through close and humble contact with chassidim who tackle their life-tasks energetically. This, then, is what is meant by the phrase, "Everything depends on the heart."

The heart, however, depends in turn on the purse. Heat alone will not suffice: it needs to be supplemented by ready cash, tangible merchandise. That is to say: the hours set aside daily for Torah study must be scrupulously guarded. Each hour of study is of consequence to oneself and to one's entire household.

There are those whose affairs at the moment are all being conducted on a credit basis. The heart is there, to be sure; it succeeds in drawing its possessor to a *chassidisher farbrengen;* he feels moreover that he is being aroused; but what is still lacking is hard cash, the fixed times set aside for Torah study.

Everyone needs to know — and everyone knows — that a Jew's good-heartedness (and in particular a chassid's good-heartedness) as expressed according to the Torah, is a well-spring of happiness in family life. This is the greatest of all blessings. It is well known that a pure family life as directed by the Torah is one of the happiest things known to all humanity. And this can be arrived at only through the fixing of times for Torah study in the company of good friends.

Though this subject has now been raised only by the way, parenthetically, it warrants close attention, for it is vital to the life of the sons and daughters of all the House of Israel, and to their children likewise.

9.

The story of the Alter Rebbe's journey to Petersburg gives us tangible testimony to the above statement that whatever happens to a *tzaddik* — and especially to a *tzaddik* who is a leader of Jewry — takes place only with his consent. When the Alter Rebbe did not want to travel further, the wagon came to a halt — and it came to a halt where and when the Alter Rebbe so desired.

Had the wagon stood still at candle-lighting time this would have been not at all remarkable. For such things we find concerning even an unwitting reaction. Take for example the incident in which the wealthy scholar R. Yehoshua Tzeitlin, seeking to put the Alter Rebbe's perception to the test, served him wine which had been handled by a gentile; when his little stratagem failed he said: "Concerning you it is written, לֹא יְאֻנֶּה לַצַּדִּיק כָּל אָוֶן — 'No evil shall befall the right-eous...'" In this incident, for example, there is nothing re-markable. But that the wagon should stand still at ten-thirty on Friday morning, and not budge, — this is one of the palpable wonders of G-d, like any overt miracle.

From all of the above it is abundantly clear to anyone, that one whose word carried weight over material things, as was the case with the Alter Rebbe, had the option of not being imprisoned at all; and of not hiding, even for a solitary hour. If he did go nevertheless, this was for the sake of a profound purpose involving the service of G-d.

Avraham Avinu opened the channel of self-sacrifice for the sanctification of the Divine Name, and the Alter Rebbe opened the channel of self-sacrifice for the service of G-d according to the teachings of *Chassidus*. From all of this one can gather that the whole episode of the Alter Rebbe's im-prisonment was only a garment worn by choice, in order to avoid making use of supernatural means.

Truth to tell, this subject warrants a detailed explana-tion, especially since this would provide at least an inkling of an appreciation of the Alter Rebbe's quintessential inner love for Jews in general — for he wanted every individual to start living with a zest in his Torah study, and in his divine service according to the teachings of *Chassidus* — and his love for

---

R. Yehoshua Tzeitlin: A prominent *misnaged* of Shklov. See Vol. II, p. 2.

No evil shall befall: *Prov.* 12:21.

Self-sacrifice for the sanctification of the Divine Name: In the original, *mesirus nefesh al Kiddush HaShem.*

chassidim in particular. And this love the Alter Rebbe planted in the Rebbes who succeeded him.

To explain this theme in passing is impossible: it deserves detailed attention in a hallowed nook all its own. I am nevertheless mentioning it in brief, so that chassidim will know that they are not (G-d forbid) alone, for such a deepseated and quintessential love is everlasting, throughout all the generations until the coming of *Mashiach,* when it will be granted us, at the time of the Resurrection of the Dead, to gaze directly upon the living and luminous countenances of the Rebbes.

10.

After the brief introduction above, as to how the imprisonment and all the suffering it involved was of no account in the eyes of the Alter Rebbe, I would like to tell you of a certain incident.

In the year 5666 (תרס"ו; 1906) my father [the Rebbe Rashab] and I were in Moscow on 24 Teves, the anniversary of the passing of the Alter Rebbe, and a *minyan* was needed for the afternoon *Minchah* prayer. It was midwinter, and the days were short. Besides, the only way to be allowed to live in Moscow in those days was by holding a document of proxy, and every Jew knew that he had to be on his guard so that he should not be recognized when walking in the streets, for fear of his life. So it was that for a number of Jews to assemble, especially at a fixed time, was exceedingly difficult. While we were waiting my father said: "If people only knew the lofty worth of responding *Amen* to the *Kaddish* which is soon to be said — what rich spiritual and material blessings and success it bestows upon all the five levels of the soul, and what blessings for children, health and livelihood it brings in its wake, to generation after generation, — then there would be a considerable number of *minyanim.*"

The anniversary of the passing: In the original, יוֹם הַהִלּוּלָא — lit., "the day of rejoicing," for on the *yahrzeit* every year the souls of the departed are granted a more elevated appreciation of G-dliness.

In the meantime people started to wander in one by one. My father was always punctilious about the proper times for prayer, especially in the afternoon, so he had already prayed the *Minchah* service. When the tenth man arrived — a chassid by the name of R. Baruch Shalom HaKohen Rudner — the *minyan* prayed the *Minchah* service, after which my father said: "There are times when *Kaddish* is recited for the sake of the departed, and there are times when *Kaddish* is recited for the benefit of those who recite it. There are times too when for the one who recites it the *Kaddish* is a ladder, while for the listener it is a channel through which divine blessings flow. The initials of the first four words of *Kaddish* [יִתְגַּדֵּל וְיִתְקַדַּשׁ שְׁמֵהּ רַבָּא] comprise the word יֹשֶׁר. May the blessing elicited by the *Kaddish* be drawn down in a manner of *Yosher*, finding expression in the kind of good which is visible and revealed."

*   *   *

On the anniversary of the Rebbe's passing a disciple is bound to him with all the five levels of his soul — *nefesh, ruach, neshamah, chayah* and *yechidah*.

Even if an ordinary person is imprisoned he becomes refined by the experience. How much more so the Alter Rebbe; and particularly since he was imprisoned over the revelation of the innermost dimension of the Torah, risking his very life for this cause; and, as is known, his daughter gave her life on this account.* Considering self-sacrifice of this order, and his *dveikus* with the Infinite One, Blessed be He, and his close communion with his saintly teachers, one will be able to appreciate the extent to which the entire incarceration did not engage his attention. From this one will likewise to be

———————

* See Sections 11 (p. 95) and 14 (p. 102) below.

Kaddish is a ladder: Speaking of the ladder in the dream of Yaakov Avinu (*Gen.* 28:12), the *Zohar* says: דָּא צְלוֹתָא — "This is prayer."

A manner of *Yosher:* A term describing one of the modes in which the *Sefiros* are manifested. See Rabbi J. I. Schochet, *Mystical Concepts in Chassidism,* Ch. III; in *Tanya,* p. 838-840.

able to understand, or at least imagine, the following divinely-ordained situation: After the Alter Rebbe had spent time in the Peter-Paul Fortress, being in the company of the Maggid, and listening to the Baal Shem Tov, how much must he have suffered during those three hours in the home of the *misnaged.*

Now the above-quoted statement which has been handed down from Rebbe to Rebbe — that those three hours caused the Alter Rebbe more anguish than the whole imprisonment — may be well understood.

11.

In the course of the five years 5548-5552 (תקמ״ח—תקנ״ב; 1788-1792) the circle of chassidim grew exceedingly, both in numbers and in quality. That is to say, all the disciples of the three *chadarim* spread out in various places. As is known, the Alter Rebbe was highly organized, both in his own life and as a leader of men, so that their mission of awakening their brethren to the teachings of *Chassidus* was closely planned. I had jotted down what I had been told on this subject, and much of this I recorded in a long letter to a certain individual. At any rate, in the course of these five years there was a great increase in the number of chassidim who were men of mellow understanding. The *misnagdim* saw that the chassidim were growing into a body to be reckoned with, and observed that the disciples whom the Alter Rebbe dispatched as emissaries to disseminate the teachings of the Baal Shem Tov were G-d-fearing men, and scholars of formidable stature. Seeing moreover that in every town they won over more individuals to the cause of *Chassidus,* their opponents once again sought to arouse the ire of the Gaon of Vilna. At first, as is known, he refused to listen to them. But the factious men among them,

---

The above-quoted statement: On p. 66 above. For further details see Rabbi
    Nissan Mindel, *Rabbi Schneur Zalman of Liadi*, p. 182-183.
The five years 5548-52: Misprint in the original; for תק״ן read תקנ״ב (cf.
    beginning of following paragraph).
Chadarim (pl. of *cheder*): See p. 67 above.

who fanned dissension, conspired to surround him with
falsehood and deceit, bringing him slanderous allegations
about the lifestyle of the chassidim in general, and in particular the charge that they disparaged the study of the Torah.

During this period — in the years 5551-5552
(תקנ״א – תקנ״ב; 1791-1792) — the rose of *Chassidus* flourished,
and the Evil One who cast his malevolent eye on the First and
on the Second *Beis HaMikdash* now made his presence felt. A
harsh edict was mooted in the Heavenly Court. During that
summer the Alter Rebbe had sent his chassid R. Yaakov of
Semilian to the *tzaddik* R. Nachum of Chernobyl, bearing a
pidyon nefesh on his behalf, and on behalf of the cause of
Chassidus in general. He then called for his daughter — the
saintly *Rebbitzin* Devorah Leah, mother of the *Tzemach Tzedek*
— and imparted to her what he had intended by the names
which he had given her (that is, after which of the many
Devorah's and Leah's he had named her). He explained her
too his life-work in disseminating the teachings of his mentors, and told her of the success with which his endeavors had
met. But this had served only as "an arrow in the eye of
Satan," for now a dire verdict against him had been passed
down in the Heavenly Court. He told her further that he
considered that the divine influence which was to be brought
down to the World Below could be directed too from the
World Above; this was the result of *avodah*, but it was not an
approach appropriate to the world-scheme of *Tikkun*.

The Alter Rebbe's daughter replied not a word. She left
the room, and later returned to tell him: "To this you ought
never agree: this — on no account!"

She then called for a few selected and discreet chassidim
of her father, told them in brief of what she had now heard
from his mouth, and declared: "My father — on no account! I
undertake to stand in his stead, so that he will be able to carry
out the intention and the will of my grandfather and my

He then called for his daughter: See also p. 102 below.
An arrow in the eye of Satan: Talmudic metaphor (Tractate *Kiddushin*
30a) for a defiant challenge.

greatgrandfather — which is also the Divine Will."

The children of the Alter Rebbe used to refer to the Maggid of Mezritch as their grandfather, and to the Baal Shem Tov as their greatgrandfather.

12.

In my father's *farbrengens* of bygone days, every word is a pearl. And as time goes by one comes nearer to an understanding of an old *vort*, a memorable dictum from long ago, and it becomes clear and luminous in quite a novel way. Each word warms one, and gives one a sense of wellbeing. Then when one ponders over it, one does not feel so lonely.

On the physical plane we see that if a person owns a number of individual pearls, they may well be valuable merchandise — but they are after all only individual pearls. If however these selfsame pearls are threaded together in a certain order, then even though there is nothing new in the pearls themselves, their beauty is now of quite a different kind. They light up their entire surroundings, and around them is created a purer air.

13.

In the year 5639 (תרל"ט; 1878) *Yud-Tes* Kislev fell on Sunday. The day before, on *Shabbos,* my grandfather the Rebbe Maharash delivered a *maamar* which opens with the words, אַתָּה אֶחָד וְשִׁמְךָ אֶחָד וּמִי כְעַמְּךָ כְּיִשְׂרָאֵל גּוֹי אֶחָד בָּאָרֶץ — "You are One, and Your Name is One, and who is like Your people, like Israel, the one nation on earth?" He explained there that the unity in the levels of G-dliness represented by אַתָּה ("You") and שִׁמְךָ ("Your Name") is brought about by the *avodah* of גּוֹי אֶחָד בָּאָרֶץ [i.e., the particular task of the Jewish people (גּוֹי) — of revealing the divine Unity (אֶחָד) underlying the material creation of This World (אָרֶץ)]. He went on to explain the difference between — on the one hand — the innate unity of אַתָּה הוּא

You are One: *II Samuel* 7:23.

קוֹדֶם שֶׁנִּבְרָא הָעוֹלָם ("You were [the same] before the world was created") and אַתָּה הוּא לְאַחַר שֶׁנִּבְרָא הָעוֹלָם ("You are [the same] since the world has been created"), and — on the other hand — the unity which is effected by *avodah*.

My grandfather used to mark *Yud-Tes* Kislev as follows. On the eve of the 19th of Kislev there was a festive gathering which was known as the *seudah* of my grandmother, the saintly *Rebbitzin* Rivkah. He would sit at the table for 15 or 20 minutes, and would say: "This is the *seudah* which the grandson is celebrating." The next evening, on the eve of the twentieth of Kislev, when the main *seudah* took place, he would remain at the table together with those present for 50 minutes or an hour. It was on one such occasion that he recounted the following.

When the Alter Rebbe was on his way from the house of the *misnaged* and saw how overjoyed his chassidim were — they were even rolling about in the streets of Petersburg — he was overcome by fear. His apprehension did not stem from his immediate circumstances, for he had been granted unqualified freedom. His fear was rather from the way in which the victory had burst forth in all directions. After prayers the next morning (on Wednesday, for *Yud-Tes* Kislev that year fell on a Tuesday), the Alter Rebbe said: "Concerning the fourth day of creation it is written, יְהִי מְאֹרֹת — 'Let there be luminaries,' and the word מְאֹרֹת is spelled there without the letter *vav*." The Alter Rebbe then cited the interpretation of *Ramban* on this verse — that the light that was created on the first day served for three days. To this the Alter Rebbe added, "Three generations: The Baal Shem Tov, the Maggid," — and stopped. He later resumed: "On the fourth day the luminaries

---

You were [the same]... You are [the same]...: Paraphrase of passage from *Tanna devei Eliyahu Rabbah*, Ch. 21, appearing in the preliminary morning prayers (*Siddur*, p. 17).

The grandson: In the original Yiddish, *einikl*, loosely meaning a descendant. (The Rebbe Maharash was in fact a greatgrandson of the Alter Rebbe.)

Let there be luminaries: *Gen.* 1:14.

were *taken away* * (בַּיּוֹם הָרְבִיעִי נִטְלוּ הַמְּאוֹרוֹת) — but on the same day the luminaries were *suspended* (נִתְלוּ הַמְּאוֹרוֹת). Everything now depends on the chassidim. Now" — he addressed them here directly — "everything depends on *you*."

In the course of that Wednesday the news of the Rebbe's liberation spread throughout the breadth of Petersburg, and as evening fell, a great number of people assembled. When the Rebbe made it known that he did not intend to deliver a chassidic discourse, two men who had jostled their way through the thick crowd approached the Alter Rebbe and said: "We have been thrown far into the depths of Russia. Yet G-d is our witness that we serve Him and fulfill whatever we know of what is written in the Torah. Rebbe! Please teach us Torah, and strengthen our hearts in the service of the Creator!"

Soon after, the Alter Rebbe went out to the courtyard and delivered the *maamar* that begins with the words, כַּמַּיִם הַפָּנִים ("As in water face answers to face, so the heart of man to man"). And even though it was bitterly cold outside where they all stood, everyone felt warm, and *the warmth permeated every last little bone.* (This was the phrase as I heard it from my father.)

Before the Alter Rebbe delivered the *maamar* he cited a

---

* The Baal Shem Tov passed away on Wednesday; see p. 74 above.

Were *suspended:* I.e., positioned in the heavens. See *Rashi* on *Gen.* 1:14 and on Tractate *Taanis* 27b.

Luminaries were *suspended*...Everything now depends...: As in English, where the words "suspend" and "depend" are related through their common root meaning "to hang," so too the Hebrew words נִתְלוּ ("were suspended") and תָּלוּי ("depends").

The luminaries were suspended: On the Wednesday that the Alter Rebbe was born near Liozna (*Chai* Elul 5505/1745), the Baal Shem Tov, then in far-off Mezhibuzh, had already quoted this same phrase (as spelled נִתְלוּ) as a prelude to his joyous announcement to his chassidim that on that day a new soul had descended to this world to illuminate it. See: Vol. III of the present work, p. 245; and R. Nissan Mindel, *op. cit.,* p. 24, and the sources given there.

As in water: *Prov.* 27:19.

verse from *Tehillim:* זֶה דוֹר דֹּרְשָׁו מְבַקְשֵׁי פָנֶיךָ יַעֲקֹב סֶלָה (lit., "Such is the generation of those that search for Him, of those among [the children of] Yaakov that seek Your Countenance forever"). This verse he now proceeded to expound phrase by phrase according to the teachings of *Chassidus,* and on the non-literal level of *derush,* as follows:

"זֶה דוֹר: This is such a generation —

"דֹּרְשָׁו: that if its leaders and mentors —

"מְבַקְשֵׁי פָנֶיךָ: seek Your Countenance, that is to say, the innermost levels *(pnimiyus)* of the Inifinite One —

"יַעֲקֹב סֶלָה: then its ordinary Jews (יַעֲקֹב — יַעֲקֹב — יַעֲקֹב) are at all places and at all times strong (סֶלָה) in the strength and eternity of the Infinite One." [The name יַעֲקֹב is comprised of two components — י, עָקֵב, signifying the indwelling of the loftiest levels of divine light *(yud* being the first letter of the Four-Letter Name of G-d) within the lowliest levels of His people *(akeiv* = "heel")].

The Alter Rebbe then quoted the phrase which describes the struggle between Yaakov and Esau's guardian angel: וַיֵּאָבֵק אִישׁ עִמּוֹ (lit., "And a man wrestled with him"), and with it quoted the comment of the *Talmud:* הֶעֱלוּ אָבָק...עַד כִּסֵּא הַכָּבוֹד ("They raised dust... up to the Throne of Glory"). On this the

---

Such is the generation: Ps. 24:6.

Its leaders: The word used here for "its leaders" is דּוֹרְשָׁיו, as in the Talmudic phrase דּוֹר דּוֹר וְדוֹרְשָׁיו — "Each generation and its Torah teachers" (Tractate *Sanhedrin* 38b). The word דּוֹרְשָׁיו literally means "its seekers," and in this sense it is used in *Iggeres HaKodesh,* beginning of Epistle 24, in which the Alter Rebbe speaks of those who in various degrees seek their Maker in prayer.

Seek Your Countenance: פְּנִימִיּוּת — "innermost level," from פָּנִים — "countenance." Hence פָנֶיךָ — "Your innermost level," i.e., the innermost levels of the Infinite One.

Strength and eternity: Cf. the Talmudic statement, כָּל מָקוֹם שֶׁנֶּאֱמַר נֶצַח סֶלָה וָעֶד אֵין לוֹ הֶפְסֵק עוֹלָמִים —"Wherever something is described by one of these terms (נֶצַח, סֶלָה, וָעֶד), it will not be intercepted forever" (Tractate *Eruvin* 54a).

And a man wrestled: Gen. 32:25, and *Rashi* there.

They raised dust: Tractate *Chullin* 91a.

Alter Rebbe asked the question: "Surely the verse should have said, וַיִּלָּחֶם אִישׁ עִמּוֹ (lit., 'And a man *fought* with him'). Why then does it say וַיֵּאָבֵק ('wrestled')?" And he answered: "This word appears because it hints at the fact that there are battles whose origin is in nothing more substantial than dust (אָבָק) — as for example, a dispute which is fomented by lovers of discord, whose life-force is sustained by dust alone."

Following this statement, the Alter Rebbe delivered the above-mentioned *maamar*.

The Rebbe Maharash once said that this *maamar* is based on a teaching of the Baal Shem Tov. My father then asked him, when speaking with him at *yechidus*, whether the Alter Rebbe had heard this *maamar* from the Maggid of Mezritch, or whether he had heard it while in prison [i.e., by direct revelation from the Baal Shem Tov].

With a smile his father chided him: "People who want to know everything grow old before their time!"

My father continued telling me of his *yechidus:* "But when my father perceived that this question was really important to me" (and this, despite the utter self-effacement of my father with respect to his father, especially at *yechidus*), "he replied: 'In the World of *Tikkun* the proper direction for *avodah* to take is working upward from below, and not through the downward revelation of what is Above.'"

*   *   *

Another discourse on the same verse, כַּמַּיִם הַפָּנִים — delivered by the Rebbe Maharash in 5639 (תרל"ט; 1879) — discusses the above-mentioned teaching on the words זֶה דוֹר. It is extant in two versions, an incomplete one recorded by my father, and a complete one by R. Moshe Leib Ginsburg.

By direct revelation from the Baal Shem Tov: See p. 66 above.
Working upward... downward revelation...: In the original, מִלְמַטָּה לְמַעְלָה... מִלְמַעְלָה לְמַטָּה...

14.

The Alter Rebbe had sent his *pidyon nefesh* to R. Nachum of Chernobyl early in the month of Elul.

On the first evening of Rosh HaShanah the Alter Rebbe came out of his study, and though, as is known, he never spoke at all on the first night of Rosh HaShanah, yet this time he asked: "Where is Devorah Leah?" And when he saw his daughter he began to say: "... לְשָׁנָה".

No sooner had he said that first word than she sprang forward and said to him: "לְשָׁנָה טוֹבָה תִּכָּתֵב וְתֵחָתֵם.* Father, please don't say anything!"

On the Second Day of Rosh HaShanah the Alter Rebbe gave a discourse on the teachings of *Chassidus* until *Havdalah* (it was his custom to deliver *maamarim* on both days). After *Havdalah* he asked his daughter Devorah Leah and her husband R. Shalom Shachna to come to his study. R. Shalom Shachna stood by the wall and sobbed: "What is one to do about a child of two years? And such a child!"

The next day, on the Fast of Gedaliah, Devorah Leah passed away. The Alter Rebbe took his grandson — later to be known as the *Tzemach Tzedek* — to sleep with him in his room, and when he turned three he arranged for him to sleep next to the Ark in which stood a *Sefer* Torah, so that he should be within four cubits of Torah.

Once, after his mother's passing, when he was in the Alter Rebbe's room, he woke up and cried: "Mother! Take me away to you!"

And his saintly mother patted him and said: "No, no. Sleep soundly. Your grandfather is here; you stay with *Zeide!*"

15.

Before my father's *bar-mitzvah,* his father (the Rebbe

---

* The established form of words, as is known, is in the singular (as above — "May you be inscribed and sealed for a good year"), and not in the plural (תִּכָּתְבוּ וְתֵחָתְמוּ). All the Rebbes too were addressed thus.

Devorah Leah passed away: See p. 96 above, and Vol. IV of the present work, p. 231.

Maharash) taught him *Tanya*. At that time he told him three things.

(a) "Thank G-d that my greatgrandfather* was arrested in 5559 (תקנ"ט; 1798) and not in 5539 (תקל"ט; 1778). For what would he have done then? He would have had to make use of supernatural means, and scorch the world. And that is not the divine intention in creating the world."

(b) "The first of the pastoral letters published under the collective heading *Iggeres HaKodesh* (lit., 'The Sacred Epistle') — the one beginning with the phrase פּוֹתְחִין בִּבְרָכָה ('We begin with a benediction') — was written and disseminated ten years before the writing of the second epistle, that beginning with the word קָטֹנְתִּי (lit., 'I have become small')."

(c) "At first the epistle beginning קָטֹנְתִּי concluded with the words וְרוּחַ נְכֵאָה ('and with a restrained spirit'). But after the Alter Rebbe had delivered the *maamar* beginning כַּמַּיִם הַפָּנִים three times in Liozna, explaining the verse according to the interpretation of *Rashi* and not according to the *Targum*, he appended to the epistle known as קָטֹנְתִּי the following words: וְכוּלֵי הַאי וְאוּלַי יִתֵּן ה' בְּלֵב אֲחֵיהֶם כַּמַּיִם הַפָּנִים וגו' (lit., 'And through all that, perhaps, G-d will put into the hearts of their brethren

---

* For my grandfather the Rebbe Maharash, "my greatgrandfather" meant the Alter Rebbe, and "my grandfather" or "our grandfather" (because my grandmother the *Rebbitzin* Rivkah was likewise a grandchild) meant the Mitteler Rebbe.

My greatgrandfather: Misprint in the original ("grandfather").
Supernatural means: In the original, *makkifim*.
Scorch the world: In the original, *brenen di velt*.
Iggeres HaKodesh: Part IV of *Likkutei-Amarim — Tanya*.
The one beginning: *Tanya*, p. 390.
The second epistle: *Ibid.*, p. 396; it is dated 1798. See p. 46 above.
The *maamar* beginning כַּמַּיִם הַפָּנִים: See p. 99 above.
The interpretation of *Rashi:* On *Prov.* 27:19; viz., "As in water face answers to face, so the heart of man to man."
According to the *Targum:* "Just as [different bodies of] water and [different] faces do not resemble each other, so the hearts of men."

that *as waters [reflect] the face...'*). And by so doing he implanted positive *middos,* character traits, in the hearts of his chassidim."

* * *

When my father taught me this epistle he told me that when his father (the Rebbe Maharash) had taught it to him, he had said: "If the Alter Rebbe had not inserted the three words בְּמִדַּת אֱמֶת לְיַעֲקֹב (lit., 'according to the attribute of "truth unto Yaakov"') he would have had another 50,000 chassidim. *But the Alter Rebbe demands the attribute of truth!"*

* * *

The Maggid of Mezritch bestowed upon the Alter Rebbe the gift of a smile with which he could have captured the world. Since however the entire mission of the Alter Rebbe was to inculcate in chassidim the practice of *avodah pnimis (avodah* which the individual himself generates at will from within), he did not want to make use of that smile, for it was an expression of the *makkifim* of the soul, stemming from the soul's superrational and transcendent faculties.

16.

The year 5600 (ת"ר; 1840) saw the first appearance of sections of *Likkutei Torah,* and of the halachic responsa which the *Tzemach Tzedek* had written to his various rabbinic correspondents.

In 5603 (תר"ג; 1843) the authorities in Petersburg compelled him to leave for the provinces. (Their intention was otherwise, but this is not the time for an explanation.) He set out in 5604 (תר"ד; 1844), accompanied by my greatuncle R. Yisrael No'ach, visiting Shklov, Mohilev, Rogachov, Zhlobin,

---

Truth unto Yaakov: *Micah* 7:20. The Alter Rebbe here demands that his chassidim be humble of spirit before every man — but truthfully so.

Sections of *Likkutei Torah:* These were edited by the *Tzemach Tzedek* from manuscript versions of *maamarim* of the Alter Rebbe.

R. Yisrael No'ach: Of Niezhin. See genealogical table on p. 36 above.

Minsk and Vilna, and returned by way of Smorgon and Dokshytz, arriving in Lubavitch via Polotzk and Vitebsk.

While they were in Shklov, at the beginning of their journey, R. Yisrael No'ach told his father that many of the young chassidim were too bashful to meet and speak with the Rebbe at *yechidus*.

Hearing these words the *Tzemach Tzedek* wept bitterly, and said: "How can one say 'bashful'? Here is literally a matter of life and death — and people are bashful?!"

R. Yisrael No'ach then said to his father: "Many of the older chassidim see in you your grandfather."

"How can one say that?" replied the *Tzemach Tzedek*. "In the days of my grandfather, when a *chassidisher* householder stood next to someone, that other fellow felt good, simply on account of his neighbor's noble character traits. And when a chassid arrived somewhere, people would crowd around him like bees around a beehive. *Chassidishe* folk in those days used to light up Jewish homes; they planted wholesome saplings to last for generations."

17.

Reading through the letters of the Rebbes, whether general (pastoral) letters or whether letters addressed to individuals, one is struck by their sheer love for their chassidim. In common parlance the greatest love is a person's love for his children. In truth, however, this is as nought when compared with the love of Rebbe for chassid.

As is known, the Alter Rebbe suffered from a debilitating nasal disease which his physicians explained as a symptom of some deep-seated yearning. This is the same longing as described by the Psalmist: נִכְסְפָה וְגַם כָּלְתָה נַפְשִׁי — "My soul yearns, yea, it faints [for the courts of G-d]."

Your grandfather: I.e., the Alter Rebbe.

A *chassidisher* householder: On the adjective, see above note on "The *avodah* of chassidim." *Baalebos* ("householder") — as distinct from a fulltime scholar.

My soul yearns: *Ps.* 84:3.

The *Tzemach Tzedek* once said that all the various kinds of self-sacrifice which his grandfather the Alter Rebbe underwent were of no consequence when compared to the self-sacrifice of having to tear himself away from cleaving to his Creator (as it is written, וְעִמְּךָ לֹא חָפַצְתִּי — "And beside You I desire nothing"), and devoting himself instead to doing someone a favor, and caring that some Jew somewhere should do *teshuvah* through his own endeavors and become a real servant of G-d.

18.

After speaking at length about the need for cultivating brotherly love, the Rebbe said the following.

I would like to make chassidim aware of this, and request this: that chassidim should become more bound up with each other, more caring about each other. Any Jew should be cherished, and especially so among chassidim. Nowadays it can happen that one does not come to hear of a joyful event in another's family for three months. May the Almighty grant that you should all be enabled to give good tidings and to receive good tidings.

Having been raised on the yeast of *ahavas Yisrael*, on the love of a fellow Jew, *temimim* in particular and chassidim in general ought to be warmer, must be warmer. The dominant spot in one's attention should be occupied by one's fellow. His joy is mine: my joy is his.

When the news reached Lubavitch that R. Elchanan Morozov was freed from conscription in the czarist army, his fellow chassid R. Hendel danced about the courtyard with a singsong: "Chonye is free!" He then walked straight into the study of my father, who always held him in high esteem, passed on the good news, and then (I was there to witness the scene) danced around exuberantly. My father stood up from his chair, laid his hand on R. Hendel's shoulder, and when

---

And beside You: Ps. 73:25. See *HaYom Yom*, entry for 18 Kislev.

they had danced around each other a few times, he said: "For this I will now share with you an exposition in *Chassidus*."

Chassidim ought to hold every Jew dear, and especially chassidim and those who are of chassidic stock. Each man ought to help his fellow in every way possible — though help should always be extended discreetly, in order to spare the recipient any humiliation. Likewise one needs to know how to rebuke one's fellow: not increasing his anguish (he already knows his own shortcomings, and his heart aches over them); but rather showing him warmth and bringing him near, first with a finger, then with a hand. And then when one is quite alone one should shed a tear over the other fellow's imperfections, and should say a little *Tehillim* for him.

19.

Ample in thought; sparing in words; prolific in deeds. And the one to be worked on is me. Such was the mettle of a chassid of bygone years.

A certain Rebbe (this was of course before he became Rebbe) asked a question of a certain Rebbe at *yechidus,* and received the following reply: "Your task in *avodah* is to work on yourself until another senses it, until the efflux of *nozlim* becomes more generous. The peasant who brings his wheat to the mill to be ground thinks that it is the spout at the outlet that provides the flour; the miller knows that if you want flour at the outlet you have to fill up the funnel at the top — provided, that is, that you fill it with wheat, not sand; if you stoke the mill with sand you don't get flour. One's *Chassidus* therefore needs to be without compromise, so that the piece

---

Bringing him near: In the original, *yenem mekarev zain.*

Imperfections: In the original, the evil in another is euphemistically referred to as his לא טוב (lit., "his not-good").

The efflux of *nozlim:* I.e., the effects of the *chochmah* and *binah* of *etzem haneshamah,* which flow into *he'aras haneshamah.* "*Nozlim*" is an allusion to an earlier *derush* on the phrase from *Shir HaShirim,* וְנוֹזְלִים מִן לְבָנוֹן (*Song of Songs* 4:15). See pp. 20-21 above. See also *HaYom Yom,* entry for 24 Adar I.

of bread that reaches one's fellow should be life-giving bread."

Chassidus demands not only that one should hear, but that one should cultivate sensitivity — to be sensitive to G-dliness, sensitive to Torah, sensitive to one's fellow.

20.

By their opposition to chassidim through deeds or words after the old style, today's *misnagdim* are causing distress to the souls of the departed geonim (*May the memory of the righteous be a blessing!*) who are in the Lands of Life. It is written: אַל תִּזְכָּר לָנוּ עֲוֹנֹת רִאשׁוֹנִים — "Do not bring to mind our former wrongdoing." Souls in the World of Truth experience intense regret over the past — for having allowed themselves to be led by fomentors of dissension and slanderers of chassidim. Those who now raise opposition to chassidim and spark off controversy are thus causing anguish to the souls of the departed *geonim*. "May G-d bless His people with peace."

21.

The Rebbe told the young men standing near him that he had heard something remarkable: the ice had carried away the bridge! (This is what had happened a few days earlier on the frozen Dvina River.) The Rebbe then proceeded to explain his meaning.

When I heard this it occurred to me that a bridge should be fearful of cold, that cold can (G-d forbid) break a bridge. Listen well, young men, for you are the bridge between the

---

Not only... hear, but... cultivate sensitivity: In the original, *nit nor her'n, nor derher'n*.

The Lands of Life: Or, "the Lands of the Living"; cf. *Ps.* 116:10. Here used as a poetic name for the state of everlasting life that follows death.

Do not bring: *Ps.* 79:8.

May G-d bless: *Ps.* 29:11.

Dvina River: Near Riga.

children and the adult generation; remember that a bridge
needs to be guarded vigilantly against destruction (G-d forbid) by cold. Keep yourselves warm with the study of Torah
and the observance of the *mitzvos* so that the bridge should
remain sound. May the Almighty grant that everyone keep to
the right, and may He make their way prosper.

22.

It brings me great joy to hear that people gather together
for group study. There is sowing and there is planting, and
both are needed. Sowing represents the study of *nigleh*, the
revealed levels of the Torah, and planting — the study of
Chassidus. In this way roots are struck deeply, roots that will
benefit one's children's children. The same is true of brotherly love, and of the comradely talk exchanged between
friends. Make yourselves strong, my friends of the chassidic
brotherhood. "Let each man help his neighbor" to set aside
times for the study of Torah and for meeting in the comrade-
ship of a *farbrengen.* And in the merit of our forefathers, the
Rebbes of blessed memory, may the Almighty help us all,
together with the entire House of Israel, and make us worthy
of hearing glad tidings, both materially and spiritually.

Sowing represents...*nigleh,*...planting...*Chassidus:* Study in the field of
    the revealed plane of the Torah yields a relatively prompt harvest — a
    knowledge of the *Talmud* and *halachah;* the hidden levels of the Torah
    demand a more prolonged effort of cultivation before the saplings
    planted there produce their fruits. (Cf. *Toras Shalom.*)
Let each man: Cf. *Isa.* 41:6.

Chapter 3

Shemini Atzeres and Simchas Torah 5694 (תרצ"ד; 1933)
[Warsaw]

1.

In days gone by, a *chassidisher farbrengen* was a cornerstone in one's life: it literally laid foundations in people's lives. After a *farbrengen* one felt cleaner. Sometimes the *farbrengen* utterly washed away the mud of undesirable traits and rinsed off the uncleanliness of various habits; sometimes these were not washed away completely. But whatever the case, all unwanted attributes became in some measure despised. A person looked at his past with pain. Not only did a *farbrengen* bring about the resolution that a man's past was not in order and his accustomed conduct unsatisfactory: it also gave rise to a firm resolve for proper conduct in the future. In other words, one's vigilance in refraining from transgression (*sur mera*), and one's diligence in the performance of the commandments (*aseh tov*), were both raised by the *farbrengen* to a higher level.

For the chassidim of long ago, evil and good were conceived of on a level utterly different from today. The obvious basic task of a chassid was to toil in order to introduce light, in order to illuminate oneself. This meant washing one's "I"

[Warsaw]: After leaving Riga, the Rebbe Rayatz lived in Warsaw for nearly two years — from *erev* Rosh Chodesh Elul 5693 (תרצ"ג; 1933) to early Tammuz 5695 (תרצ"ה; 1935).

Unwanted attributes: In the euphemistic Yiddish original, *nit gute zachn* ("not-good things").

Refraining...(*sur mera*)...performance...(*aseh tov*): From the verse in *Tehillim*, סוּר מֵרָע וַעֲשֵׂה טוֹב — "Turn away from evil and do good" (*Ps.* 34:15). These two phrases commonly signify the observance of the negative and positive commandments respectively.

with the light of the labor of self-cultivation, with the light of real and actual *avodah*.

In those days a chassid longed to hear a chassidic thought. People would yearn their eyes out in search of an elder chassid. People were eager to hear a live word of *Chassidus*. And when through the grace of the Almighty one came to hear such a thought, it infused new life.

The chassidim of bygone days dedicated themselves to living their lives as chassidim. The aura of *Chassidus* and the life of *Chassidus* encompassed them and permeated them. Any practice which one observed in the conduct of an elder chassid was law. There were no whys and wherefores. It simply went without saying that this was how things ought to be done, and that with precisely this kind of conduct one could be a chassid.

Whenever the early chassidim heard a *vort*, they would as a matter of course devote all their energies to implanting it in their hearts. They would exploit that resource while making their way to market or to a neighboring village. With this *vort* they lived all the twenty-four hours of their day. With this *vort* in mind they read *Kerias Shema* before going to bed at night, and with this *vort* in mind they opened their eyes in the morning. With this *vort* they said their prayers and with this *vort* they lived, each according to his occupation and source of livelihood.

Among my childhood jottings there is a note recorded in the winter of 5654 (תרנ״ד; 1893-94). My *melamed* at the time, the Rashbatz of blessed memory, described for me the conduct of the elder chassidim who in their youth had visited or studied under the Alter Rebbe in Liadi. He had seen them in

---

In those days a chassid: In the original, "... *a chassidisher yungerman.*"
Longed to hear...a live word: Cf. beginning of the Compiler's Foreword to *Tanya* (p. xii): The immediacy of "*listening* to words of moral advice is not the same as seeing and reading them in books."
A chassidic thought: In the original, *a vort Chassidus,* i.e., "a word of chassidic teaching."
The Rashbatz (רַשְׁבַּ״ץ): Acronym for Rabbi Shmuel Betzalel (Sheftel).

his hometown of Sventzian in the year 5603 (תר"ג; 1843). One of them was R. Yitzchak the Tailor, who in the course of his work used to discuss with his employees theoretical topics in *Chassidus.*

Not only among chassidim, but among G-d-fearing Jews in general at the time, their spiritual life was of prime importance and their material life was secondary. The basic material requisites of life were bounded within certain limits. True enough, people used to occupy themselves with the demands of their livelihoods; they conducted households, and raised and guided their children; they owned their own houses and property; they were dressed cleanly and well; they supported their married children who were Torah scholars *oif kest.* In brief, people lived a serene and honest life, each according to his place. But the "I" of a Jew was Torah and *mitzvos* and *Chassidus.* There were also (heaven forfend) poor folk, people who were heavily preoccupied with eking out a livelihood and who lived in very straitened circumstances — but none of this impinged on their real "I". For their true "I" was Torah and the fear of heaven.

In those days there was no such thing as a partition of pride separating people from each other. Of course there were differences and gradations. But everything was taken in earnest. And just as there were no partitions between the pauper and the regular householder and the rich man (people were measured in those days not according to their silver and

---

The year 5603 (תר"ג; 1843): I.e., 30 years after the passing of the Alter Rebbe in 5573 (תקע"ג; 1812).

R. Yitzchak the Tailor: In the original Yiddish, Reb Yitzchak *der Schneider.*

In the course of his work...theoretical topics: The Alter Rebbe once said that it was his wish that when any two chassidim met in the street, they would discuss *atik* and *arich* (— two abstruse concepts in *Chassidus,* referring respectively to the internal and external aspects of G-d's Will).

Spiritual...prime...material...secondary: I.e., הַגְבָּרַת הַצּוּרָה עַל הַחוֹמֶר, — "causing Form to dominate Matter."

No...partition of pride: This innovation of the Baal Shem Tov aroused the ire of the scholarly opponents of the new movement.

gold thread, but according to criteria of intellect and character, irrespective of their financial status), so too was there no
partition between the simple Jew and the learned *ben-Torah*, or
the *chassidisher Yid*. In his soul the common ignoramus sensed
the worth of a Torah scholar or a chassid. And the greatest
chassid for his part was able to appreciate the loftiness of the
unsophisticated faith which underlies every move of the
simplest Jew.

More than the simple Jew envied the *maskil* or *oved*, the
oved envied the simple Jew. In him he saw truth, and innate
piety; he saw zest in the performance of a *mitzvah*, and delight
in the exercise of a positive character trait; and he saw too the
sweetness of brotherly love.

The simple Jew was a healthy tree sprouting from a
sound upbringing — an education toward the fear of heaven
and toward *kabbalas ol*, an education which engraved and
inculcated in every child that the first step which a Jew should
make on rising in the morning is directed towards the *beis
midrash*, there to read a little *Tehillim* and worship with the
congregation.

The time-honored tradition of studying *Aggadah* in the
local *beis midrash* during the twilight interval between *Minchah*
and *Maariv* gave us clean, fine Jews, men with clean hearts and
clean thoughts, men of charity, men with a warm sensitivity
to the love of the Torah and the love of a fellow Jew. The "I" of
every Jew, great or small, was Torah, the fear of heaven, and
positive traits of character. It followed as a matter of course
that the atmosphere in which such people lived was something different, something cleaner. Then the Rebbes arrived
on the scene with the teachings of *Chassidus* and opened people's eyes, and of course their conceptions of good and evil as
seen in the light of *Chassidus* were on quite a new level. And at

---

Studying *Aggadah:* Cf. the counsel of the Sages: ?רְצוֹנְךָ שֶׁתַּכִּיר אֶת מִי שֶׁאָמַר וְהָיָה הָעוֹלָם
לְמֹד אַגָּדָה! — "Do you wish to know He-Who-spoke-and-the-world-came-
into-being? — Study *Aggadah!*" (*Sifri, Parshas Eikev*, Sec. 49.)

every *farbrengen* the meaning and the understanding of good grew until people attained to such levels of spiritual development that what had previously been regarded as good now became spurned as evil; in the spirit of the verse that says, וְיָשָׁן מִפְּנֵי חָדָשׁ תּוֹצִיאוּ — "And you shall remove the old [harvests] because of the new."

The *chassidisher farbrengen* of yesteryear was a blessing from Above. It opened up windows into each man's dark corners, illuminating them with the delight of *Chassidus.*

A *farbrengen* was a cornerstone in one's material life and a cornerstone in one's spiritual life. Both the elder chassid who was the guide and mentor and the younger chassid who was being guided and led knew their spiritual status. Among the chassidim in general there was a profound respect for an elder chassid. Everyone knew his own place, and the elder chassidim too knew their obligations to the other chassidim.

In those days people used to have "ears that hear," and many were the chassidim who furthermore had ears of sensitive perception.

At a *farbrengen* one would discuss concepts in *Chassidus.* All talk was directed to the comprehension of a concept — analyzing a *vort,* showing how one should understand it. The younger chassidim would ask, the older ones would answer. For this is the approach that characterizes a true learner: when he ought to be hearing he toils to hear. And as is well

---

And you shall remove: Lev. 26:10.

Knew their spiritual status: Cf. הַמַּכִּיר אֶת מְקוֹמוֹ — One of the 48 ways by which the Torah may be acquired is "to know one's place" (Tractate *Avos* 6:6).

Ears that hear: A literal translation of the Aramaic phrase אוּדְנִין דְּשַׁמְעִין, i.e., attentive ears; from the statement of R. Shimon bar Yochai in the *Zohar:* "Happy the man whose words fall on ears that hear."

Sensitive perception: In *Toras Shalom* of the Rebbe *Rashab,* the spelling of the word חָסִיד is explained as follows: a חָסִיד is חֶסֶד, with a nucleus (י) of *chochmah* within.

Ears that hear,...ears of sensitive perception: In the rhyming Yiddish translation and comment, *oieren vos heren,... oieren vos derheren.*

A true learner: In the original, *a mekabel amiti.*

known, it takes serious exertion to become a recipient. To be a disciple demands *avodah*, and the more one labors to become a disciple capable of receiving, the more one becomes a vessel capable of containing. All this refers to those times when one is learning. But when one ought to be talking and asking, *then one should talk* — and do so in clear words. And as to the kind of chassid who constantly stands prepared only to receive, it is questionable whether he is a recipient even in those times when one should be only a recipient.

2.

There are four modes of connection between Rebbe and chassid. (a) *Rav* and *talmid* (teacher and student), or, in other words, *mashpia* and *mekabel*. (b) *Hiskashrus* and *dveikus* (lit., "being bound" and "cleaving"). This refers to the fusing of chassid and Rebbe, both becoming bound together in a complete unity through their Torah study and their *avodah*. This relates to the well-known answer which my saintly father gave to a certain individual who at a *yechidus* said that he wanted to be bound (*mekushar*) to him: "All *hiskashrus* is through the study of Torah. Study the *Chassidus* which I expound, and you will become *mekushar*." (c) Rebbe and chassid as *av* and *ben* (father and son). (d) Rebbe and chassid as *maor* and *or* (luminary and light).

Now even in the mode of luminary and light, which is the highest of the above levels, what is crucial is the state of being bound inwardly and with one's very being. We are not speak-

---

To become a recipient: In the original, *a mekabel*.

When one is learning: I.e., when one is a silent recipient, as when listening to *divrei* Torah from one's Rebbe.

When one ought to be talking and asking: This, by contrast, refers to when one is at the kind of *farbrengen* among chassidim described above.

Then one should talk: Cf. וְלֹא הַבַּיְשָׁן לָמֵד — "A bashful person cannot learn" (Tractate *Avos* 2:5).

The *Chassidus* which I expound: The context implies the teachings contained in the speaker's original *maamarim*.

ing only of the kind of bond in which the chassid constantly remembers the Rebbe and the Rebbe constantly remembers the chassid. We are speaking of a state of being utterly intertwined at all spiritual levels, in such a way that both chassid and Rebbe complement the true essence of each other like *or* and *maor*, light and luminary. The luminary reveals a light from its very being (*or atzmi*), and such light is a revelation of the luminary. Each is dependent on the other, just as with Rebbe and chassid. And this entire bond finds expression in a manner of inner love.

3.

The silent confession during the Sounding of the *Shofar* represents the highest point within that level of revealed repentance which is called "lower-level repentance." For *teshuvah* comprises two levels — "lower-level repentance" *(teshuvah tata'ah)* and "higher-level repentance" *(teshuvah ila'ah)*. And though they have a common direction, yet each has its own definition. "Lower-level repentance" is definable in terms of revelation, and every kind of revelation is expressed loudly and with *hispaalus,* an unloosing of emotions.

Hispaalus too has it own boundaries, and these lie at two opposite extremes — on the one hand noise and tumult, and on the other, a sensation of being faint, drained, and weak. This can be seen in practice — that every unloosing of emotions begins with noise and upheaval, and ends with a quiet stillness. This quiet stillness is the exhausting of the person's energies.

The kind of bond: In the original Yiddish, *tzugebundenkait.*
Being utterly intertwined at all spiritual levels: In the original Yiddish, *oisgebundenkait.*
The silent confession: In the original, *der yisvadde belachash* (Yid./ Heb.); from the instruction which appears in the *Machzor* (festival prayer-book) for Rosh HaShanah — that "one should confess in silence" at certain points during the Sounding of the *Shofar.*
Lower-level... higher-level repentance: See *Iggeres HaTeshuvah,* Chs. 6 and 9, in *Tanya,* p. 363ff. and p. 375ff.

The silent confession is the climax and practical application of the entire *avodah* of *teshuvah* which begins with Rosh
Chodesh Elul, the whole process being a chain of levels in
teshuvah.

During a recent chassidic discourse (in the *maamar* beginning *BaYom HaShemini*) a certain parable was explained. A man
owns a precious vessel which becomes soiled, or even dam-
aged. He sighs, and is anxious; then he washes it, and finally
mends it, restoring it to perfection.

Rosh Chodesh Elul is the time of spiritual stocktaking.
And soon after, when the time comes for *Selichos,* a person
washes his vessel with the tears that he sheds over the state
of his spiritual life. And the *avodah* of Rosh HaShanah repairs
the vessel through one's acceptance of the yoke of heaven.

The Sounding of the *Shofar* is the time of *teshuvah* — in a
revealed state — which finds expression through an outcry
from within, originating in the innermost point of the heart.
The parable taught by the Baal Shem Tov to illustrate this is
well known — in which the son cries out, "Father, father,
have pity on me! Father, father, save me!"

When a son has given offense to his father through
damaging an exceedingly precious vessel, then in addition to
the father's anguish at its loss, he is distressed doubly and
trebly by the fact that the one responsible is his own son. The
mere fact that the son is insensitive to the value of the vessel
would cause pain; how much more so when he has sunk so
low that he could even have destroyed it.

The Sounding of the *Shofar* is the time which the Infinite
One, Blessed be He, has set aside for all Jews to give account

---

The climax and practical application: In the original, דער בְּכֵן (i.e., the וּבְכֵן; ·
lit., the "Therefore:—..."); a favorite chassidic idiom reflecting the
insistent need to translate every noble resolve into an immediate and
tangible deed.
Spiritual stocktaking: In the original, *cheshbon hanefesh.*
Acceptance of the yoke of heaven: In the original, *kabbalas ol malchus shamayim.*
The son cries out: This is not a cry of pain, but an entreaty. See *Sefer
HaMaamarim* — 5705 (Kehot, N.Y., 1980), p. 1.

for all the arguments and charges presented by the evil angels, and concerning which they testify.

Rosh HaShanah is a time of trial and judgment for everyone. At this point the individual takes stock of where he stands as regards the fulfillment of the Torah and its *mitzvos*, and where he stands as regards the labor of refining the various traits of his character. He takes account of the fact that [in the Heavenly Court] the prosecuting angels, who are called "sons of G-d," bring to mind and verify the existence of all the sins, iniquities and transgressions of which he was guilty in the course of the year, and demand that he be sentenced to harsh and bitter punishment. He further considers that if at this time he truthfully regrets his past, this will alter things for him.

Now if a person meditates along the above lines, two opposite reactions result. On the one hand, a reaction of tumult, caused by the anguish experienced over the undesirable situations he has brought about — both the destruction of valuable things, and the distress which he has caused (as it were) Above. This anguish is all the more intense when he considers Whom it is that he has distressed — a father so devoted that even when there are grievous prosecutors his fatherly love is so great that he grants his child a chance to experience regret.

This latter reaction is the silent confession. It is a level of yearning: the child is now longing to draw close to his father. The repentance which was tumultuous was the person's regret over the undesirable things that he had done; the silent confession is the son's inward yearning for his father.

The Sounding of the *Shofar* is a propitious time, and within that propitious time, the silent confession occupies the most propitious moment. It is the time of the Sounding of the *Shofar* that sees the revelation of the verse, וְלֹא אָבָה ה' אֱלֹקֶיךָ לִשְׁמֹעַ אֶל בִּלְעָם -- "And the L-rd your G-d did not want to listen to Bil'am." It

Called "sons of G-d": *Gen.* 6:2.
A propitious time: In the original, *eis ratzon*.
And the L-rd... to Bil'am: *Deut.* 23:6.

is explained in *Likkutei Torah* that Bil'am (Balaam) is the one who seeks to act as prosecuting attorney (G-d forbid) towards Israel — and the sound of the *Shofar* confuses him. And the silent confession, the most propitious of propitious moments, is the moment when the penitent son becomes united with our blessed Father in heaven.

4.

On Simchas Torah every man grasps hold of the wooden roller of a Torah Scroll, and joins in the Torah's dance. The great and the small, the scholarly and the simple, — all are swept up in the joy of the Torah; all are firmly locked hand in hand in the utmost affection and brotherly love.

Each of the wooden rods around which the parchment is wound is everywhere called *etz chaim* ("a tree of life"). Since the Torah is something involving wisdom and understanding, one would have expected them to have borrowed the name of the Tree of Knowledge. Yet they are universally known by the name of the Tree of Life — for the Torah is "a tree of life for those who hold fast to it" (עֵץ חַיִּים הִיא לַמַּחֲזִיקִים בָּהּ): those who hold fast to it, live. When it comes to understanding, people are at different levels, one higher, one lower. But when we are speaking of being alive, there are no differences: whoever holds fast to the Tree of Life — the Torah — lives.

On Simchas Torah, then, people seize the *etz chaim* of a *Sefer* Torah and leap right into the Torah's dance. People dance with the Torah — they are making the Torah happy. In the midst of this joy, however, one needs to do some thinking. True, we are happy with the Torah. But is the Torah happy with *us*?

In the material world, even if a person is capable of taking an object without weighing whether it wants to be taken or not, this kind of taking possession is termed "taking by force,"

The Tree of Knowledge... the Tree of Life: *Gen.* 2:9.

A tree... hold fast to it: *Prov.* 6:18.

Taking by force: In the original, לְקִיחָה בִּזְרוֹעַ (lit., "taking by the [force of one's] arm); cf. Tractate *Pesachim* 57a.

and this is not legally classified as taking possession. The thing has not been taken: it has been forced. And if this is the case in the world of material objects, how much more so in the spiritual realm is a thing taken by force not really taken.

We are happy with the Torah — *but is the Torah happy with us?* In practice one should of course dance with the Torah, and joyfully so. But at the same time one should ponder this question, as to whether the Torah is happy with *us*. Such meditation arouses a noble resolve concerning one's acceptance of the yoke of heaven — setting aside fixed times for Torah study, and a workplan for one's *avodah* throughout the forthcoming year.

There are people who become warmly aroused with the joy of the Torah whenever Simchas Torah comes around. This is no doubt felt genuinely, for at this time the innermost point of their soul is revealed. Indeed, it is a delight to see how happy they are in the joy of the Torah. But this awakening must be channeled into real and actual *avodah* — so that they set aside fixed times for the group study of the Torah throughout the year.

5.

"How long shall we stand in a situation that rests on one support?"

Within our brotherhood there are a number of chassidim who could be men of quite some stature. That is, they could well be the kinds of people that *Chassidus* would like them to be. The only trouble is that they satisfy themselves with a level of *avodah* which belongs to the order of *makkif* [i.e., their spiritual endeavors encompass them as if from a sphere outside themselves, rather than being internalized (i.e., brought to the level of *pnimiyus*) through the systematic and intellectual regulation of their *avodah*]. They do not have a workplan

---

How long... on one support: In the original Aramaic, עַד מָתַי נִיקוּם בְּקִיּוּמָא דְחַד סַמְכָא; a rhetorical question appearing in the *Zohar*, addressed by R. Shimon bar Yochai to his disciples.

for their *avodah*, involving self-cultivation on the level of *pnimiyus*, and proceeding by gradated stages. Instead, everything is done on the level of *makkif*, as if sporadically.

When Rosh Chodesh Elul comes such people are aroused in a positive manner. They take stock of how the year has passed, sum up their accounts, and in conclusion make practical resolutions. Arriving at this balance-sheet gives rise to heartache and anguish over their spiritual status. One senses how poor and naked he is. One knows that he is a year older — but in what has the year passed?

One feels pained thinking about what will finally come of such a chaotic life, a life of *Tohu* — a life which is constantly thinking about "tomorrow", and because of this, every day loses its "today". In this way one forgets to think in terms of בָּרוּךְ ה' יוֹם יוֹם — "Blessed be G-d, day by day," being preoccupied instead with what will be tomorrow.

But Elul is the month of mercy, when the Thirteen Attributes of Mercy shine forth, and it is a propitious time. The spiritual stocktaking therefore brings about an intense longing for the acceptance of the yoke of heaven which characterizes Rosh HaShanah. The individual makes a firm resolve that in future things will be completely different.

And indeed when Rosh HaShanah and Yom Kippur come around, he is in quite a fine state. His time is carefully invested, and he is never idle. So when Sukkos and Simchas Torah come, he is in a decidedly joyful frame of mind. Things aren't too bad at all. There is only one thing wrong: everything is in a manner of *makkif*. He has indeed experienced a *hispaalus*, an emotional arousal, in the awe of heaven; a *hispaalus* of *teshuvah*; a *hispaalus* of joy; — but it is all in a manner of *makkif*.

That which is *makkif* may be observed in either of two ways — coming from either the loftiest heights or the nethermost depths. Light and power which are *makkif* are more intense than their counterparts which are *pnimi*. As discussed in *Chas-*

Blessed... day by day: *Ps.* 68:20.

sidus, makkif and *pnimi* correspond to *sovev* and *memaleh.* That which is *memaleh* is an *or pnimi.* The kind of light which is *or pnimi* is present according to the measure of the recipient vessel, and (as it were) fills it. When light and vessel unite, the vessel becomes refined to such a degree that it is possible for the vessel itself to become light.

As stated above, the light and power of *makkif* are more intense than light and power which are *pnimi.* They cannot be bounded by a vessel, but they can give life-force to the light which is *pnimi.* When they unite with the *or pnimi,* the latter increases greatly in strength.

Intellect *(seichel)* is light which is *pnimi.* Will *(ratzon)* and pleasure *(oneg)* are lights which are *makkif.* The intellect is limited to the vessel of the brain. Will and pleasure, however, cannot be delimited to a vessel, for they are "encompassing lights" *(oros makkifim).* They illumine the intellect, and the *middos,* and practical activity as well. But wherever they may be, by their very presence they give life-force to the *or pnimi* of the faculty in which they are to be found, and this faculty becomes animated with greater vigor than it would have had alone.

This may be observed from tangible experience. One cannot compare the manner in which a person studies a subject when prompted by *understanding* alone, that is, because he is a man of intellect, and such a man by nature wants to understand, — with the manner in which a person studies a subject either because *he wants* to master its reasoning, or because he derives *pleasure* from his study. In the latter two cases, in addition to the fact that his very comprehension of the subject will be on a higher level, deeper and richer intellectually, his whole grasp of the subject will be intensely animated. This results from the revelation of *ratzon* and *oneg,* which are powers of *makkif,* in *seichel,* which is a power of *pnimi.*

There are specified ways in which a light or power which

Memaleh... or pnimi... fills it: מְמַלֵּא — lit., "fills".
Becomes refined: I.e., more spiritual.

is *makkif* can become revealed in a light or power which is *pnimi*. This however demands a certain preparation on the part of that which is *pnimi*, to enable it to absorb the light which is *makkif*. Without such preparation, not only will the light which is *makkif* not enhance and invigorate its *pnimi* counterpart, but it will crush and destroy it.

The above explanation will enable us to understand why, when speaking of the revelation of an *or makkif* the expression used in *Chassidus* is: "the *or makkif* strikes the *pnimi*." The use of the term "strikes" is surprising. If we are speaking of a revelation of light, one would have expected to hear that the *or makkif* "is revealed" in the *pnimi*, or that it "illuminates" the *pnimi*. The reason for the use of the term "strikes" is that in *or makkif* there is no middle path, for it is an extremely intense light. Since it knows no middle path, "revelation" and "illumination" are not appropriate to it. Indeed, in this subsists the difference between *or makkif* and *or pnimi*. With the latter, the terms "revelation" (*hisgalus*) and "illumination" (*he'arah*) are in place. The *or pnimi* becomes revealed in a revelation of light and illuminates — unlike *or makkif*, which has no [such] middle path.

Or makkif affects its recipient in one of two ways. If it has a prepared place, encountering the proper preparation of the *or pnimi* which is to receive it, then it is utilized to the highest extent possible. This means that whereas the *or pnimi* was previously unable to reach a particular level, with the powerful influence of the *or makkif* it is now enabled to attain it. If, however, the proper preparation of the *or pnimi* is lacking, then the *or makkif* shatters the *or pnimi*.

This, then, explains the use of the expression, "the *or makkif* strikes the *or pnimi*." For the only manner in which *or makkif* operates is striking with force. This can sometimes give rise to the attainment of the loftiest levels; sometimes it can lead downward (G-d forbid) to the lowest depths.

The discussion so far has been about *makkif* in general terms. As far as the ordered explanation of its details is concerned, I am certain that those who study *Chassidus* are well acquainted with this subject, especially as regards the details of its analogy in the faculties of the soul — regarding *seichel* and *middos*, which are powers of *pnimi*, and regarding *ratzon* and *oneg*, which are powers of *makkif*. Even though all this is Torah, and the main consideration in the comprehension of *Chassidus* is that each concept should be articulated clearly, and this includes the repeated discussion of even the most familiar concepts in *Chassidus*, for the very speaking of them invigorates, — nevertheless now is not the appropriate time for lengthy explanations in general, and of familiar concepts in particular.

Everyone knows from their tangible experience that when *ratzon* ("will") strikes the *seichel* ("intellect"), the latter becomes elevated to a degree which stands in no relation to its potential in its own right. The same is the case when *oneg* ("pleasure") is revealed. If, however, the *ratzon* is not internalized, in a manner of *pnimi*, but remains as *ratzon*, then it destroys (G-d forbid) all of the faculties which are *pnimi*.

In bygone days, a person whose *avodah* remained at the level of *makkif* used to be called a *chitzon*. In the eyes of the *temimim*, the kind of character thus described was despised and out of bounds. There were a number of quite fine students, who toiled earnestly in their [Talmudic] studies, spent their time conscientiously in the study of *Chassidus*, comprehended their studies (each according to his abilities), and prayed with commendable warmth. But all this was experienced in an outward manner, in a manner of *chitzoniyus*.

Chitzoniyus is related to that which is *makkif*. Whatever is *makkif* is not only outward, or external; this characteristic indeed represents the advantage of that which is *makkif* over its *pnimi* equivalent. For the latter is received within a vessel, which is impossible for a light or power which is *makkif*. But when we say, as above, that *chitzoniyus* is related to that which is *makkif*, this is not meant (so to speak) in a complimentary way. For it is easier to err with regard to something *makkif*

A person whose *avodah* remained at the level of *makkif*: In the original Yiddish, *a makkifdikn*.

than to its *pnimi* counterpart. A person who is characterized by *chitzoniyus* lives in delusion — he deludes himself; one who is a *pnimi* does not live in delusion. He knows where he stands, and what the particular concept before him means, and is preoccupied with making himself more of a vessel that will be able to absorb the things which occupy him.

A *chitzon*, by contrast, is deluded both as regards himself and as regards whatever concept confronts him. His error can take one of several forms, sometimes veering too much in the direction of ascent, and sometimes too much in the direction of descent. This may be readily observed. There are times when he describes a thing in glowing terms that are well beyond its justifiable proportions, and there are times when he disparages a thing more than is warranted. For a *chitzon* in general is one who exaggerates. It is not that the exaggeration stems from falsehood: it comes from the fact that he is a person who lives in delusion. He fools himself. He grasps concepts superficially, without the inward dimension of *pnimiyus*. And "just as he absorbs, so he exudes."

A *chitzon* studies *nigleh,* the revealed levels of the Torah; he studies *Chassidus;* quite often in the course of his prayers he meditates on the *Chassidus* he has been studying; — and all of this is done with warmth. Indeed there are such whose warmth may be perceived more than that of a *pnimi*. A *pnimi* needs time. He cannot hurry. First he studies; then he meditates on the concept he has been studying; he absorbs it inwardly; until eventually he is warmed by it, and is aroused by it. And this all takes time.

A *chitzon* — with his spiritual situation characterized by the forces of *makkif* — does not need so much time. When he has studied his fill he thinks that he knows his subject. He is so

---

Absorbs... exudes: In the original, כְּבוֹלְעוֹ כָּךְ פּוֹלְטוֹ; Tractate *Pesachim* 30b. The metaphor is borrowed from the laws dealing with the *kashering* of various vessels.

In the course... studying: In the original Yiddish, *davent* (lit., "he prays"). In *Chabad* usage this often implies not merely saying one's prayers, but being involved in the prolonged kind of *avodah* here described.

deluded within himself that he truthfully thinks, with the
outward truth of his *chitzoniyus*, that he has mastered it.
Moreover he is already warm — but his warmth is the outward warmth of *chitzoniyus*.

Whatever a *chitzon* studies, be it in *nigleh* or *Chassidus*, — as
soon as he has finished studying, and has not yet even had
time to thoroughly digest his subject, he already begins to
expound upon it, propounding opinions and arguments, and
can even insist on the validity of his own interpretation.

With him, every item of spiritual knowledge and comprehension is inextricably encrusted with coarseness of spirit. To
borrow the expression of *Likkutei Torah,* "his spirituality is
coarse." Accordingly, when he proposes a learned argument,
he insists on its validity. In the study of *Chassidus* — which is
the *pnimiyus,* the inner dimension of the Torah — his failing,
of belonging only to *chitzoniyus* and *makkif,* is even more apparent. When a *chitzon* studies *Chassidus* it may well be said of him,
"Just as he absorbs, so he exudes."

Moreover, a *chitzon* can even be an *oved* — but in this too he
is deluded. A *pnimi* knows that *avodah* demands time. It takes a
great deal of toil indeed until one transforms a *middah,* a
character trait; and even when one has already brought oneself to the point of doing so, one still needs to check oneself
critically lest the unwanted trait awakens again. A *chitzon,*
however, is not involved with *avodah* on the level of *pnimiyus,*
with carrying through a task to its very end, as one should;
with him everything remains at the level of *chitzoniyus* and
makkif. His innate character traits, therefore, remain as they
were.

On *Yud-Beis* Tammuz I told you that a little note is extant
which records the questions that my greatgrandfather the

Inextricably encrusted with coarseness of spirit: Lit., "its fetal sac and
placenta are coarseness of spirit"; i.e., even the *spiritual* fruits of the
chitzon are inevitably obscured by this accompanying husk —
coarseness.

Awakens again: In the original, חוֹזֵר וְנֵעוֹר; another metaphor borrowed
from the laws of *kashrus;* see Tractate *Avodah Zarah* 73a.

Tzemach Tzedek once posed to his grandfather the Alter Rebbe at *yechidus.* The note appears to date from the years 5565-5568 (תקס״ה-תקס״ח; 1805-1808). One of the questions asks: "What is the ultimate point of *Chassidus?"* And the Alter Rebbe replied: "The entire point of *Chassidus* is that one should transform the nature of his character traits."

It should be noted that my greatgrandfather's question was: "What is the ultimate point of *Chassidus?"* — and not: "What is *Chassidus?"* My greatgrandfather knew what *Chassidus* is — a divine level of wisdom, the inner dimension of the Torah. His question was: "What is the ultimate point of *Chassidus?"* And it was to this question that the Alter Rebbe answered that "the entire point of *Chassidus* is that one should transform the nature of his *middos."*

In the Written Torah we count letters: each letter expresses divine light in its very essence. In a dictum of the Alter Rebbe we should count letters. And the Alter Rebbe said that "the entire point of *Chassidus* is that one should transform the nature of his *middos."*

Now everyone understands with absolute clarity the difference between "his natural *middos"* and "the nature of his *middos."* That much requires no explanation.

What *Chassidus* demands is that one should transform the nature of one's *middos. Chassidus* demands of everyone who studies its teachings that he should transform the nature of his *middos.* For *Chassidus* is not only a schoolmaster who teaches one *how* to transform the nature of his *middos.*

It is clear to everyone that the Alter Rebbe's reply reaches up to the loftiest heights of *Chassidus.* That is to say: His reply describes the uppermost extreme of *Chassidus.* In every *or yashar (sic)* whose direction is from below upward, the lowermost extreme is the beginning, and the uppermost extreme is its true consummation.

Transform the nature of his character traits: In the original, לְשַׁנּוֹת טִבְעִיּוּת מִדּוֹתָיו.

Divine light in its very essence: In the original, *or atzmi.*

The Alter Rebbe's answer, then, as to what constitutes the ultimate point of *Chassidus*, is a description of the uppermost extreme of *Chassidus*. And the uppermost extreme of *Chassidus*, the ultimate purpose of *Chassidus*, is that one should transform the nature of one's *middos*.

All the richest sequences of concepts in the teachings of *Chassidus*; the most broadly-based comprehension of the ideas of *Chassidus*; the profoundest depths plumbed in the teachings of *Chassidus*, that encompass all of the three faculties — *chochmah*, *binah* and *daas* — of the divine soul, which is "truly a part of G-d above"; — the intention of all of this is that a person should transform the nature of his *middos*.

"Turn it over and over — for everything is in it." In this [above-quoted dictum of the Alter Rebbe] lies the entire point of *Chassidus*. *Chassidus* opens one's eyes and shows one the truth in each thing. *Chassidus* explains that in the phrase חֵטְא וְעָוֹן [usually translated "sin and iniquity"], *chet* implies a "lack", and *avon* derives from the noun עֲוִית, meaning "distortion".

A reminder: One must not forget for a moment that if a person is lacking in the self-refining labor of practical *avodah*, then the entire point of *Chassidus* is missing. As for those who study *Chassidus* and occupy themselves with comprehending it, but without being brought by their study to practical *avodah*, — this is an indication that their study of *Chassidus* has become distorted, and has veered away from its proper path. For the entire point of *Chassidus* is that one should transform the nature of his *middos*, and this can be accomplished only through inward *avodah* day by day, working on all of the three "garments" [i.e., means of expression] of the soul — thought, word and deed.

Truly a part of G-d above: *Tanya*, beginning of Ch. 2.
Turn it over: I.e., Study the Torah over and over; Tractate *Avos* 5:21.
Sin and iniquity: See *Vidui*, the confession of Yom Kippur.
Implies a "lack": See *Rashi* on *I Kings* 1:21. Note that the alternative renditions of *chet* and *avon* imply subtler faults than do the standard translations.

6.

At the conclusion of the above talk on *makkif* and *pnimi* in *avodah*, which left a considerable impact on the listeners, one of the chassidim who felt a nearness to the Rebbe asked for his blessing — "that the Almighty should help [us to bring these ideas into practice]."
The Rebbe replied as follows.

Of course one needs a blessing that the Almighty should help. But at the same time we need to know, without any self-delusion, that with a blessing alone we will not advance in our way through the world. A blessing is a very fine thing, valuable indeed. But it is effective only when one takes action. In the Torah it is written, וּבֵרַכְךָ ה' אֱלֹקֶיךָ בְּכֹל אֲשֶׁר תַּעֲשֶׂה — "The L-rd your G-d will bless you *in all that you do.*" There has to be real and actual *avodah*. This labor includes plowing and sowing — plowing one's ego, casting away the stones which prevent effective sowing, and then sowing within oneself the kinds of seed that will sprout well.

Avodah begins with one's "I". One needs to make a truthful account: Who am I, and what am I?

Who am I? — A divine soul; and this is חֵלֶק אֱלֹוקַּ מִמַּעַל — "a part of G-d above," or, as the Alter Rebbe cites this verse in *Tanya,* חֵלֶק אֱלֹוקַּ מִמַּעַל מַמָּשׁ — "*truly* a part of G-d above." Not satisfied with the general statement that the second soul of a Jew is "a part of G-d," the Alter Rebbe adds the word מַמָּשׁ — "truly and actually." All men of understanding know full well what the word מַמָּשׁ signifies. Actual G-dliness — this is one's "I". Next, one needs to know *who* is this "I"; to ponder deeply *what* is this "I" — that is, in what is it occupied; what should this "I" want; and what does the "I" want.

The L-rd...you do: Deut. 15:18.
A part of G-d above: Job 31:2.
Cites... in *Tanya*: Ch. 2.

This kind of detailed meditation is a plowing. It plows up the hardness, and the stones that make up one's stony heart are laid bare. This makes it possible for one to clear the field where the *avodah* is to take place, and to sow good seeds in it.

If a person occupies himself with orderly *avodah*, as *Chassidus* demands and teaches one to do, then a blessing is effective and achieves results out of all due proportion. In the verses which promise divine rewards "if you will walk in the way of My statutes" (אִם בְּחֻקֹּתַי תֵּלֵכוּ), the expression used is that "the land will yield its harvest" (וְנָתְנָה הָאָרֶץ יְבוּלָהּ). In the verses which warn of divine retribution — "Take care lest your heart be lured away" (הִשָּׁמְרוּ לָכֶם פֶּן יִפְתֶּה לְבַבְכֶם), the expression used is that "the soil will not yield its harvest" (וְהָאֲדָמָה לֹא תִתֵּן אֶת יְבוּלָהּ). The former verse uses the word אֶרֶץ ("land"), while the latter says אֲדָמָה ("soil"). In the language of *Chassidus, eretz* signifies *ratzon* ("will"), while *adamah* signifies *seichel* ("intellect"). And of the four terms which the Torah uses for man (אָדָם, אִישׁ, אֱנוֹשׁ, גֶּבֶר), the first (אָדָם) signifies *seichel,* and the second (אִישׁ) indicates *middos,* character traits.

The *Gemara* says that "the Jews in the Diaspora practice idolatry [lit., 'perform an alien service'] in a state of purity." *Rashi* explains: "That is to say, [their divine service is] without devout intent, and without taking it to heart." In the light of the teachings of *Chassidus* this may be understood as follows. If a thing is done without *kavanah* and without its being taken to heart, then it is *avodah zarah,* an alien worship. For real *avodah* is only that which is done with *kavanah* and with attentive care. Hence [the promises contained in] the verse, וְהָיָה

Stony heart: Cf. (e.g.) *Ezek.* 11:19.
If you will walk: *Lev.* 26:3.
The land will yield: *Ibid.* v.4.
Take care: *Deut.* 11:16.
The soil will not yield: *Ibid.* v.17.
Eretz signifies *ratzon* ("will"): Cf. *Bereishis Rabbah* 5:7: "Why is it called *eretz* (אֶרֶץ)? — Because it wanted (שֶׁרָצְתָה) to do the will (רָצוֹן) of its Maker."
Adamah signifies *seichel*: Cf. the phrase, אֲדַמֶּה לְעֶלְיוֹן (*Isa.* 14:14).
The Jews in the Diaspora: Tractate *Avodah Zarah* 8a.

אִם שָׁמֹעַ תִּשְׁמְעוּ — "And it shall come to pass, if you will diligently obey..."* This is an *avodah* to be done with *kavanah* — a labor of the intellect, to meditate on this G-dly subject; and an *avodah* that must be taken to heart — the labor of refining one's character traits. If the *avodah* is done in this way, then come the promises of וְאָכַלְתָּ וְשָׂבָעְתָּ — "You shall eat and be satiated." But if it is done without *kavanah*, and without its being taken to heart — and this is what is termed *avodah zarah*, "alien worship" — then even the *adamah* will not yield its harvest [and *adamah*, as we have seen, signifies intellect]. That is to say, that even if a person whose *avodah* is such is exceedingly learned in *Chassidus* and master of numerous concepts, then even when he expounds *Chassidus* and offers explanations and expositions of its teachings, *there will be no fruit.* There will be "clouds and wind, but no rain." There will be arrogance and coarseness of spirit — but no real, practical *avodah*.

If, on the other hand, "you walk in My statutes," with *avodah* which is orderly, comprising divine service both by the intellect and by the heart, then there follows the consequence: וְנָתְנָה הָאָרֶץ יְבוּלָהּ — "the land will yield its produce." In such a case, not only will the *adamah* (signifying intellect) be fertile, but so too will the *eretz* (signifying will) yield its produce.

It was explained a short while ago that there is a light which is *pnimi,* and a light which is *makkif;* that the *or makkif* is more intense than the *or pnimi;* in the context of the faculties of the soul, *or makkif* and *or pnimi* represent respectively *ratzon* ("will") and *seichel* ("intellect"); when the *or makkif* becomes united with the *or pnimi,* the latter becomes stronger — but only because of the influence and revelation within it of the *or makkif.* The produce that is yielded, then, the fruit that comes forth, stems from the *or pnimi.*

---

* This is explained in the *maamar* beginning with the words אֲנִי לְדוֹדִי (5693/ תרצ"ג; 1933), in connection with the concept of empty and full vessels.

And it shall come to pass: *Deut.* 11:13.
You shall eat: *Deut.* 8:10.
Clouds and wind: *Prov.* 25:14.

To sum up: The "produce of the *eretz*" refers to the direct results of the *or makkif* itself, not merely to its effects on the *or pnimi*. In terms of *avodah*, this is [the level of the love of G-d which is] called *re'usa deliba;* in terms of *haskalah*, it refers to understanding both the essence of a concept, and the G-dly content which lies in that concept.

This is the point of the blessing that "the land (*eretz*) will yield its produce." It is palpably observable that *ratzon* ("will") comprises more than what in fact comes down into practice. This, then, is the point of this threefold blessing: [Firstly:] That one's will should yield produce, and not remain restricted to will alone. [Secondly:] That this harvest should find expression in actual deeds; not being confined to a sound understanding of the subject, merely "sermonizing beautifully," as is the case with one who studies a great deal of *Chassidus* without its affecting his actions, but doing good deeds, "fulfilling beautifully." [Thirdly:] Since the influence of the will is an *or makkif*, concerning which it is easier for one to delude oneself [as to one's actual spiritual standing] than in the case of *avodah* animated by an *or pnimi*, the concluding part of the blessing is — that one's *avodah* should be done truthfully.

One of those present asked: "If so, what is the difference between a blessing and prayer?"

The questioner evidently sought to imply that prayer entails *avodah*, whereas a blessing effects a drawing down from Above by means other than *avodah*.

To this question the Rebbe replied as follows.

Regarding the general difference between a prayer and a blessing, it is well known that blessing refers to a *hamshachah*, a drawing down from Above. Its aim is that that which is present in the source, set aside to be drawn down, should

---

Re'usa deliba (רְעוּתָא דְלִבָּא): Lit., "the desire of the heart"; i.e., the desire of the innermost point of the heart.

Sermonizing beautifully: In the original, נָאֶה דּוֹרֵשׁ; Tractate *Yevamos* 63b.

Fulfilling beautifully: In the original, נָאֶה מְקַיֵּם; *ibid.*

Present in the source: I.e., potential energy.

indeed be drawn down — without any hindrance, and to its proper place.

For example: Our Father and our King has given us, all of Israel, a good year, with health and sustenance. Our Sages teach us that "a person's livelihood is determined for him from Rosh HaShanah" (כָּל מְזוֹנוֹתָיו שֶׁל אָדָם קְצוּבִים לוֹ מֵרֹאשׁ הַשָּׁנָה), and it has been explained in *Chassidus* that the word for "livelihood" (מְזוֹנוֹתָיו), in the plural form, implies both forms of sustenance, physical food and spiritual food, as it is written, כִּי חֹק לְיִשְׂרָאֵל הוּא מִשְׁפָּט לֵאלֹקֵי יַעֲקֹב — "For it is a decree for Israel, a [day of] judgment for the G-d of Jacob."

In this context, the purpose of a blessing is that the physical and spiritual sustenance which has been set aside this Rosh HaShanah for all of Israel throughout the world should come down in a *revealed* kind of good (טוֹב גָּלוּי) — in the form of children, health, and ample sustenance, and the study of the Torah and the fulfillment of the *mitzvos* through the awe of heaven. And when we say "good", we mean "good" in the way that we created beings understand it. In the prayers of Yom Kippur we ask: וְאוֹצָרְךָ הַטּוֹב לָנוּ תִּפְתַּח — "And Thy good treasure-house, open Thou for us!" In this phrase the pause should come after the *first* word [instead of after the second word; hence, instead of the adjective הַטּוֹב ("good") *itself* qualifying the preceding noun, as in the usual translation given above, it joins the following word, so that the request now reads: "וְאוֹצָרְךָ — And Thy treasure-house, הַטּוֹב לָנוּ — which is good for *us*, i.e., good in *our* eyes, תִּפְתַּח — open Thou!"].

It is explained thoroughly in *Chassidus* that "Thy treasure-house," the treasure-house Above, is goodness in its entirety. However, within the realm of good itself there is a hidden good, the kind of good of which the Alter Rebbe speaks in *Iggeres HaKodesh*, in the epistle beginning לְהַשְׂכִּילְךָ בִּינָה.

A person's livelihood: Tractate *Beitzah* 16a.
For it is a decree: *Ps.* 81:5.
Prayers of Yom Kippur: In the concluding *Ne'ilah* service.
A hidden good: I.e., suffering in its various forms, the benefits of which are visible to the spiritual eye alone.
The epistle: See *Tanya*, p. 446.

What we request is *revealed* good. And revealed good is that which is visible and revealed in the form of children, health, and ample sustenance, and the study of Torah with the *avodah* which *Chassidus* demands. May the material and spiritual sustenance come down to all of Israel without any hindrance, and to its proper place.

This is the meaning of blessing.

Prayer is a request that something new be drawn down, in the shape of a livelihood, health, salvation, the ultimate Redemption — things which were not yet existent in the source.

This is the general difference between a blessing and a prayer. A blessing seeks that that which is present in the source should indeed be drawn down in practice without any hindrances, as it is written, עַד מְהֵרָה יָרוּץ דְּבָרוֹ — "His word runs most swiftly"; it seeks that the word of G-d with its flow of material and spiritual good should be drawn down speedily. Prayer seeks to effect a desire Above that something should be drawn down from a higher level than the source.

Both approaches, however, both blessing and prayer, require plowing and sowing. Though these preparations are different in the two cases, yet plowing and sowing there must be. One must toil. And may the Almighty grant that this toil should yield fruit, fruit which is good both spiritually and materially.

7.

When one of our brotherhood or one of the *temimim* arrives here from some township and I ask him if *Chassidus* is being studied over there, and whether there is a time set aside in the local synagogues for the study of *Chassidus* and of *nigleh*, the revealed levels of the Torah, there are those who answer that there is no one to study with. So I ask: "Is there absolutely no one?" And they answer that there *are* one or two, perhaps even three. This is the answer to my question as to

---

His word runs most swiftly: *Ps.* 147:15.

the public study of *Chassidus*. I ask further: "*Nu*, and what about a study session in *Gemara*, a chapter of *Shulchan Aruch*, and the like?" Again the same answer: "There's no one to study with."

If some effort had been made, then seven or eight people would have met for group study, perhaps even a *minyan*.

I am duty-bound to make it known to all those who satisfy themselves with the excuse that "there is no one to learn with" that they bear a weighty responsibility. This they need to know. The truth is that if a person lives in a small township or village where there are no Torah scholars, if he has a will to do so he can see to it that Torah should be studied publicly.

Experience has shown that if only there is a person who is actively devoted to awakening the people around him to the need for public Torah study, things move, thank G-d. Everyone, even the simplest and most ignorant of Jews, is eager to hear a word of Torah. Everyone is happy to hear a saying of our Sages, a passage from the *Aggadah*, a *Midrash*, a Torah law. There are those too who want to hear a word of *Chassidus*. It all depends only on the one who proposes such study — one to whom the outcome really matters. And the obligation to initiate these things lies on each member of the chassidic fraternity and on each one of the *temimim*.

Let everyone keep in mind the following statements of our Sages: כָּל הַמְקַיֵּם נֶפֶשׁ אַחַת מִיִשְׂרָאֵל... כְּאִילּוּ קִיֵּם עוֹלָם מָלֵא — "Whoever saves one soul among Israel [is regarded by the Torah] as if he saved an entire world"; and again: כָּל הַמְלַמֵּד אֶת בֶּן חֲבֵרוֹ תּוֹרָה ... — "Whoever teaches Torah to his friend's child [is regarded as if he was his father]." The Sages do not speak of "saving souls" or "teaching his friend's children," in the plural; for one soul, one child, is an entire world.

The times which are fixed for the public study of the Torah are the *etz chaims*, the wooden rollers of the Torah

---

Whoever saves: Tractate *Sanhedrin* 37a.
Whoever teaches: Tractate *Sanhedrin* 19b.

which are known as the Trees of Life, to which every individual should hold fast throughout the year. Then the Torah will be happy with us. That will *literally* be Simchas Torah — the Rejoicing of the Torah, for the Torah will rejoice with the Jewish people.

As to whoever will devote himself to rousing the people around him to set up public study sessions, it is obvious that the Almighty will grant him success in his material endeavors. The Torah will not remain in debt to him.

The Torah is called תּוֹרַת חֶסֶד — "a Torah of lovingkindness," because it always arouses mercy for the Jewish people. For this reason too the Torah is called כּוֹס שֶׁל בְּרָכָה — "a cup of blessing," for by her entreaties to the Almighty she secures for them an abundance of blessings. He who dedicates himself utterly to sparking off the establishment of regular Torah study sessions in public, him will the Torah bring an abundance of good, both materially and spiritually.

8.

Praise and gratitude to the Almighty for the revelation of the light of *Chassidus* in general, and for the revelation of the luminary in particular — our predecessors, the Rebbes.

Every expression of praise and gratitude should be articulated in clear words, every word of which shines forth and is heard. Blessed, then, be our G-d, Who has placed our lot among the living. We in this world belong to generations in which the light of *Chassidus* is following a direction of revelation, and the luminary — the Rebbe — is following a direction of revelation, and the luminary — the Rebbe — is to be found in a phase of self-revelation.

Since the day that the Holy One, Blessed be He, created man on the earth there have been *Chassidus* and Rebbes. The first man in the world was a chassid, as the *Gemara* says, אָדָם

A Torah of lovingkindness: E.g., in *Prov.* 31:26.
A cup of blessing: Cf. *Midrash Rabbah* on *Parshas Zos HaBerachah* 11:4: "וְזֹאת הַבְּרָכָה" — זוֹ תּוֹרָה.

הָרִאשׁוֹן חָסִיד גָּדוֹל הָיָה — "Adam was a great chassid (pious man)."

In every generation there were Rebbes and chassidim, but only in a concealed manner — there were hidden *tzaddikim* — until the Almighty began a direction of revelation, so that there should be revealed Rebbes and chassidim, and He revealed for us the saintly Baal Shem Tov.

From that luminous day on which the Baal Shem Tov became revealed, the light of *Chassidus* began to shine forth in a revealed manner; then began a trend of the "revelation of the luminary," and then began the nearing of the luminary to the spark.

Until the time of the Baal Shem Tov, and for a certain period of his lifetime as well, there were indeed Rebbes and chassidim, but only hidden ones. With the revelation of the Baal Shem Tov, the Tree of Life was revealed, with all of its branches — Rebbes, who like luminaries give forth light among Israel.

Everyone knows the inner meaning of the words which R. Yehudah Leib HaKohen writes in his approbation to *Tanya*: וְכָעֵת יִשְׂמַח יִשְׂרָאֵל בְּהִגָּלוֹת דִּבְרֵי קָדְשׁוֹ — "Israel shall now rejoice as his saintly words are revealed" [alluding to R. Israel Baal Shem Tov]. By revealing the teachings of the *Chassidus* of *Chabad*, the Alter Rebbe opened up a new world for chassidim.

The Alter Rebbe's *Chassidus*, however, is the Written Law of *Chassidus*. "Great is G-d, and exceedingly exalted," therefore (גָּדוֹל ה' וּמְהֻלָּל מְאֹד), for having granted us this beautiful gift, and for having given us Rebbes who explain us the Written Law of the Alter Rebbe.

Our Rebbes have opened (and open) for us the "well-

Adam was a great chassid: Tractate *Eruvin* 18b.

The nearing of the luminary to the spark: In this context (see next para.), this refers to the relation between Rebbe and chassid. (See also Section 2, above.)

Israel shall now rejoice: *Tanya*, p. viii-ix.

However, is the Written Law: Hence demanding authoritative interpretation.

Great is G-d: *Ps.* 145:3.

springs of the great depths" — in the comprehension and knowledge of G-dliness, and in the service of the Almighty. They open up doors for us in all the worlds up to the highest levels, enabling one to have an intellectual grasp, as if in a tangible manner, of G-dliness. They bring a G-dly lamp into the fleshly, material world, and show us the union of this lowly world with the worlds Above.

9.

Everyone knows that the spiritual domain is utterly different from the material domain. As was discussed in the *maamarim* of Rosh HaShanah and *Yom-Tov*, we material and created beings have no grasp of that which is spiritual. We do however have an inkling of that which is spiritual, and this appraisal gives us some image of it. This does not mean that we have a grasp of it: it does mean that we have attained some clarity as to what we do not know. For just as *knowing* has its definition and its image — a defined image, which one knows — so too does *not knowing* have its defined image, of that which we do not know.

By way of illustration, let us compare an ignorant person who does not understand a certain topic in the *Gemara*, with a scholar of stature who has encountered the difficulty of an apparent internal contradiction in the text, which he is unable to resolve. True enough, neither of them understands — yet they are utterly different. The ignoramus knows nothing; that is, he does not even know what it is that he does not know. The scholar, though he too does not understand, knows what it is that he does not know. The latter situation can be called a *clear not-knowing.* And this too can be reckoned as a kind of knowing, for at least it brings about some kind of appraisal. We created and material beings *know* that which is spiritual; that is, we have some appraisal of spiritual things through the experience of the faculties of the soul; and

---

Wellsprings of the great depths: *Gen.* 7:11.
Inkling... appraisal: In the original, הַעֲרָכָה.

though we do not *know* *them* either, nevertheless they are *known to us.*

There is a difference between our *knowing* something (הַשָּׂגָה) and its *being known* to us (יָדוּעַ). Wherein lies the difference? In the former case we know the known thing by virtue of itself; in the latter, we know it through something else.

For example, we know the spiritual world *(ruchniyus)* through the faculties of the soul. We do not know the spiritual world itself. But since the faculties of the soul are spiritual, and we know them through the ways in which they manifest themselves, it may be said that the spiritual world is known to us.

A thing's *being known* to us does not quite mean that we *know* it; on the contrary, this state causes anguish. For just as grasping something gives rise to delight and pleasure, so too one's *not* knowing something thoroughly gives rise to pain and distress. This is plain to see. One who has thoroughly grasped a certain idea is filled with joy to the point of satiety; quite the opposite of one who has not grasped the idea, who is distressed.

But even after this entire distinction has been made, being at the level at which spiritual things are *known* to us does enable us to draw nearer to the level of *knowing* them. It gives some hope that one will perhaps be granted the possibility of understanding.

[At this point the Rebbe Rayatz quotes an exposition of his father, the Rebbe Rashab, on the difference between the material domain and the spiritual domain. The former passes through phases of motion and rest, whereas one's spiritual life, one's *ruchniyus*, is constantly active within itself even when one is unconscious of it. (In the Yiddish original, *Seichel seichelt-zich ven du herst nit oich.)* The discourse of the Rebbe Rashab, the continuation of which ranges over the more abstruse reaches of the terminology of *Chassidus*, includes an explanation of the statement in the *Zohar* that "the gates of *Gan Eden* are closed at night."]

10.

Rambam opens one of the chapters of his *Hilchos Deos* as follows: "Just as the sage is distinguishable in his wisdom and in his mental attitudes..., so should he be distinguishable in his actions."

On *Yud-Beis* Tammuz it was explained in detail that one who is a *pnimi* is orderly, and one who is well ordered is ordered well in all of his affairs. With him, the very order of things is itself orderly.

In divine service, *hachanah* ("preparation") is one of the indispensable factors, for *hachanah* is part of *hachsharah*, making oneself fit to become a vessel capable of receiving what it needs to hold. The preparation itself needs to be done in a methodical way. Indeed, sometimes the mere setting of things in order suffices to show that no preparation is called for; that is, there are things which do not need to be preceded by lengthy preparation.

There were times when in the *avodah* of certain chassidim, men of commendable standing inwardly, preparations did not play a role. Instead there was *haatakah*, which means moving oneself across from one place to another. This can be done in a number of ways. Moving oneself [mentally] away from circumstances that disturb one's *avodah* may also be called *haatakah* — but of quite a modest order. Properly speaking, *haatakah* means moving oneself away from one field of *avodah* to another field, in which he now chooses to be occupied. And what is crucial here is that *one be able to give oneself a decisive directive* to move where necessary — and this is an ability that every chassid needs.

We have explained that one's *avodah* should not be confined to the level of *makkif*, and that one must not live in self-delusion. Accordingly, since most of us have not yet

---

Hilchos Deos: Ch. 5.

One be able to give oneself a decisive directive: In the original, אז מען איז א בעל-דעה אויף זיך.

We have explained: See Section 5, on p. 121ff. above.

attained those levels of *haatakah* that involve (as it were) moving oneself away, in the meantime we should toil at the task of *hafanah* (lit., "emptying oneself").

It is unnecessary to explain the difference between *hafanah* and *haatakah*. *Chassidus* sharpens one's intellectual tools well, so that one can understand a concept with absolute clarity. And though *haatakah* is an advanced level in *avodah*, one should nevertheless strive towards it. One should want to be able to be there. And when a person toils with a will and a desire, the Almighty helps him along.

11.

May the Almighty grant that the Torah be happy with *us;* that there be a *Simchas* Torah, a *Rejoicing* of the Torah, in the sense that the *Torah* should rejoice. And if the Torah rejoices, then it will be Simchas Torah all the year round. This rejoicing of the Torah will illuminate all the countries in which Jews are to be found, and will fill all Jewish homes with happiness.

The *Mishnah* teaches: כָּל הַמְקַיֵּם אֶת הַתּוֹרָה מֵעֹנִי סוֹפוֹ לְקַיְּמָה מֵעֹשֶׁר — "Whoever fulfills the Torah in poverty will ultimately fulfill it in wealth." As we said earlier: The Torah does not remain a debtor to whoever studies it, nor to whoever exerts himself to arrange for the communal study of the Torah. Exhausted though he may be after a long day's toil, scorched by the heat of the sun, or frozen by the winter's cold, and yet he sits down in the evening for his nightly *shiur*, — the Torah itself pleads in the Heavenly Court on behalf of such a Jew, that he and his household be judged with mercy.

Simchas Torah — the Rejoicing of the Torah — is present only when one studies it. It is then that it rejoices, and intercedes for the bestowal of blessings upon the entire House of Israel. And when this takes place, the lives of Jews every-where will be lit up materially and spiritually.

Hafanah (lit., "emptying oneself"): I.e., freeing oneself of distracting influences.
Whoever fulfills the Torah: Tractate *Avos* 4:9.

Needless to say, the above promise to "Whoever studies the Torah..." refers not only to its study but to its fulfillment as well — including both the observance of its *mitzvos* in actual practice, and the regulation of one's interpersonal conduct in the light of proper character traits, as the Torah requires. The prologue to fulfillment, however, is study. And when one's study is imbued with the awe of heaven — that is, when one's regular studies are accompanied by the study of *Mussar* and *Chassidus* — one's studies then find their way into one's heart, and the study of the Torah leads to its fulfillment.

Every individual who has a sense of *ahavas Yisrael*, who simply likes a fellow Jew and is anxious for the spiritual and material welfare of Jewry at large, should explain to his friends and aquaintances the moral obligation that lies on everyone to study Torah daily. Each person according to his own status ought to be a member of a group that studies at a fixed time every day.

"The People of the G-d of Avraham" have always stood (and, thank G-d, today too stand) at a high level of intellectual development — "a wise and understanding nation" in every sense of the phrase. Every Jew — including even one whose childhood learning, due to various family circumstances, was scant — has the intellectual potential to master a page of *Gemara* and follow a reasoned explanation.

Every Jew is eager to hear a word of Torah, and to understand it too. It sticks to him; he finds a certain delight in it; it makes him feel good.

A Jew must have spiritual nourishment: he cannot be satisfied with physicality alone. Every Jew has a sensitivity to spiritual things and the spirit within him aspires to higher things, just as he seeks the fleshly life of This World.

* * *

Every Jew cherishes his lineage, the "rock from which he is hewn." From the depths of his soul he respects his fore-

---

The People of the G-d of Avraham: *Ps.* 47:10.
A wise and understanding nation: *Deut.* 4:6.
Rock from which he is hewn: Cf. *Isa.* 51:1.

bears, and at every opportunity he is happy to point out his descent from rabbis and Torah scholars. To be sure, with some people this is truer than with others, but even in the case of a Jew who is (G-d forbid) well and truly frozen, there is a spark of life that from time to time casts up within him memories of his roots, and he seeks out names of relatives who were rabbis and Torah students. There is no need to dwell on this at length, for within everyone's frequent experience there are individuals who themselves are (*poor fellows!*) far removed from the Torah, and yet with the greatest enthusiasm tell all about their parents and relatives who were Torah scholars.

We were in Rostov, Russia, in the winter of 5681 (חרפ״א; 1920-21), during the famine years. The situation at the time is common knowledge: the new regime was in its early years, and the Yevsektzia was beginning to make its presence felt. Prospects looked grim for the survival of the various religious organizations, Torah institutions and *mikvaos*. Until that time all these religious bodies were organized at a level that would be hard to find in a major Jewish community, let alone in such a town on the River Don where Jews were barred.

The fact is that it would be a *mitzvah* to recount all of this in detail, for it enables one to see the beauty of the natural face of Jewry.

Rostov was a town in which only craftsmen and those holding diplomas of higher education were allowed to live. It goes without saying that Torah scholars and truly G-d-fearing Jews never went to the town, and in any case the authorities did not allow Jews in general to go there.

Jewish craftsmen from the good old days, who had been raised on a genuine, healthy Torah-education, laid the foundations for the local religious institutions, the synagogues, and a *mikveh*, all of which eventually flourished, and these causes, together with a variety of charitable bodies, all enjoyed the material support which the unobservant Jews

---

Poor fellows!: In the original Yiddish, *nebbich.*

with a secular education gave them with the greatest degree
of involvement and energy.

At the first opportunity for a permit, which untiring
endeavors with the czarist authorities had finally managed to
secure, the little community had brought itself a scholarly *rav*
and a number of G-d-fearing *shochatim*.

Despite the fact that only a short while earlier the czarist
regime had annulled the restrictions on Jewish residence in
the town, we and a large number of Polish Jews who had fled
the war zones and arrived there found that all the religious
organizations were in good order.(They also included *chadarim*
where children were taught just as in the regular Jewish
communities.) The hospitality shown by all the local Jews
without exception, whether observant or non-observant, is
indescribable. None of the new arrivals (thank G-d) was in
need of any material help, but the friendly goodwill raised
everyone's morale.

The head of the community and several members of the
council, who were a far cry from the Torah scholars who
were the leading lights in the Jewish towns, at their first
meeting expressed their pleasure at the arrival of the observant families. They stated that they were prepared to set up
synagogues for those who desired to maintain their own
nussach, as well as Torah schools for their children in the spirit
of their previous education. They asked the newly-arrived
families to make themselves just as much at home as they had
felt in their own Polish towns. Moreover, they invited them
to play a part in the local religious institutions, and to give
their cooperation to the *rav* as well as to all of those who were
involved in strengthening their various organizations.

In all the above one can see the natural Jew face to face.
The beautiful feelings of a Jew are not (G-d forbid) swept
away in the tempest of life in This World; they are not lost in
the turmoil of the workaday world. In the course of the few
years that elapsed until the rise of the new regime, the Jewish
life of Rostov flourished.

One winter's day during my stay there, there arrived a
firm directive that the local *mikveh* be closed down. A commis-

sion was immediately set up, headed by a certain doctor, and it came to the conclusion that the *mikveh* was not clean. The truth which everyone knew and saw — that the *mikveh* could not be in that state — interested no one.

Within a few days word came through as to the doctor's identity. The reports about him were bleak: he was one of the greatest destroyers of the faith. It was decided in the community that I should invite the doctor and plead our cause with him. This was one of the hardest things imaginable for those times — yet it happened. We spent a winter's evening together conversing on various subjects, until finally the doctor began telling of his family background, and who his grandfather was... and out of this conversation the opportunity arose for the *mikveh* question to be aired. And, thank G-d, it worked. In fact he himself offered advice as to how we could secure a permit for the *mikveh*.

Such cases abound in their thousands, that demonstrate what a Jew is, and what kind of a spiritual nucleus a Jew possesses. That man has never existed — and never will exist — who can measure the extent of what a Jewish heart contains.

It is true that at times light and darkness, good and evil, alternate erratically. At times there are wayward deeds that derive from the nethermost depths — but there are also noble deeds inspired by the loftiest heights. In the most unlettered of Jews we can find beautiful sensibilities that are hard to find in highly educated non-Jews.

For this we are obliged to the healthy Jewish education of yesteryear, to the love of the Torah and of good character traits which grandfathers and greatgrandfathers bequeathed to their children and grandchildren.

We spoke earlier of the Jews of wholesome sensitivity who were produced for our people by the group study of *Ein Yaakov* in synagogues between the *Minchah* and *Maariv* services; what a pure type of person was given us by the custom of reciting *Tehillim* in the *beis midrash* before daybreak; how great was the contribution of the *yeshivos* with their Torah students, which yielded scholars and sages of world standing — the veritable crown of Israel's glory.

The spark of *ahavas Yisrael* in every Jew should rouse itself and set up circles for Torah study. Every Jew gives money for Torah causes. True, this is a personal obligation devolving on every Jew — but it must be known that one cannot discharge one's obligation as a Jew by donations alone. One must support the Torah with one's time, with one's very self; one must keep up with the entire House of Israel; one must himself study every day. By not studying, one becomes coarsened and ignoramus'd, and does harm thereby to all of Israel.

Every Jew has a sacred obligation to exert himself for the sake of Jewry in general, to enhance the crown of Israel's glory. And this can be done only through Torah study. Accordingly, each individual ought to devote time and effort to enrolling members in the various study groups, to influencing his acquaintances to seat themselves at the study tables — and then indeed there will be light in all the dwelling-places of the Children of Israel.

12.

We are rejoicing with the joy of the Torah, in the hope that with the Almighty's help the Torah will be happy with *us* — for then there will be a consummate joy, both spiritually and materially.

The truth is that we do have what to be happy about; even now, in a situation in which spiritual matters are a little clouded over, we should be joyful. We are at the very eve of the footsteps of *Mashiach*, and now is the time at which the ultimate purpose originally conceived comes to its realization.

We of the generation of the footsteps of *Mashiach* are realizing the divine purpose in this bitter exile which weighs upon us from within and without, and people are (thank G-d) studying Torah and praying with devotion. If people study a

---

Light in all the dwelling-places: Paraphrase of *Ex.* 10:23.
A little clouded over: The year was 1933.
Ultimate purpose... realization: In the original, נְעִיצַת הַתְחָלָה בַּסוֹף.

word of *Chassidus* and digest it, and then employ it in prayer, "the service of the heart," then there is what to be happy about.

It is explained in *Chassidus* that the difference between the material world and the spiritual world is that in the former, in *gashmiyus,* the foundation is below and the edifice is above it, whereas in the latter, in *ruchniyus,* the foundation is above, and the edifice below. Jews in this exile, therefore, are realizing the divine purpose — to make a dwelling-place for Him among mortals.

In the times of my greatgrandfather, the *Tzemach Tzedek,* the learned Reb Aizik of Homil was a chassid of considerable stature. Earlier, in the times of the Alter Rebbe, he was one of the young chassidim, but while yet a young man he knew how to receive.

My father once asked my grandfather what it means to be an *atzmi,* and in reply my grandfather described Reb Aizik. And once Reb Aizik had already lived at that level for some years, even though he used to make the journey to my great-grandfather in Lubavitch as a chassid, nevertheless he did this out of *kabbalas ol,* out of a noble sense of duty.

Once when Reb Aizik was on a visit to Lubavitch for *Shavuos* in the year 5608 (ח"רת; 1848) or 5609 (ט"רת; 1849), my greatgrandfather called for him — either because of the closeness which he felt toward him, or (according to the alternative version, which was confirmed by my father) because of Reb Aizik's extreme devotedness to my greatgrandfather. Having summoned him he said: "I am going to repeat for you a discourse in *Chassidus* which I heard from my grandfather the Alter Rebbe — a teaching of the Baal Shem Tov, transmitted letter by letter, with my grandfather's explanation of it."

On his way out of the Rebbe's study Reb Aizik encountered a number of young men and youths who were students in my greatgrandfather's *yeshivah,* and danced around with them and embraced them. The chassidim all found it quite remarkable that one so steeped in profound intellectuality as Reb Aizik should be carried away with such abandon. It was clear to them all that something of consequence had taken place, but none of them took the liberty of asking him for the meaning of his exultation.

It was the custom of the elder chassidim that whenever they came to Lubavitch they would meet informally for a *farbrengen* together. On one such occasion Reb Aizik, referring to himself in the third person, said: "When *Mashiach* comes they'll put Aizel on their hand (as if he were some tiny creature) and they'll say: 'See this? This used to study Torah; this used to meditate on *Chassidus* during his prayers!'"

Reb Aizik's belittling his own standing in the realm of intellectual perception and *avodah* should have taken place within himself. When the *Kohen Gadol* had to immerse himself in the *mikveh* and in preparation for this examined himself lest his immersion be disqualified because some foreign object had adhered to his body, we are told that "they spread out a sheet between him and the people." A great man too must scrutinize himself lest his purification be hampered by unwanted obstructions — but this should be done privately.

  - The Alter Rebbe's explanation of the use of the term "chassid" is well known — that it is based on the statement of *Tosafos* that a chassid acts for another's good even in a matter that harms himself. Reb Aizik spoke as he did for the sake of chassidim in general, so that people should learn how to conduct themselves.

The ultimate purpose of the beginning [of a divinely-ordained process] is realized only at the end. The divine intention — that "the Holy One, Blessed be He, desired to have a dwelling-place among the nether creatures" — is now being realized by Jews in exile. Every year that passes brings

---

Aizel: Familiar diminutive of Aizik, a Yiddish equivalent of Yitzchak.

See this?... his prayers: In the original Yiddish, אָט דאָס האָט געלערענט, אָט דאָס האָט געדאַווינט.

They spread out a sheet: Tractate *Yoma* 30a.

Acts for another's good: Tractate *Niddah* 17a.

The ultimate... only at the end: In the original, נְעִיצַת הַתְחָלָה אִיז בַּסוֹף דַוְקָא.

Dwelling-place among the nether creatures: *Midrash Tanchuma, Parshas Naso,* Sec. 16.

us nearer to the time of the Coming of *Mashiach (May it be speedily and in our own days, Amen!)* and to the revelation of the *or atzmi*. We should therefore be exceedingly joyful.

Before dawn comes, the darkness of night thickens, and it is when daybreak is imminent that a heavy slumber descends upon one. We can see this from our own experience, when one stays up throughout a long winter's night when there is time to steep oneself in some profound concept, and as dawn draws near a heavy sleep threatens to weigh one down. It is then that one needs to gather strength, so that one will not fall asleep.

The light is about to come, thank G-d; daybreak is beginning. Now is therefore the time when we should invest every effort and exertion to ensure that we are not overtaken by sleep. Chassidim should study *Chassidus* in public. In all chassidic synagogues times should be fixed for the group study of *Chassidus*. And with the Almighty's help we will be spared to see in serene joy the light of day, and "the light, that is good," will be revealed to all of Israel.

13.

All material things are an analogy for the understanding of G-dliness. In truth, of course, everything is G-dliness and G-dliness is everything. But in order to make this comprehensible the Almighty created a physical world comprising many components, each of which is an analogy for the understanding of G-dliness.

Imagine a huge cauldron which is filled with hundreds of buckets of water. Since water is by nature cold, and it is difficult to warm such a quantity all at once, one first heats one gallon of water to the highest degree that its container can stand without bursting. Having been heated over its own

---

The light, that is good: Cf. *Gen.* 1:4.

G-dliness: Not in the sense of the emulation of G-d by mortals; the word is here used to translate אֱלֹקוּת, and refers to the Creator Himself.

One gallon: In the original, "one *se'ah*."

fire, the vessel with its boiling water is now placed in the huge cauldron, whose hundreds of buckets of water are gradually warmed.

Water is Torah. Lithuania is, thank G-d, a huge cauldron full of Torah scholars *(May they continue to increase!)*. In addition to news gleaned from letters and conversations with people who come from there, I have happy memories of the times when I was the guest of our folk in Lithuania. From my meetings with various rabbis and Torah scholars who are not of our circles, as well as from questions of all kinds which reach me from quite ordinary householders, the same impression is gained — of Lithuanian Jewry's love of Torah.

In fact when I was in Riga I told the people there that in addition to their commendable attainments in the field of *tzedakah* and mutual help, they should learn this attribute — the love of Torah — from the Lithuanians. Lithuania takes pride in a Torah scholar; with them a *yeshivah* student occupies his rightful place. Their adult scholars are immersed in their studies, and exert themselves to advance their scholastic attainments. But the nature of water is cold — and it's cold there, freezing cold. Though it is not in the nature of water to stagnate, this is nevertheless possible. If, however, water bubbles and flows, then it does not stagnate — and what keeps water in motion is heat. In brief, the cauldron needs to be warmed up.

Each student of the Tomchei Temimim Yeshivah, each chassid worthy of the name, is such a vessel, a gallon of

---

Water is Torah: I.e., the Torah is likened by the Sages to water *(Derech Eretz Zuta* 8).

May they...increase: In the original, כֵּן יִרְבּוּ.

Not of our circles: In the original, עולמ'שע; a Yiddish adjective improvised from the Hebrew noun *olam* ("world"); i.e., "of the [non-chassidic] world at large."

Householders: As opposed to fulltime Torah scholars.

It's cold there, freezing cold: Adjective traditionally applied by chassidim to Lithuanian Jews ("Litvaks"), and signifying a lack of ardor and spontaneity in divine service.

boiling water with the capacity of being heated from within. The *temimim* who are in Lithuania should be happy that they are living in an atmosphere of the love of Torah, for the *yeshivos* there are its life-giving waters. At the same time they, together with the other chàssidim who live in the towns of Lithuania, ought to strengthen the establishment of regular study sessions for the study of *Chassidus.*

At this point the Rebbe addressed a remark to a *tamim* by the name of Yehoshua Aizik who had come for *Yom-Tov* from Kovno:

Your letter on the organizing of the study of *Chassidus* among the *temimim* and *Anash* in various Lithuanian towns caused me considerable pleasure. A child is a continuation of his father. My pleasure is my father's pleasure, and my father's pleasure is a source of spiritual life and blessing to all those who occupy themselves with Torah and *avodah.* Please convey our greetings to all the *temimim* and *Anash* of Lithuania and see to it that you consolidate the regular sessions for the public study of *Chassidus.* And may the Almighty help you all materially and spiritually.

Someone asked a question: "It would appear from the analogy that not only is it impossible for a person to occupy himself with another's spiritual welfare until he himself has attained the level expected of him, but moreover the cold water could prevail over the hot."

To this the Rebbe replied:

Though it is true that the nature and details of all material things should serve us as analogies for the understanding of spiritual matters, one should nevertheless keep in mind that an analogy is only an analogy. Even though this fact is obvious, the very awareness of it serves to free an analogy of unwanted limitation and corporealization.

So it is in our analogy of the cauldron of cold water, where the analogy is not absolutely comparable to the subject being illustrated. In the analogy, one cannot in fact put the hot water into the cold without its being cooled unless one first boils it properly. This is so because whatever is material has no real existence, and its heat is not of its essence; it can therefore cool down. In the case of a spiritual value, however, through its very encounter with something cold which it seeks to warm, its quintessential inner strength is aroused. We are not speaking here of the arousing of this inner strength through its determination to vanquish an opposing power; here the arousal is effected by its purposeful activity alone.

One can find a way of using every material thing for the understanding of a spiritual subject. It goes without saying that the analogy will not match the subject in all its details, and one needs to exercise discernment as to what to select and what to ignore. This is what is meant by the common abbreviation, וְדַ"ל (וְדַי לַמֵּבִין), for a mere remark suffices to light the way for a man of understanding.

14.

The way it is now conducted, your Yagdil Torah School in Kovno lays a firm foundation in the fear of heaven. May the Almighty bestow an abundance of material and spiritual blessings on all those who are involved in it and who support it, and give them the desire to strengthen and enlarge it, so that it will increase its enrollment of students who are able and conscientious in their study of the Torah and in the fear of heaven. And from the Yagdil Torah (lit., "an increase in Torah") may there come an increase in G-d-fearers.

15.

There are certain words in the *Tanach*, in the Written Law, which have two forms — the *kri*, the way the word is to be pronounced, and the *ksiv*, the way it is spelled. In the Oral Law the Sages sometimes interpret the content of a word by means of the instruction *Al tikrei* ("Do not read... but..."), as

---

Do not read: This instruction refers to the verse, וְכָל בָּנַיִךְ לִמּוּדֵי ה' וְרַב שְׁלוֹם בָּנָיִךְ —
  "And all your children shall be learners of [the Torah of] G-d, and great shall be the peace of your children" (*Isa.* 54:13).

in the phrase, אַל תִּקְרֵי בָּנַיִךְ אֶלָּא בּוֹנַיִךְ —"Do not read *banayich*, 'your children,' but *bonayich*, 'your builders.'" In *Chassidus*, the instruction *Al tikrei* is the inner life of a 'word: it brings the word to life, both on the intellectual plane of *haskalah*, and on the plane of *avodah*.

On Simchas Torah last year one of the functionaries of the Tomchei Temimim Yeshivah was given the honor of reading aloud the verse, וְיִהְיוּ נָא אֲמָרֵנוּ לְרָצוֹן לִפְנֵי אֲדוֹן כֹּל —"May our words find favor before the Master of all things." It was explained at the time that the word אֲמָרֵנוּ can be interpreted in the manner of *kri* and *ksiv*, as if to say: "Do not read 'our words,' but 'our deeds and our labor'" — "May our *deeds* find favor." One cannot support a *yeshivah* with words alone: one has to take action.

As far as the *yeshivah* is concerned, whether materially or spiritually, thought and speech alone cannot be counted as action. We once explained the statement of the Sages, מַחֲשָׁבָה טוֹבָה: הקב"ה מְצָרְפָהּ לְמַעֲשֶׂה — "The Almighty joins a good thought to a deed" [or: "reckons a good thought as a deed"]. This is for the Almighty to do ; as far as *people* are concerned, the deed has to be actually done.

Question: "The verse in *Yeshayahu* says אַף עֲשִׂיתִיו — 'and, moreover, I have made it,' implying that in translating an intention into action (מַעֲשֶׂה) one is confronted by spiritual obstacles which obscure the way. As far as one's *avodah* with oneself is concerned, *Chassidus* offers advice. But when it comes to influencing another, how does one cope with these obstructions?"

The Rebbe replied as follows:

In *Chassidus* there is sound advice on all matters of con-

On Simchas Torah: On this paragraph, see pp. 15-16 above.
The Almighty joins: Tractate *Kiddushin* 40a.
And, moreover, I have made it: *Isa.* 43:7. Of the series of verbs in this verse, signifying successive stages of descent through the Four Worlds, it is only the last — עֲשִׂיתִיו, akin to מַעֲשֶׂה and עֲשִׂיָּה — that is preceded by אַף ("and, moreover"). Hence the implication regarding obstacles.

duct and guidance, both with regard to one's own conduct and with regard to the conduct and guidance of another. *Tanya* is called *Likkutei Amarim* ("Selected Sayings"), because it is entirely composed of answers given to questions asked at *yechidus;* it is the source of the spring of living waters, that purifies.

The relationship between *rav* and *talmid* ("teacher" and "student") is more than simply a relationship of *mashpia* and *mekabel* ("mentor" and "recipient", i.e., disciple). The task of the *rav* should be to make of his student a recipient, to extend the bounds of his sensitivity and of his abilities. This demands a certain dedication on the part of the *mashpia* towards his *mekabel.* It requires great effort, and constant prayer — that it be granted him to raise G-d-fearing disciples. And then the Almighty helps one to find the real ways and means of turning one's student into a true recipient.

16.

A chassid must be well ordered.

(Because time is short* we will have to be brief, and the expression of brevity is always somewhat pungent. Generally speaking, concepts are by preference explained at length, with ample details and instances, and each additional positive or negative illustration enhances their comprehension. But just as every concept must have a beginning and source, so must it have an end. The beginning of a concept is a point; the end of a concept is brevity. Even though the point precedes the concept and brevity comes at the end of the concept, and moreover the two extremes are by definition different from each other, yet this they have in common — that each when expressed gives rise to a certain degree of pungency.)

---

* This talk was delivered at the *Kiddush* on Simchas Torah, and those present had to hurry in order to allow time for the *Minchah* prayer and the *Yom-Tov* meal before sunset.

Composed of answers: See *Tanya*, Compiler's Foreword.
Rav and *talmid:* Cf. Section 2, on pp. 116-117 above.

To revert to our subject. — A chassid without order loses the very semblance of a chassid. Without order, not only will he be constantly losing his way and not arriving at any destination, but even what he does do will not be properly done; it will be dead, without vitality.

A chassid should carefully observe elder chassidim in order to learn from their conduct, but should first measure himself well to determine whether he is already at a level at which it is proper for him to emulate a particular practice.

Suppose someone observes another who is in a state of spiritual awakening in the course of his prayers, and is himself aroused at the sight — but he is not yet really at that level. One must not cool anyone down, but at the same time a person should know that this particular *avodah* is not yet appropriate for himself. For the moment the observation should be pocketed, until such time that it becomes appropriate for him to put to use.

In the meantime, a passage of *Tehillim* with tears asks the Almighty for help in attaining the desired awakening. There is a lot of entreating to do — that one's prayers should come forth spontaneously, that one should be helped to cultivate an open and sensitive heart.

My father once said to someone: "Washing each hand three times before meals, and holding the handle of the dipper with a towel, is not a practice that is appropriate to you. When you are at that level, then you will do it." To someone else he said: "As to washing each hand three times before meals, and holding the vessel with a towel, you should not wait until you have attained to a certain level, but should do so out of *kabbalas ol* because that is what the law requires."

That one's prayers should come forth spontaneously: In the Yiddish original (which has no Hebrew or English equivalent), *es zol zich davenen;* a reflexive form of the verb "to pray" (and with no subject), suggesting that the action takes place of its own accord.

Washing... three times... towel: In Lubavitch circles, washing as here described has come to be regarded no longer as a *hiddur*, a mark of unusually loving and punctilious observance, but as standard practice.

A chassid has to be well ordered both in his study and in his *avodah*. In fact these depend on each other: if one is orderly in his study then he is orderly in his *avodah* too.

17.

The Rebbe asked those present to say *LeChaim!* over a drop of *mashke,* and added that there was no need to talk about this, because talk of this kind displaced subjects that did need to be talked about. He then amplified this theme, as follows.

Each soul that is about to descend to this world is allotted a certain number of letters of speech which it will utter in the course of its lifetime. These letters are uncombined, for free will in the choice of combinations is left to each individual, who decides for himself which words to speak.

The superiority of man over the whole of Creation lies in speech — to the point that mankind at large is termed *medaber* ("the speaker"), a name that indicates the highest level of humanity. One would have thought at first glance that the superiority of man lies in his intelligence. The distinctive quality of intelligence, however, is to be perceived when it finds expression in speech.

According to the dictates of worldly wisdom, speech may be divided into four categories; according to the Torah, following the opinion of *Rambam,* it falls into five categories: (a) speech which is a *mitzvah,* such as reading words of Torah and prayer; (b) speech which is beloved, as in praise of the quality of intellect and good character; (c) speech which is permitted, such as that involving a person's needs of food and livelihood; (d) speech which is forbidden, such as falsehood, slander and tale-mongering; and (e) speech which is repugnant — idle talk and pointless narrative.

Chassidus discusses and clarifies these five categories at various levels, throwing light on their foundations; reveals the inner mystery hidden in speech; and explains how the tongue is the quill of the heart, and speech is the servant of intellect and character.

With the divine light in *Chassidus* we can see the clarity of the above five distinctions, the quality and nobility of speech which is a *mitzvah* and which is beloved, the vulgarity of forbidden speech, and the lowliness of repugnant speech.

Chassidus clarifies the meaning of permitted speech, explaining first what is meant by permissibility. According to the teachings of *Chassidus*, permissibility is a very closely-defined concept. Before partaking of what is permissible one is first required to establish whether it is needed. If the object is not needed, but merely desired, then *Chassidus* teaches that even if it is permissible of itself, the desire for it is absolute evil, requiring *teshuvah*.

Everyone needs to be vigilant with speech — that is, with the third category, permitted speech, for it commonly leads to the fifth category, the repugnant speech of pointless prattle, which is turn leads to the fourth category, forbidden speech.

Especial care needs to be taken by businesspeople, for the superfluous talk of commerce is a well-trodden threshold leading to all kinds of evil. By superfluous talk is meant that every delectable detail of a subject is repeated over and over again with gusto. And this kind of talk can lead to evil consequences.

The Mitteler Rebbe says that businesspeople have an advantage over fulltime Torah scholars, for they see the tangible workings of Divine Providence in practice. But the inflated talk of commerce draws cataracts over one's eyes, so that not only does it blind a person from perceiving the workings of Divine Providence, but moreover it removes his delight in spiritual things, making him coarsened by materiality. People in the business world, then, should vigilantly shun this kind of talk.

Whether he is standing in his shop or in the marketplace, every businessman should have a book in his pocket — such as a *Chumash, Tanya, Mishnayos* or *Tehillim* — so that whenever he has a free moment he can read a verse of *Chumash*, or a few lines of *Tanya*, or a *mishnah*, or a passage of *Tehillim*.

The words directed above to businessfolk are not addressed only by one who guides and warns a certain part of our people *(May they all enjoy good health!)*; as one who loves all of Israel I offer these words as a piece of good advice. If people act on it the Almighty will grant His help, and an abundance of blessings will flow in through their very doors and windows.

This is a matter which affects not only each individual separately, but also the entire House of Israel, for a word which a Jew utters — in Torah, prayer, supplication, or request — opens up all the pipelines of divine blessing, silences charges levelled in the Heavenly Court, rescinds harsh edicts, and blesses one's endeavors with success.

Let me tell you a story. The Baal Shem Tov once saw that the entire House of Israel stood under a dire threat which was being weighed in the Heavenly Court. He consulted with his saintly disciples, but despite their many fasts they were unable to revoke the impending decree. They managed to persuade the local *rav* to ordain a public fast — not because he understood the inner meaning of what was at hand, but on the pretext of certain overt circumstances. At a certain point in the course of the fast, when all the men and women of the community had assembled for the reading of *Tehillim*, the Baal Shem Tov saw that the decree of the Heavenly Court still stood intact. Soon after he turned joyfully to R. Nachman of Horodenka and with a radiant face told him that the sentence had been revoked. The joy of his disciples was unbounded.

When they next sat at his table, the Baal Shem Tov told them that one woman had caused the edict to be rescinded. In the midst of all the *Tehillim* and the wailing in the synagogue the arguments of the Accusing Angel had risen to a pitch: it was an hour of woe for Israel. But in the women's gallery of that synagogue there sat one simple peasant-woman who was so ignorant that she could not even read *Tehillim*. When she heard the sobbing and weeping all around her she cried out: "Master of the universe! Aren't You our Father? Your children are asking something of You with bitter tears. I've got five little ones at home, and when they all start crying I can't bear to hear them. So You on High, Who have *so* many children, even if You had the heart of a Tartar You'd have to answer them. Father: answer Your children!"

*   *   *

A story should be not only heard, but rather sensed. In fact at any time one ought to have אוּדְנִין דְּשַׁמְעִין — "ears that hear," and hearing is worthy of the name only when it leads to sensitive perception.

This story tells us how potent is a word uttered by a Jew, how cherished is the reading of a passage of *Tehillim*. Though he live in the remotest corner of the world, yet with a word of Torah or *Tehillim* he can open up the pipelines of livelihood for the entire House of Israel.

However, he who is intellectually able to comprehend the unity of G-d — both how everything is G-dliness and how G-dliness is everything — cannot discharge his responsibilities by *Tehillim* alone. If he seeks to do so, this is no less than casting off the yoke of heaven.

18.

There is a verse in *Tehillim* in which King David says: לְךָ דֻמִיָּה תְהִלָּה אֱלֹקִים בְּצִיּוֹן וּלְךָ יְשֻׁלַּם נֶדֶר. This means [in paraphrase]: "To You, G-d, *dumiyah* [for the moment translatable as 'silence'] is praise; G-dliness is in Tzion; and to You, G-d, shall the vow be fulfilled." There are three statements here: two which David HaMelech addresses to the Creator — (a) "Your praise is through silence," and (b) "To You, G-d, shall the vow be fulfilled" — and a third which he addresses to the world at large, so that all should know that "G-dliness is in Tzion." In the following verse he makes a fourth statement: שֹׁמֵעַ תְּפִלָּה עָדֶיךָ כָּל בָּשָׂר יָבֹאוּ — "You, the One Who hears prayer, to You shall

---

Not only heard, but rather sensed: In the rhyming Yiddish original, *nit nor her'n, nor takke derher'n.*

Ears that hear: I.e., attentive ears; cf. R. Shimon bar Yochai in the *Zohar:* "Happy the man whose words fall on ears that hear."

To You, G-d: *Ps.* 65:2.

You, the One: *Ibid.,* v.3.

all flesh come." This idea is similar to that expressed in the paragraph in *Shemoneh Esreh* which begins with the words *Shema koleinu:* כִּי אַתָּה שׁוֹמֵעַ תְּפִלַּת כָּל פֶּה — "For You hear the prayer of every mouth."

At first glance the connection between these four statements is incomprehensible. We begin with a seeming contradiction. On the one hand, לְךָ דֻמִיָּה תְהִלָּה: we are told that "Your praise is through silence"; on the other hand, שֹׁמֵעַ תְּפִלָּה עָדֶיךָ כָּל בָּשָׂר יָבֹאוּ: a reference to prayer, which is through speech.

Next, what is the meaning of the phrase, וּלְךָ יְשֻׁלַּם נֶדֶר — "To You shall the vow be fulfilled"? These words appear to refer to some well-known vow which every Jew is obliged to fulfill. Indeed, from the word יְשֻׁלַּם (lit., "shall be paid"), it would seem that the verse is addressing the Almighty as follows: "G-d, You may rest assured that the debt which is owing to You will be paid." What *is* this debt of which David HaMelech speaks with such certainty, as if he were speaking of some debt which must be paid, whether through goodwill and pleasure, or through duress and suffering?

Finally, what is the nature of the public announcement that David HaMelech makes: אֱלֹקִים בְּצִיּוֹן — that "G-d is in Tzion"?

[Let us first consider the opening phrase: לְךָ דֻמִיָּה תְהִלָּה, tentatively translated above as follows: "To You, silence is praise."] The word תְּהִלָּה means "praise" — as, for example, when some person praises a great *talmid chacham*, describing his stature in the study of Torah and in the fear of heaven, repeating the learned discourses and moral teachings which he has heard from his mouth, and dwelling upon his noble attributes of humility, truth, lovingkindness, charity, and his love of his fellow Jew. Suppose now that this person recalls an entire address which he once heard from this *talmid chacham*, and which he now repeats, as follows: "My children, my friends! If your child falls ill with convulsions or whatever disease, you are at your wit's end, and in tears, and your poor hearts are sore *(May He Who is in heaven protect you and the whole of Israel from all evil!)*. Parents tear their hair; the situation is so desperate that G-d alone can have mercy. Total strangers are unnerved at the sight of a wee soul, a budding little body, collapsing all of a sudden, convulsing, and wrestling with death; it struggles, it wants to live, but the dread disease drags the little body away. How great, then, must be the heartache when some fathers and mothers are themselves (heaven forfend) the Angels of Death of their own little ones, through not observing *taharas hamishpachah,* the laws of family purity, with immersion at its due time in a *mikveh* which is kosher."

Suppose that the speaker further recalls how that same *talmid chacham,* continuing his address, had gone on to speak about *ahavas Yisrael,* about how one should cherish every fellow Jew, both in a mundane sense and (even more so) in a spiritual sense; about how one should be prepared for self-sacrifice in order to do a favor to a fellow Jew, sparing neither time nor effort; and about how this applies in heightened measure to the dissemination of Torah among one's brethren — a task which warrants literal self-sacrifice.

Approaching his listeners in gentle terms, the sage had explained at the time what a weighty responsibility lies upon parents to bring up their children in the straight path of Torah and *mitzvos,* by following which they will be protected from the crooked paths of dishonesty and violence, and their parents — after 120 years in This World — will leave behind them *Kaddeishim* of whom they can be proud. Indeed, the good deeds of the children will open up for their departed parents the portals and the palaces of *Gan Eden.* The *talmid chacham* had also warned of the contrary possibility: if parents did not take due care and enroll their children in *chadarim* and *yeshivos* imbued with the awe of heaven, they would bring misfortune both upon themselves and upon their children.

*   *   *

After 120 years: A euphemism for "after their demise," 120 years being the traditional maximum lifespan (cf. *Gen.* 6:3).

Kaddeishim: Popular plural form of *Kaddish,* prayer recited by sons after their parents' passing; extended in common parlance to mean the sons themselves.

Now when a person repeats an address such as the above, not only does he relive anew the original experience of standing and listening to it from the mouth of the sage, but moreover the very repetition sets up a certain bond between himself and the original speaker. For the fact is that speaking of the worthy character and the Torah teachings of a *talmid chacham* arouses within the narrator himself a noble sensation of warm nearness to him.

This too is what constitutes the Book of *Tehillim* — the songs of praise which David HaMelech sings to the Almighty, whether expressed in words of thirst and yearning, as in the verse, צָמְאָה לְךָ נַפְשִׁי כָּמַהּ לְךָ בְשָׂרִי — "My soul thirsts for you, my flesh longs for you"; or whether expressed in piteous entreaties for help, as in the verse, אֵ־לִי אֵ־לִי לָמָה עֲזַבְתָּנִי — "My G-d, my G-d, why have You forsaken me?" — and as in the plea [of one struggling to stay afloat in a turbulent world], הוֹשִׁיעֵנִי אֱלֹקִים כִּי בָאוּ מַיִם עַד נָפֶשׁ — "Save me, O G-d, for the waters have reached up to my very soul"; or whether expressed in cries of woe, as in the following verses: בָּאוּ גוֹיִם בְּנַחֲלָתֶךָ טִמְּאוּ אֶת הֵיכַל קָדְשֶׁךָ — "Nations have come into Your inheritance, and have defiled Your holy Temple"; עַל עַמְּךָ יַעֲרִימוּ סוֹד וְיִתְיָעֲצוּ עַל צְפוּנֶיךָ — "They take crafty counsel against Your people, and conspire against Your hidden ones"; אָמְרוּ לְכוּ וְנַכְחִידֵם מִגּוֹי וְלֹא יִזָּכֵר שֵׁם יִשְׂרָאֵל עוֹד — "They have said, 'Come, let us cut them off from being a nation, so that the name of Israel be no more remembered'"; or whether expressed in a surge of hope, as in the verse, זָכַר חַסְדּוֹ וֶאֱמוּנָתוֹ לְבֵית יִשְׂרָאֵל רָאוּ כָל אַפְסֵי אָרֶץ אֵת יְשׁוּעַת אֱלֹקֵינוּ — "He has remembered His lovingkindness and His faithfulnesss towards the House of Israel: from the farthest corners of the world all have witnessed the deliverance by our G-d."

My soul thirsts: *Ps.* 63:2.
My G-d, my G-d: *Ibid.* 22:2.
Save me, O G-d: *Ibid.* 69:2.
Nations have come: *Ibid.* 79:2.
They take crafty counsel: *Ibid.* 83:4.
They have said, Come: *Ibid.*, v. 5.
He has remembered: *Ibid.* 98:3.

This, then, is the meaning of the word תְּהִלָּה — the kind of praising and recounting that gives rise to a bond of nearness between the speaker and the one being praised.

Affinity of this type is readily observable. If someone describes in glowing detail how he once happened to see all the glory that a certain country bestowed upon its ruler on one of its national festive days, with all its sumptuousness, and all the nobility of the realm, — then the very description brings him to a state of elation, which alone suffices to raise him out of his workaday existence: he transcends it, he is nobler.

This explains why prayer is called a ladder, as it is written, וְהִנֵּה סֻלָּם מֻצָּב אַרְצָה וְרֹאשׁוֹ מַגִּיעַ הַשָּׁמָיְמָה — "And behold a ladder standing on the earth, its top reaching up to the heavens." Prayer is the ladder which connects the worshiper with the Holy One, Blessed be He; the bond between them comes into being through the praises in prayer.

The phrase we have been considering is, לְךָ דֻמִיָּה תְהִלָּה — "To You, silence is praise" [, and we have seen the word תְּהִלָּה implies a connection established through praise]. The first word in the verse — לְךָ — addresses itself to *Atzmus Ein-Sof*, the very Being of the Infinite One. The phrase thus states that the worshiper's connection with *Atzmus Ein-Sof* comes about through דֻמִיָּה ("silence"). What, then, *is* this state of דֻמִיָּה, that is capable of connecting man with *Atzmus Ein-Sof?*

* * *

A real *massig*, a person of true understanding, is not deluded: he does not fool himself. Indeed, this is part of his very definition. With him, everything is clear and explicit. Such a person, a *baal hassagah*, relates to every concept in one of two ways — either he understands it, or he sees that it cannot be understood; both of these states, however, are grasped perfectly. Just as in the former case the concept is

Prayer is called a ladder: In the *Zohar*, on Jacob's dream.
And behold a ladder: *Gen.* 28:12.
Understands…cannot be understood: Cf. p. 139 above.

clear to him, in that he knows exactly what he understands, so too in the latter case does he know with perfect clarity exactly what it is that cannot be understood. With him, indeed, the latter knowledge is sometimes accompanied by a rational explanation as to why the concept in question cannot be understood.

A *baal hassagah* understands furthermore that the fact that he *has* understood something does not yet mean that he has understood it in its entirety; his present understanding is merely a prelude to a real understanding. In other words, his understanding of the positive dimension of a subject is a prelude to his understanding of its negative dimension. Or, in yet other words, clothing oneself in intellect leads to abstracting oneself from intellect.

There is something further that a real *massig* can understand, and that is, that understanding must be set aside in the face of that which transcends it, namely, *gefihl* — spiritual sensitivity or perceptivity, for the insight that arises out of the intellectual process transcends it.

Haskalah, here meaning the intellectual process, can be brought down into terms of rational explanation, unlike *gefihl*, which often cannot be explained; if the person is challenged on grounds of illogicality or a seeming contradiction he will not have words at his disposal with which to rebut the objection, yet his *gefihl* tells him nevertheless that things are as he said. This means that *haskalah* descends (as it were) into the vehicle of words, thereby assuming a measure of obscurity — for every *kashe*, every logical objection of the above kind, is a form of obscurity. Not so is the case of *gefihl* (or, in Hebrew, *hergesh*), which does not descend (as it were) into lengthy verbalization and does not become veiled by obscurity. It follows that an idea intellectually conceived is strengthened by confirmatory evidence and weakened by a logical objection; an idea which is spiritually perceived is neither strengthened by evidence nor weakened by an objection.

We find an instance of this in the *Gemara*, in Tractate

In Tractate *Beitzah:* 6a, and *Rashi* there.

Beitzah, where Rav states a law — that a chicken hatched on *Yom-Tov* is not permissible for food because it is *muktzeh*. It should be borne in mind that very law, every *halachah*, is the end product of a reasoned argument. Accordingly, two of Rav's disciples, Rav Kahana and Rav Assei, challenged him: Why should the law in the case of the chicken hatched on *Yom-Tov* be different from the law governing a calf born on *Yom-Tov*? To this question Rav gave an answer. Rav Kahana and Rav Assei asked further: But why should the law of the chicken hatched on *Yom-Tov* be different from the law governing a calf born on *Yom-Tov* to a *[treifah]* cow which even though it be properly slaughtered cannot be rendered kosher? Rav remained silent, and gave them no answer — but he did not retract from his decision on the *halachah*, and the *Gemara* goes on to discuss why he offered no reply to their second question.

On careful analysis of the various lines of argument involved in this discussion we see that Rav's thinking on the subject of the chicken hatched on *Yom-Tov* was a product not only of reason, but of *gefihl*. In its early stages, a line of thinking which proceeds from *gefihl* also comprises reasoning which can be explained. This explains why Rav answered the first question of Rav Kahana and Rav Assei, pointing out that the chicken is *muktzeh* while the calf is not. The second question, however, which queries the distinction that was based on a line of thinking proceeding from *gefihl* alone, Rav was

-----

Not permissible ... *muktzeh:* I.e., because it is not regarded as having been set aside or prepared for food at the onset of the festival.

Rav gave an answer: After *shechitah* the calf born on *Yom-Tov* is permissible for eating, because when it was yet unborn the *shechitah* of its mother would have simultaneously rendered it fit and prepared for food; because of this potential preparedness it is now not *muktzeh*.

To a *[treifah]* cow: The unborn calf is considered part of its mother, and in this case it cannot be rendered kosher by the *shechitah* of the cow; nevertheless we find that its own *shechitah* does render it kosher, even in the absence of Rav's above-stated rationale. Why, then, should Rav hold that the chicken is forbidden?

unable to answer — for a reasoned argument *can* be (as it were) brought down into verbal explanation, but this is not the case with a line of thinking based on *gefihl*. No matter how much it be explained the *gefihl* remains, unexhausted and unplumbed. As was said above, a line of thinking based on reason can be rebutted by a logical objection; a line of thinking proceeding from *gefihl* weathers such objections.

With a real *massig*, the lines of thinking that proceed from *gefihl* are far loftier and far more delectable than the lines of thinking that are based on his reason. Hence a *baal hassagah* can set aside a profoundly comprehended conception out of deference for a *gefihl*. By "set aside" is meant that he transforms that entire conception into a seed from which *gefihl* will sprout, and this *gefihl* in turn connects him with the very essence of the conception which cannot find expression in words — but in *gefihl* alone.

Gefihl is an epithet regarding which one may be particularly vulnerable to self-deception. For so scant is our explanatory vocabulary that we are reduced to using one and the same expression for a variety of instances of the soul's manifestation; so weak is our intellectual perceptiveness [of these various instances] that they impinge on each other. One thus needs to exert considerable intellectual effort in order to define each descriptive word in its precisely correct and clear connotation.

More clearly expressed: Every epithet includes an instance in which it is used only in a borrowed sense, as a *to'ar hamush'al*, and not in its own essential sense, as a *to'ar atzmi*. But even the latter category can be subdivided. Sometimes an epithet in this category is used only as a servant *(meshares)*, that is, as a garment *(levush)* [— a means of expression] for the faculty *(ko'ach)* which clothes itself in it, and at other times it is used in its own primary sense [— the *atzmi* of the *atzmi*, as it were].

As with epithets in general, so too the epithet *hergesh* or *gefihl* can be used either in a borrowed sense or in its own essential sense; and the latter usage itself can be further subdivided — into usage as a *levush*, and usage in its own primary sense.

[The Rebbe illustrates this by contrasting four pairs of Hebrew/Yiddish phrases. On the one hand: *a kerper* ("body") - *gefihl, a middos-gefihl, a seichel-gefihl, a nefesh-gefihl;* on the other hand: *a gefihl in kerper, a gefihl in middos, a gefihl in seichel, a gefihl in nefesh.* For example: *a middos-gefihl,* as opposed to *a gefihl in middos.* The former phrase signifies "an emotional sensation"; the latter signifies "a sense of (or: an insight into) emotion." In the former phrase *(a middos-gefihl),* though *"middos"* appears to be an adjective qualifying *"gefihl",* it is *"gefihl"* in this phrase that is defined as the *levush* (lit., the "garment"), ancillary to *"middos".* In the latter phrase *(a gefihl in middos),* by contrast, *gefihl* is defined as the *melubash* (lit., "that which is clothed"), i.e., the object.

The Rebbe goes on to show how this distinction — as to whether *gefihl* is the subject or the object — does not obtain equally when this term is paired with *kerper* or *middos,* as in the case when it is paired with *seichel* or *nefesh.*

Proceeding to draw ever subtler distinctions, the Rebbe now points out that the inner dimension of *gefihl* (i.e., *gefihl* when it is a *melubash,* the object), though it is a spiritual faculty, itself comprises (as it were) body and soul. Its *metzius* ("existence") is its body, and its *mehus* ("essence") is its soul. Moreover, each of these two grades may be further divisible into its own respective *metzius* and *mehus.* At this point the *baal hassagah* pauses — for though when speaking of the *metzius* of *gefihl* gradated levels are conceivable, the *mehus* of the inner dimension of *gefihl* is in all cases identical and indivisible; "for this is a *gilui atzmi."* (The phrase *gilui atzmi* here means: a revelation of the innermost self of the *baal hassagah;* and since his *atzmi* is a חֵלֶק אֱלוֹק מִמַּעַל מַמָּשׁ, "truly a part of G-d above," it is of course identical with the *Atzmus* of Him of Whom he is a part.)

Truly a part of G-d above: Cf. *Job* 31:2; and see *Tanya,* Ch. 2.

Throughout the entire train of thought outlined above, instead of expounding the ideas as his own the Rebbe presents them as if they are the conclusions which a hypothetical *baal hassagah* arrives at, stage by stage, in the course of his own meditation. Accordingly, at this point we find this *baal hassagah* contemplating the phrase *"gilui atzmi"* in all its possible depth, and in the course of so doing transcending the bounds of *seichel*, of intellect, and beginning to perceive the above concepts through the heightened spiritual insights of *gefihl*.]

Poised on the threshold leading from the chamber of understanding to the chamber of *gefihl*, the moment of transfer from one to the other is characterized in the *baal hassagah* by three states of being — silence, waiting, and hoping.

And this brings us to understand the meaning of the phrase with which we began: לְךָ דֻמִיָּה תְהִלָּה — "To You, silence is praise." The bond between לְךָ [here referring not to the Almighty, but addressed to the individual listener or reader] and *Elokus*, Divinity, is established only through דֻמִיָּה. This word bears three connotations — silence, waiting, and hoping — all of which are components of *gefihl*. The first step is — silence; this step means divesting oneself of *seichel dehalbashah*, concrete intellect [as opposed to intellect in the abstract]. The second step is — waiting; the individual yearns and waits, waits and [as the third step] hopes for a *gilui atzmi*, an intuitive illumination from the innermost point of his *hergesh*. And no matter at whatever level he stands, he constantly hopes to attain heights yet loftier.

[The verse which we have been expounding now proceeds:] אֱלֹקִים בְּצִיּוֹן. [This was translated literally above as, "G-d

---

Three connotations — silence, waiting, and hoping: The root דמם means both to be silent and to stand still; the third meaning is suggested by the verse, דּוֹם לַה׳ וְהִתְחוֹלֵל לוֹ — "Rest in G-d, and place your hope in Him" (*Ps.* 37:7).

Concrete intellect: Lit., "intellect when it serves as a garment."

is in Tzion."] Tzion signifies *etzem haneshamah*, the innermost point of the soul. Accordingly, אֱלֹקִים בְּצִיּוֹן signifies the *Elokus* of the soul. As is known, the *etzem haneshamah* is not clothed in the body; the levels of the soul which are clothed in the body are only a reflection *(he'arah)* of the *neshamah*, while the *etzem haneshamah* remains Above. Thus we read in the *Midrash* that the soul is known by five names — נֶפֶשׁ, רוּחַ, נְשָׁמָה, חַיָּה, יְחִידָה. The lower three levels, known by the acrostic נר"ן, are those described by the adjective *pnimiyim;* these are the indwelling or permeating levels of the soul. The other two, whose acrostic is ח"י, are known as *makkifim*, the "encompassing" or superrational levels of the soul. It is the highest level — *yechidah* — that is known by the name Tzion; this is the level hinted at by the phrase אֱלֹקִים בְּצִיּוֹן, in the sense of "the *Elokus* of the soul." And this level of the soul is called יְחִידָה because its Source is the level of *Elokus* known as יָחִיד [i.e., *Atzmus*].

[Our verse concludes with the phrase,] וּלְךָ יְשֻׁלַּם נֶדֶר — "To You shall the vow be fulfilled." This refers to the oath administered to the soul of every Jew before its descent into a body in this world. In the words of the *Gemara*, מַשְׁבִּיעִים אוֹתוֹ תְּהִי צַדִּיק וְאַל תְּהִי רָשָׁע — "An oath is administered to him: 'Be righteous and be not wicked.'" This vow everyone must fulfill, whether willingly or under duress, and it is in order to make this possible that souls descend to this world a number of times in transmigration.

There are people who claim that for various reasons they cannot fulfill what is expected of them with regard to fixing set times for Torah study, and with regard to prayer, the service of the heart. Excuses there are aplenty, but people forget the truth — and nothing can make it budge — that the vow must be paid up.

The first stage in *avodah* is, in the above-quoted words of

Tzion signifies *etzem haneshamah*: See Introduction to *Shaar HaEmunah*, in *Ner Mitzvah veTorah Or* of the Mitteler Rebbe.

Soul is... יְחִידָה... Source is... יָחִיד: See *Shaar HaYichud*, in *Ner Mitzvah veTorah Or* of the Mitteler Rebbe, Ch. 10.

Transmigration: In the original, *gilgulim*.

Tehillim, עָדֶיךָ כָּל בָּשָׂר יָבֹאוּ — "To You shall all flesh come"; that is,
a person needs to bring his own bundle of flesh before Him
"Who hearkens to prayer." As we have seen above, תְּפִלָּה
("prayer") signifies joining. And it is revealed and known to
Him "Who hearkens to prayer" that it is the desire of every
Jew, in the innermost point of his heart, to be bound in utter
unity with *Elokus.* The starting-point of *avodah,* then, is to
bring one's bundle of flesh before Him "Who hearkens to
prayer" — to pray with a congregation and to set aside fixed
times for the study of Torah.

We now understand what King David is saying. He is
telling us the truth — that וּלְךָ יְשֻׁלַּם נֶדֶר: the vow that the soul
undertakes, to "be righteous" through the fulfillment of the
Torah and its commandments, must be fulfilled. Listen to
what he is saying: וּלְךָ יְשֻׁלַּם נֶדֶר. One must pay up this vow. And
it will be paid, whether willingly or (G-d forbid) otherwise. As
to those who imagine that various obstacles hinder them
from doing their duty in prayer and Torah, let them be well
reminded that אֱלֹקִים בְּצִיּוֹן; that is, the *Elokus* to be found in every
soul is not only powerful enough to remove all the obstacles
and hindrances that life in this world raises up against the
observance of Torah and *mitzvos,* but, moreover, it even contains the potential to enable the person to elevate himself to
the bond implied by the words לְךָ דֻמִיָּה תְהִלָּה. To realize this
latter potential, however, demands a level of *avodah* that is not
within the reach of every man. The first step in *avodah* nevertheless remains: עָדֶיךָ כָּל בָּשָׂר יָבֹאוּ — to bring oneself before Him
"Who hearkens to prayer," by praying with a congregation
and fixing times for Torah study, this being a cup of blessing
that overflows with material and spiritual bounty.

Signifies joining: One of the meanings of תפל, which is one of the roots of
תְּפִלָּה, is identical with one of the meanings of the root טפל — "to join"
(as with mortar; cf. אֵין תּוֹפְלִין אוֹתָן בְּחַרְסִית; *Tosefta Pesachim* 5:9).

Chapter 4a

The Eve of Yud-Tes Kislev 5694 (תרצ״ד; 1933)
[Warsaw]

1.

Yud-Tes Kislev is the Festival of Liberation, which tens of thousands of families (*May they increase!*) celebrate with joyous feasting in all corners of the globe. It is a worldwide festival, which our people have this year been blessed with for the 135th time. This *Yom-Tov* marks the release from imprisonment of the Rebbe who founded the *Chabad*-Lubavitch dynasty, R. Shneur Zalman of Liadi, the author of *Tanya* and of *Shulchan Aruch HaRav*, who is known among *Chabad* chassidim as the Alter Rebbe. After having been imprisoned in the Peter-Paul Fortress for 52 or 53 days, he was liberated on this day in the year 5559 (תקנ״ט; 1798).

The Alter Rebbe's imprisonment and liberation are not only an instance of the workings of Divine Providence; in addition they most certainly provide us with guidance in the service of our Maker.

Without any shadow of a doubt, anyone capable of thinking can understand that the Alter Rebbe's imprisonment and liberation are to be counted among the divine wonders that have been shown to Jewry; this was an episode that ultimately brought about a distinctive turn of good fortune upon the entire House of Israel.

Counting from 5536 (תקל״ו; 1775), 158 years have passed

Yud-Tes Kislev: See p. 27ff. above, and footnotes there.
For 52 or 53 days: On the correspondence of this prison term with the 53 chapters of *Tanya*, see *Kitzurim VeHearos LeSefer Likkutei Amarim* by the *Tzemach Tzedek* (Merkos, N.Y., 1948), p. 122.
Counting from...1775: On the dating, see p. 67 above, and footnotes there.

since — through the grace of heaven — the teachings of *Chabad* were first revealed. Their innermost content is the requirement that one cause form to prevail over matter, through the *avodah* of "mind ruling heart" — that the intellect should cultivate and refine the attributes of the heart, the *middos*. This is no easy task, but *Chassidus Chabad* supplies all the means that are needed. The first piece of assistance is the ability to look at any matter with the eyes of intellect, without the heat of *middos*, for the *avodah* of chassidim over these 150-odd years has caused the very substance of the brain and of the heart to develop in such a way that they are enabled to help each other.

A conversation comes to mind from winter of the year 5663 (תרס"ג; 1902-3). On account of his ill health, my father had travelled to Vienna to consult one of the leading medical specialists there, and in order to arrive at a clear diagnosis this gentleman asked for the details of my father's daily program, including the hours he worked and the way his work was arranged. And when *Chassidus* was mentioned he wanted to know what kind of scholarly discipline this was.

My father replied: "The discipline of *Chassidus* requires that the head explain the heart what the person should want, and that the heart implement in the person's life that which the head understands."

"How can that be done?" asked the specialist. "Are head and heart not two continents separated by a vast ocean?"

To this my father answered: "The task is to build a bridge that will span these two continents, or at least to connect them with telephone lines and electric wires so that the light of the head should reach the heart. As a result of various observations and discoveries, I must add that in those who are

----

Form to prevail over matter: In the original, הַגְבָּרַת הַצוּרָה עַל הַחוֹמֶר.
Mind ruling heart: In the original, מוֹחַ שָׁלִיט עַל הַלֵּב; see *Tanya*, Chs. 12 and 51, based on the *Zohar, Raya Mehemna, Parshas Pinchas*.
The heat of *middos:* In *Chassidus*, intellectual perception is represented as being cold; the *middos* are emotional attributes stemming from the heart, and are represented as being hot. See *Tanya*, Ch. 3.

born into this branch of learning" — my father referred here to chassidim — "the substance of the brain, in which their psychological and intellectual faculties reside, and the substance of the heart, have an innate aptitude for this branch of learning and for the tasks it demands."

2.

Chassidim have an innate ability to cause form to prevail over matter, and to perceive the essence of a subject with the utmost clarity. Even in matters in which the first glance sets the heart aflame, chassidim are able to set this emotional arousal aside and to consider the subject with the eyes of the intellect. This is a faculty which *Chassidus Chabad* brought into being.

And it is with this precise and disciplined look which *Chassidus* has produced that we should perceive and consider the meaning of the Alter Rebbe's imprisonment and liberation.

The episode of the ascent of the Baal Shem Tov's soul on high on Rosh HaShanah 5507 (תק"ז; 1746) is well known. He told his disciples thereafter that the world would be illuminated by *shnei or* — "two lights," the light of *nigleh*, the revealed plane of the Torah, and the light of *Chassidus*. According to the tradition handed down by our forefathers, the Rebbes, the Alter Rebbe at the time of his passing — 24 Teves 5573 (תקע"ג; 1812) — was 68 years old,* the letter equivalents of which

---

* The author of *Beis Rebbe* [Chaim Meir Heilman; Berditchev, 1900] writes that the Alter Rebbe was born in 5507 (תק"ז; 1747), but according to the accepted tradition he was [in his third year] by then.

Set this emotional arousal aside...intellect: In the Introduction to his *Kuntreis HaHispaalus,* the Mitteler Rebbe protests that some chassidim are so excessively wary of allowing their souls to ignite and flare up in the spiritual rapture of *hispaalus,* that "they regard it as being as *treif* as a carcass" (אֲסוּרָה כִּנְבֵלָה)! Some, indeed, are so zealous in keeping their intellects in dour control of their spiritual passions, that when they sit down to *daven,* they fall asleep....

Shnei or: Hence the Alter Rebbe's first name, Shneur (שְׁנֵיאוּר).

spell out the word חַיִּים ("life"). At the time of the Baal Shem Tov's above-mentioned *aliyas haneshamah,* therefore, he was three years old — and the Baal Shem Tov could see the luminary who was to radiate two kinds of light.

Consider the situation. This renowned sage and Rebbe — who at the age of 26 had been chosen by the Maggid of Mezritch to compile the *Shulchan Aruch,* and of whom the Maggid had said הִלְכְתָא כְּרַב, that the law would be decided in accordance with his ruling, for his *Shulchan Aruch* would find acceptance throughout all the places where Jews are dispersed, — this Rebbe was imprisoned.

As has been said above, chassidim ought to always seek the truth in any matter, to understand its essence clearly. One must set aside one's burning heart and make one's calculations with the plain intellect alone. Who caused the imprisonment of this great Rebbe, who worked with self-sacrifice for the dissemination of the teachings of the Baal Shem Tov? — The greatest scholars of Israel, men who would have been prepared to sacrifice their own lives for the sake of the observance of the Torah and its *mitzvos,* men whose intentions were, without even a fleeting doubt, for the sake of heaven.

There are things which one may not say; things which one should not say; things which one does not want to say. As to this matter, neither may one speak of it, nor should one speak of it, nor do I want to speak of it. But the subject must nevertheless be clarified in a few brief words. There was a certain mistaken suspicion — a grievous error, a most painful one — but the intention of those involved was unadulteratedly *leshem shamayim,* for the sake of heaven, for the sake of the observance of the Torah and the commandments.

This all shows us that it was the Hand of G-d that directed those events. It was Divine Providence that brought about the imprisonment of the Alter Rebbe, and it was Divine Providence that released him.

The Maggid had said: The phrase הִלְכְתָא כְּרַב is borrowed from Tractate *Bechoros* 49b, referring to the Talmudic sage known as Rav. Here its meaning is: "The law is according to [this] *rav.*" See p. 209 below.

3.

The concept of הַשְׁגָּחָה פְּרָטִית, Divine Providence, as it is explained by the Baal Shem Tov, is well known — that even a wisp of straw and a plucked leaf that kick about in the open are governed by a divine ruling that determines how many times they are to turn about and where they are to be thrown around.

The Baal Shem Tov teaches that the Holy One, Blessed be He, arranges sets of circumstances of various kinds in order to implement the Divine Providence that governs a minute creation, in order that a fallen leaf that has been rolling about since last year in some backyard or other, or a bit of straw from a stalk which someone used when thatching a cottage roof a few years ago, should now be moved from their places to somewhere else. To accomplish this a stormwind breaks out, shaking heaven and earth in the middle of a warm and sunny day — and thereby brings to fulfillment the Divine Providence that governs the little stray leaf and the old wisp of straw.

* * *

For ten years the Baal Shem Tov studied the Written Torah from the mouth of Achiyah HaShiloni. So writes the Baal Shem Tov from Mezhibuzh in a letter to his disciple, the author of *Toldos Yaakov Yosef,* dated Tuesday of the week of

---

Hashgachah peratis: The author explains elsewhere that this comprises two levels: (a) everything has a purpose (as, in this instance, the stormwind); (b) the slightest change in the universe is ultimately connected with the total purpose of Creation.

The Written Torah: In the original, תּוֹרָה שֶׁבִּכְתָב.

Achiyah HaShiloni: See p. 72 above, and footnotes there.

A letter to his disciple: (Footnote in the original:) Reprinted in *Ginzei Nistaros* (Jerusalem, 5684 (תרפ"ד; 1924)); Letter No. 28 in the section entitled *Or Yisrael.*

   Reprinted in *HaTamim,* p. 348, Letter No. 89; and see p. 72 above.

The author of *Toldos Yaakov Yosef:* See above, *ibid.*

Parshas Miketz (28 Kislev) in the year 5513 (תק״יג; 1752). I have this letter, among the many letters which were taken out of the Kherson and Kiev Archives in the years 5678-5679 (תרע״ח-תרע״ט; 1918-1919). And even the simplest person can appreciate the meaning of ten years' study of the Written Torah from the mouth of Achiyah HaShiloni.

As explained in *Rambam's* Introduction to *Mishneh Torah,* Achiyah HaShiloni belonged to the seventh generation in the chain of tradition of those who handed down the Torah in turn: Moshe received the Torah at Sinai and passed it on to Yehoshua; Yehoshua to Pinchas; Pinchas to Eli; Eli to Shmuel; Shmuel to David; and David to Achiyah. "Achiyah HaShiloni saw Amram," says the *Gemara;* he was one of those who left Egypt; he was present at the splitting of the Red Sea, and at the Giving of the Torah; and he was a member of the *beis din* of King David.

The Baal Shem Tov explains that every single created thing has its own worth Above, each according to its essence. That which is *domem* ("still life") is different to that which is *tzome'ach* ("vegetative matter"); this in turn is different to that which is *chai* (belonging to the animal kingdom); this in turn is different to *medaber* ("the speaker" — man); and within the realm of *medaber,* the people of Israel are "the people close to Him." Divine Providence nevertheless applies even to the minutest detail; and the Baal Shem Tov concludes by saying that the degree to which Divine Providence applies to "the people close to Him" cannot even be imagined. For if a question as petty as whether the straw or the leaf will remain in their present place or be moved elsewhere is determined by Divine Providence, then how much more so must that which affects one of His people be determined by a Divine Providence that transcends our understanding.

In the year 5513: The date 5517 in the Yiddish original is a misprint.
The Kherson and Kiev Archives: See above, *ibid.*
Achiyah HaShiloni saw Amram: Tractate *Bava Basra* 121b.
The people close to Him: In the original, עַם קְרֹבוֹ; *Ps.* 148:14.

4.

In everything, even in the minutest circumstance which we created beings reckon as nothing and do not take at all into account, there is a divine intention, a divine will; and Divine Providence arranges the circumstances that will enable this intention to be realized in a certain way.

One day in the summer of 5656 (תרנ״ו; 1896) I was strolling with my father in a field in the country resort of Bolivke, near Lubavitch. The crops were almost ripe, and the grain and the grass were nodding in a gentle breeze.

"Behold G-dliness!" said my father. "Each movement of every single ear of grain and blade of grass was included in the Primal Thought of the *partzuf* of *Adam Kadmon*,* in Him Who watches and gazes until the end of all the generations; and Divine Providence brings this thought to realization for the sake of a certain divine intention."

As we walked on we found ourselves in a forest. Deep in contemplation of what I had now been told concerning Divine Providence, and overwhelmed by the gentleness and the earnestness of my father's explanation, I plucked a leaf from a tree that I passed by, and held it for a while in my hand. As people often do and without taking particular notice, I tore off little pieces from the leaf every so often as I walked on, ensconced in thought, and tossed them to the ground.

My father now said: "The *Arizal* says that not only is every leaf of a tree a creature with divine vitality, which the Almighty created with a certain end as part of the ultimate purpose of Creation; but, moreover, every single leaf contains the spark of a soul that descends to This World for the

---

* These terms are familiar to those schooled in the teachings of *Chassidus*.

Watches...all the generations: In the original, צוֹפֶה וּמַבִּיט עַד סוֹף כָּל הַדּוֹרוֹת.
    The phrase is borrowed from the *Musaf* prayer *(Zichronos)* of Rosh HaShanah.

With divine vitality: In the original, מיט אַ חיות אֶלקי.

For the sake of a *tikkun*: See Rabbi J.I. Schochet, *Mystical Concepts in Chassidism*, Ch. XI (also appearing in the Soncino *Tanya*, pp. 882-884).

sake of a *tikkun* — in order to attain restitution.

"Just see how 'man is always liable for damages, whether awake or asleep.' The difference between being awake amd asleep is to be found in the inward faculties of *seichel* and *middos*, in the person's intellect and in his emotional attributes. The external faculties are to be found in a sleeping person too; only his inward faculties are confused — which explains the presence of the paradoxes to be found in dreams. And where does the difference between a person awake or asleep become apparent? — In the faculty of vision. One who is asleep does not see; one who is awake can see.

"When a person is awake he sees G-dliness; when he is asleep, he does not.

"But 'man is always liable for damages, whether awake or asleep.' Just now we discussed the subject of Divine Providence — and quite without thinking you plucked a leaf, held it in your hand, played with it, turned it around, squashed it, tore it up in little pieces, and scattered it in various places.

"How can a person be so lightminded in relation to a creature of the Almighty? This leaf is something created by the Almighty for a particular reason. It has a G-d-given vitality, it has a body, and it has its life. In what way is the leaf's 'I' smaller than *your* 'I'?

"True, the difference is a big one. The leaf is *tzome'ach* and you are *medaber*, and there is a great difference between the two categories. Nevertheless, one should always remember the mission and the divine intention of every created thing — what is the task that the *tzome'ach* has to fulfill in this world, and what is the task that the *medaber* has to fulfill in this world."

*   *   *

Man is always liable: In the original, אָדָם מוּעָד לְעוֹלָם בֵּין עֵר וּבֵין יָשֵׁן; Tractate *Bava Kama* 3b.

The leaf's 'I': *Tzavaas HaRivash* likewise records a teaching of the Baal Shem Tov that one should regard oneself as no greater than one's fellow creatures, such as ants.

It was on this occasion too that my father expounded the Talmudic phrase, יַתּוּשׁ קְדָמְךָ — "The gnat has precedence over you," explaining that there is a way in which creatures belonging to the mineral, vegetable and animal kingdoms are superior to man, in that each of them fulfills the mission assigned to it by the divine intention.

Whenever we went strolling together throughout the following several days my father discussed this theme, until he arrived at the subject of divine knowledge and mortal free will — how the course of action which a man will choose is revealed and known Above, yet this divine foreknowledge does not direct the choice, for a man is granted free will to choose good and spurn evil.

5.

There is a maxim which says: "The past is the teacher of the present" — i.e., it explains current happenings — "and the guide of the future."

Picture the situation. The Alter Rebbe is spreading the teachings of the Baal Shem Tov in the world around him; he is traveling about and founding circles of chassidim; thousands of people are becoming chassidim and dozens of towns find themselves drawn to the teachings of *Chassidus*. And Divine Providence puts him in prison.

The above maxim, however, will help us gain some grasp of the whole point of the Alter Rebbe's imprisonment.

The *Gemara* says that "Avraham Avinu was imprisoned for ten years" — for disseminating a belief in G-d. For there is

---

The gnat has precedence: Lit., "The gnat preceded you"; Tractate *Sanhedrin* 38a. (Popularly pronounced, יַתּוּשׁ קְדָמְךָ.)

Superior to man: Cf. *Tanya*, Ch. 29.

Divine knowledge and mortal free will: In the original classical phrase, יְדִיעָה וּבְחִירָה.

A maxim: In the original, מַאֲמַר הֶחָכָם, a phrase that generally signifies a quotation from the medieval anthology entitled *Mivchar HaPeninim*.

Avraham Avinu (אַבְרָהָם אָבִינוּ): Lit., "our father Abraham."

Imprisoned for ten years: Tractate *Bava Basra* 91a.

a verse that says:וַיִּקְרָא שָׁם בְּשֵׁם ה׳ אֵ־ל עוֹלָם — "There he called upon the Name of G-d, the everlasting G-d," and this the Sages understand to mean that Avraham Avinu "caused the Name of the Holy One, Blessed be He, to be called upon by the mouth of every passerby." He did not wait until he was approached, but himself made the first move, seeking to explain the idea of One Creator to even the very simplest of people.

He devoted himself to the dissemination of G-dliness — to spreading the recognition that there exists One Who is the Creator of the universe and Who directs all created beings — with his body, and with whatever he possessed, borrowing money for traveling expenses and for the costs of extending hospitality. This hospitality was utilized for one purpose only — spreading G-dliness in the world, by seeing to it that each gentile wayfarer pronounced a blessing, praising the sole Creator and Master of the universe. And if he declined, the beloved and kindly Avraham grew stern, and presented him with a costly account for all the delicacies and beverages which he had been served, arguing that in the desert wilds they were more expensive than in inhabited regions. Recognizing his predicament, the guest had no option but to listen to what Avraham Avinu explained him about the Creator of the universe, taking great pains to convey the concept of His Unity. Avraham Avinu was not satisfied with simply having the gentile recite the words of the blessing, but wanted him to actually understand what G-dliness is all about. He proceeded therefore to offer such a range of explanations that even the commonest of coarsened Levantine nomads could understand the meaning of G-dliness.

This is what is meant when it is said that Avraham Avinu

There he called: *Gen.* 21:33.

Caused the Name...to be called upon: Tractate *Sotah* 10a-b, where the verb וַיִּקְרָא ("he called") is understood on the level of *derush* as if it were in the causative form, וַיַּקְרֵא (lit., "he caused to call").

G-dliness: Not in the sense of the emulation of G-d by mortals; the word is here used to translate אֱלֹקוּת, and refers to the Creator Himself.

was generous with his money, with his body and with his soul. Whatever money he had he spent on hospitality; he exerted himself physically in order to tend to the needs of his guests; and he forewent his greatest spiritual pleasure. For he was a profound sage, and the greatest pleasure of such a man is to be ensconced alone in the contemplation of ideas. Yet this he sacrificed, setting aside his own intellectual pleasure, and devoting his time instead to explaining to ordinary folk the Unity of the Creator.

Here, then, is Avraham Avinu, devoting his entire resources, body and soul to the propagation of the knowledge of G-d in the world — and Divine Providence puts him in prison. There he sits for ten years, until Divine Providence releases him with a victory of which the whole world hears, and from his liberation comes forth the people of Israel.

6.

The prison terms of Avraham Avinu and of the Alter Rebbe need to be understood, for in them lies a comprehensive Torah teaching.*

It is axiomatic among all thinkers that in every single thing there is a mixture of good and evil, such that there is no good without evil and no evil without good. That is to say, in good there are to be found elements of evil, and in evil there are to be found elements of good. In the mixture of good and evil, moreover, just as the elements of evil that are present in good are utterly evil, so too are the elements of good that are present in evil utterly good.

Tranquillity is good; imprisonment is evil. In the good and evil of these two states there is an admixture of evil in the

---

* See the *Sichah* of *Yud-Tes* Kislev in *Sefer HaMaamarim — Kuntreisim*, Vol. I, *Kuntreis* 16.

Of Avraham Avinu and of the Alter Rebbe: The juxtaposition calls to mind the saying of the Alter Rebbe — "From [acting on the advice of] *Tanya* one can become a chassid like Avraham Avinu." (Cf. Rabbi Zalman Duchman, *LeSheima Ozen* (N.Y., 1963; Heb.), p. 22).

good and of good in the evil. This means that in tranquillity, which is good, there are elements of evil, and in imprisonment, which is evil, there are elements of good. And, as stated above, the elements of good and evil which are to be found in things which are good and evil are absolute: the evil which is mixed with good is utterly, absolutely and expressly evil, and the good which is mixed with evil is utterly, absolutely and expressly good.

That tranquillity is good we can see from an explicit verse in the Torah: וַיַּרְא מְנֻחָה כִּי טוֹב — "He saw that rest was good." In this good, however, there are elements of evil, utter evil. For all evil desires, theft, robbery, bloodshed, bodily excesses and undesirable character traits stem from tranquillity. The *Gemara* expresses this in a penetrating metaphor: "A lion does not roar over a pile of straw but over a pile of meat." The aroma of meat makes him wild and crazed; or, in the words of *Rashi*, "He is happy, and crazed, and does damage."

The *Gemara* does not stop at this statement, but R. Oshiya and R. Yochanan each spell it out by means of a parable in order to make it even clearer.

"R. Oshiya said: This is like a man who had a lean but big-boned cow which he fed on leeks, and it began to kick him. He said to her: 'What caused you to kick me if not the leeks which I gave you?'"

This parable speaks of the body. For the body is an animal, striving after material and animalistic things — except that when it is lean, and not pampered, then even if it is big-boned and coarse it is still tolerable. If, however, it is fed on leeks, sated with succulent delicacies, then this big-boned animal begins to kick, and do damage.

R. Yochanan seeks to go further, and offers an alternative parable: "This may be likened to a man who had a son. He washed him and perfumed him, gave him food and drink, hung a purse around his neck, and sat him down next to the

---

He saw that rest: *Gen.* 49:15.
A lion does not roar: Tractate *Berachos* 32a.

door of harlots. Now how can that son not sin?"

Anyone who understands the workings of the soul can perceive how faithfully these three quotations delineate the path of a *yored* and *nofel*, G-d forbid; of one who is slipping from his spiritual level, or falling from it. It all begins with the pile of meat. One does not run wild because of a pile of straw; a pile of meat, however, can make a person wild and crazy, so that he becomes a *yored*. He can start kicking against the merciful Father, until he even becomes a *nofel*.

R. Oshiya and R. Yochanan teach their parables in order to enable every individual to find within himself exactly what kind of undesirable trait — or, to be more distinct, what kind of evil trait — his own wildness lies in.

It is difficult and redundant to spell out in more explicit and detailed terms what is meant by *yored* and *nofel*. There are such that think that only when someone falls down from the fifth storey and breaks his arms and legs is he called a *nofel*, whereas it is quite possible for a person to fall down a few steps and lose his reason, G-d forbid.

There are certain kinds of people who behold the counterfeit smiles, the superficial gentility, of the so-called New World, and grow ashamed of their lineage, of the fact that they are children who were born into chassidic families.

Without any shadow of a doubt, every such son and daughter prizes and cherishes their childhood memories, and many of them no doubt preserve luminous glimpses of chassidic conduct, so that if they were to compare their parents' home with their own, they would find nothing to be ashamed of in their family background, in the name "chassid".

The pile of meat which makes one wild and crazy varies from lion to lion; there are lions whom any measure whatever of material things causes him to "be happy, go crazy, and do damage."

Now how can that son not sin?: In the original, מַה יַּעֲשֶׂה אוֹתוֹ הַבֵּן שֶׁלֹּא יֶחֱטָא.

7.

Yissachar was wise indeed: "He saw that rest was good." Good, as we have seen, includes elements of utter evil, so Yissachar sought a means of being rid of them. And since, as our Sages teach us, יָגַעְתִּי וּמָצָאתִי תַּאֲמִין — "If someone tells you: '... I exerted myself, and I found,' believe him," it follows that Yissachar, having undertaken his search earnestly, was successful in it. And the way he found to cope with the elements of evil which are present in tranquillity is indicated in the continuation of the above-quoted verse: וַיֵּט שִׁכְמוֹ לִסְבֹּל — "He bent his shoulder to bear." What load did he bear? *Rashi* answers: עוֹל תּוֹרָה — "The yoke of the Torah."

At first glance this expression is puzzling. Torah, after all, is wisdom, something which everyone relishes; everyone wants to be wise. Moreover, people commonly consider themselves to be wise, as we see from the traditional interpretation of the verse describing King Solomon: וַיֶּחְכַּם מִכָּל הָאָדָם — "He was wiser than all men," according to which this verse means that he was "even wiser than the fools." For even fools concede that Shlomo HaMelech is wiser than they — except that they consider themselves too to be wise.

If, then, wisdom is so prized, why is Torah called a yoke?

The simple truth is that the essence of Torah is the obligation of bearing its yoke, of studying Torah every day. And this is a yoke which must be undertaken by every individual, every group, and every community.

It is true that our brethren (thank G-d) bear the yoke of the Torah by supporting Torah schools and *yeshivos;* this is very fine, though here too there is more to be done. But not through this alone can one fulfill the above verse: "He bent

---

I exerted myself, and I found: Tractate *Megillah* 6b.
He bent his shoulder: *Gen.* 49:15.
Rashi answers: *Loc. cit.*
Traditional interpretation: Based on statements in *Midrash Tehillim* and elsewhere.
He was wiser: *I Kings* 5:11.

his shoulder to bear" the yoke of the Torah. Everyone needs to study personally. Every individual, irrespective of whether he is young, middle-aged, or quite old, and regardless of whether he is wealthy or not, a businessman or a laborer, is obliged to study Torah every day.

These are the words of the opening section of Chapter 246 of *Hilchos Talmud Torah* ("The Laws of Torah Study") in the *Shulchan Aruch, Yoreh De'ah:* "The obligation of Torah study devolves on every man of Israel, whether poor or rich, robust or ailing, young or aged. Even a pauper who knocks on doors, and one who has a wife and children, is obligated to fix times for the study of Torah by day and by night, as it is written, וְהָגִיתָ בּוֹ יוֹמָם וָלַיְלָה — 'You shall meditate upon it day and night.'"

The yoke of the Torah is the means of coping with the elements of evil which are interspersed within the good of tranquillity; it sears the spirit of wildness which emerges from the good which is tranquillity.

8.

Just as in the good of tranquillity there are elements of evil, utter evil, so that one needs to seek ways and means of somehow becoming rid of them, so too in the evil of imprisonment are there elements of good, utter good, which grant the person involved considerable benefits, things of real use in his life.

In the epistle opening with the words לְהַשְׂכִּילְךָ בִּינָה in *Iggeres HaKodesh*, the Alter Rebbe discusses physical suffering — involving one's children, health, or livelihood — and says that it is not proper that a person should desire the life of flesh, and children, and sustenance; he explains further how visible physical suffering is in fact a hidden good, and how through simple faith it is transformed into good.

In other words, the Alter Rebbe is saying here that physical suffering is really not suffering: it is hidden good. That,

---

You shall meditate: *Joshua* 1:8.
In the epistle: Epistle 11; *Tanya,* p. 446.

however, refers to its root. But as to the state in which it becomes apparent in this world, laborious *avodah* is called for if one is to uncover the elements of good which are to be found in physical suffering — and then the evil becomes transformed into good.

Broadly speaking, the good which is in physical suffering is the fact that it is an atonement for sin; the "lessening of fat and blood" which suffering brings about makes an effective sacrifice. The undesirable fat becomes lean; the grossness described in the rebuke, שָׁמַנְתָּ עָבִיתָ כָּשִׂיתָ — "You have grown fat, thick, and fleshy," which is present in some degree in every individual, according to his spiritual level, — this grossness melts away; and the seething heat of one's unwholesome blood is cooled.

Everyone knows to what extent unworthy elements are compounded in his own fat and blood, and how vitally he is in need of a certain degree of cleansing.

9.

Truth to tell, one should be very wary of rebuking another. Concerning this there are laws in the Torah as to when one should — or, rather, when one must — do so. But even in such cases, in particular with offenses committed publicly, and even more so with instances of *Chillul HaShem,* a desecration of the Divine Name, must one also be exceedingly careful not to shame the person being rebuked. For if this does happen, G-d forbid, then not only does one not achieve the aim of having the offender improve his ways, but in addition gross harm is done to the speaker, in whom the trait of meanness may thereby emerge.

We encounter a comparable situation in the physical world, and, as has been mentioned on another occasion, the

---

Lessening of fat... sacrifice: Cf. *Zohar II,* 119b: מְעוּט חֶלְבָּא וְדָמָא דְּתַעֲנִיתָא אִיהוּ חָשִׁיב יַתִּיר מִקּוּרְבָּנָא — "The lessening of fat and blood through fasting is valued more than a sacrifice." See too p. 222ff. below.
You have grown fat: *Deut.* 32:15.

life of the body serves as a parable that can teach us how to conduct our spiritual lives.

Before we come to our parable: May the Almighty grant that all our brethren enjoy good health, and may He send a complete recovery to those who are not well! If, however, one has to perform a surgical operation, then one simply has to do it, for it is the greatest favor that can be done to the patient.

Performing an operation requires a certain strength. It is no easy matter. True enough, one needs to sympathize with the patient, but at the same time one must have this certain strength, together with a hope in G-d that the operation will be successful.

The fact is that a doctor needs to tread a path in *avodah* that is all his own. He grows accustomed to seeing sick folk, and his sense of compassion can dry up, so that if he is to preserve a due humanity he must make strenuous efforts and be aware of his responsibility.

10.

In the *Mishnah* in Tractate *Kiddushin*, R. Yehudah in the name of Abba Guria tells us of the character traits and the spiritual life that typify certain kinds of people.

He says: "Most camel-drivers are upright people." *Rashi* explains: "Because they travel through deserts where wild beasts and robbers are to be found, they are afraid for their lives, and their hearts are contrite (lit., 'broken') before G-d."

He goes on: "Most sailors are pious," and *Rashi* explains that this is "because they go away to a place of danger and are forever trembling."

Further: "The best of doctors is destined for *Gehinnom*." Here *Rashi* comments: "He is not afraid of illness; his diet is [imprudently] that of healthy people; his heart is not contrite before G-d; sometimes he takes people's lives; and it can

---

Most camel-drivers: Tractate *Kiddushin* 4:14.
Upright people: In the original, כְּשֵׁרִים.
Are pious: In the original, חֲסִידִים.

happen that he has the opportunity to cure a poor man but does not treat him."

Abba Guria speaks here of three kinds of people, three categories which embrace a great proportion of humanity. Let us not take note of their occupations, but only of their attributes of character and their spiritual level, for this is how *Rashi* understands the three categories.

The first category, people whom Abba Guria describes as honest men, are those who make their hearts contrite ("broken") before G-d. True enough, such a man arrives at this state because of a certain reason — his place of work is dangerous — but the practical consequence is a good one: his heart is pliable, and a person with such a heart deserves to be called "an honest man."

A man in the second category is called "pious", his brokenheartedness being expressed in trembling. He is a G-d-fearing man, and is always trembling lest he sin. His heart is not only pliable, but contrite, or "broken", and such a man is worthy of being called "pious".

The third kind of person is one who fears no illness; he eats and drinks; the fear of heaven does not move his heart; and his occupation sometimes brings him to bloodshed. To this kind of man Abba Guria applies no name at all; he merely indicates where his place is, where he belongs. For a man of this kind belongs in *Gehinnom*.

This last and worst kind of person is the great exponent of tranquillity, of complacency. Of him it is written, יָעֹז בְּהַוָּתוֹ, which the *Targum* understands to mean that he is conceited on account of his wealth. His ego — his "I need" and "I want" — gives him a certain self-assuredness that David HaMelech calls הֵעָזָה, or insolence.

If, however, a doctor is of the kind that humbles his heart before G-d, and heals the poor, then things are as they should be, though he still needs a strong heart. As to the faults listed

---

Of him it is written: *Ps.* 52:9. (Lit., "He strengthens himself in his wickedness.")

in the *Mishnah*, they occur because his work makes him grow accustomed to the sight of people in ill health, and that is why his responsibility to them must constantly be brought to mind.

11.

Just as there is such a thing as physical illness so is there spiritual illness, and one who rebukes another must relate to it just as the doctor relates to physical illness. But if the physician of the soul — the person who is rebuking — is himself unafraid of illness, seeing no malady in himself and recklessly eating and drinking as if he were in ideal health, and thinking himself to be so merely because he is a Torah scholar, not humbling his heart before G-d, — then he is (G-d forbid) a destroyer of souls, because the rebuke of another must be governed only by the directives of the Torah.

Let me tell you about a conversation that took place between a few elder chassidim at a *farbrengen* in Lubavitch in the winter of 5649 (תרמ"ט; 1888-1889). Those involved were R. Hendel, R. Aharon and R. Yekusiel, the last two being *melamdim* from Dokshytz, and all three *baalei avodah* whose labors of self-refinement had permeated their entire being.

The discussion turned to the subject of rebuke — how the time-honored custom of chassidim at a *farbrengen* among themselves is to analyze various character traits thoroughly and candidly, and how sometimes this airing is effective and sometimes not.

At this point R. Yekusiel the *melamed* told his friends how once when he was a young man he was making his way to Lubavitch — by foot, as usual — and arrived in the nearby town of Dubrovna. As he entered the *beis midrash* of the local Lubavitcher chassidim he found that it was packed to capacity. Someone was repeating a discourse of *Chassidus*. It was the Rebbe's personal emissary, R. Gershon Dov, who in his younger years had been a chassid first of the *Tzemach Tzedek* and then of the Rebbe Maharash.

Physical illness...spiritual illness: Cf. *Rambam, Hilchos Deos* 2:1.

When he had completed the *maamar* all those present sang together, and in the course of the *farbrengen* that followed, R. Gershon Dov related that at a *farbrengen* during one of his journeys the illustrious R. Hillel* had said: "I once heard from the Rebbe (the *Tzemach Tzedek*) that הוֹכֵחַ תּוֹכִיחַ is like הַמּוֹל יִמּוֹל. [The former commandment means, 'You shall surely rebuke'; and the latter means, '(He) shall surely be circumcised.'] Just as the commandment of circumcising another can be fulfilled only by one who is himself circumcised, so too can the commandment of rebuking another be fulfilled only by a person who has first rebuked *himself*, and only then proceeds to rebuke his fellow.'"

To this R. Hillel had added: "And only on this condition is rebuking effective."

*   *   *

Whoever rebukes himself — and this is an obligation that lies on every individual personally — knows full well what manner of man he is, and how vitally he needs a cleansing of the grossness of his having "grown fat, and thick," and of his seething blood.

And all of this is cleansed through (heaven forfend!) physical suffering.

---

* R. Hillel of Paritch, outstanding chassid of the *Tzemach Tzedek,* and author of *Pelach HaRimon* and *Likkutei Biurim.*

You shall surely rebuke: *Lev.* 19:17.
Shall surely be circumcised: *Gen.* 17:13.
Can be fulfilled only...himself circumcised: On this interpretation of the dual Hebrew verb, see *Rashi* on Tractate *Avodah Zarah* 27a.
First rebuked *himself:* Based on a teaching of the Baal Shem Tov — that הוֹכֵחַ means rebuking oneself, and *then* תּוֹכִיחַ means rebuking another.
Whoever rebukes himself: Cf. *Klalei HaChinuch VehaHadrachah* ("Principles of Education and Guidance") by the Rebbe Rayatz, where the first prerequisite for being an educator is — sober self-criticism.
An obligation...personally: In the original, חוֹבַת גַּבְרָא.

12.

Everyone has his own שָׁמַנְתָּ עָבִיתָ כָּשִׂיתָ, his own "growing fat, thick, and fleshy." Not only does it blind him from perceiving his actual spiritual state; moreover, it is a foul wellspring from which flow all kinds of negative traits.

This form of grossness needs to be removed — by each individual's own efforts. Every individual ought to think deeply in order to devise means of rescuing himself from the fearsome, stagnant swamp of "growing fat, and thick," for this is a question on which one's very life depends.

In the course of our prayers we ask the Almighty: "May it be Your will that I sin no more. The sins that I have committed, erase in Your abounding mercies, but not through suffering or severe illnesses."

This is our request, and it is of course made earnestly. After all, it appears in the confessional prayer of *Al chet* which we say before retiring every night, before returning the deposit [i.e., the soul] which was lodged with us for safekeeping, and which we say in particular in the prayers of Yom Kippur. But beyond requesting, something needs to be *done* — in two directions: settling debts from the past, and living a healthy present.

In the material world we see that if (G-d forbid) someone's livelihood totters and he slips into debt, and asks his creditors to pardon his tardiness in paying, then provided that he pays off his debts in installments they continue to supply him with merchandise.

Old debts must be paid up — even in installments, but they must be paid up. There is no way out. We once discussed this at length* in connection with the phrase, וּלֵךְ יְשַׁלֵּם נֶדֶר. The

---

* On Simchas Torah 5694 (תרצ״ד; 1933). [See p. 170ff. above.]

May it be Your will: *Siddur,* p. 305.

Al chet...every night: In point of fact, this is not a standard component of the prayers before retiring at night; in the *Siddur* (p. 121) it is introduced as follows: "If one wishes to say *Al chet,* it is to be found on p. 302."

divine intention underlying the descent of the soul into the body must be realized — if not through kindly means, then (G-d forbid) through suffering.

The *maamarim** which begin with the words זֶה הַיּוֹם and מִן הַמֵּצַר discuss at length the concept of a trial which involves both prosecution and defense attorneys. A parable is set out from an ordinary courtcase, and a distinction is drawn between the trial of every man that takes place on Rosh HaShanah and the trial that takes place after his passing. In addition, definitions are given of four levels at which a person's *avodah* may be — the level of *meisim* ("the dead"), the level of *noflim* ("those who are falling"), the level of *cholim* ("the sick"), and the level of *asurim* ("those who are imprisoned").

The ethical teachings and the guidance in the service of G-d which are to be found in *Chassidus* are intended for all Jews, not only for chassidim. *Every* Jew ought to listen closely to the voice of G-d which has been revealed through our forefathers, the Rebbes.

It is difficult to speak of this often. One would far prefer speaking only of happy things, never mentioning any harsh or stern words. But everyone should well remember [the warnings which follow] the verse, אִם בְּחֻקֹּתַי תֵּלֵכוּ — "If you walk in My statutes." And may the Almighty grant that the verse [of blessing] be fulfilled: וְנָתַתִּי גִשְׁמֵיכֶם — "And I will give your rains...," and that our brethren be blessed with an abundance of good, both materially and spiritually.

---

* Delivered in New York on Rosh HaShanah of the year 5690 (תר"ץ; 1929), and published the same year.

Meisim...noflim...cholim...asurim: The terms are borrowed from the second paragraph of *Shemoneh Esreh.*
If you walk in My statutes: *Lev.* 26:3.
And I will give your rains: *Lev.* 26:4.
Your rains...an abundance of good: In the language of *Chassidus,* גִשְׁמֵיכֶם refers to all material things, since גַּשְׁמִיּוּת stems from the word גֶּשֶׁם, which means both "rain" and "materiality".

13.

The point that has been made thus far — that in the evil of suffering there is a good — refers to a general benefit, in that it constitutes an atonement for sinful deeds, words or thoughts, for suffering reduces the kind of fat and blood that comes into being through one's שָׁמַנְתָּ עָבִיתָ כָּשִׂיתָ, through one's having "grown fat, thick, and fleshy."

The atonement of sin, however, is only a *tikkun* of the past; i.e., through one's suffering the past is rectified. But in fact the evil of suffering comprises elements of good which are utterly and absolutely good.

It is characteristic of the teachings of *Chassidus* to illuminate any subject with the understanding of נֵר ה' נִשְׁמַת אָדָם — "The soul of man [which] is a lamp of G-d," until one has it in one's grasp: clearly, with vitality welling from within, and in a manner that produces results — for such understanding points out a path in actual, practical *avodah*.

To apply this thinking to our subject. — Suffering brings about two kinds of benefit. One is the reduction of the fat and blood of materiality, and hence the atonement of sin, the rectification of the past. The second benefit is that it makes a person more spiritual, more refined, nearer to his soul.

Guf and *nefesh* represent material reality (*gashmiyus*) and spiritual reality (*ruchniyus*). *Guf* and *nefesh* are body and life. *Chassidus* explains how in every body there is a soul. In the category of *domem* [the so-called "inanimate" creations in the universe], in which our eyes of flesh see no more than a body, there is a soul as well. And in a thing as spiritual as the soul

---

The soul of man: *Prov.* 20:27.
With vitality welling from within: In the original, מיט אַ חיות פְּנִימִי.
And in a manner that produces results: In the original, און אַ בְּכֵן.
Rectification of the past...more spiritual: The benefit coming in two
    stages, referring respectively to the past and the future, calls to mind
    the words of *Rashi* (on *Ex.* 3:3), אָסֻרָה מִכַּאן לְהִתְקָרֵב לְשָׁם — "I shall turn aside
    from here to come nearer to there." (See p. 304ff. below.)

there is also a body. And just as our eye cannot see the soul of an "inanimate" object, so can our brain not grasp the concept of a body in the *nefesh*.

Both body and soul are the handiwork of the Creator. His way is that of מַפְלִיא לַעֲשׂוֹת — "He works wonders," joining the spiritual soul with the physical body.

14.

Man is the elect of creatures and, like all other creatures, is compounded of body and soul. In two respects, however, the manner in which these two elements are compounded in man differs from that of all other creatures.

In the first place, though in all creatures including man the body is a material creation and the soul a spiritual one, yet he is utterly different from them all in that his body and soul each stem from the extreme point of their respective sources. Soul and body, as we have said, are *ruchniyus* and *gashmiyus*. The soul of man, then, stems from the loftiest level to be found in *ruchniyus*, such that it is called חֵלֶק אֱלוֹק מִמָּעַל — "a part of G-d above," while the body stems from the lowliest level to be found in *gashmiyus*.

In the second place, the manner in which these two elements are compounded is itself different in man. In all other creatures the combination of body and soul — of matter and form — subsists only in the fact that the body lives by virtue of the soul: the soul gives life to the body. They do not influence each other. In man, by contrast, body and soul are

---

He works wonders, joining...soul with...body: See *Rashi* on Tractate *Berachos* 60b, and *Siddur*, p. 6.

Man...is utterly different...respective sources: Going back to the Six Days of Creation, it will be noticed that the creation of man springs from two sources, and takes place in two stages (see *Gen.* 2:7); in the case of all other created beings, each species is the result of a single divine fiat (e.g., *Gen.* 1:24).

Loftiest level...lowest level: Reminiscent of the verse, אָחוֹר וָקֶדֶם צַרְתָּנִי (*Ps.* 139:5).

A part of G-d above: *Job* 31:2.

compounded in such a way that matter and form are engaged in perpetual battle.

Before a man even knows how to choose good and detest evil, the battle between body and soul has begun. Both natures, his physical nature and his spiritual nature, are at work within him. His physical nature perceives whatever is good and pleasurable in bodily things alone, whereas his spiritual nature perceives the good and the delight and the refinement of noble character traits, and appreciates the beauty of understanding.

Gashmiyus and *ruchniyus* are at war. The physical body seeks to override the spiritual soul: matter prevailing over form; the spiritual soul seeks to gain mastery over the physical body: form prevailing over matter.

*   *   *

The second kind of benefit to be gained from suffering [i.e., becoming thereby more spiritual and more refined] is the absolute good which is to be found in the evil of suffering. This is a kind of good that one ought to yearn for; it is a distinctive and unique kind of good, a kind of good that is simply not to be found in that which comprises good alone.

And much yet remains to be said about the lofty quality of the manifestations of the second kind of benefit which are to be found in the evil of suffering.

15.

Imprisonment is evil, but within it there are elements which are good, utter and absolute good. In fact, this is a dual

---

Battle between body and soul: Body and soul here in fact signify the נֶפֶשׁ הַבַּהֲמִית (the animal soul) and the נֶפֶשׁ הָאֱלֹקִית (the G-dly soul) respectively. (This is clear from the following sentence in the text.) In this contest, the prize is the body: Who will gain dominion over it? Cf. *Tanya*, Ch. 9.

Unique kind of good: Cf. כִּיתְרוֹן הָאוֹר מִן הַחֹשֶׁךְ ("...like the superiority of light over darkness"; *Eccl.* 2:13), as explained in *Tanya*, Ch. 26 — "...light that proceeds *from* darkness."

good, since it comprises both kinds of benefit which are to be gained from suffering — the simple benefit which accrues from the lessening of fat and blood, and, more importantly, the second benefit discussed above.

In the suffering brought on by illness, G-d forbid, pain hinders a person from being rapt in thoughts of repentance and spiritual stocktaking and whatever else he should be thinking about. Likewise, worries involving one's children, health and livelihood make a person confused and preoccupied, by ensnaring him in the foolishness of devising stratagems, and the like.

None of these disadvantages, however, are to be found in the evil of the suffering of imprisonment.

16.

In prison a person becomes closed off from the entire turbulent and tempestuous world. Every minute is an hour; every hour is a month; every day is a year.

In prison a person becomes acquainted with the utmost depth of evil which malevolent geniuses can engineer. The experience gives one a limited but precise picture of what Hell means, and of what is meant by Angels of Destruction.

From one's first step inside, and one's first glance at one's cell, all bodily desires vanish, and in the first few minutes during which one is left alone, there flutters through a ray of delight at the temporary respite from the torture and humiliation which one has undergone at the hands of the wardens and the interrogator.

At one's very first attempt to reflect on what has transpired, when one has the full image of the governors of the prison clear before one's eyes, one stands overawed by the sheer depth of evil which can be found in the creature called

---

In prison...tempestuous world: Throughout this passage, the Rebbe Rayatz was speaking from firsthand experience. For an account of his seven prison terms, see the letter (addressed "to one of his sons-in-law") in Vol. IV of the present work, p. 143.

"man". One becomes minute and lowly in one's own eyes as one beholds the scum of humanity.

There are learned works that discuss the varying natures of different kinds of creatures, and consider the cruel habits of those that prey with tooth and claw — the predators of the towns and the wilds, the snakes and scorpions of the deserts, the fearsome denizens of the seas and the skies — and they come to the conclusion that the most pernicious beast in the whole of creation is man.

But it is only when one is in prison that one comes to know the evil of this wild beast. It is there that one sees his real face, and hears his vulgar voice and harsh speech. It is there that with bloodshot eyes one witnesses a man's calm enjoyment from shedding blood.

The most difficult time in prison is at night. For those who have already experienced the taste of prison it is quite unnecessary to explain that daytime in prison is far quieter than midnight in the smallest of hamlets. But for those who are caught up in the hubbub of the world it is difficult to imagine the deathly silence that reigns in prison even by day, and more so by night, when the wardens and all the officials are at rest.

In the midst of this dead stillness one hears metallic footsteps and the clatter of keys in one of the iron doors. Involuntarily one shudders, for one knows full well what a night visit signifies. At best it means a summons to the interrogator, with all the dire tortures that accompany it. A more dread experience is to overhear an exchange of conversation between a prisoner and the warden who is escorting him to the place of execution.

17.

Prison is a fine little retreat for private meditation. Here

A fine little retreat for private meditation: In the original, אַ גוטע התבּוֹדְדוּת-שטיבּל. Cf. the well-known story, retold by the Rebbe, that underlies the haunting melody known as "Shamihl".

one is spared the customary bother of having to close one's eyes in order that one should not see things that one ought not see, of blocking one's ears against things that one ought not hear, and of guarding one's tongue from undesirable speech.

This is a place where a person can rediscover his own equilibrium, where he can make a really honest self-appraisal, where he can thoroughly consider his past, joyfully accept the suffering of the present, and firmly resolve how he will live his future as soon as the Almighty lifts him from bondage into freedom.

The good which is to be found in the evil of the sufferings of imprisonment sets a man up on a higher rung in life; it has a salutary influence on certain faculties of the soul which develop only by such means; and provided that all this is utilized for the service of G-d, this is a most useful experience.

18.

All of this is true of ordinary people, that tranquillity is good and imprisonment is evil. But in the case of consummate *tzaddikim,* the fathers of the world, whatever things they encounter are various paths in the service of G-d.

The imprisonment of Avraham Avinu took place in order that he should blaze the trail of utter self-sacrifice for G-d-liness, for *Elokus.* The imprisonment of the Alter Rebbe took place in order that he should blaze the path of utter self-sacrifice for the service of G-d according to the teachings of *Chassidus.*

Rediscover his own equilibrium: In the original, קומען צו זיך.

Salutary influence: The Rebbe Rayatz once said that he would not undergo another second of imprisonment for all the treasures in the world — but neither, for all the treasures in the world, would he in retrospect *forgo* a single second of it. Moreover (in the beginning of Chapter 34, referred to in an earlier note), the Rebbe Rayatz wrote that he used to set aside time for recalling old memories, especially of his last imprisonment.

Blaze the trail...blaze the path, etc.: Lit., "open the pipe" (צנור).

The Baal Shem Tov said before his passing that the alternative was open to him of leaving this world in the manner of Eliyahu HaNavi, of whom it is written, ...וַיַּעַל בַּסְּעָרָה הַשָּׁמָיִם — "[He] ascended heavenward in a storm," but he did not want to forgo what was written in the verse, כִּי עָפָר אַתָּה וְאֶל עָפָר תָּשׁוּב — "For dust you are, and to dust shall you return."

The Alter Rebbe, who was chosen from Above to disseminate the teachings of the Baal Shem Tov according to the path of *Chabad*, was given from Above the power to open up the spiritual faculties of *chochmah, binah* and *daas* in his fellow Jews, in order to make them vehicles for *Elokus*. [To this end,] the Alter Rebbe had to experience all the possible paths in divine service.

In order to open the gates of one's *chochmah, binah* and *daas* so that these faculties should illuminate one's heart in the course of one's practical *avodah*, one must have actual *mesirus nefesh*. In *Chassidus* this term [usually translated "self-sacrifice"] is explained as meaning *mesiras haratzon*, the setting aside of one's own will. And it was the Alter Rebbe who cleared a path to *mesirus nefesh* for the sake of *avodah*.

As one contemplates the inner meaning of the Alter Rebbe's imprisonment and release, one lights upon new ways of understanding and fresh insights as to what paths in *avodah* they opened up.

By virtue of the merit of our forefathers, the Rebbes of blessed memory, may the Almighty grant us and all of Israel the understanding and the strength to walk — with hearts joyful in both a material and a spiritual sense — in the ways of divine service which the Alter Rebbe opened up through his *mesirus nefesh*. May the promise of the verse be realized: יָפֻצוּ

Eliyahu HaNavi (אֵלִיָּהוּ הַנָּבִיא): The prophet Elijah.

He ascended heavenward: *II Kings* 2:11.

For dust you are: *Gen.* 3:19.

Mesirus nefesh...mesiras haratzon: Chassidus points out verses in which *nefesh* signifies "will"; e.g., *Gen.* 23:8, and *Rashi* there.

מַעְיְנֹתֶיךָ חוּצָה — "Your wellsprings [the teachings of *Chassidus*] shall be spread far and wide." And may *Mashiach*, the king, come speedily and in our own days, Amen.

Your wellsprings: *Prov.* 5:16. Once when the soul of the Baal Shem Tov ascended to the heavenly abode of *Mashiach* and asked him when he was going to come, *Mashiach* replied with a paraphrase of this verse: "When your wellsprings shall be spread far and wide" — in reference to the dissemination of the teachings of *Chassidus* which the Baal Shem Tov had revealed to the world. (See *On the Essence of Chassidus* (*Inyanah shel Toras HaChassidus* in English translation; Kehot, N.Y., 1978), p. 15, footnote 23.)

Chapter 4b

The Eve of 20 Kislev 5694 (תרצ"ד ;1933)

[Warsaw]

1.

As is well known, the Alter Rebbe used to read a number of chapters of *Tehillim* every day, according to the alternative division of the book into the days of the month; the Rebbes who succeeded him did likewise.

The first verse of the allotment of *Tehillim* for *Yud-Tes* Kislev is as follows: תְּפִלָּה לְמֹשֶׁה אִישׁ הָאֱלֹקִים ה׳ מָעוֹן אַתָּה הָיִיתָ לָנוּ בְּדֹר וָדֹר — "A prayer of Moshe, the man of G-d. L-rd, You have been an abode for us in generation after generation." David, King of Israel, had received a tradition that Moshe Rabbeinu had composed this Psalm. In the words of the *Midrash Shocher Tov*: "Moshe Rabbeinu uttered eleven Psalms, corresponding to eleven tribes. To begin with, the Psalm opening with the phrase 'A prayer of Moshe' includes the verse, תָּשֵׁב אֱנוֹשׁ עַד דַּכָּא וַתֹּאמֶר שׁוּבוּ בְנֵי אָדָם — 'You bring man low until he is crushed, and You say: Return, you children of man.' This corresponds to

---

Tehillim every day: See note "Concerning the Reciting of *Tehillim*" that is appended to all editions of *Tehillim Ohel Yosef Yitzchak*.

Alternative division: I.e., in addition to reciting *Tehillim* daily according to the division of the Book into the days of the week.

A prayer of Moshe: *Ps.* 90:1.

An abode: Or, "a haven," but "abode" better suits the *derush* at the end of this Section.

Moshe Rabbeinu uttered eleven Psalms: *Midrash Shocher Tov* (=Midrash *Tehillim*) 90:3.

Corresponding to eleven tribes: *Rashi* on *Ps.* 90:1 explains that "Moshe Rabbeinu uttered these Psalms, parallel to the eleven blessings that he bestowed on eleven tribes in *Parshas Zos HaBerachah*" (*Deut.* 33:6-24).

You bring man low: *Ps.* 90:3.

203

204 LIKKUTEI DIBBURIM

the blessing of Reuven: יְחִי רְאוּבֵן וְאַל יָמֹת — 'May Reuven live, and not die.'"

In the allusions, such as the above, in the Book of *Tehillim*, there is to be found instruction for one's divine service, for every word of Torah and prayer ought to give a person a certain degree of guidance as to how to conduct himself in all the areas of his daily life.

This is why the occasion has often arisen for an explanation of the fact that תּוֹרָה ("Torah") means הוֹרָאָה ("a teaching") — to show a person how to arrange all spheres of his mundane life, both in his family affairs, such as the conduct of his home and the upbringing of his children, and in his social life.

In the above allusions in the Book of *Tehillim*, then, there is guidance for one's divine service.

The above Psalm comprises four main points: (a) man is exhorted to contemplate how fleeting is the lifespan of this fleshly, material world; (b) he is told how he is given help from Above to follow the path of Torah and *mitzvos*, and (c) how by various means he is directed from Above toward the ways of repentance; (d) he is given a solid reminder that things of this world should not bring him to conceit.

This Psalm opens with the words: ה' מָעוֹן אַתָּה הָיִיתָ לָּנוּ בְּדֹר וָדֹר — "L-rd, You have been an abode for us in generation after generation." It closes with the words: וִיהִי נֹעַם ה' אֱלֹקֵינוּ עָלֵינוּ וּמַעֲשֵׂה יָדֵינוּ כּוֹנְנָה עָלֵינוּ וּמַעֲשֵׂה יָדֵינוּ כּוֹנְנֵהוּ — "And may the pleasantness of the L-rd our G-d be upon us; establish for us the work of our hands; the work of our hands, yea, establish it for us." Now the word מָעוֹן ("abode") and the word נֹעַם ("pleasantness") are composed of the same letters, except that the statement

---

The blessing of Reuven: *Deut.* 33:6.

And not die: The correspondence of this Psalm with Reuven's blessing is clarified by the comment of *Rashi* on the phrase, "and not die": "I.e., in the Next World, when the incident of Bilhah (see *Gen.* 35:22 and *Rashi* there) will not be recalled to his discredit" — because he repented (cf. *Bereishis Rabbah* 84:19); and "Return, you children of man" in the above-quoted verse is a call to repentance.

This Psalm opens: I.e., after its introductory phrase.

Composed of the same letters: Theoretically, for both may be spelled either with or without the letter *vav*.

מָעוֹן אַתָּה הָיִיתָ לָּנוּ בְּדֹר וָדֹר ("You have been an abode for us in generation after generation") appears at the beginning of the Psalm, while the request introduced by the words וִיהִי נֹעַם ("And may the pleasantness") appears at its end. This Psalm, then, embraces the entire life of a man on this world — from the moment that the soul enters its abode, the body, until it returns to the place called נֹעַם ("pleasantness"), for, as it is written in the Zohar, עָלְמָא דְאָתֵי אִקְרֵי נֹעַם — "The World to Come is called pleasantness."

2.

It was on Yud-Tes Kislev, then, that the Alter Rebbe said this chapter of Tehillim — the day that marked the hillula of the Maggid of Mezritch, the anniversary of his passing, and the day that was to be his own hillula, the day of his liberation from imprisonment.

Among my notes of stories which I heard from my father in the summer of 5655 (תרנ"ה; 1895), there are many about the Alter Rebbe which have been handed down the generations from Rebbe to Rebbe. Some of them were passed down in a whisper, with earnest warnings that they were not to be revealed except for the benefit of avodah.

My greatgrandfather, the Tzemach Tzedek, was exceedingly particular that stories should be transmitted with the greatest of care.*

My grandfather, the Rebbe Maharash, kept notebooks of stories that he had heard from his father and from older relatives who then lived in Lubavitch, as well as from elder chassidim whom he had known as a child. He was well organized and had an extraordinary memory, and at the age of ten began to write down whatever he heard.

In his first jottings he records how his father, the Tzemach Tzedek, went to Petersburg** in the summer of 5603 (תר"ג;

---

* See below, end of this Section.
** For the Rabbinical Conference convened by the government.

1843), and before setting out he instructed his children* that every day, including *Shabbos*, they and their mother** should read three chapters of *Tehillim* in his study. He also sent Hershel the *meshares* with a *pidyon* to be taken to the burial place of his mother in Liozna.***

With his accustomed brevity, my grandfather the Rebbe Maharash records: (a) the discussions surrounding the sending of emissaries to Haditch and Niezhin, the burial places of the Alter Rebbe and the Mitteler Rebbe respectively; (b) a few stories that his father the *Tzemach Tzedek* had told him about how the Alter Rebbe had made the journey to Petersburg;**** (c) a statement made by his father the *Tzemach Tzedek* concerning the Alter Rebbe and himself: "My grandfather was *taken* to Petersburg; I am going myself"; (d) another statement made by his father concerning the Alter Rebbe: "My grandfather experienced self-sacrifice for the sake of the teachings of the Baal Shem Tov and for the sake of chassidim; for us this self-sacrifice should be a beaten path."

Astonishing stories are recorded there of the Alter Rebbe's stay in Peter-Paul Fortress, stories that have been handed down from generation to generation in hallowed purity.

When my father used to speak of the Alter Rebbe he would say that quite apart from the remarkable spiritual level of his soul, he was an *atzmi* [i.e., one who is absolutely true to

---

* R. Baruch Shalom (הרב"ש); R. Yehudah Leib (הרי"ל); R. Chaim Shneur Zalman (הרש"ז); R. Yisrael Noach (הרי"נ); R. Yosef Yitzchak (הריי"צ); R. Yaakov (הרי"); and R. Shmuel (הר"ש; the Rebbe Maharash).

** *Rebbitzin* Chayah Mussia, daughter of the Mitteler Rebbe and granddaughter of the Alter Rebbe.

*** *Rebbitzin* Devorah Leah, daughter of the Alter Rebbe and mother of the *Tzemach Tzedek*. The events surrounding her passing, during the lifetime of her father, are recounted at length on pp. 95-102 above.

**** During his first arrest in 5559 (תקנ"ט; 1798), and during his second arrest in 5561 (תקס"א; 1800).

The sending of emissaries: On similar missions to that of Hershel.
For the sake of the teachings: I.e., for their dissemination.
Atzmi [i.e., one who is...]: Though this is the meaning here, עצמי is sometimes used loosely in the original, as if synonymous with *atzmiyus*, in the sense of "the quality of being an *atzmi*."

his true self, or *etzem*], and wherever an *atzmi* may be, he is an *atzmi*.

The concept of being an *atzmi* involves two points: (a) an *atzmi* is what he is; (b) whatever an *atzmi* is, he is that at all times and in all places equally; changes in space and time are immaterial to him.

The light of the sun, the heat of the sun, and the influence of the sun — whether in relation to the vegetable kingdom, the animal kingom, or humanity — are each only *hispashtus*, an "extension" of the sun, and not *atzmus*, the "self" of the sun. This is why they vary under the influence of changes in time and space. That which is at the level of *hispashtus* can be delimited, obscured, withheld or hindered.

With an *atzmi*, however, changes of space and time are of no consequence. The *etzem* of the sun is equal in all places and at all times. As to the divine command, וְהָיוּ לִמְאוֹרֹת בִּרְקִיעַ הַשָּׁמַיִם לְהָאִיר עַל הָאָרֶץ — "They shall be luminaries in the firmament of heaven to give light upon the earth," signifying that "the realm of this one shall be daytime and the realm of the other shall be nighttime," — this delineation refers only to the *hispashtus* of the luminaries. That which is *atzmi*, by contrast, is unbounded, for the realm of *atzmi* is unaffected by changes of time and space.

The Alter Rebbe was an *atzmi*, and an *atzmi*, as we have said above, is unaffected by changes of time and space. Once inside the office of the Peter-Paul Fortress where he was to be crossexamined, as soon as dawn came (for he had been brought there before daybreak) he took out his *tallis* and began to examine its *tzitzis*, whereupon all the clerks there were overwhelmed by dread* — for wherever an *atzmi* may be, he is an *atzmi*.

In fact, however, the *etzem* of the sun is not exactly analo-

---

* The story has been told at length, and this is not the place to repeat it.

Vegetable... animal...humanity: In the original, צוֹמֵחַ, חַי, מְדַבֵּר.

They shall be luminaries: *Gen.* 1:15.

This one...daytime...the other...nighttime: Cf. *Midrash Tanchuma* on *Parshas Korach*, Section 5, paraphrased by *Rashi* on *Num.* 16:5.

gous to the *atzmiyus* of the Alter Rebbe, for a *nivra*, a created being, cannot provide an exact analogy with a *neshamah*, a soul. Though the *atzmi* of a *maor* (lit., "a luminary") and the *atzmi* of *chiyus* ("life-force") are both *atzmi*, they are nevertheless different.

Wherever the Alter Rebbe was, he remained just as he had been. His stay in prison constitutes entire Torah teachings that can and should provide us with direction and encouragement in the study of *Chassidus*, a path in the *avodah* of the heart required by prayer, and zeal in following the ways of *Chassidus*.

My greatuncle R. Baruch Shalom, the son of the *Tzemach Tzedek*, was gifted with a musical talent. When he was eight years old the Alter Rebbe taught him the tunes for the cantillation of the Torah, the Prophets and the Writings. Concerning the latter, the cantillation for the *Kesuvim*, he said that this was the song of the Levites in the *Beis HaMikdash*. At the same time he told him two stories that he had heard from his Rebbe, the Maggid of Mezritch, and concluded with these words: "When we used to hear a Torah discourse from the Rebbe, we saw this as the Oral Law, and when we heard a story from his mouth, this was our Written Law."

The Alter Rebbe, then, is saying here that a story heard from one's Rebbe is Torah *Shebichsav*, whereas a Torah teaching heard from one's Rebbe is Torah *Shebe'al peh*. One should listen attentively to the depth and richness of these words, for a statement of the Alter Rebbe is a wellspring of life-giving waters.

The full weight of a *vort* of the Alter Rebbe, and how it ought to be studied, may be clearly seen in *Likkutei Torah*.*

---

* A collection of *maamarim* of the Alter Rebbe on *Vayikra, Bamidbar, Devarim* and *Shir HaShirim*, annotated by the *Tzemach Tzedek*; first published in Zhitomir in 5608 (תר"ח; 1848).

When he was eight years old: This was in the last year of the life of his greatgrandfather, the Alter Rebbe.

When we used to hear: This refers to the Alter Rebbe and his colleagues, the disciples of the Maggid.

There we see how my greatgrandfather the *Tzemach Tzedek* studies each statement of the Alter Rebbe, illuminating it by reference to *Talmud Bavli*, *Talmud Yerushalmi*, *Zohar* and *Midrashim*.

*   *   *

And from all the above it is now perfectly clear for what soundly-based reason my greatgrandfather was most particular that stories should be transmitted with the greatest of care.

3.

My grandfather the Rebbe of Ovrutch* once told my father** something that he had heard from his saintly grandfather, R. Mordechai of Chernobyl, in these words:

My father (R. Nachum of Chernobyl) once told me that the Rebbe (the Maggid of Mezritch) regarded the *Rav* (the Alter Rebbe) as a child.

The Maggid had once said to R. Zusya:*** "Write to our sage *(gaon)*, Reb Zalmanyu Litvak ('the Lithuanian'), and tell him to make the journey here."

And from that time on, his colleagues of the *Chevraya* called him "the Rav." One of them, R. Avraham "the Malach" ("the angel"), the son of the Maggid, told his father of this and this was the answer: "The holy brotherhood concur with the truth. A name carries significance, and in the   *Halachah*, the law is determined

---

* R. Yosef Yitzchak, son of the *Tzemach Tzedek* and son-in-law of R. Yaakov Yisrael of Chercass.
** The Rebbe Rashab, son-in-law of the Rebbe of Ovrutch.
*** R. Zusya of Hanipoli; brother of R. Elimelech of Lyzhansk.

R. Nachum of Chernobyl: R. (Menachem) Nachum of Chernobyl was himself one of the disciples of the Maggid, like the other protagonists figuring in the following episode.

Zalmanyu: Affectionate diminutive Yiddish form of the Alter Rebbe's second name, Zalman.

Chevraya: Short for *Chevraya Kaddisha* ("the holy brotherhood"; Aram.); the disciples of the Maggid.

A name carries significance: Cf. Tractate *Berachos* 7b.

The law is determined...'*Rav*': See p. 167 above, and footnote there.

according to him who is called 'Rav'. The Shulchan Aruch
(Code of Jewish Law) of the Rav will find acceptance
throughout all the scattered communities of the House
of Israel."

When the Rav arrived, R. Zusya told him that the
Maggid had referred to him as "our gaon." The Rav
sighed deeply, and fainted. When he came to he was
exceedingly weak, and had to remain in bed.

This took place in Rovno, at the time of the big
meeting.* The members of the brotherhood were afraid
to tell the Rebbe, the Maggid. R. Mendele (R. Menachem
Mendel) of Vitebsk held that it was out of the question
for them to do so, because of the anguish involved. The
members of the brotherhood would have to find some
means themselves of making a pidyon for the Rav. R. Levi
Yitzchak of Berditchev argued otherwise, and ultimately
persuaded the other disciples to inform the Maggid. This
they did through a deputation of three: R. Mendele, R.
Zusya, and R. Levi Yitzchak.

The Maggid answered in the following words: "And
G-d hid it from me! He has the sensitivity of a son. I was
like a son to my Rebbe (the Baal Shem Tov), and he is like
a son to me."

None of us understood what these words of the
Rebbe conveyed — until a few days before his passing**
he told us: "What you sense now, R. Zalmanyu already
sensed last summer..."

And before his passing he took the Rav's hand in his
own and said: "Yud-Tes Kislev is our hillula" (day of
rejoicing).

---

* In the summer of 5532 (תקל"ב; 1772).
** In Kislev 5533 (תקל"ג; 1772).

Rovno: The Maggid lived there for the last few years of his life, until
     soon before his passing.
The big meeting: The disciples had met to consider possible counter-
     measures to the excommunication of Chassidism that had been pub-
     lished by the misnagdim.

And, indeed, the Tuesday of the week of *Parshas Vayeishev*, 5533 (חקל"ג; 1772) was the *hillula* of the Maggid of Mezritch, the day of his passing, while the same day 26 years later — the Tuesday of the week of *Parshas Vayeishev*, 5559 (חקנ"ט; 1798) — was the *hillula* of the Alter Rebbe, the day of his liberation from imprisonment.*

Speaking of this once at a *farbrengen*, the well-known chassid R. Shmuel Dov of Borisov** said that the 26 years between these two events correspond to the four letters of the Name of G-d, whose numerical value totals 26. "The Alter Rebbe," he said, "revealed the path of *yichuda ila'a*."

When I was imprisoned in the Spalerke*** I was reminded of the above *farbrengen*, which my father had told me about. I recalled too that when he had once entered the study of his father the Rebbe Maharash for *yechidus*, his father had expounded a certain concept in *Chassidus*, and had meanwhile said: "My greatgrandfather (the Alter Rebbe) underwent self-sacrifice so that chassidim should have a perception of *yichuda ila'a* and an understanding of *daas elyon*."

4.

The Psalm referred to above opens with these words: תְּפִלָּה לְמֹשֶׁה אִישׁ הָאֱלֹקִים — "A prayer of Moshe, the man of G-d." Commenting on the latter phrase, the *Midrash* asks: "If 'man', why 'G-d'? And if 'G-d', why 'man'?" And one of the answers which it gives to its own question is the following: "When he ascended on high he was a man...; flesh and blood ascended to

---

* I.e., his first imprisonment in Petersburg; 19 Kislev 5559 (חקנ"ט; 1798).
** Prominent chassid of the *Tzemach Tzedek*. Borisov is in the Minsk region.
*** Major prison in Petersburg. The writer was arrested [15] Sivan 5687 (תרפ"ז; 1927). [See: Vol. IV of the present work, Chapter 34; and Vol. VI, passim.]

R. Shmuel Dov: His name appears more often in its more familiar Yiddish form as R. Shmuel Ber.
If 'man', why 'G-d': *Midrash Shocher Tov* 90:5, which is paraphrased in the original.

the presence of the Holy One, Blessed be He, Who is all fire, and Whose angelic messengers are fire. Moshe ascended to Him and is called 'man', and when he descended he is called 'G-d'."

Two points are made here: one is that when Moshe Rabbeinu ascended on high he is called "man" and when he descended he is called "G-d"; the other is that it is in relation to the angels that he is given the name "man". For though angels are called אֵשׁ ("fire"), the souls of mortals are called אִישׁ ("man"). The superiority of *neshamos* ("souls") over angels may be seen in the very word אִישׁ, which comprises the word אֵשׁ and the letter י. Moreover, the added letter י is *within* the אֵשׁ, reflecting the superiority of אִישׁ over אֵשׁ.

Now to explain. The letter י signifies *chochmah*. This is a vast concept, discussed at length in all the classical works on Kabbalah. Briefly, nevertheless: One's initial comprehension of any concept appears as a swift and brief revelation. We observe, for example, that in the case of someone toiling to resolve a problem encountered in his studies, the first intimation of a solution comes to him as a brief flash. This is why *chochmah* is known as the בָּרָק הַמַּבְרִיק ("lightning flash") of the essence of the concept.

The smallest of all the letters is י, but [the writing of] every letter must begin with it, for *yud* is a point (*nekudah*), and everything begins with a point.

The fence (גֶּדֶר; i.e., the defining characteristic) of *chochmah* is *bittul* ("self-effacement"). Indeed, "the fence (סְיָג; i.e., the safeguard) for wisdom is silence" (סְיָג לַחָכְמָה שְׁתִיקָה). The fence (סְיָג) of something is not the thing itself. For example, in the statement, וַעֲשׂוּ סְיָג לַתּוֹרָה — "Make a fence around the Torah," we see that the fence and the Torah are distinct from each other, though the fence does have a connection with the Torah in that it safeguards it. The same applies in relation to *chochmah*, where the fence (גֶּדֶר) — i.e., the vessel — for *chochmah* is *bittul*.

Every letter: Of the script used for a *Sefer* Torah, *tefillin* and *mezuzos*.
The fence...is silence: Tractate *Avos* 3:13.
Fence around the Torah: Tractate *Avos* 1:1.

The essence of *bittul* is hearing and accepting what another says. A wise man (חָכָם) listens to everyone. He is a wise man who from every situation and from every man, whether great or small, can learn a little something.

5.

Every single aspect of my father's conduct had a basis in the *Halachah* or in Kabbalah. And any custom observed by his forebears, the Rebbes, which he had either seen himself, or which he had heard of on reliable authority, was regarded by him as a statute.

Our Sages tell us: חַיָב אָדָם לוֹמַר בִּלְשׁוֹן רַבּוֹ — "One is obligated to quote a statement in the very words of his teacher." With my father, this principle of faithful transmission applied not only to a custom, but even to every nuance of a *niggun* — how each melody was sung, and when it was sung.

The singing of *niggunim* plays a serious part in the way of life of chassidim. Everyone knows, for example, the ten *niggunim* composed by the Alter Rebbe, to be sung on particular occasions. My father taught us the great *niggun* comprising four themes, and explained* that they correspond in ascending order to the Four Worlds — *Atzilus, Beriah, Yetzirah* and *Asiyah*. I have kept a *hanachah*** which I recorded of this talk at the time.

Some of these ten *niggunim* are quite short — single motifs which he would sing at certain times. And in Lubavitch the great *niggun* was sung only on special occasions: on *Yud-Tes*

---

* On *Yud-Tes* Kislev 5663 (תרס"ג; 1902), at the festive meal held with the students of the Tomchei Temimim Yeshivah to celebrate the Alter Rebbe's liberation.

** In Lubavitch this meant the notes of a formal discourse or talk of one of the Rebbes, as recorded by a listener. A discourse committed to writing by the Rebbe and handed to the chassidim for copying was known as a *maamar* or a *ksav*.

From every man: Cf. Tractate *Avos* 4:1, and see p. 225ff. below.

A statute: In the original, חֹק אֲ.

One is obligated...words of his teacher: Tractate *Eduyos* 1:3.

Atzilus...Asiyah: Listed here in descending order (despite the context) because of the familiar acronym, אֲבִי"ע.

Kislev, at the celebration of a circumcision, *bar mitzvah* or wedding, and on Rosh Chodesh Elul.

My teacher the Rashbatz, R. Shmuel Betzalel, once told me something that he himself had heard from the mouth of the *Tzemach Tzedek* at the wedding of R.Shneur-R.Nachum's,* as follows: "Our Sages tell us, הָאוֹמֵר שְׁמוּעָה בְּשֵׁם אוֹמְרָהּ יִרְאֶה בַּעַל שְׁמוּעָה כְּאִלּוּ עוֹמֵד לְנֶגְדּוֹ — 'One who quotes a teaching in the name of another should regard the original speaker as if standing before him.' When one repeats a Torah teaching, one unites oneself with the *Naran (nefesh, ruach, neshamah)* of the one who taught it; when one sings a *niggun* which one has heard from him, one unites oneself with his *chayah* and *yechidah*." The *Tzemach Tzedek* had then proceeded to sing the Alter Rebbe's celebrated *niggun* with the earnest rapture of *dveikus*. His sons sang with him, and all those present shed contrite tears of *teshuvah*.

My grandfather (the Rebbe Maharash) used to sing certain *niggunim* to himself: in the course of *davenen* — during *pesukei dezimrah* and the blessings of the Reading of *Shema*, and while putting on the *tefillin* of Rabbeinu Tam; while he was putting on his *Shabbos* clothes, and again after *Shabbos* as he took them off; and at the *Shabbos* table, by evening and by day.

Among my notes there is a *vort* that I heard my father telling R. Shmuel Dov on the way home from Yalta in 5647

---

* R. Shneur was the son of R. Nachum, son of the Mitteler Rebbe. The year was about 5609 (תר"ט; 1849) or 5610 (תר"י; 1850).

R.Shneur-R.Nachum's: In the generation following the passing of the Alter Rebbe, there were of course many chassidim (and not only descendants) called Shneur. In the absence of commonly-used family names, this familiar Yiddish hyphenated form identifies which Shneur is intended.

Original speaker...standing before him: *Talmud Yerushalmi*, Tractate *Shekalim* 2:5.

Yalta: Port town in Crimea. Due to his delicate health, the Rebbe Rashab spent the greater part of the years 1885-1889 in visiting seaside resorts and health spas in warmer lands — in France, Germany, Holland, Austria and Italy.

(תרמ"ז; 1887) — that a *niggun*, a discourse of *Chassidus*, and *yechidus*, correspond respectively to thought, speech, and action.

Now to clarify. It has been explained* that the bond and union between Rebbe and chassid subsists at various levels.

When a chassid speaks with his Rebbe at *yechidus*, two forces are at play. Firstly, the word *yechidus* means the state of being sole, as in the statement in the *Mishnah*, אֱמֹר מַה שֶׁאָמַרְתָּ לִי בְּיִחוּד — "Say what you said to me when we were alone." Secondly, *yechidus* implies clarity, as in another statement of the *Mishnah*, וְיָדְעוּ בְּיִחוּד כִּי שָׁם הָאָרוֹן נִגְנַז — "And they knew *clearly* [as defined by R. Ovadiah of Bartenura] that the Ark was hidden there." *Yechidus*, then, means not only the union of chassid and Rebbe — which is a product of the bond of the chassid to the Rebbe, and of the innate love which the Rebbe feels for the chassid — but in addition it means clarity. The essential content of *yechidus* is a union that gives rise to clarity in the mind of the chassid as to what course of action he should take. For when a person first begins to tackle the subject of *avodah* and draws up an account of his spiritual situation, his spirits wilt, and confusion sets in. He does not know what his first step should be towards *tikkun*, towards rehabilitating his spiritual condition methodically and effectively.

It is this much-needed clarity that a chassid finds in *yechidus*, through union with his Rebbe. When he tells his

---

* See above, Simchas Torah 5634 [on p. 116ff.].

A discourse of *Chassidus*: In the Old-World usage of the Yiddish original, אַ חֲסִידוּת. In more recent times it would be termed *a maamar*.

Say...when we were alone: Tractate *Sanhedrin* 7:10. R. Ovadiah of Bartenura explains בְּיִחוּד to mean, "There was no one with us."

Knew *clearly*...Ark was hidden: Tractate *Shekalim* 6:2.

Innate love: An approximation for the original, viz., *ahavah atzmis*. This corresponds to the higher of the two levels of *ahavas Yisrael* described in *Derech Mitzvosecha* by the *Tzemach Tzedek* — the level at which one spontaneously overlooks another's imperfections because one loves him to the same degree that one loves one*self*; i.e., because one sees all souls as an extension of one*self*.

Rebbe of his inner spiritual condition, the Rebbe tells him how he should begin the labor of *tikkun.*

The term *maaseh* (translated above as "action") does not refer only to a piece of work such as making a vessel or writing and drawing — instances of motor activity. Rather, *maaseh* is a term that describes a function. The function, or effect, of every faculty of the soul — whether we are speaking of the intellectual faculties of *chochmah, binah* and *daas,* or the emotive attributes of love and awe, *chessed* and *gevurah,* or the faculties of sight and hearing, thought and speech — is called *maaseh.*

This, then, is the explanation of the above *vort* — that a *niggun,* a discourse of *Chassidus,* and *yechidus,* correspond respectively to thought, speech, and action (*maaseh*). When a chassid brings the entire content of his *yechidus* to realization, his bond with his Rebbe extends to the furthest level of *maaseh.* (This subject warrants a deep-reaching explanation, which will be forthcoming when the Almighty provides the opportunity.) When a chassid repeats the *Chassidus* heard from his Rebbe, there is created a union on the level of speech. And through a *niggun,* there comes into being a union on the level of thought.

6.

It was the private custom of each of our forebears, the Rebbes, to deliver certain *maamarim* in the presence of their children. As has been mentioned before, *Biurei Zohar,** the *Siddur,*** and certain *maamarim* in *Pirush HaMilos**** are based on the *maamarim* which the Alter Rebbe delivered for the most

---

* By the Mitteler Rebbe; first published in Kopust in 5576 (רע"ק; 1816).
** Also by the Mitteler Rebbe; first published in Berditchev in 5578 (חע"ק; 1818).
*** As above; first published in Warsaw in 5630 (תר"ל; 1870), though twice as much again remains in ms.

Maaseh (translated above): See p. 215 above.
*Maamarim...*Alter Rebbe...children alone: This took place at the Friday evening meal, while the public *maamarim* were delivered at *Seudah Shelishis,* the Third Meal. "Children" in fact included his sons-in-law, and sometimes a chosen few elder chassidim as well. Some *maamarim*

part in the presence of his children alone.

Likewise, the Alter Rebbe repeated for the *Tzemach Tzedek* alone the *maamarim* which he had first delivered either before the latter's birth or in his early childhood. So, too, my great-grandfather (the *Tzemach Tzedek*) delivered certain *maamarim* for my grandfather (the Rebbe Maharash). And my grandfather delivered certain *maamarim* for my father (the Rebbe Rashab), as well as a number of expository *maamarim* explaining the discourses which he had delivered publicly.

In preparation for my *bar-mitzvah** I had to memorize and master three *maamarim*, one short and two long. My father directed me to repeat one of the long ones on Monday of the week of *Parshas Balak*, which was the twelfth of Tammuz, at the burial places of my grandfather and greatgrandfather.** He told me to repeat the short one publicly, at the festive table on the same day after prayers, and the third *maamar* at a certain time which is recorded in my notes of that time.

No one was to know of this third *maamar*. In those days I saw this as a major trial — but this too I withstood, even though it entailed a major battle with myself. Indeed, my life in that period presented a number of such fresh challenges that seemed to demand more of a struggle than my childhood strength could muster.

From the year 5651 (תרנ"א; 1891) onwards, a new world

---

* On 12 (*Yud-Beis*) Tammuz 5653 (תרנ"ג; 1893).

** The Rebbe Maharash and the *Tzemach Tzedek* respectively, both buried in Lubavitch.

    were addressed to his daughter Freide alone, and her brother — later the Mitteler Rebbe — had to entreat her to repeat them to him (see Chaim Meir Heilman, *Beis Rebbe* (Berditchev, 1900), p. 114). Some of these *maamarim* she committed to writing.

Repeat the short one: This is the familiar *maamar* that is customarily heard at a Lubavitcher *bar-mitzvah*. It begins with the words, אִיתָא בְּמִדְרָשׁ תִּילִים, and was first delivered by the Rebbe Rashab at his own *bar-mitzvah*, 20 Cheshvan 5634 (תרל"ד; 1873).

The third *maamar*: This he repeated in his father's study.

From the year 5651: The writer was then ten years old.

opened up before me, a world of notions that were somehow spiritual. It was at this time that my father began to teach me *Chassidus*, and that I began to feel somehow that there exist comprehensible concepts whose effect is that one should not desire the things which one spontaneously desires, and that one should desire the things which one does not spontaneously desire.

7.

There were three people at the time of whom I was particularly fond. The first, and the one I loved most of all, was my teacher, R. Nissan. From the very first day that I started studying under him I found him lovable. He captivated me with the whole of my heart of childhood innocence — by his clear explanations of the *Gemara* with its commentaries of *Rashi* and *Tosafos*, by the good-natured patience with which he listened to my childish queries, by his fiery joy, by his explanations of the *Aggadah*, and by every move that reflected the refined character traits of a true chassid. R. Nissan the *Melamed* was the first to open my eyes to perceive how in the realm of human conduct good and evil are to be found jumbled together, and the first to explain to me how one ought to abhor evil and choose good.

The second of the beloved people was R. Chanoch Hendel Kurnitzer, and the third was R. Meir Mordechai Borisover. I owe them a great deal for the influence they had on me in my early childhood years, when I was seven or eight years old.

After Pesach 5647 (תרמ"ז; 1887) we were on our way home from Yalta, where my father had been from the middle of Elul 5646 (תרמ"ו; 1886), and spent about three weeks in Kharkov. There, for the first time in my life, I saw assembled in one place all the celebrated chassidim of stature — such as R. Chaim Ber Vilenski (from Kremenchug); R. Dov Ber [Ze'ev] Kozevnikov (from Yekaterinoslav), who was known as the Radaz; R. David Zvi Chein (from Chernigov) — the Radatz; R. Yaakov Mordechai Bespalov (from Poltava) — the Rim; as well as a host of *rabbanim* and well-to-do chassidim. All of this made a strong impression on me, particularly the self-effacement and the respect shown by all these hoary *rabbanim* and chassidim in the presence of my father. Every move of every single one of them became deeply engraved in my young mind, especially the honor accorded my father by the *rav* of Kharkov, R. Yechezkel Arlozorov, a scholar renowned in the rabbinic world, and by his brother R. Eliezer, the well-known *rav* of Ramen.

In honor of Lag BaOmer a festive meal was arranged, which was attended by all of the above-mentioned men of stature, and by so many chassidim that the large room was packed. I clambered on to a chest of drawers that stood at the side, and witnessed the profound respect shown by all those present. I observed their happy faces, as their warm hearts found expression in enthused melodies. Then suddenly they all fell silent, and my father began to expound *Chassidus.*

Back in Lubavitch in time for Shavuos I found myself strongly drawn to R. Hendel. I began to make a special point of listening to whatever he said, and watching him as he prayed.

That Shavuos I began to take an interest in the chassidim who had made the journey to Lubavitch for *Yom-Tov.* All around me I heard names — R. Gershon Ber, R. Shalom-R.Hillel's, R. Zalman Neimark, R. Avraham Ber of Bobruisk, R. Shmuel Ber of Borisov, R. Yoel of Podobranka, R. Avraham of Zhebin.

Then there was R. Pinchas Leib. He had been my grandfather's *gabbai sheni,* an assistant of the *gabbai* R. Levi Yitzchak. R. Pinchas Leib was a true chassid — *a chassidisher Yid* — and a really good friend. Nowadays he spent most of his time in our house, because he was busy copying various manuscript *maamarim* for my father — almost my father's aide. He used to speak to me warmly, telling me stories about my grandfather, and setting out the praiseworthy attributes of each of the above-mentioned elder chassidim.

I clambered on to a chest of drawers: The writer was almost seven years old
    at the time.

That Shavuos was the first *Yom-Tov* on which I was present for the whole time during which *Chassidus* was being expounded in the *minyan* that was held in the little hall* where my father used to deliver his *maamarim* on Shavuos (unlike *Shabbos*, when this would take place in his home). I understood nothing, but I observed everything closely; the proceedings interested me intensely.

Since I had learned little during my almost three-quarters of a year in Yalta, my studies had fallen behind the expectations for my age. A temporary private tutor was therefore hired for me, by the name of R. Yitzchak Gershon, whose task was to prepare me in the few months remaining until the new term for admission to the *cheder* of the advanced *Gemara* class.

At this point an extraordinary assiduity developed within me, and in those few months I managed with G-d's help to attain the standard required for admission to the class of an efficient teacher — R. Shimshon the *Melamed* — under whom I studied for three years. As a teacher, he carried out his tasks well in all respects, but as a person he was far from good-natured, so that through various circumstances I was brought even closer to R. Hendel Kurnitzer and R. Meir Mordechai Borisover. Whenever I had free time from *cheder* I would sit down next to them to hear a story or a *vort*.

R. Hendel's *davenen*, the way he read *Tehillim*, his admirable character; R. Meir Mordechai's settling down at certain times to study (he was a businessman who had time available only in the evenings, when he would take a seat in the little hall and study — in such a pleasant manner!); — all these left a mighty impact on me. I felt a special degree of attentiveness and respect towards them, and would find delight in serving R. Hendel a cup of tea, or bringing a little something for R. Meir Mordechai.

---

* In Lubavitch, this *(der kleiner zal)* was the name of the hall in which prayers took place, while the hall in which the students of the Tomchei Temimim Yeshivah studied was known as "the big hall" *(der groisser zal)*.

Quite often R. Meir Mordechai would listen to my recitation of the *Gemara* that I had studied. When he saw that I had grasped a particular passage properly, he would afford me pleasure by teaching me the novel interpretation of one of the commentators. And R. Hendel would often listen as I recited the *Mishnayos* that I had committed to memory.

The greatest joy of all was listening to R. Hendel telling of how he had grown up among elder chassidim. In fact he had even known chassidim of the Alter Rebbe. From every story or custom that he recounted of the chassidim of bygone years he would derive a moral, a lesson in proper conduct. With him, the love of a fellow Jew was one of the key lessons. Whatever he said sprang from a heart inflamed by the enthusiasm of a chassid, and found expression in mild words which sank deep into the listener's heart.

8.

By the winter term of the year 5650 (תר"ן; 1889-1890) I had been admitted to the class of the above-mentioned R. Nissan the *Melamed*. With him I began to experience the first really happy days of my childhood, and all three — R. Nissan, R. Hendel and R. Meir Mordechai — had become the dearly-loved folk with whom I had to share my every glad moment. It goes without saying, then, that keeping my big secret of the two *maamarim* that I now had to master for my *bar-mitzvah* entailed a major battle. But my father's injunction that no one should know of them was observed minutely: no one even detected that I had a secret.

After my *bar-mitzvah* my father would every so often deliver a *maamar* for me alone. These private discourses were generally unrelated to the *maamarim* that he would deliver on

---

Novel interpretation: In the original, *a chiddush.*
Chassidim of the Alter Rebbe: Some 74 years had elapsed since his passing in 1812.
A moral: in the Heb./Yid. original, א. בְּכֵן.
By the winter term: The writer was then nine years old.

Shabbos to the chassidim at large, though a minor portion of one of them was occasionally included. Most of them were very short, dealt with topics in *avodah*, and included parables expounded at length. Among other things he would point out exactly which details of each parable were relevant to the lesson being illustrated. Moreover, apart from teaching me each *maamar*, systematically explaining every concept according to the extent of my grasp, he taught me how to study.

On Sunday of the week of *Parshas Pinchas* [i.e., six days after my *bar-mitzvah*] my father called me into his study and said: "It is true that this is a deferred fast, but it is the first fast of your 'being a man'."

This was a reference to the *maamar* that my father had delivered two months earlier, based on the verse, וְחָזַקְתָּ וְהָיִיתָ לְאִישׁ — "Be strong, and be a man." It was then Sunday of the week of *Parshas Acharei-Mos-Kedoshim*, 11 Iyar 5653 (תרנ"ג; 1893), and the occasion was my *yom chinuch* ("the day of my training") — i.e., the day on which (to all appearances) I began to put on *tefillin*. In fact I had begun to put on *tefillin* much earlier.*

That *maamar* had discussed the four terms for "man" — *adam, enosh, ish, gever*. In it my father described an admirable *adam* and a fine *ish*, and showed how being termed *enosh* or *gever* depends on each man alone.

Adam and *ish*, he pointed out, are terms describing the essential level of the individual concerned. Specifically: *Adam*

---

* One of those present asked when the Rebbe had begun, to which the reply was: "It's a well-known rule [quoting a Yiddish folk expression]: 'One doesn't tell tales out of *cheder*.'"

A deferred fast: When the 17th of Tammuz falls on a ·*Shabbos*, the fast is deferred to Sunday, whereby it loses a certain degree of stringency.

Be strong: *I Kings* 2:2.

Began to put on *tefillin*: According to the usual custom in Lubavitch circles, one begins to put on *tefillin* two months before the date of the *bar-mitzvah*, though without a *berachah* for the first few weeks. (See *HaYom Yom*, entry for 2 Menachem Av.)

Terms describing the essential level...: In the original, תּוֹאֲרִים עַצְמִיִּים.

speaks of *mochin,* i.e., the level of *avodah* which focuses on *Chabad* — divine service that is generated by intellectual activity. *Ish* speaks of *middos,* i.e., the level of *avodah* which focuses on the emotive attributes of the soul and on the refinement of one's character traits. *Enosh* and *gever* are (as it were) adjectival terms describing the essential levels of *adam* and *ish.* Specifically: *Enosh* indicates weakness, while *gever* indicates strength. That is to say, that if the level of *avodah* characterized as that of *adam* or of *ish* is executed in a weak manner, then it may be described by the term *enosh.* If, however, an *adam* or an *ish* executes the *avodah* expected of him energetically, then it may be described by the term *gever.* This, then, is the meaning of my father's above statement that being termed *enosh* or *gever* depends on each man alone.

That was the first *maamar* in which I experienced a pleasure that was distinctively personal. In that *maamar* I sensed the meaning of "Rebbe" according to my understanding of those days, and felt the meaning of "father".

I remember the *farbrengen* at which the above three chassidim sat together after that *maamar,* each of them explaining it to me in his own style. R. Meir Mordechai explained the level of *adam* as spoken of there, R. Hendel discussed the level of *ish,* and my teacher R. Nissan clarified the use of the terms *enosh* and *gever,* pointing out how one's weakness and strength depend only on the manner in which one's *avodah* is carried out in practice.

[Now, two months later, soon after my *bar-mitzvah,* my father took up the subject of fasting.]

"On one's first fast-day," he said, "one should fast — and I mean fasting, not losing weight."

And he proceeded to explain himself: "Abstention from eating and drinking is called losing weight, whereas if one toils away at one's studies while not eating and drinking, that is called fasting."

Losing weight: In the Yid. original, *dar'n* ("dieting").

"Today," he went on, "you will review mentally all three
maamarim that you have prepared for your *bar-mitzvah*, as well
as a certain number of chapters of *Mishnayos* which you will
memorize" — this was in addition to the allotment of chapters
of *Mishnayos* that I had to memorize every day — "and at four
you will come to see me in my study."

When I came, he told me to recite all three *maamarim* from
memory. Since this took a good few hours he told me to go
and rest a little while between one *maamar* and the next.

The warmth that my father showed me gave me the
greatest of pleasure: I felt no difficulty in fasting at all. Before
I left his study he warned me that no one was to know that I
was fasting.

On fast-days in Lubavitch we used to *daven Minchah* late,
and intentionally so. I don't mean after sunset, but in the late
afternoon, such as eight o'clock on Shivah-Asar BeTammuz
and seven o'clock on Tishah BeAv. When I went to *shul* for
Minchah, then, I very much wanted it to be known that I was
now a grown-up, that I was fasting. But [I saw to it that] no
one noticed.

From Monday of the week of *Parshas Pinchas*, the 19th of
Tammuz, until *Shabbos Parshas Vaeschanan*, my daily task was to
review and recite to myself from memory one of the three
maamarim in a certain order.

On Tuesday of the week of *Parshas Eikev*, the 19th of
Menachem-Av, my father called me into his study and said
that I should tell my *melamed*, R. Nissan, that my father had
told me that I should see him that afternoon, so would he
excuse me from *cheder* for a few hours. My *melamed* gave his
permission at once. But I was restless, curious as to what was
in store for me, and it was with impatience that I waited out
the time until Mendel the *Meshares* came to the *cheder* to say
that my father was calling for me.

From Monday: The day after the fast.
Until *Shabbos Parshas Vaeschanan*: I.e., for almost four weeks.
On Tuesday: Three days later.

When I entered his study my father said: "We're getting close to Elul. This is your first Elul since becoming a man (*ish*), so one needs to prepare for it. I'm going to say a *maamar* for you, and then I'll help you commit it to memory so that you'll know it well. Then you'll recite it from memory by yourself and review it mentally. But no one is to know of it."

My father then delivered for me a brief discourse that began by quoting the verse, וְהֵסִיר ה' מִמְּךָ כָּל חֹלִי — "G-d will remove all illness from you." I spent the whole afternoon with my father, until I had mastered that *maamar* thoroughly. On the following *Shabbos*, *Parshas Eikev*, he publicly delivered an expanded version of the same *maamar*, though it was the original version that he instructed me to continue reviewing until he would say another *maamar* for me.

This recurred from time to time. For example: In the summer of 5654 (תרנ"ד; 1894), when my father travelled to Liman* for health reasons, he took me along to accompany him as far as the Smolensk station. (There we would have to wait a few hours for the Oreol-Odessa train, quietly: no one in Smolensk knew that my father was passing through.) And in the railway carriage on the way from Rudny** to Smolensk my father delivered a short *maamar* for me that began with the quotation, בֶּן ג' שָׁנִים הִכִּיר אַבְרָהָם אֶת בּוֹרְאוֹ — "At three years of age Avraham recognized his Creator."

9.

When my father was about to set out in the train headed for Oreol he said: "Our Sages teach, אֵיזֶהוּ חָכָם הַלּוֹמֵד מִכָּל אָדָם — 'Who is wise? He who learns from every man.' Now one

---

* Health resort near Odessa, at the mouth of the Dniester on the Black Sea.
** This was the nearest railway station to Lubavitch, the 12 kilometers from which one would travel by wagon.

G-d will remove: *Deut.* 7:15.
At three years: Tractate *Nedarim* 32a.
Who is wise: Tractate *Avos* 4:1; and see p. 213 above.

doesn't have to be wise to be a learner, for learning is the very
definition of the level called 'man' (adam): a man is someone
who learns, and one who does not learn is not a man. But he
who learns *from every man* is wise. That is, a wise man is he who
in every person finds something good from which to learn."

Learning is an expression of *seichel* (intellect), and *seichel*
involves deliberateness. The term *ish* ("man") refers to *middos*,
but only to *middos* that are guided by the *seichel*. One's natural
middos, by contrast, are a fiery flame, whereas אִישׁ *(ish)* is made
up of the word אֵשׁ *(esh*, meaning "fire") and the letter י *(yud,*
which indicates the intellect). That is to say, אִישׁ signifies the
kind of fire in which the qualities indicated by י — *chochmah* and
seichel — are to be found.

Now this superiority of אִישׁ is significant only when a
contrast is drawn with the angels, who are called אֵשׁ, while
souls [i.e., of people] are at the level of אִישׁ. In fact, however,
the real superiority of souls lies in their belonging to the level
of *adam,* and not that of *ish.*

The pre-eminence of Moshe Rabbeinu [, nevertheless,] is
stated in terms of his being at the level of *ish.* Thus we read:
וְהָאִישׁ מֹשֶׁה עָנָו מְאֹד מִכֹּל הָאָדָם אֲשֶׁר עַל פְּנֵי הָאֲדָמָה — "Now the man *(ish)*
Moshe was very humble, more so than all the men on the face
of the earth." This is paradoxical. Since *adam* refers to man as
an intellectual being, and *ish* refers to the *middos,* the level of
adam is clearly loftier than that of *ish.* Moreover, the Torah
proceeds to speak in praise of Moshe Rabbeinu as follows: בְּכָל
בֵּיתִי נֶאֱמָן הוּא — "Throughout My house he is a trusted servant."
On this Ibn Ezra comments: "Like a member of the household
[who enters and makes his requests at will]." And, in the next
verse: פֶּה אֶל פֶּה אֲדַבֶּר בּוֹ — "With him I speak face to face." Ibn

---

Deliberateness: In the original, מְתִינוּת.

Ish...refers to *middos:* Throughout this Section, *middos* means the man-
     ifestation of a person's emotive attributes — love, fear, and the like —
     and character traits.

Now the man Moshe: *Num.* 12:3.

Throughout My house: *Num.* 12:7.

With him I speak: *Num.* 12:8.

Ezra's comment: "With no intermediary." Yet a man of this stature is described by the term *ish* rather than *adam!*

This paradox is explained in *Chassidus.* The term *adam*, as we have seen, refers to *seichel.* Now *seichel* is a lofty thing — but it is not a consummation. The term *ish* refers to *middos,* and good *middos* do reflect the attainment of perfection. For after all the superlatives that the Almighty employs concerning Moshe Rabbeinu, attesting to his being at the level of *adam* — that to the Almighty he is "like a member of the household," for he is at the level of *chochmah deAtzilus;* that "with him I speak face to face," without intermediaries, because the level of *chochmah* signifies *bittul,* utter self-effacement (as the Alter Rebbe says in *Tanya* when characterizing the lofty level of the *sefirah* of *chochmah)* — the noblest level attributed to him is that of *ish.* Hence, the more profound the *chochmah,* the more does it find expression in the perfection of the *middos.*

On Shavuos 5679 (תרע״ט; 1919), when we were in Rostov* on the Don, my father delivered three *maamarim,*** all long and complex. The third *maamar* included a discussion on the advantage gained (as it were) by the Divine Plan when the ultimate purpose of the beginning of a process is realized only at its end. In the course of this discussion my father said: "This is what is meant by the verse, וְהָאִישׁ מֹשֶׁה עָנָו מְאֹד מִכֹּל הָאָדָם אֲשֶׁר

---

* In the month of MarCheshvan 5676 (תרע״ו; 1915), when the German army reached the border of White Russia, the Rebbe Rashab left Lubavitch and settled in Rostov on the Don, where he passed away, on 2 Nissan 5680 (תר״פ; 1920), and where he lies buried. [See p. 42 above.]
** On the first night of Shavuos, the *maamar* opening with the words, אָנֹכִי ה' אֱלֹקֶיךָ — "I am the L-rd your G-d"; on the second night, the *maamar* וַיְדַבֵּר אֱלֹקִים אֵת כָּל הַדְּבָרִים הָאֵלֶּה — "And G-d spoke all these words"; at the midday meal of the second day, וַיֹּאמֶר מֹשֶׁה אֶל הָעָם אַל תִּירָאוּ — "And Moshe said to the people: 'Do not fear.'"

The Alter Rebbe says in *Tanya:* Ch. 43.
Ultimate purpose... only at its end: In the original, נְעִיצַת הַתְּחָלָה בַּסּוֹף (lit., "the beginning being wedged in the end" — when the wheel comes full circle, so to speak).
This is what is meant: The meaning is spelled out at the end of this paragraph.

עַל פְּנֵי הָאֲדָמָה — 'Now the man Moshe was very humble, more so
than all the men on the face of the earth.' For Moshe Rabbeinu saw the Book of Adam. There he saw that in the last
years before the footsteps of *Mashiach* there would be a generation of people devoid of G-dly understanding, i.e., that their
understanding could not be defined as such, in particular
when compared to the understanding of Moshe Rabbeinu,
next to which their attainments would be reckoned as
nought. He saw moreover that there would not be real *avodah*
in the mind and the heart, but only the fulfillment of the
mitzvos in actual practice. He saw, however, that this would be
accomplished through self-sacrifice — that there would be
numerous physical and spiritual obstacles obscuring their
path, but that they would withstand every hindrance and
survive every trial, and fulfill the commandments with *mesirus
nefesh*. It was in this that Moshe Rabbeinu saw the ultimate
purpose of the beginning — of the beginning that sprang
from the innermost essence of the Infinite One. And contemplating all the above, he grew exceedingly humble, since the
people of that generation were so much higher than he."

Every year, on the second day of Shavuos* after the
midday meal, my father would come to visit me. In the course
of the *farbrengen* in my home that Shavuos he discussed the
concept of וְהָאִישׁ מֹשֶׁה — "the man (*ish*) Moshe." He pointed out
that the distinctive quality of Moshe Rabbeinu lay in the
perfection of his *middos* in keeping with the level of *adam* that
he had attained in keeping with the transcendent reaches of

---

* From Sukkos 5658 (תרנ"ח; 1897), after the marriage of the writer, until the
year 5680 (תר"פ; 1919), the Rebbe Rashab used to visit his son the Rebbe
Rayatz every *Yom-Tov* and on *Yud-Tes* Kislev.

The Book of Adam: In the original, סִפְרוֹ שֶׁל אָדָם הָרִאשׁוֹן. The *Arizal* writes
   that the souls of all generations are comprised in Adam. (See the
   Tzemach Tzedek on the *mitzvah* of *ahavas Yisrael* in *Derech Mitzvosecha.*)

The footsteps of *Mashiach:* In the original, בְּעִקְּבוֹת מְשִׁיחָא.

He saw, however: In the original, וְגַם (lit., "also"), but this meaning is
   clear from the context.

The transcendent reaches of *chochmah:* In the original, בְּמַעֲלַת הַפְלָאַת הַחָכְמָה.

chochmah that he had attained. (It is explained in *Chassidus*, in one of its more abstruse areas, that this transcendent quality of *chochmah* — כֹּחַ הַהַפְלָאָה שֶׁבַּחָכְמָה — undergoes two stages, which are known literally as enrobing and disrobing.)

10.

The above discussion will give us a new insight into the verse which we looked at a little while ago. It will be recalled that, commenting on the description of Moshe Rabbeinu as אִישׁ הָאֱלֹקִים — "the man of G-d," the *Midrash* says that "when he ascended on high he was a man *(ish)*." That is to say: When he was in the midst of his loftiest flights of divine understanding he remembered that he was at the level of *ish*, a man of *middos*.

There are people who in the course of serving G-d through prayer set about their meditation in a way that involves a solid grasp of their subject. One can see that they are *davenen* as one ought to, and that they are duly aroused. But when after *davenen* such a person steps into the big world, he is almost like someone else: he can stumble in various ways involving *middos*, which are not at all in keeping with his *davenen*.

The reason for this is that while he was *davenen* he did not work on himself, toiling toward the refinement of his own *middos*. Prayer today replaces the sacrifices, and a sacrifice has to be accompanied by a verbalized confession. Prayer without self-directed *avodah* is a sacrifice without a confession. In such a case, a person is close [to his Source] during prayer, but when he comes in contact with the outside world after prayer he is deficient.

This then is what is meant by the statement of the *Midrash* that "when Moshe Rabbeinu ascended on high he was

---

Disrobing: In the original, כֹּחַ הַהַפְשָׁטָה — abstraction. Enrobing: In the original, כֹּחַ הַהַלְבָּשָׁה — perceiving *makkif* in reality.

It will be recalled: See p. 211ff. above.

Prayer today replaces the sacrifices: Cf. וּנְשַׁלְּמָה פָרִים שְׂפָתֵינוּ — "We will render [the prayer of] our lips in place of [the sacrifice of] bullocks" (*Hosea* 14:3).

a man *(ish)"*: he remembered that he had *middos*, and that they had to be refined.

Now the above-quoted *Midrash* went on to say that when Moshe Rabbeinu descended from the heavens he is called "G-d" (אֱלֹקִים). The name *Elokim* signifies power, judgment, and *tzimtzum*. There is a verse that says: וְלֹא נָחָם אֱלֹקִים דֶּרֶךְ אֶרֶץ פְּלִשְׁתִּים כִּי קָרוֹב הוּא — "G-d (*Elokim*) did not lead them by way of the land of the Philistines (Plishtim), for it was near." On this verse the Alter Rebbe comments in *Torah Or** that פְּלִשְׁתִּים signifies expansiveness — being broad and wide open, like an open-ended alley (מָבוֹי מְפוּלָשׁ).

On the one hand, the characteristic of Plishtim is to be found in the realm of holiness (פְּלִשְׁתִּים דִּקְדוּשָׁה). Thus, the unbounded and open-ended joy with which a person gives expression to his cleaving to G-d belongs to the level of loving Him בְּכָל מְאֹדֶךָ — "with all your might." On the other hand, the parallel characteristic of Plishtim is to be found in the realm of impurity (פְּלִשְׁתִּים דִּקְלִיפָּה). This finds expression in the evil attribute known as scoffing (לֵצָנוּת) — wisecracking, empty-headed hilarity, and idle chatter. The Psalmist writes, וּבְמוֹשַׁב לֵצִים לֹא יָשָׁב — "[Happy is the man...] who does not sit where scoffers sit," and on this phrase the Sages comment: אֵלּוּ פְּלִשְׁתִּים — "This refers to Plishtim."

There is thus a lesson to be learned from the above-quoted verse: "G-d did not lead them by way of the land of the Plishtim, for it was near, [for G-d said: Lest the people regret] when they see war, and return to Egypt." It is not the way of G-d to be in a state of excessively revealed joy as soon as one gets out of [one's personal] Egypt. For אֶת זֶה לְעֻמַּת זֶה עָשָׂה הָאֱלֹקִים —

---

* A volume of *maamarim* of the Alter Rebbe, first published in Kopust in 5597 (תקצ"ז; 1837).

G-d did not lead them: *Ex.* 13:17.

Expansiveness...open-ended alley: On this concept see p. 47 above, and footnote there.

Happy is the man: *Ps.* 1:1.

This refers to Plishtim: Cf. Tractate *Avodah Zarah* 19a.

Out of [one's personal] Egypt: On this spiritual liberation, see *Tanya,* Ch. 47.

"G-d created one side opposite the other" [i.e., everything on the holy side of the universe has its counterpart in the realm of impurity]. Thus, counterpoised to the joy that stems from holiness there is a *kelippah* — the joy derived from vanities.

The verse includes the phrase, כִּי קָרוֹב הוּא — "For it was near." The shell or peel (Heb., *kelippah*) envelops a fruit totally, and so too is the animal soul closely bound up with a person. Moreover, the *Gemara* calls the Evil Inclination "a skilled craftsman." He is most accomplished in his work. He begins by getting a person [over-]involved in things that are permitted — as can readily be seen, and as every individual *(nebbich)* senses the situation within himself.

It is hard to speak — but it is painful to remain silent.

How is it possible that a person who has just been involved in his *davenen,* his *dveikus* finding expression ardently in the sweetness of his voice, should now — when he comes out into the world — not only bring along nothing, but moreover be jolly, with a wisecrack to spare, and be *pleased with himself?* This very self-satisfaction is the Plishtim of the *kelippah,* of the unholy side of the universe.

Every peel or shell (*kelippah*) bears a relation to the fruit that it covers. There are fruits whose *kelippah* can also be eaten — but only after being cooked. Though the fruit may be edible raw, the *kelippah* will not be digestible unless it is first scalded and stewed.

There is no need for this to be explained at length: everyone knows what is intended. This is the thrust of the statement of the Sages, that when Moshe Rabbeinu descended from the heavens he is called *Elokim.* For [after the *avodah* of *davenen*] a person needs to employ powerful restraints, to stand in judgment over himself, and to delimit himself *(tzimtzum)* — in order to know what his tasks are in this world.

G-d created one side: *Eccles.* 7:14.
Animal soul closely bound up: See *Tanya,* Ch. 29 (אֲבָל בֵּינוֹנִי כו').
A skilled craftsman: Cf. שֶׁכַּךְ אוּמָנְתוֹ שֶׁל יֵצֶר הָרָע (Tractate *Shabbos* 105b).
Restraints…judgment…*tzimtzum:* See p. 230 above.

This is the path blazed by the Rebbe whose liberation we are celebrating now, in order to enable everyone to become involved in the dual *avodah* implied by the words אִישׁ הָאֱלֹקִים — during one's *avodah* of intellectual endeavor, to be working simultaneously at the level of *ish (middos)*; after one's *davenen*, when one resumes one's daily life, to be a judge over oneself.

Now to consider the words of our verse afresh: תְּפִלָּה לְמֹשֶׁה אִישׁ הָאֱלֹקִים. The word תְּפִלָּה implies joining, bonding. The spiritual leaders of Israel are called "Moshe", as in the well-known quotation, אִתְפַּשְׁטוּתָא דְמֹשֶׁה בְּכָל דָּרָא — "An extension of Moshe is to be found in every generation." Our verse thus intimates that each such Moshe bonds the people of Israel to the Almighty, bringing them to the level at which every one of them can become אִישׁ הָאֱלֹקִים, in the dual sense explained above.

The Rebbe whose liberation: I.e., the Alter Rebbe.

Implies joining: See p. 171 above, and footnote there.

An extension of Moshe: *Zohar*, paraphrased in *Iggeres HaKodesh*, end of Epistle 27.

Chapter 5a

Pesach 5694 (תרצ״ד; 1934)

[Warsaw]

1.

In the life of the townsfolk of Lubavitch, pride of place was occupied by the festivals of the year. Great and small alike — that is to say, from the most erudite to the most unsophisticated — were involved first in the preparations for each *Yom-Tov* and then in the *Yom-Tov* itself, with all their faculties and senses, minds and hearts, mouths and ears, hands and feet.

The tenor of life in the *shtetlach* — the provincial towns, as some people like to call them — was clearly distinguishable from that of the typical city. In the townlet, earnestness and truth were more in evidence. This is especially true when we are speaking of a bygone era, when in all circles these qualities were prized to quite a different degree. Even 40 or 50 years ago the little *shtetl* radiated its pristine aura. On the face of every small-town Jew one could clearly perceive our noble lineage of 3000 years, the lineage of the sons of Avraham, Yitzchak and Yaakov.

True enough, the *shtetl* had to take the advice of our Sages — that one should not become overly familiar with those in power — very seriously indeed. In fact people lived in dread of "the sound of a rustling leaf." If anyone caught sight of some government official walking down the street, his heart fluttered within him. On the other hand, though, there was delight and moral beauty to be sensed in the secure and placid

---

Overly familiar with those in power: Tractate *Avos* 1:10. This sentence is of course a euphemistic understatement.
Sound of a rustling leaf: *Lev.* 26:36.

lifestyle of the *shtetl* which in a certain measure was the result of people's contentedness with whatever they had.

The humblest townlet could boast its own charitable institutions and voluntary mutual-aid societies — its *Talmud Torah* for teaching the young, its *Bikkur Cholim* society for visiting the sick, its *Lechem LaEvyonim* society for feeding the poor, its *Malbish Arumim* brotherhood for clothing the threadbare, its *Gemilus Chessed* fund for interest-free loans, its annual *Moas Chittim* appeal to provide *matzos* for the needy, and so on. And without exception, every single townsman had a share in each one of these causes by his frequent contributions of a kopek or a *tzveier*. It was a clean life, an expression of solid character traits.

The *Ein Yaakov* that was studied around the *shul* table between *Minchah* and *Maariv* every evening at dusk, the *Midrash* and the *Pirkei Avos* that were taught in *shul* every *Shabbos*, — these were a wellspring of life-giving waters, a fount of noble *middos,* and a guidepost for all the simple townsfolk, letting people know for what reason they were living in this world.

What a spiritual delight it was in summer to observe how late on a *Shabbos* afternoon, after a few hours' Torah study indoors, little groups of people would gather outside the

---

Talmud Torah: Torah school for children before *yeshivah* age; lit., "the study of Torah" — a Talmudic phrase, as in *Pe'ah* 1:1 (paraphrased in the Morning Blessings, in the paragraph beginning *Elu devarim*).

Bikkur Cholim: Lit., "visiting the sick"; source: as above.

Lechem LaEvyonim: Lit., "bread for the poor"; cf. *Ps.* 132:15.

Malbish Arumim: Lit., "clothing the naked"; the phrase is borrowed from one of the Morning Blessings.

Gemilus Chessed: Lit., "performing deeds of kindness." In addition to this broader meaning, usage has given this phrase — and so too the acronym of its Hebrew initials, pronounced *"Gmach"* — the additional specific meaning of (a) an interest-free loan, or (b) a fund offering such loans. Source: as for *Talmud Torah* (above).

Maos Chittim: Lit., "money for wheat."

An expression of solid character traits: This phrase translates the *ad hoc* Hebrew-Yiddish adjective, *middos-tovos-diker*.

various *batei midrash*. Over here Shmuel the Tailor is telling his cronies what R. Yaakov Leizer quoted from the *Midrash* about Korach's claims against Aharon and Moshe Rabbeinu. Over there Avraham Donye the Butcher is repeating for a little knot of friends what he has just heard from R. Mendel the *Melamed* — how one day, in the times of the *Mishnah*, R. Yochanan asked his disciples which in their opinion was the most beautiful virtue that a man could choose to pursue.

Over the generations, the public teaching of *Ein Yaakov*, *Midrash* and *Pirkei Avos* has furnished our people with countless multitudes of upright men and loyal Jews. Whether they were on their way to a nearby village — and many townsfolk used to do business with the surrounding villages — or whether they were standing at their stalls in the marketplace, they would ponder over what they had heard in the *beis midrash* the previous evening between *Minchah* and *Maariv*. It was with marked impatience that they would wait for *Shabbos* to come around, for then there would be a more relaxed opportunity to hear a new Torah thought, and perhaps an insightful anecdote about a *tanna*, or an *amora*, or a *gaon*.

In days gone by, every Torah thought, every story from *Ein Yaakov*, every passage from the *Midrash*, every narrative from the life of a *tzaddik*, found its due niche in every Jewish heart. The same is true of a *vort* from the teachings of *Chassidus*. By its very nature abstract, such a *vort* was certainly not easy for an unlettered person to grasp. It was nevertheless so potent that it infused vitality into his daily reading of the *Psalms* and into his performance of the *mitzvos*. And wherever one turned one could sense a deep-seated respect for the Torah scholar, and an all-encompassing love for the Torah itself.

2.

Thought and imagination can place a person in whatever

Midrash about Korach's claims: Cf. *Rashi* on *Num.* 16:1ff.
R. Yochanan asked: Tractate *Avos* 2:10.

time and location he chooses. If he so desires, then through thought and imagination he can place himself in the past of decades ago, and experience it in his present time and location just as he experienced it then.

Our mentor the Baal Shem Tov says that "a man is where his will is." For this reason one needs to exercise even greater vigilance with one's thought than with one's speech. *Chassidus* discusses at length the differences between the three faculties — thought, speech, and deed — that are known as the garments of the soul. They are so called — *levushim* — not only because they are the faculties in which the soul is clothed, just as the body is clothed in garments, but because through them the soul manifests itself. When we say by way of parable that the body is a garment to the soul, we do not only mean that the soul is clothed in the body; we also mean that through this garment — the body — the soul reveals itself in its true essence: we see that its very being is life, and that its function is to give life. So it is with thought, speech, and deed: through these three garments the soul manifests itself.

Of these three garments — *machshavah, dibbur,* and *maaseh* — the most subtle is thought. It is known as *levush hameuchad,* because it is constantly united with the soul. The outermost garment, the garment of action, is a *levush hanifrad,* a garment separate from the soul, and speech is *levush hamechubar,* a garment connected with the soul — though connected only intermittently, for, as it is written, "There is a time to remain silent, and a time to speak." Thought, however, is a garment that is united with the soul constantly.

In the innermost garment, thought, the tension between good and evil is of more moment than it is in the other

---

A man is where his will is: Lit., "Where a man's will is, there he is himself." Another version reads: "...where his thought is." See p. 1 above.

Even greater vigilance: See *Tanya, Iggeres HaKodesh,* end of Epistle 22.

Garments of the soul: Cf. *Tanya,* Ch. 4.

A time to remain silent: *Eccles.* 3:7, paraphrased in the original.

garments — deed and speech. An improper thought constitutes a blemish, as is made clear in the explanation that
Chassidus gives of the statement in the *Gemara* that "the
contemplation of sin is more reprehensible than is sin itself."

Not only do thought and imagination have the power to
place a person in the distant past, to the point that here, in his
present situation, he is enabled to experience things long
since seen with the same sensations as he then experienced,
but moreover, now that he is older and more experienced,
with a certain lifetime behind him, he is able to view the same
events more perceptively.

In my thoughts and my imagination I often relive sights
which I first saw in Lubavitch at different times. Sometimes
these were sights of lofty things — the Rebbe, my father,
delivering a discourse of *Chassidus;* the variety of paths in
avodah exemplified by the chassidim around me; chassidim
sitting together at a *farbrengen;* or the way in which ordinary
baalei batim and well-to-do guests would listen to the teaching
of *Chassidus.* Sometimes these were sights of more modest
subjects, such as the way in which the homespun folk of the
shtetl conducted their lives day by day. But whichever sights I
recall, I arrive at the fundamental conclusion that the light of
Chassidus infuses life into whoever is in its range. This is true
even of those who are not permeated by the life of *Chassidus,*
but who are encompassed by its aura, in the manner of an *or
makkif.* They too find that their performance of the *mitzvos* is
invigorated by a unique vitality.

The plain *baalei batim* and common craftsmen who lived in
Lubavitch were no doubt quite ordinary people, like all the
Jews of all the Jewish townlets. The *chassidisher* atmosphere
nevertheless left its clear impression on them, and as was the
case in all such places, it was especially in evidence in the
course of the preparations for each festival, and during the
Yom-Tov itself.

Contemplation of sin: Tractate *Yoma* 29a, and see *Iggeres HaKodesh, loc. cit.*

3.

In Lubavitch, each *Yom-Tov* had its own distinctive preludes and preparations, its customs, and its pious superadditions to customs. I am not referring to the *hiddurim* with which Jews throughout the world commonly enhance their observance of laws and customs, nor am I referring to the customs which are practiced by chassidim at large. I am speaking of a genre of distinctive customs that were popularly labelled in these terms: "This is what R. Yankel *Zip* used to do"; "This is how R. Yisrael *der Lebediker* ('the lively one') used to do it."

In the days when people used to be measured by their scholastic attainments, these two townsmen of Lubavitch would have been reckoned as ordinary people with a certain scholarly background. The field in which they shone was their deeds. In bygone years men of good deeds were not only more numerous, but of a different class: whatever they did was done in a spirit of innocent integrity. There were men of deeds who in that field were men of stature.

The saintly R. Yissachar Dov Kobilniker, the one-time *maggid* of Lubavitch, was one of the unassuming disciples of the Baal Shem Tov, and a teacher of the Alter Rebbe in his childhood. R. Yissachar Dov once related that when he first came to Lubavitch around the year 5485 (תפ״ה; 1725) as the new son-in-law of one of the local townsmen, he even then managed to make the acquaintance of R. Yisrael *der Lebediker*, by that time a man of ninety or more. And he recalled that whenever R. Yisrael would *daven* or memorize chapters from the *Tanach* or *Mishnayos*, he would do so with all the vigor of a lively young man.

R. Yisrael often used to say: "A *mitzvah* performed with-

In a spirit of innocent integrity: In the original, בִּתְמִימוּת.

R. Yissachar Dov Kobilniker: The Alter Rebbe once referred to him as "the treasure of my heart and soul; he is a friend and brother to me" (*Igros Kodesh*, Letters of the Alter Rebbe, p. 42).

A *mitzvah* ∴ without *kavanah*: This statement on *mitzvos* paraphrases a classic dictum on prayer. See *Tanya*, Ch. 38, in explanation of *Shnei Luchos HaBris*, Vol. I, p. 249b.

out *kavanah*, without due intent, is like a body without a soul. What *kavanah* should a person have in mind when he's fulfilling a commandment? — That this *mitzvah* (commandment) comes from the *metzaveh* (Commander). Who is the Commander? — 'I am the L-rd your G-d Who brought you out of the Land of Egypt'; that is, the Creator, Who drags us all out of our various quagmires. So if I, Yisrolik Nobody, have been privileged to fulfill a commandment that proceeds from the One G-d, I should be leaping and dancing out of sheer joy!"

Whenever R. Yisrael saw someone suffering from melancholy or simply in low spirits, he would not let him go until he had explained clearly that this state of affairs would never do. This explanation was normally given with gentle words. There were however times when he could speak quite sharply.

"Look here," he might say to someone with a long face. "Why are you so upset because you're poor or sick" (or, G-d forbid, whatever other misfortune might have struck him)? "Tell me, do you deserve any better? You yourself know that you deserve all this. Don't be a fool. Kiss the rod, accept it all lovingly — and your Father will surely give you a candy."

Such were R. Yissachar Dov's recollections of R. Yisrael *der Lebediker.*

R. Yisrael, in turn, used to relate that in Lubavitch there had once lived an ordinary individual by the name of R. Yaakov — no great scholar, but a man who had committed the entire *Tanach* to memory, letter perfect, and who was thoroughly familiar with the details of all the laws in *Orach Chaim* — right from the beginning of the section dealing with one's rising in the morning until the last paragraph of the laws of the 14th and 15th of Adar Rishon. In summer he made stoves and in winter he made *volikess*, furlined boots. From these crafts he made a comfortable living, and in addition he owned

---

I am the L-rd: *Ex.* 20:2 — the First Commandment, paraphrased in
    the original.
Yisrolik Nobody: In the original, *Yisrolik Gornisht.*

a large garden that provided him with vegetables throughout the year. And while at work he would repeat to himself from memory entire chapters of *Tanach* and sections of *Orach Chaim*.

This R. Yaakov was generous, and in all respects a man of fine character. He once recalled that when he was newly married and had to support a family he went along to consult a certain person — known as R. Chaim *der Zeier* ("the sower") — for advice on what kind of livelihood he should pursue. R. Chaim's answer was simple enough: "Earn your living from crafts that will make your fellow Jews feel warm."

And that was why he used to make stoves and *volikess*.

R. Yaakov used to like giving children fruit from the trees that grew in his garden — apples, plums, cherries, and so forth — and teaching them which blessings to recite over them. Every afternoon he would gather together a number of people, pour them each a glass of kvass, and tell them of laws that were written in *Orach Chaim*. From all of this activity there came into being a number of customs and embellishments of customs that bore his name, R. Yankel *Zip*. And why was he nicknamed *Zip*, which means a sieve? — Because every law that he taught came out clear and clean as if it had been strained and refined through a fine *zip*.

Now R. Yisrael *der Lebediker* was a faithful disciple of R. Yaakov *Zip*. He had already received a number of well-trodden customs that he would hand on in the name of his teacher, and in the course of time these became enhanced by certain *hiddurim* of his own. So it was that the townsmen of Lubavitch had accumulated a number of *minhagim* that were the heritage of generations.

4.

In the 102 years that Lubavitch was the capital of the Rebbes of *Chabad*,* the township became the source-book for

---

* It is recorded in my notes that the Mitteler Rebbe settled in Lubavitch in MarCheshvan 5574 (תקע״ד; 1813), and passed away on 9 Kislev 5588 (תקפ״ח; 1827); the second generation in Lubavitch was the *Tzemach Tzedek*, who passed away on 13 Nissan 5626 (תרכ״ו; 1866); the third generation — the

the spiritual lifestyle that *Chassidus* prompts, and for the customs that chassidim practice. This is true of the workaday life
of the whole year, but especially so with regard to the
festivals.

In Lubavitch, even though the *Shabbos* preceding the
month of Elul — *Shabbos Mevarchim* — would still be a clear and
sunny day, the air felt different. There was a smell of Elul in
the air; you could feel the first stirrings of a *teshuvah*-breeze.
Every person there was beginning to grow a little more deliberate, a little more thoughtful, and allowing his weekday
affairs to fade from his memory.

During the two midsummer months from Shavuos until
Shabbos Nachamu — except for a certain break during the Three
Weeks, which were days of real mourning, the laws of this
period being punctiliously observed in all their details —
people would sometimes take a little stroll across the marketplace between *Minchah* and *Maariv*. No one ever went out for a
walk between Pesach and Shavuos, but from then on people
took the opportunity of enjoying the pleasant summer
weather.

From *Shabbos Nachamu* onwards, groups would begin to
form for study sessions held after *Maariv,* in the spirit of the
verse that says, קוּמִי רֹנִּי בַלַּיְלָה — "Arise, cry out in the night." By
the time *Shabbos Mevarchim* Elul came around one could already
sense the atmosphere of Elul. Anxiously, people now awaited
the first recitation of the *Psalm* that begins, לְדָוִד ה' אוֹרִי וְיִשְׁעִי —

Rebbe Maharash, who passed away on 13 Tishrei 5643 (תרמ"ג; 1882); the
fourth generation — the Rebbe Rashab, who left Lubavitch like an exile on
16 MarCheshvan 5676 (תרע"ו; 1915), and went to Rostov on the River Don.

(Footnote:) On 16 MarCheshvan: Misprint in the original gives "15 MarCheshvan," which was *Shabbos.* Cf. p. 42 above, which in describing the journey
specifies Sunday, 16 MarCheshvan.

From *Shabbos Nachamu...* study sessions: On increasing one's study time
as of 15 Av, which always falls within a few days of this *Shabbos,* see
Tractate *Taanis* 31a, and *Rashi* there.

Arise, cry out in the night: *Lam.* 2:19; a reference to Torah study, as
in Tractate *Tamid* 32b.

"By David: G-d is my light and my salvation"; eagerly, they awaited the first blast of the *shofar* that would announce that the gates of the Month of Mercy had been thrown open.

The stamp of Elul could already be detected in the *Chassidus** that the Rebbe delivered on *Shabbos Mevarchim Elul*, with its traditional opening phrase, אֲנִי לְדוֹדִי וְדוֹדִי לִי: ר"ת אֱלוּל — "'I am my Beloved's, and my Beloved is mine': The initials of these words constitute the word 'Elul'"; or with the phrase, הַשָּׁמַיִם כִּסְאִי — "Heaven is My throne"; or with the phrase, רְאֵה אָנֹכִי נֹתֵן לִפְנֵיכֶם הַיּוֹם — "Behold, I set before you this day...." Every day of Elul was quite unlike every other day of the year. Lying in bed at six o'clock in the morning, you could hear that the first daybreak-*minyan* in the *beis midrash* had already finished its morning prayers. You could hear the *shofar*. It woke you up to the fact that the world was now pervaded by Elul. You dress hastily, a trifle dissatisfied with yourself for having somehow slept in so late. Through your mind flits the recollection that this was the period that Moshe Rabbeinu spent on Mt. Sinai. These are propitious days, days in which you can accomplish more than usual. You tell yourself that you really should become a *mensch:* you cannot let these hours be lost on sleep.

By the time you arrive at the *beis midrash* you find quite a

---

* This was the term used in Lubavitch for the discourse [*maamar*] that the various Rebbes would deliver to the audience of chassidim on a *Shabbos* or other festive occasion.

By David: *Ps.* 27, recited twice daily from the first day of Rosh Chodesh Elul through Hoshana Rabbah (cf. *Midrash Tehillim* 27:4).

First blast: The *shofar* is blown daily as a call to repentance from the second day of Rosh Chodesh through the second-last day of Elul.

The stamp of Elul...in the *Chassidus*: In the original, *Di Chassidus...iz shoyn givehn a Eluldikke.*

I am my Beloved's: *Song* 6:3.

Heaven is My throne: *Isa.* 66:1.

Behold, I set: *Deut.* 11:26.

Daybreak-*minyan*: In the original, *vasikin-minyan;* cf. Tractate *Berachos* 9b.

Moshe Rabbeinu...Mt. Sinai: See *Rashi* on *Ex.* 33:11.

crowd already there. Some are reading *Tehillim*, some are studying *Chassidus*, some are reading *Tikkunei Zohar*, while others, whether standing or sitting, are at prayer.

5.

In the entire framework of divine service defined by the teachings of *Chabad*, a most prominent place is occupied by *davenen*, that is, *avodah shebalev* — the service of the heart. In Lubavitch there were individuals known as *baalei avodah*, who used to *daven* for hours on end even on ordinary weekdays throughout the year, but during the month of Elul in its own distinctive manner.

As you entered the anteroom of the *minyan* you would be struck by the wondrous sight that met your eyes. Everyone you see is in a quiet state of profound concentration, cleaving raptly to his Maker, and neither hearing nor seeing whatever surrounds him. The first has been humming a meditative *Chabad* melody, and to the strains of that *niggun* he now reads

---

Reading *Tikkunei Zohar:* There is a custom (cited in most editions) of completing the study of this work from Rosh Chodesh Elul through Yom Kippur.

Davenen: In *Chabad* circles, this word (even without qualification) signifies not only praying, but more particularly the measured meditation that animates it.

Avodah shebalev: See Tractate *Taanis* 2a, and *Rashi* on *Deut.* 11:13.

Anteroom of the *minyan:* In the original, *cheder sheni* (lit., "second room"). Since this is the place *par excellence* for divine service through the exercise of *Chabad* (in its original connotation — as the acronym of *chochmah, binah* and *daas,* the intellective faculties of the soul), such a room is also affectionately known by the Yiddish nickname of *"Chabadnitze".* Indeed, the Mitteler Rebbe is reported to have said hyperbolically that a *shul* which does not have one may not be entered. (Cf. *On Learning Chassidus* (*Kuntreis Limud HaChassidus* in English translation; Kehot, N.Y., 1959), pp. 22-23.)

In a quiet state of profound concentration: The Heb./Yid. original — *farmoichet* (from Heb. *mo'ach,* meaning "brain") — is far less formal, something like "all brained up."

Cleaving raptly to his Maker: In the Heb./Yid. original, *fardveiket* (from Heb. *dveikus*).

the words, בָּרוּךְ גּוֹזֵר וּמְקַיֵּם — "Blessed be He Who decrees and fulfills"; the second is pondering over the words, חַנּוּן וְרַחוּם — "Gracious and compassionate"; a third is saying, וְכוּלָם ... מְשַׁבְּחִים וּמְפָאֲרִים — "And they all... praise and glorify"; a fourth, having arrived at the palpably rich entreaties of *Ahavas Olam*, breathes out its words one at a time. Nourished by the sap of sound comprehension, these words now sprout forth their meaning with such sweetness, with such a yearning to cleave, with such a sound of supplication, that you feel that every word is raising this worshiper a rung higher. He is growing nearer to his innermost point; he is about to attain his goal.

The motif of supplication that accompanies his reading of the words, מַהֵר וְהָבֵא עָלֵינוּ בְּרָכָה וְשָׁלוֹם — "Hasten, and bring upon us blessing and peace"; the soft quietude of the melody with which he makes his request, וְתוֹלִיכֵנוּ מְהֵרָה קוֹמְמִיּוּת לְאַרְצֵנוּ — "Speedily lead us upright to our Land"; the confident rhythm with which he affirms, כִּי אֵ-ל פּוֹעֵל יְשׁוּעוֹת אָתָּה — "For You are G-d Who performs acts of deliverance"; the joyful voice with which he expresses his gratitude, וְקֵרַבְתָּנוּ מַלְכֵּנוּ לְשִׁמְךָ הַגָּדוֹל — "You have brought us near, O our King, to Your great Name"; — all these together give him the strength to say *Shema Yisrael*.

*   *   *

Every day brought you nearer to the *Shabbos* before *Seli-chos*. The *Chassidus* that was delivered that *Shabbos* was listened to with a special degree of concentration. On that Friday night people usually slept less than usual. Quite spontaneously you woke up early, a little restless, and you went to the *mikveh* before dawn.

Blessed be He Who decrees: These quotations are sampled from progressive stages of *Shacharis*, leading up to *Shema Yisrael*. The first is from the passage that opens with the words, *Baruch she'amar*.

Gracious and compassionate: From *Ashrei* (Ps. 145:8).

And they all... praise: From *Tisbarech lanetzach*.

The palpably rich entreaties: In the original, *di samme gedichte*.

Hasten, and bring: This and the following three phrases are from *Ahavas olam*.

Arriving there you found quite a number who had come before you, and all of them seemed to be in a hurry. You could see it on their faces: this *Shabbos* was different to all others. This was the *Shabbos* before *Selichos*.

All kinds of ideas are running around in your own head, too. One thought that suddenly presents itself is a clarion call: לְךָ ה' הַצְּדָקָה — "Righteousness belongs to You." But more insistently than that, you are now reminded of the continuation of that verse: וְלָנוּ בֹּשֶׁת הַפָּנִים — "And we are marked by shamefacedness." With a contrite heart you immerse in the *mikveh*, asking yourself meanwhile whether this *tevilah* is a real immersion of *teshuvah*, accompanied by remorse over the past and a resolve for the future, or whether it is perhaps (G-d forbid) an instance of טוֹבֵל וְשֶׁרֶץ בְּיָדוֹ — one who immerses in the *mikveh*, but while still grasping a reptile in his hand.

As you passed by the various *minyanim* — the *beis midrash* and Binyamin's *shtibl* — you could hear large groups of people saying *Tehillim*.

The way people read their *Tehillim* on this *Shabbos* was also different to the way they read *Tehillim* throughout the year. The same people, to be sure — plain folk who used to get together early every morning to read *Tehillim*, joined on *Shabbos* by those whose livelihoods made them spend their weekdays in the surrounding villages and townships. But they too view this *Shabbos* as being different to every other *Shabbos*. Every one of them is occupied with *himself*. Emerging from the sounds of their *Tehillim* you can hear an inner voice that proceeds from the all-embracing *chassidisher* atmosphere.

Righteousness belongs to You: Or, "charitability"; *Dan. 9:7.*

And we...shamefacedness: *Ibid.* The *Selichos* service proper opens with this verse.

Immerses...reptile in his hand: In the original טוֹבֵל וְשֶׁרֶץ בְּיָדוֹ (*Rambam, Hilchos Teshuvah* 2:3, which is a paraphrase of Tractate *Taanis* 16a). A dead reptile imparts *tum'ah*, ritual impurity; hence this metaphor for equivocal repentance.

An inner voice...from the all-embracing *chassidisher* atmosphere: In the succinct and allusive original, *hert zich a kol pnimi fun a chassidishn makkif.* See p. 237 above.

Having been at the *mikveh* you now went off to *shul* to
commit the new *maamar* to memory. That would take a good
few hours. What usually happened was that you would go in
for the repetition of the *maamar*, then resume your memoriz-
ing, and *daven;* at about three o'clock you would eat the *Shabbos*
midday meal.

At the table of my father, the Rebbe, the midday
meal of the *Shabbos* preceding *Selichos* was much shorter than
that of any other *Shabbos*. Generally speaking, meals in Lubavitch did not occupy much time, except that on occasion they
would develop into a *farbrengen,* when a story might be told or
a *vort* repeated.

The *Shabbos* meals in Lubavitch, then, followed a certain
pattern. Indeed, Lubavitch had a pattern and an order in
everything it did, an order that was defined by the fixed
limitations of time and place. Thus it was that the midday
meal of the *Shabbos* preceding *Selichos* was brief, for the scent of
the imminent Days of Awe was all-pervasive.

6.

The *avodah* of making preparations for *Shabbos* and *Yom-
Tov,* in particular for Pesach, was highly regarded by my
father, and he often spoke in praise of those who took it
seriously.

In Lubavitch, the preparations for Pesach were already
underway by midsummer. There was a certain place some 30
viorsts away on the road leading to Dubrovna — the Cherbiner farm, an estate belonging to a *paritz* — where wheat was

---

Go in for the repetition of the *maamar:* The *maamar* had been delivered
by the Rebbe to the assembled chassidim the previous evening,
between *Minchah* and *Maariv.* The next morning a select group of
chozrim ("repeaters") would "go in" — i.e., to the Rebbe's study — for
chazarah ("repetition"), a session during which the Rebbe would first
listen to their reconstruction of the *maamar* from memory, and then
amplify and elucidate. (Rabbi Raphael N.Kahan, *Lubavitch VeChayaleha*
(Kfar Chabad, 1983; Heb.), pp. 23-24.)
Meals in Lubavitch: I.e., at the Rebbe's table.

always harvested for *shemurah matzah*. Its long-term lease was held by a scholarly chassid, a man who was noble both in intellect and character. Chassidim, however, are never too particular about addressing people with honorific titles. So, regardless of the fact that this R. Zalman was master of the *Talmud Bavli* and very much at home in the *Yerushalmi* and the *Turim*, expert as well in the *Zohar*, the writings of the *Arizal* and all the works on *Chabad Chassidus* that had appeared in print, and a most generous philanthropist besides, he was addressed simply as Zalman Cherbiner — Zalman from Cherbin.

By the time I knew him he was already some 70 years old, and the dignity of his appearance was indescribable. The lines of his face suggested that here was both an active mind, and a likeable and easygoing kindliness. All in all, he stands as one of the most respected personalities in my album of childhood memories.

In addition to his being a worthy example of the wise countryfolk of long ago — men of truth and refined character — he was one of the revered chassidim of my greatgrandfather, the *Tzemach Tzedek*, and one of the closest chassidim of my grandfather, the Rebbe Maharash. From his mouth I heard dozens of stories, stories that reflect the lives and characteristic lifestyles of many kinds of chassidim of the fourth and fifth generations of *Chassidus Chabad*.

When R. Zalman told a story, he relayed it punctiliously, with neither additions nor explanations. Before he began it, however, he would describe the place and time and circumstances in which the particular episode took place, so that his listener received a complete representation of the event. Listening to him telling a story, you felt that you were in that very environment of those chassidim of long ago; with your

---

Chassidim of the fourth and fifth generations: I.e., the disciples of the aforementioned Rebbes of the third and fourth generations respectively (viz., the *Tzemach Tzedek* and the Rebbe Maharash).

Chassidus Chabad: Word order as in Heb.; in this phrase, the second word is an adjective qualifying the first.

own eyes you could see my greatgrandfather or my grandfather sitting with them.

Every person has certain things that are engraved and
chiselled in his memory and his heart, things that are unfor-
gettable throughout a lifetime. Wherever he might be, to
whatever land and whatever environment Divine Providence
leads him in the stream of life, when he recalls such a thing
this recollection drags him out of his unsanctified, workaday
life and places him in that innocent, luminous childhood life
from which it stems. Though standing now in the tumultuous din of his life of later years, he relives those clear and
sunny days.

We are bidden to "Remember the days of yore, ponder
the years of each generation." For chassidim this instruction
has a distinctive meaning. Every *chassidisher* home is saturated
with upright values, with the love of the Almighty, the love
of the Torah, and the love of a fellow Jew. The home of every
chassid, regardless of whether he was rich or poor, has always
been "a meeting-place for Torah sages."

As to the continuation of the verse — "Ask your father
and he will recount it to you" — among chassidim there used
to be no need for such a command: fathers used to narrate of
their own accord. They did not regard it as recounting a story.
It was a vital element in their lives: the narration issued
spontaneously. But in that narration there lay a life. Such a
narration must remain engraved for a lifetime.

The verse goes on: "And your elders, and they will tell
you." How beautifully this was observed among chassidim.
We have already mentioned on a number of occasions that the
elder chassidim of bygone days saw themselves as being
responsible for invigorating the lives of their younger
colleagues.

Remember the days: *Deut.* 32:7.
A meeting-place for Torah sages: Tractate *Avos* 1:4.
Ask your father: *Deut.* 32:7.
The narration issued spontaneously: In the Yid. original, *es hot zich
    dertzeilt.*

To be sure, the *chassidishe yungelait* of bygone days had attentive ears, and an intense longing to hear a *vort* from an elder chassid. Whole days and nights were devoted to this, and once one had heard a *vort*, one repeated it on dozens of occasions. All in all, *yungelait* appreciated the value of an elder chassid, and in the "revealed rebuke" of his stern words of guidance one could detect his "hidden love" for his younger listener.

7.

One of my scores of childhood memories is the lustrous picture of a reunion that took place between a little group of elder chassidim on one of the nights of Chanukah in the year 5650 (תר"ן; 1890) — my teacher the Rashbatz, R. Hendel, R. Aharon and R. Yekusiel from Dokshytz, and R. Zalman Cherbiner. They soon began to reminisce of years long past, when they had been young chassidim of my greatgrandfather, the *Tzemach Tzedek.* All of a sudden R. Zalman stood up from his seat and began to sing the sublime melody to which my greatgrandfather used to intone the *Mussaf* prayers on Rosh HaShanah. At this, the other elder chassidim stood up too, and sang with him.

Then they came to the stirring theme, so well known among chassidim, to which my greatgrandfather used to sing the words, אַשְׁרֵי אִישׁ שֶׁלֹּא יִשְׁכָּחֶךָ וּבֶן אָדָם יִתְאַמֶּץ בָּךְ — "Happy is the man who does not forget You, the son of man who holds fast to You." They were now in such a state of ecstasy that their faces were enflamed, and tears streamed down their cheeks. One could see that at this point these men were reliving those hallowed and luminous moments. There is not the slightest

---

Revealed rebuke...hidden love: *Prov.* 27:5.

1890: The writer was then 9 ½ years old.

R. Hendel: R. Chanoch Hendel Kurnitzer; see p. 218ff. above.

Stirring theme: See *Sefer HaNiggunim* (Nichoach, N.Y., 1957), Vol. II, p. 3 (Notation No. 179).

Happy is the man: From the opening passage of *Zichronos.*

doubt that at that time each one of them felt that he was standing right near the *Tzemach Tzedek,* seeing and hearing the Rebbe as he was *davenen.*

Having had my greatgrandfather's *beis midrash* described to me many times before, I knew exactly what it looked like and where he stood while *davenen.* Thus it was that the voice and the mien of these five hoary chassidim made such an intense impression on me that I was swept along with their ecstasy. In my mind's eye, I too witnessed the sight of my greatgrandfather — wrapped in his *tallis,* dressed in his white garments, with a white *yarmulke* on his head — as he said, אַשְרֵי אִישׁ שֶלֹא יִשְׁכָּחֶךָ — "Happy is the man who does not forget You"; I too heard his voice of holy yearning, as he said, וּבֶן אָדָם יִתְאַמֶּץ בָּךְ — "the son of man who holds fast to You."

Having been plentifully nourished with stories of how souls of *tzaddikim* had revealed themselves — whether in an apparent or a hidden manner — to their descendants and disciples, it was clear to me that my greatgrandfather was certainly here. This thought both gladdened and terrified me. I was utterly enveloped in a sublime sensation that cannot be expressed in words, a sensation springing from the loftiest chambers of the heart of which no man can write.

At that time I experienced it with all the pure innocence of childhood. As I grew older and began to study *Chassidus,* and better grasped the meaning of the bond of a chassid and his Rebbe, I understood it well — that such an occurrence, chassidim cleaving in thought to a Rebbe, has the power to cause the Rebbe to come to his chassidim.

True enough, in today's life of tumult it is hard to imagine and grasp how it is possible that a cleaving in thought should have such a far-reaching effect, but in the pure and deliberate life that was lived in former years this was well understood, and felt.

A unique reverence for these chassidim grew within me. With my own eyes I had seen how they possessed the mighty spiritual power of divesting themselves of their workaday

---

Chambers of the heart: Tractate *Niddah* 20b, and *Rashi* there.

lives and attaining such an ascent of the soul, such an *aliyas haneshamah,* that in their intense fervor they were able to be drawn into the distant past.

What a surge of life and spirit such a *chassidisher farbrengen* gives one! It burns away all the thorns of one's fleshly life; it pours a dose of spiritual life into one's daily existence, so that the temporal life of this material world is transmuted, refined and cleansed.

Such *chassidishe farbrengens* purify the atmosphere and create a luminous environment; they point out paths in one's service of the Almighty; they set a young man firmly on a basis of truth; and they become forever engraved in his mind and heart.

Succulent recollections of this kind are no doubt to be found among all those who stem from chassidim. Every *chassidisher* son, daughter and grandchild, in addition to his being animated by the blood, the brain and the spiritual sap of his *chassidishe* parents and forebears, carries within him memories of things seen and heard from them in his childhood.

8.

At certain moments, such memories can spark off a cataclysm in one's life, can protect one from harm, and set a whole family on the path of an authentically Jewish life.

In Petersburg there once lived a very wealthy man of about 45 or 50 who was born into a family of chassidim hailing from the Mohilev region. At the age of 14 he had already found his way somehow to the big city where he had succumbed to the pressures of the time and the place, until eventually he even desecrated *Shabbos,* ate *treifah* food, and so on. Nevertheless, since his roots had been in a family of prominent disciples of the Rebbes of *Chabad,* when the portrait of the Alter Rebbe was first reproduced in print he commissioned a celebrated artist to make a large copy of it,

---

A dose of spiritual life: In the original, *a revi'is mit chayim.*

together with a copy of the portrait of my greatgrandfather, the *Tzemach Tzedek*. He paid the artist generously, and when the paintings were ready he placed them in the library that adjoined his study.

Years passed, and his business affairs prospered. He gave his children Jewish names at birth, but these were soon enough replaced by Russian ones. His extravagant household pursued all the pleasures and luxuries of This World with a passion and, predictably enough, his social circle was composed mainly of Christians, or of Jews who had long since forgotten their Jewish roots.

It so happened — through the workings of Divine Providence — that one day the urgency of a certain business matter involving a local chassid demanded that he go to see him personally at home. As he walked inside, he saw ample rooms filled with people sitting around set tables, and the whole household rollicking with joyful singing. A familiar sight, he thought, as he recalled his early childhood years in the home of his chassidic parents.

Seeing his guest arriving, the host immediately rose to welcome him, ushered him into his office, and they discussed their business affairs. He had known his guest's parents, and had also heard how far this son of theirs had strayed.

When their discussion was over the guest said: "Excuse me, but what is the celebration in there? Is it perhaps a family occasion, for which I could wish you *Mazel Tov?*"

"Yes," replied the host, "it is indeed a family *simchah*. Right now we are conversing by telephone with our fathers and grandfathers in *Gan Eden*. And we were so glad to hear warm regards from there that we decided to celebrate this evening with a feast."

The guest stood perplexed at this unintelligible explanation.

Seeing his embarrassment the host continued: "You see, today is *Yud-Tes* Kislev* (— for that much his guest remem-

---

* See p. 173 above.

Yud-Tes Kislev: See p. 27 above, and footnotes there.

bered clearly). In *Gan Eden*, in the abode of the Alter Rebbe, there is a great deal of rejoicing. All the *tzaddikim* have assembled there in order to wish him *Mazel Tov* on his liberation and on the salvation that he brought about, through which tens of thousands of people have become chassidim. Our fathers and grandfathers who used to travel long distances to visit the Rebbes of their respective generations are there too for the big celebration, and we, their children and grandchildren, are rejoicing together with them over this *Yom-Tov* which is both theirs and ours."

9.

Hearing these few but pregnant words, the magnate felt a violent urge to join those chassidim in their *farbrengen* — just for a little while. But then again, he felt himself to be so strange and remote from their lifestyle that he could not summon the strength to express his wish. In fact he felt ashamed of himself. How could he, who ate *treifah* food, and so on and so forth, join in with this pious brotherhood?

Reading these thoughts from his guest's face, the host had the sensitivity to rise to the occasion unasked. Inviting the stranger to join the celebration for a moment, he added: "By the way, my friend, while you're in there with us you'll get regards from your father and your grandfather too...."

And the chassidic host saw to it that his guest should feel completely at home.

Now it is clear that seasoned chassidim do not have to be told what a *seudas mitzvah* among chassidim looks like, especially if we are talking about a *seudah* held in honor of *Yud-Tes* Kislev, which is now celebrated in all kinds of cities and townships around the world. But this *seudas Yud-Tes* Kislev was held in Petersburg itself, in the very place where the miracle occurred. Moreover, it took place over 40 years ago,

---

Very place...miracle occurred: Cf. Tractate *Berachos* 9:1.
Over 40 years ago: This takes us back to about 1892 (cf. below, end of this Section). The events of *Yud-Tes* Kislev took place in 1798.

when aged chassidim (including R. Yitzchak and R. Zalman Rubashov) who themselves had known the hoary elders — both among the chassidim and among the *misnagdim* — who were present *at the time* were still alive. It goes without saying, therefore, that this *Yud-Tes* Kislev feast was celebrated with an enthusiasm, with a holy joy, quite out of the ordinary.

An hour passed, two hours, three. The magnate even forgot that he had booked theater tickets for himself and some important officials of his acquaintance. He was drawn so deeply into the life of the chassidic brotherhood of that moment that for a while it seemed to him that he was back in his parents' home. For this was all an echo of his childhood. He recalled the festive meal which was prepared every *Yud-Tes* Kislev in his grandfather's little *shul*. He remembered too the *seudah* which his grandfather used to hold whenever he came home together with his friends after a visit to his Rebbe in far-off Lubavitch. His grandmother used to fuss happily over the preparations for that meal, and his mother and aunts all shared in helping for that joyous occasion. Lost recollections from long ago now sprang to life from when he was ten and twelve years old, and from his *bar-mitzvah* too. He recalled the *chassidisher* teacher of his boyhood; R. Baruch Asher the *Melamed* was his name.

After quite some hours had passed, he finally went home. A close friend of his told me in the year 5657 (תרנ״ז; 1897), some five years after the event, that the first thing he did when he arrived there was to walk into his library, and *daven* the *Maariv* prayer with sobs that came from deep within him.

Within a few days he had bought new dishes and had made his kitchen utterly kosher, and was himself well on the way to becoming a new man.

*   *   *

The very *teshuvah* that can be brought about (G-d forbid) through a pogrom or through a ruler or minister as severe as Haman can be sparked off by a *chassidisher farbrengen*, or by memories of a *chassidisher* home — but with kindness, and without suffering, G-d forbid.

10.

With R. Zalman Cherbiner, the harvesting of wheat for the baking of *shemurah matzah* followed a fixed and traditional routine. The first step was a thorough examination of all his fields to see which would yield the finest grain. Then the day for the harvest was chosen according to three criteria — clear weather, a hot sun, and three dry days preceding it. The wheat was always reaped from twelve noon until two or two-thirty in the afternoon.

When the grain was almost ripe R. Zalman would pay a visit to Lubavitch to organize matters. Since no one could know in advance exactly which day would answer to all the requirements, he would come with a number of wagons in which he would take home the men who would be doing the reaping. In fact most of the work was done by R. Zalman and his family, together with other Jewish farmers who lived with their families on his estate. But for good measure these were always joined by several of the *zitzers* ("sitters"), the young men who studied full time in the Rebbe's *beis midrash*. Together with them R. Zalman usually took home to the farm a number of the chassidim from other parts of the country who were visiting Lubavitch at that season. Sometimes they would all wait together at Cherbin for a week or ten days — until there came a day that answered the demands of all the above *hiddurim*.

As for R. Zalman, all of this constituted a veritable *avodah* — in fact, a time of threefold joy. First of all was the fact that it was time to reap wheat for the Rebbe's *shemurah matzah*. Secondly, he gained on the side the *mitzvah* of providing hospitality to such a number of chassidim for several days, and this was not only a *mitzvah* that he particularly cherished, but also one in which he had the right touch. Thirdly, to crown all, he would soon be privileged to have as his guest the Rebbe himself, who always came in person to participate in the reaping. In his younger days this was my grandfather, and in later years — the period I remember — the visitor was my father. These visits gave him years' worth of vigor.

From the day that R. Zalman set out from Lubavitch with his wagonloads of *shluchei mitzvah* until the great day came, people talked about the weather every single day. People were always gazing at the sky. (Was this a *dry* wind? Couldn't you feel a touch of moisture in the air?) And the whole township was abuzz with dozens of earnest speculations as to the next day's weather. Day by day everyone watched out for the special messenger from Cherbin who would bring word that this was indeed the day.

The ride to Cherbin with my father, which took up to two hours, with all of its surrounding experiences, made a deep impression on me. (Every incident I encountered at the time found in my child's mind a parallel story in the *Tanach* or in the *Aggados* that I knew.) These are among the experiences that I recorded, in varying degrees of detail, in my childhood memoirs.

11.

The reaping and threshing were carried out in a spirit of great joyfulness — but tempered by a sober earnestness that could be seen on all faces. Every man there wore his *gartl* around his waist, every head was covered by both a *yarmulke* and a hat. Despite the heat everything was done energetically, as if the workers were all accustomed to this kind of activity.

R. Zalman, with his ample patriarchal beard, and a countenance shining for sheer joy, was already advancing in years. But here he was, sickle in hand, darting in and out among the workers, as if he were the youngest man present. You could see that it was joy that was lifting him off the ground. His light shoes with their white socks flitted in the air as if they were spiritual beings, like the feet of Naftali on a G-d-given

---

Wore his *gartl:* As for the most solemn of religious observances.
Both a *yarmulke* and a hat: As above.
Feet of Naftali: *Gen.* 49:21, and *Rashi* there.

mission, in a way that is possible only with a true servant of G-d, an *oved Elokim* — with a man of whom it may be said that the very soles of his feet experienced the same intense joy that his brain did, and were animated by the same inner will that animated the desire of his heart in its performance of this *avodah*.

Some men reaped while others sang, and all around the sunny steppes their lusty song resounded. That entire vista basked in a resplendent holiness. At a little distance, all decked out in their *Shabbos* best, stood the women and children of the families who lived in Cherbin. Their faces all shone with an awareness that what they were witnessing that day was no common spectacle.

As soon as the reaping and threshing were over, some of the men went off with R. Zalman to bathe. He then put on his *Shabbos* clothes and led the *Minchah* prayers — but to the vigorous rhythms of the prayers of Simchas Torah. And in keeping with the festive mood of the day, they all omitted the penitential verses of *Tachanun*. R. Zalman reserved a special rollicking melody for the concluding passage — *Aleinu*. When he arrived at *Oseh shalom*, the very last sentence of the final *Kaddish*, you could tell that he was waiting eagerly for some pair of burly young stalwarts to honor a lighthearted old custom — to sneak up behind the congregant who has just finished leading the service, lock their arms suddenly around his waist, and deftly give him an unsolicited somersault in the air. If there were no volunteers, because of the reverence in which he was held, he would say *Nu!* so often, and delay the three backward steps of *Oseh shalom* for so long, that someone

---

The very soles of his feet: The *Chabad* teachings that underlie this statement are explained in: Rabbi S.Y. Zevin, *A Treasury of Chassidic Stories on the Torah* (Mesorah Publications/Hillel Press), Vol. II, pp. 494-8.

Joy: In the original, *oneg*.

Inner will: In the original, *ratzon pnimi*.

A resplendent holiness: *Ps.* 29:2.

Give him an unsolicited somersault: In the original, *iberkulyen*.

Would say *Nu!*: In the original, *nuken*.

would simply *have* to oblige. Back on his feet, he would then
join the rest of the worshipers in a lively dance. As they
danced, he would sing the four verses that follow *Aleinu* at the
top of his voice, stretching out the words to match the length
of his tune. And he danced with such abandon that when he
reached the very last couple of words of *Ach tzaddikim* he
would somersault three times back and forth for sheer joy.

In a clearing between his fruit trees R. Zalman's family
always had prepared a long table covered with a rich assort-
ment of dairy products for a festive meal, in the course of
which my father would deliver a *maamar*. After a couple of
hours at the table together it was evening, and time to recite
the *Maariv* prayers. My father would then retire to rest in a
room that had been prepared for him, while the chassidim
gathered. again around the table in tranquil camaraderie,
humming familiar melodies and exchanging favorite stories
until daybreak.

In the morning we all found a *minyan* for the *Shacharis*
prayers, and at about ten my father and certain others would
return to Lubavitch. R. Zalman would not arrive there till late
in the afternoon, bringing with him the rest of the chassidim,
and the sack of wheat, which he would suspend from the
ceiling on a special hook in a room that had been set aside for
the purpose.

12.

Years passed, R. Zalman passed away, and the wheat for
my father's *shemurah matzah* was now harvested from the
farms in the Jewish colonies of the Kherson region. The
estate chosen was sometimes that of a wealthy chassid called
R. Nachman Dulitzki. The farm was nicknamed Nechayevke,
and the work there was supervised by the late R. Zvi Sanin.
From the year 5657 (תרנ"ז; 1897), when the Tomchei Temimim
Yeshivah was founded in Lubavitch, all the stages in the
preparation of the *shemurah matzah* that follow the reaping and
threshing were entrusted to the students of the *yeshivah*.

In the early years the wheat was ground in a water-mill.

Every possible *hiddur* was undertaken to ensure that the flour would be unquestionably dry and fit for making *shemurah*. For example, only new millstones were used. But since this year the owners of the mill modernized their plant and introduced *mechanized* rollers, the chassidim set up their own handmill to grind the flour. The preparations for milling would start on Rosh Chodesh Adar, but not before the wheat had been sorted and examined three times over — this too according to a fixed routine.

When it came to producing *matzas mitzvah*, the *matzah* to be made on *erev* Pesach, there was a distinct order of events to be followed, both with regard to the drawing of *mayim shelanu*, the water which was kept cool in preparation for the baking, and with regard to the baking proper. The senior students of the *yeshivah* were now given earnest instructions as to each of the other stages as well, including the preliminary heating of the oven to ensure that it was absolutely kosher, and the precise arrangements for kneading and baking, and for supervising the entire process.

Now it once happened that a prospective student arrived at the *yeshivah* — an intelligent and erudite young man — and the board of examiners accepted him willingly. At the beginning of each academic year a list of all the newly-accepted students was always drawn up. As the executive director of the *yeshivah* I would present this list to my father, together with a comment on each student by the board of examiners, as well as by other confidential advisors.

Modernized...*mechanized* rollers: *Matzos* thus manufactured became known in Russian Yiddish as *mashinove matzos* (as opposed to *hant matzos*). With the advent of technological progress, the railway too eventually reached within a wagon-ride of Lubavitch, and chassidim began to succumb to the soft life, preferring to travel there in hours by train instead of for weeks on foot. Thus it was that the hardy oldtimers used to nickname their weakling colleagues: *"mashinove chassidim."*

Executive director of the *yeshivah:* The author was appointed to this position *(menahel poel)* in 1898, at the age of 18.

My father interested himself in every single student, but in particular in this young man, whose talents showed promise. There was only one problem: the confidential comment pointed out a certain lack of refinement in the young man's character, and this coarseness was reflected in his features.

After pondering the report at length, and rereading it, my father said: "We should accept him, but we'll have to take him well in hand."

As soon as the list of students was approved, at about the middle of Cheshvan, I structured a particularly demanding program for this young man. This I entrusted to the two *mashgichim,* one of whom was responsible for supervising the study of *nigleh* and the other for the study of *Chassidus,* with the request that they observe him with a close eye. And this is what happened throughout the winter semester.

13.

On Rosh Chodesh Teves that year my father left for abroad. When it was around Rosh Chodesh Adar and time to begin sorting the wheat to be used in baking, I received a letter from my father instructing me to entrust all the hard work in the preparation of the *shemurah* to that young man, and to write back reporting how he performed his tasks. My father was not due to return to Lubavitch that year until several days before Pesach.

I obeyed my instructions meticulously. All the heaviest tasks were imposed on this student — sorting the wheat, setting up the handmill, grinding — to the point that for two solid weeks, day and night, I gave him not a moment's rest. However, this was all organized in such a way that he would not detect that all his exertion came as the result of any particular directive.

Middle of Cheshvan: The month following Tishrei; i.e., soon after studies were resumed.

Rosh Chodesh Adar: I.e., two months after Rosh Chodesh Teves, and six weeks before Pesach.

Meticulously: In the tongue-in-cheek original, *behiddur.*

In fact it was universally true of the students of the Tomchei Temimim Yeshivah in Lubavitch that they did not ask *Why?*, but willingly did what they were asked to do.

The *yeshivah* was built on four foundations: truth, love, loyalty and devotedness. The *yeshivah* regarded each of its students as its child. The brotherly love among the students was remarkable, and the loyalty and devotedness of the students to those who headed the *yeshivah*, and vice versa, was felt in the fullest sense of those words. And, indeed, only such norms of conduct could have yielded such students (May G-d bless them!) as did the Tomchei Temimim Yeshivah.

The time came for the baking of *shemurah*, and of *matzah* for the whole household. Now too, though all of the students participated, I loaded this young man with the heaviest work. At this point my father arrived, and in addition to the reports that I had written him he made detailed inquiries about this young man's progress.

When the time came to prepare for the baking of *matzas mitzvah* on the eve of Pesach, I honored him — in addition to this work — with the task of *bedikas chametz* in the *shul*, in the office, and in the *yeshivah*. The search for leaven in these three places was enough to keep him busy until two or three in the morning — and at seven he had to be on duty at the bakery in order to stoke the oven for one more kashering in preparation for the last batch of *shemurah*.

The labors of *erev* Pesach were finally completed, and by five in the afternoon the young men had returned from their immersion in the *mikveh*. I now called for this same student and told him that he was to diligently study the *maamar* based on the verse, שֵׁשֶׁת יָמִים תֹּאכַל מַצּוֹת — "Six days shall you eat *matzos*" — which appears in the *Siddur* of the Alter Rebbe. Having mastered that, he was to come to see me at seven the next

---

In the *shul:* In the original, *minyan.*

Six days...*matzos: Deut.* 16:8.

Siddur of the Alter Rebbe: I.e., *Seder Tefillos Mikol HaShanah* (Kehot, N.Y., 1965).

morning, the first day of Pesach, when I would study this same *maamar* with him.

I knew that he was to be one of the monitors responsible for waiting on the students in the big study hall,* and that his duties would occupy him until after the *Seder* was over — no doubt until two in the morning, without a free quarter-of-an-hour for study. But the whole intention of the exercise to which he had been subjected was to test to what extent the study of *Chassidus* mattered to him.

At seven o'clock he nevertheless appeared as arranged, with the intricacies of that discourse duly digested and ordered in his mind — relative, that is, to his grasp of *Chassidus* at the time.

Having studied with him until eight I reported on the episode to my father, who said with visible satisfaction: "We have, thank G-d, planted a tree that will bear fruit. I hope that one day he will be able to benefit others. It will take a long time, but ultimately he will sprout forth with prolific branches bearing fruit, whose seed will in turn yield further fruit."

On the last day of Pesach, at the students' festive table** in the big study hall, my father motioned to me and said: "Yosef Yitzchak! Just look what a powerful thing is *perspiring for a mitzvah!* Look — he has acquired different features altogether. The coarseness has vanished: what has now appeared is the face of a *mensch...*"

---

* In Lubavitch, *der groysser zal* was the name of the hall in which the students of the Tomchei Temimim Yeshivah studied throughout the year, and in which they ate together throughout Pesach. Each student had his fixed seat at one of the numbered tables for the eight days of the festival, and each table was waited on by one of its students, known as the *memuneh.*

** On the last day of Pesach the students would invite my father to join them in their festive meal, which would extend until late at night. At the table my father would deliver a *maamar,* and the whole assemblage would later break forth in spontaneous dancing.

14.

In the year 5650 (תר"ן; 1890) my father wrote a letter of serious conceptual content to our relative R. Shneur, the son of R. Mordechai Dov Slonim of Hebron. In it my father sets forth the virtues of meditating on *Chassidus* as a prelude to prayer, when one is already wearing one's *tallis* and *tefillin*. All in all, this letter constitutes a profound theoretical exposition of *avodah*.

It remained in the hands of R. Shneur. He showed it to his father and another few chassidim, who copied it out in manuscript, but outside *Eretz Yisrael* no one knew of its existence.

The subjects discussed there demand intensive study: a *farbrengen* is not the place to discuss them, except for several major themes.

R. Shneur had come to visit Lubavitch for the first time in the year 5645 (תרמ"ה; 1885), and had remained for some months as a resident scholar, his program of studies being mapped out by my father. In the winter of 5646 (תרמ"ו; late

---

A letter of serious conceptual content: In the original, *a Chassidus-briv*. It has since been published in *Igros Kodesh* (Letters of the Rebbe Rashab), ed. R. Shalom Dober Levin (5 vols., Kehot Publication Society, N.Y., 5742/1982), where it appears, though differently dated, as No. 16 in Vol. I. The subject referred to in this paragraph occupies pp. 24-29 thereof.

R. Shneur: The Rebbe Rashab used to refer to R. Shneur as נֶכְדִּי ("my grandson"). The anecdote that explains this nickname appears in *Igros Kodesh (op. cit.)*, footnote on p. 11.

Hebron: The Mitteler Rebbe had founded a colony of *Chabad* chassidim there in 1816-1817.

Meditating on *Chassidus:* In the original, *trachtn Chassidus*.

A profound theoretical exposition of *avodah:* In the original, *a tiffe haskalah in avodah*.

Resident scholar: In the original, *a yoshev* (lit., "a sitter").

In the winter of 5646: For a summary of the difficulties in dating the journey to Yalta, and the related anomalies in the chronology of the early childhood years of the Rebbe Rayatz, see: *Igros Kodesh (op. cit.)*, footnote on p. 7; and *Sefer HaToldos* (the Rebbe Rayatz), Vol. I, footnote on p. 17.

1885) my father asked R. Shneur to accompany him to Yalta, and often studied *Chassidus* with him. After studying a printed text they would review its subject matter orally, my father meanwhile adding explanations.

With the approach of Pesach 5646 (תרמ"ו; 1886) R. Shneur returned to *Eretz Yisrael*, and from this time there began an exchange of correspondence, R. Shneur asking for clarification of particular points in the teachings of *Chassidus*, and my father answering. In the course of several years this amounted to quite a number of letters, containing profound explanations of the *haskalah* of *Chassidus*, and directives in *avodah*. Together they constitute a veritable guide as to how the study of *Chassidus* and the practice of *avodah* should be approached; one of them is the letter mentioned above.

The fact is that it would be exceedingly worthwhile to assemble these letters, and so too the many other letters that I have (thank G-d) in my possession. Each one of them is a treasure-house of subjects that infuse the life of a chassid with inner vitality.

In the course of the above-mentioned letter, for example, my father writes that meditating on concepts in *Chassidus* while one is wearing one's *tallis* and *tefillin* has an effect on the way one lives one's whole day after the prayers are over; such meditation during prayer, moreover, is of far greater worth than at any other time; and in this connection my father explains the theme of כִּי קָרוֹב אֵלֶיךָ... בְּפִיךָ וּבִלְבָבְךָ — "For this thing is very near to you, in your mouth and in your heart" — as discussed in Ch. 17 of *Tanya*.

Not only does this letter expound the *haskalah* of *avodah*, but its every word breathes life. Its very script demands and pleads, showing the reader what his spiritual condition is at present, and telling him what it should be.

Among other things, this letter discusses hidden evil. That is to say, that one can find an individual who to all

---

To assemble these letters: The wish of the Rebbe Rayatz was ultimately fulfilled with the publication in 1982 of *Igros Kodesh* (op. cit.).

external appearances is G-d-fearing, while in fact he is lined with deceit. Such a person is a veritable לָבָן הָאֲרַמִּי — Lavan the Aramean. For outwardly he is all snow-white [Heb.: לָבָן means "white"]; inwardly, however, he is a cheat [Heb.: רַמָּאי, transposed, equals אֲרַמִּי].

This remark was not made out of any desire (G-d forbid) to cause pain or to incriminate. On the contrary, it sprang from the compassion that was felt for the nature of such a person who can harbor so much foulness within him.

The same letter devotes an entire passage to discussing the yoke of earning a living, a burden with which both laymen and full-time scholars become preoccupied. The fact is that both categories of chassidim would like to engage in *avodah shebalev* — "the service of the heart" [i.e., *davenen* at length, the reading of the passages in the *Siddur* being interspersed with pauses for disciplined meditation from memory on related texts in *Chassidus*]. The only trouble is that people argue that first they must set up a means of making a livelihood — until eventually they find themselves caught up in the yoke of earning a living. In the course of this discussion, then, my father describes how the counsels of the Evil Inclination conspire to divert a person from the path of truth, blinding his eyes with numerous cares that constitute the yoke of making a living.

This brings to mind something we once spoke about* — that the superfluous talk to be heard among businesspeople, that is, the abundance of pointless prattle that they utter, is a threshold leading to evil speech and gossip; it destroys a man's spiritual stature utterly.

----

* See p. 157ff. above.

Lavan the Aramean: *Gen.* 29-31.

A cheat: "Lavan is the father of all cheats" (*Midrash Tanchuma, Parshas Vayishlach,* 1).

The yoke of earning a living: In the original, *ol derech eretz* (cf. *Pirkei Avos* 3:5).

Avodah shebalev: See Tractate *Taanis* 2a, and *Rashi* on *Deut.* 11:13.

A means of making a livelihood: In the original, אַ כְּלִי לְפַרְנָסָה.

To return to the letter. My father there interprets — on the non-literal level of *derush* — a sentence from the *Mishnah* which speaks of a man at prayer: אֲפִילוּ נָחָשׁ כָּרוּךְ עַל עֲקֵבוֹ לֹא יַפְסִיק — "Even if a snake is coiled around his ankle, he should not interrupt [his prayers]." That is to say: In the era of the footsteps of the *Mashiach* (בְּעִקְּבוֹת מְשִׁיחָא), in the present generations which are so swamped by the worldly burdens of earning a living, *this* is the snake coiled around a person from within and without. And the remedy for this predicament is — not to interrupt one's prayers.

Indeed, my father saw this "service of the heart" as the greatest remedy for all kinds of mortal ailments and blemishes. He perceived the *avodah* of prayer as the best and broadest highway leading up to the House of G-d.

In this connection he used to say: "Our Sages teach us, תְּפִלָּה בִּמְקוֹם קָרְבָּן — 'The prayers compensate for sacrifices.' Just as there are various categories in the sacrificial service — the guilt-offering, the sin-offering, the burnt-offering, the peace-offering, the thanksgiving-offering, the meal-offering of the poor man and the meal-offering of the rich — so too are there distinct categories in the divine service of prayer, which replaces the sacrifices."

15.

The above-mentioned R. Mordechai Dov Slonim, grandson of the Mitteler Rebbe and father of R. Shneur, arrived in Lubavitch in time for Shavuos 5651 (תרנ"א; 1891), as too did many other mellow scholars of *Chassidus*, and brought with him a copy of the letter that my father had written to his son.

Even if a snake: Tractate *Berachos* 5:1.

The *Mashiach*...the snake: A classical *gematria* points out that נָחָשׁ equals מָשִׁיחַ, for the serpent is the evil counterpart of *Mashiach*. (*Meorei Or*, the earliest of the *Sifrei HaArachim*, and based on the writings of the *Arizal*; Letter *Mem*, Sec. 93.)

The prayers compensate for sacrifices: Tractate *Berachos* 26a. Cf. וּנְשַׁלְּמָה פָרִים שְׂפָתֵינוּ — "We will render [the prayer of] our lips in place of [the sacrifice of] bullocks" (*Hosea* 14:3).

In the course of the few weeks that he spent there, he became very friendly with three elder chassidim who were always to be found within the precincts of my father's *beis midrash* — R. Chanoch Hendel Kurnitzer, R. Shmuel Baruch Varshever, and R. Meir Mordechai Borisover — and showed them his letter confidentially.

R. Shmuel Baruch was one of the outstanding *maskilim* of the time, a chassid of highly-developed sensibility and a profound scholar. He was a man of hoary old age. *How* old he was at the time I do not know: I fancy he did not know either. At any rate, whenever anyone asked him his age he would only say: "It's long since time to forget."

He had first come to Lubavitch in the year that my grandfather was born — 5594 (תקצ"ד; 1834) — and had not gone home until 5606 (תר"ו; 1846). In 5610 (תר"י; 1850) he had come again, remaining until 5626 (תרכ"ו; 1866), when after the passing of my greatgrandfather he had again gone home. Finally, in 5632 (תרל"ב; 1872) he had returned to Lubavitch, where he stayed for the rest of his life.

He had a complete mastery of all the published works of *Chassidus*, almost to the point of having memorized them — such as *Torah Or, Likkutei Torah,* the *Siddur* of the Alter Rebbe, and the published works of the Mitteler Rebbe. He spoke sparingly, but when on occasion he offered an explanation of a concept, it was rich.

R. Meir Mordechai had been a longstanding disciple of the well-known chassid, R. Shmuel Borisover, under whom

---

Precincts of...*beis midrash:* In the Yid. original, *hoyf* (and in Heb., *chatzer*); lit., "courtyard", but signifying more broadly the whole cluster of buildings which together constituted the nerve-center of the chassidic community.

R. Chanoch Hendel Kurnitzer...R. Meir Mordechai Borisover; see p. 218ff. above.

Varshever: Yid., "from Warsaw" (and so too with most of the other names appearing in this work). In familiar usage family names were almost unknown at the time.

My grandfather: I.e., the Rebbe Maharash.

My greatgrandfather: I.e., the *Tzemach Tzedek.*

he had studied *Chassidus* for ten years. He was a scholar, expert in very many tractates of the *Gemara*, and for twenty years he had been the *melamed* of small groups of children. In the year of which I speak — 5650 (תר"ן; 1890) — he worked in Lubavitch as a cashier in the business of my uncle R. Zalman Aharon, and assiduously devoted all his other hours to the study of *nigleh* and *Chassidus*.

R. Chanoch Hendel was one of the select *baalei avodah*. He was no outstanding theoretician in the study of *Chassidus* — but his heart was all aflame, his character was refined beyond compare, and the extent to which he loved his fellow Jew is indescribable. All in all, he is one of those few elder chassidim who figure prominently in my childhood memories.

Now when these three chassidim saw this copy of R. Mordechai Dov's letter they settled down to studying it, first separately and then together. In fact for a few weeks they did nothing but study and discuss the contents of that letter. So it was that it became known in Lubavitch without my father's knowledge.

16.

In the month of Tammuz my father and my uncle R. Zalman Aharon returned from Luka,* where they had gone to see about a match for their sister, my aunt and in-law Chayah Mushka — namely, my uncle and and in-law, R. Moshe HaKohen Horenstein. After a couple of weeks' correspondence the two families came to an agreement about the *shidduch,* and fixed a time for celebrating the *tena'im.*

Among the elder chassidim who came to Lubavitch for the occasion were the emissary R. Gershon Dov [Pahrer], the

---

* Town in Kiev province where the well-to-do chassid R. Zalman Horenstein had his sugar factory.

A match for their sister: Her father, the Rebbe Maharash, had passed away in 1882, when she was still a child.

In-law...Horenstein: In the original, *mechutan.* Their son, R. Menachem Mendel, was later to marry Sheine, third daughter of the Rebbe Rayatz.

R. Gershon Dov: Prominent chassid of the *Tzemach Tzedek* and then of the Rebbe Maharash.

emissary R. Shalom-R. Hillel's, the scholarly R. Zalman Neimark of Nevel, the learned R. Yoel of Podobranka, the kabbalist R. Leib Hoffman, R. Monye [Menachem Manes]
Monensohn, and R. Leib Chassidov. They soon caught wind
of the above letter, and were all struck both by the *haskalah*
expounded there and by its directives for the "service of the
heart."

After the betrothal agreement had been sealed there was
a festive meal that developed into a *chassidisher farbrengen*. (As I
have related in detail on another occasion, my childhood life
had by this time undergone a certain change. I was now
drawn strongly to any quite ordinary *farbrengen*, especially if
my father was among those present.) At this gathering a
certain chassid — I would rather not mention his name —
remarked that *Chassidus* is basically *haskalah* [i.e., intellective];
that *seichel* is always in place — not only before *davenen* and in
the midst of *davenen*, but whenever a person is engrossed in
cerebration, quite independently of *davenen*.

The speaker was a man of understanding, a man of
scholarly achievement with an extensive knowledge of *Chassidus*, a man of high intellectual capacity and a profound
thinker, a speaker of rare eloquence and a person of upstanding character — but not an *oved*. In fact he would generally
daven together with the congregation, even on *Shabbos*.

A weighty discussion ensued, in the course of which a
number of the more serious thinkers present — such as R.
Gershon Dov, R. Zalman Neimark, R. [Avraham] Abba Persohn, and R. Yoel of Podobranka — expressed the view that
the mainstay of *Chassidus* is *avodah*. In support of their
remarks, they each told a story that they had heard from elder
chassidim they had known. R. Gershon Dov (who still had
early recollections of R. Betzalel Ozaritcher) repeated tradi-

---

On another occasion. See p. 250ff. above.

My childhood life: The author was near his tenth birthday at the time.

With the congregation, even on *Shabbos*: I.e., instead of *davenen* at length, as
explained on p. 265ff. above.

tions that he had received from the *tzaddik* R. Hillel [of Paritch]
and R. Aizik Homiler; R. Abba Persohn repeated things he
had heard from his father-in-law's father R. Velvel Vilenker
and from R. Moshe Vilenker; and R. Yoel of Podobranka
handed on words that he had heard from the mouth of R.
Pesach Molostovker.

From their narratives the novel contribution of the Alter
Rebbe to the teachings of *Chassidus* became apparent; likewise,
the approach to *avodah* — that is, the relation between *Chassidus* and *avodah* — as perceived by R. Menachem Mendel of
Vitebsk on the one hand, and the Maggid of Mezritch on the
other. Moreover, their stories reflected the lives and aspirations of the great *maskilim* and *baalei avodah* of the four generations of the school of *Chabad* that had passed until that time.

Being then a child, and by nature always finding in my
imagination a parallel to every experience, and now beholding
at this *farbrengen* such an assemblage of hoary-headed chassidim, their countenances all dignified, convivial and holy, their
words all uttered with such a tranquil deliberateness, — it
seemed to me, as I recall, that the scene before me resembled
the scene described to me by my *melamed,* R. Moshe Binyamin,
of how the *tzaddikim* sit in the Garden of Eden, and bask in the
radiance of the Divine Presence. Only in later years, as I grew
older, did I begin to fully appreciate the value of such a
farbrengen. For this is the true exemplification of the teaching
of our Sages: גְּדוֹלָה שִׁמּוּשָׁהּ שֶׁל תּוֹרָה יוֹתֵר מִלִּמּוּדָהּ — "Attendance on
[men steeped in] Torah is [even] more praiseworthy than the
study of Torah."

We once spoke* of what my greatuncle, R. Baruch Sha-

------

* See p. 208 above.

The *tzaddikim* sit: Cf. Tractate *Berachos* 17a.

Attendance...more praiseworthy: Tractate *Berachos* 7b. This theme is
    discussed in Section 2 of the *maamar* (beginning לְכָה דוֹדִי) which in
    Lubavitch custom is delivered by a bridegroom immediately before
    his *chuppah.*

R. Baruch Shalom: Eldest son of the *Tzemach Tzedek,* and greatgrandson
    of the Alter Rebbe.

lom, transmitted from the mouth of the Alter Rebbe — of the lofty worth of a story, provided that the narrator hands down its language meticulously. And indeed, such narratives and such teachings quicken the very soul.

17.

My father was very pleased with the stories that he had now heard at the table, for each of them had been handed down directly, mouth to mouth. In the meantime each of the elder chassidim present had taken another drop of *mashke,* and they now sang together.

Their melody came to an end, and my father said: "This very concept, that the mainstay of *Chassidus* is *avodah,* itself needs to be understood in the terms of *haskalah. Chassidus* is divine intellect. *Chassidus* is not only *haskalah,* mere intellection: it is *divine* intellect, the glory and the splendor of intellect; that is to say, the higher-than-intellect that is to be found in intellect. And it is this intellect-that-transcends-intellect that one's physical brain must grasp. But the physical brain can be enabled to comprehend divine intellect only by means of *avodah,* by laboring in the 'service of the heart' which is prayer — for prayer is the time and place at which the verse וְיִקְחוּ לִי ('They shall take *unto* Me') comes to life in the meaning which the Sages perceive there, namely, 'They shall take *Me,'* as if to say: אוֹתִי אַתֶּם לוֹקְחִים —'It is *Me* Whom you are taking.' The Essence of the Infinite One says to every man who serves Him through the *avodah* of prayer: 'It is *Me* Whom you are taking.'

"However, in order that one's prayer should be true *avodah,* so that one attains the level at which one is granted this permission ('It is *Me* Whom you are taking'), there must first be the preparations intimated by the verse, חוֹמַת בַּת צִיּוֹן

Divine intellect: In the original, שֵׂכֶל אֱלֹקִי.
The glory and the splendor of intellect: In the original, הַהוֹד וְהֶהָדָר שֶׁבַּשֵּׂכֶל.
They shall take *unto* Me: Ex. 25:2.
It is *Me* Whom you are taking: *Vayikra Rabbah* 30:13.

הוֹרִידִי כַנַחַל דִּמְעָה—'O wall of the Daughter of Zion, let tears run down like a river,' and by the verse, הָיְתָה לִּי דִמְעָתִי לֶחֶם יוֹמָם וָלָיְלָה — 'My tears have been my bread dáy and night.' No matter how profound one's *haskalah* may be, concepts comprehended through *haskalah* do not alone suffice — in the absence of tears, and in the absence of the perspiration generated by the actual practice of the *mitzvos* — to make one a servant of G-d through the *avodah* of prayer.

"It is even possible," my father continued, "that a person should study a subject of *haskalah* in *Chassidus* and understand it well, really and truly well, and indeed reach a point at which not only is the subject within him but he in turn is within the subject" (and here my father explained the terms מַקִּיף ('encompassing') and מוּקָף ('being encompassed') as used in this sense in Ch. 5 of *Tanya*); "moreover, with this subject in mind he prays his way through quite a fine *Maariv* and does his *[Tikkun] Chatzos*; furthermore, when he lies down he cannot fall asleep because he is so closely bound to his subject; — yet nevertheless, when (after all the due preparations of *mikveh* and meditation of *Chassidus* before *davenen*) he proceeds to *daven*, he contemplates the intellectual delight to be found in his subject, *but its divine element he does not sense.*

"Now this *maskil* is well aware of the clear difference between the perception of intellect and the perception of G-d-liness. Indeed, his absence of feeling for the divine element in his intellectually-perceived *haskalah* causes him no end of anguish. He pleads; he cries; he bemoans his plight; — but to no avail. All the doors and gates are locked in his face. Once and for all, *No!* From Above they say to Him: 'Do you want to be a *maskil*? So *be* a *maskil*. But divine light you won't be given!'

O wall: *Lam.* 2:18.

My tears...my bread: *Ps.* 42:4.

The perspiration...of the *mitzvos*: In the original, זֵעָה שֶׁל מִצְוָה.

He prays his way through... *Maariv*: In the original, *davent-er-op...* *Maariv*.

He proceeds to *daven*: I.e., *Shacharis*, for the *oved* the prayer service *par excellence*.

"Do you know what this means?" my father turned to the chassidim at the table. "From Above they say to the *maskilim:* כִּי תָבֹאוּ לֵרָאוֹת פָּנָי — 'When you come to appear before Me' — that is to say: 'If you want to behold the Countenance of G-d by means of your intellectual exercises, seeking by means of *haskalah* to sense the divine light, then *out of here!'* As the verse continues: מִי בִקֵשׁ זֹאת מִיֶּדְכֶם רְמֹס חֲצֵרָי — 'Who asked this of you, to trample My courts?' That is to say 'Who gave you the right to take hold of intellect divine, and to trample it with your earthy mortal intellect?' And a later verse continues the rebuke: חָדְשֵׁיכֶם וּמוֹעֲדֵיכֶם שָׂנְאָה נַפְשִׁי — 'Your new moons *(chadashim)* and your festivals *(moadim)* My soul hates.' That is to say [again on the non-literal level of *derush*]: 'The *chiddushim* (the novellae in *haskalah*) that you so ingeniously propound, and that turn you into *muadim* (incorrigibly dangerous oxen, goring one another in scholarly combat in order to flaunt your prowess in the *haskalah* of *Chassidus*), — *this My soul hates.'* And therefore, as the next verse goes on to say, גַּם כִּי תַרְבּוּ תְפִלָּה אֵינֶנִּי שֹׁמֵעַ —'Even if you make many prayers I will not hear.'"

My father now concluded: "*Davenen,* the service of the heart, first requires a preparation. In addition to preparation through *Kerias Shema* as it is said before retiring at night, and *Tikkun Chatzos,* the prerequisite to prayer is a readying of the heart, and this can come about only by means of the perspiration generated by the ardent and practical performance of the commandments. Indeed, it is through this that one responds to the plea of the prophet in the following verse: רַחֲצוּ הִזַּכּוּ — 'Bathe yourselves, cleanse yourselves!' One should bathe in sweat and cleanse oneself in tears — and *then* one can perceive

---

When you come...before Me: *Isa.* 1:12.

Who asked...to trample My courts: *Isa.* 1:12.

Your new moons...My soul hates: *Op. cit.,* v.14.

Even if you make...will not hear: *Op. cit.,* v.15.

Preparation through *Kerias Shema...* before retiring: Apart from the *Shema* itself, the theme of most of the accompanying passages is penitence.

Bathe yourselves, cleanse yourselves: *Isa.* 1:16.

the divine light that is to be found in the divine intellect of *Chassidus*."

And with that my father rose from his place. Within an instant his listeners had all joined him — in a dance that made of many men, one man.

Chapter 5b

Pesach 5694 (תרצ"ד; 1934)

[Warsaw]

18.

For my father's work — and this includes his activities on behalf of Jewry at large — the year 5669 (תרס"ט; 1908-09) was a time of outstanding importance.

In the month of MarCheshvan (late 1908) a secret meeting presided over by my father took place in Lubavitch. The participants were a number of *rabbanim,* as well as some wealthy businessmen with a sound grasp of communal endeavors; the objective was to hear and discuss a report involving several weighty issues.

Since I was my father's private secretary, the co-ordinator of the office, and one of its five active workers, I was directed by my father to acquaint those present with the following three main questions: (a) how to organize the ground-work and the elections for the forthcoming rabbinical conference; (b) the manner and extent of our involvement in the preparations and elections for the forthcoming Duma, the Russian parliament; and (c) amendments to the regulations that had been instituted by the *rabbanim* of Germany, led by HaRav Breuer, for *Machzikei HaDas,* the organization which my father had left two years earlier.

Private secretary: The writer had served in this capacity from the age of 15.

Forthcoming rabbinical conference: Held for a month in Petersburg early in 1910. For details, see *Igros Kodesh* (Letters of the Rebbe Rashab), Vol. I, pp. 35-41.

Machzikei HaDas: "Society to Uphold the Faith," established by the joint efforts of the rabbinical and communal leaders of chassidim and *misnagdim* in 1879, in an attempt to stave off the inroads of assimilation by means of political action on the national and communal levels.

The meeting lasted for five days, in the course of which decisions were reached on all the above subjects. The office was charged with executing them, and the necessary budget was seen to.

The winter months were spent in dealing with the above responsible tasks, as well as in routine representations in government circles on questions involving the economic situation of Russian Jewry. My father spent the last three winter months in various health spas abroad, and during his stay in Germany discussed the platform of *Machzikei HaDas* with *rabbanim* and communal workers. These several weeks of exertion weakened my father considerably, so that he was compelled to extend his stay abroad by several days.

Finally, on Wednesday morning, the ninth of Nissan, we left Berlin via Koenigsburg, Dvinsk, Vitebsk and Rudny, and at six on Thursday evening, the tenth of Nissan, we arrived at Lubavitch.

19.

As we drove through a few of the Jewish streets of the township of Rudny we saw tables and benches outside every house, some already washed, some being washed. In the gentile streets there was nothing to be seen.

As we drove out of the town, taking the road to Lubavitch, my father said: "I will tell you a story that I heard from my father some 30 or 32 years ago."

Now every story should teach one a lesson in *avodah*, and open up one's heart and mind in *haskalah;* every story should smooth out and straighten the crookedness in one's heart. The Book of *Bereishis* is largely composed of narratives, and is accordingly known as *Sefer HaYashar* [lit., "the straight book"],

---

Some already washed: In preparation for Pesach a few days later.*

Heard from my father: I.e., the Rebbe Maharash.

30 or 32 years ago: I.e., 1877-1879.

Known as *Sefer HaYashar:* See *Rashi* on *II Sam.* 1:18: "...*Sefer Bereishis*, which is the book of the righteous — Avraham, Yitzchak and Yaakov."

because its holy stories straighten out a man's heart and mind, enabling them to become vessels fit to contain Torah and *avodah*. So too every story should do something useful for the advancement of one's *haskalah* and *avodah*.

My father now told me something that he had heard from my grandfather, the Rebbe Maharash, that he in turn had heard from *his* father, the *Tzemach Tzedek*, who had heard it from the mouth of the Alter Rebbe — that the stories of *tzaddikim* that chassidim exchange when sitting together at a *farbrengen* are an illustration of the verse, טַל אוֹרֹת טַלֶּךָ — "Your dew is a dew of lights," for stories of this kind infuse vitality both into one's *haskalah* and into one's *avodah*.

"Rain," my father now began to explain, "enhances growth. The nature of water, which is to 'promote the growth of all kinds of pleasure-giving things,' improves both crops that are sown and those that are planted. And the water which augments the growth of field and vineyard alike rains down in four forms — *geshem, matar, yoreh* (early rain) and *malkosh* (late rain). All of these, however, benefit only the *substance* of the grain and fruit harvests; the contribution of dew is to their flavor and their nutritional value.

"With this we can better understand the above-quoted verse, טַל אוֹרֹת טַלֶּךָ. For [, to paraphrase a teaching of our Sages on these words], כָּל הַמְשְׁתַּמֵשׁ בְּטַל תּוֹרָה טַל תּוֹרָה מְחַיֵּהוּ וְכָל שֶׁאֵינוֹ מִשְׁתַּמֵשׁ בְּטַל תּוֹרָה אֵין טַל תּוֹרָה מְחַיֵּהוּ — 'Whoever makes use of the dew of the

---

Stories of *tzaddikim*...Your dew: The quotation is from *Isa.* 26:19.

A dew of lights: Translated according to the interpretation of *Rashi*, which the present teaching matches.

Promote the growth: *Tanya*, end of Ch. 1.

Crops... sown and... planted: See p. 109 above, and the footnote there.

The dew of the Torah: The original Talmudic teaching (Tractate *Kesubbos* 111b) has "the light of the Torah," which is a *derush* on the above-quoted verse (*Isa.* 26:19), while its paraphrase appearing here echoes the *language* of the verse — as too in *Tanya* (end of Ch. 36), following *Yalkut Shimoni* on the verse, and elsewhere. (See *Likkutei Sichos*, Vol. XI, p. 193, footnote there.) Cf. also next note (below). As to the connection between the two terms, אוֹר תּוֹרָה and טַל תּוֹרָה represent רָזִין דְּאוֹרַיְיתָא and רָזִין דְּרָזִין דְּאוֹרַיְיתָא respectively (*Likkutei Torah*).

Torah, the dew of the Torah revives [in the context: 'resur-rects'] him, and whoever does not make use of the dew of the Torah, the dew of the Torah does not revive him.' The stories and the informal talk that are heard at a *chassidisher farbrengen* are the *dew* of Torah, a dew that gives vitality. Rain, as we have said, benefits the *body* of the grain and fruit harvests, while dew makes them more delicious and more nutritious.

"What we have said so far in praise of the stories and conversation of chassidim has related to their innate value, without particular reference to the stature of the narrator. After all, what counts is the story. But the stature of the narrator has its importance too — not insofar as the story itself is concerned, but certainly as far as the *effect* of the story is concerned.

"When my father related something," my father con-cluded, by way of introduction to his father's story, "one had to listen attentively with all ten faculties of one's soul, noting the choice of every single letter — for every word of his was meaningful to all the ten faculties of one's soul."

20.

Here, then, is the story, as my grandfather told it to my father.

*   *   *

When I was in Marienbad I decided that I would travel home via Vienna and Warsaw, visiting Berditchev on the way, though without anyone's knowing: I would be accom-panied only by Pinchas Leib.*

---

* The assistant *gabbai* of the Rebbe Maharash.

Revives...resurrects: Cf.: "the dew with which in time to come the Holy One, Blessed be He, will resurrect the dead" (Tractate *Chagigah* 12b; *Shabbos* 88b).

Marienbad: Town in W. Bohemia (Czechoslovakia) renowned for its health spas. The Rebbe Maharash used to utilize his visits there for consultations with overseas rabbinic and communal leaders on mat-ters of public concern.

Arriving in Berditchev very early in the morning, I drove off to a hotel, prayed *Shacharis,* and went to the resting place of the Rav of Berditchev.

When I left the *ohel* I went to see the *shtiblach* of the local Polish chassidim. In the first little *shul* I visited I found quite a number of people sitting and studying, while others were indulging in the conversation of chassidim, or exchanging stories. From there I went on to a second and a third *shtibl,* everywhere finding old and young alike studying, and likewise spending their time in positive talk. This went on for quite some time, as I wandered from one *kloiz* to the next. I engaged a few individuals here and there in conversation — some of them older chassidim, some of them younger — asking them questions about whatever they happened to be studying at the time, and often receiving answers that evidenced a firm grasp of their subject.

I was about to return to my hotel to rest, for there remained a few hours until my train was due to depart, when I caught sight of several elderly chassidim with white beards. Though it was not a warm day, their long coats were tucked up, and on their feet they wore nothing more than shoes and socks. They were carrying a big bucket of water, and talking excitedly. This scene attracted my interest: I could tell that these were no common water-carriers. Moreover, as they walked, the younger people who accompanied them kept on offering to carry the bucket instead of them, but were constantly refused.

After quite a long walk they turned into an alley, where a few houses down the way I saw several elderly folk who had all taken off the long black coats that usually covered their *tallis katan;* they had rolled up their sleeves, and were busy washing the floor and the walls of the house at which we had arrived.

I found out after a moment's wonderment that this was a *shtibl* of Tolna chassidim. Speaking with a couple of those who

---

The Rav of Berditchev: R. Levi Yitzchak of Berditchev.

had brought the water here, I saw at once that these were real
Torah scholars, and chassidim through and through. When I
asked them what was going on they told me that since their
Rebbe was due to visit their town the next day, they wanted
to put their *kloiz* in order, in fit condition to receive such an
honored guest.

"So why are you doing all of this yourselves," I asked
them, "instead of giving the younger men a turn? After all,
young people do need to be brought up in the ways of chassidim, don't they, and for their sake older chassidim ought to
have *mesirus nefesh*, self-sacrifice."

"The reason that we are doing this ourselves," they answered, "and not through hired laborers, is that we want to
have healthy angels to help out the advocating angels who
come out of the *tekios*, out of the blasts of the *shofar*."

One of them explained: "You know the *Yehi ratzon* which
is said after the *tekios* of Rosh HaShanah, the one that men-
tions 'the angels that are formed from the blowing of the
shofar, and from the *tekiah*, the *shevarim*, the *teruah*, and the
tekiah, and from the קשר"ק '[i.e., the initials of these four
Hebrew names of the various kinds of sounds of the *shofar*]?
Well, one Rosh HaShanah the holy Rav of Berditchev said:
'Sweet Father, compassionate Father! Just in case the angels
that proceed from the *shofar* that Levi Yitzchak the son of
Sarah has just blown, are weak angels, then let their place be
taken by the holy, healthy angels that were created by the toil
of Your people in preparation for Pesach, as they cleaned
their kitchen utensils in order to fulfill their *mitzvah* as perfectly as possible, *kratzen* (scouring), *shobben* (scraping), *reiben*
(rubbing), and *kasheren* (making kosher)!' [— for the initials of
these four Yiddish words are likewise קשר"ק].

"As for us," the old chassid concluded, "we are doing all of

The *Yehi ratzon: Machzor*, p. 128; *Siddur*, p. 281.
Levi Yitzchak the son of Sarah: The·speaker here refers to himself
in the self-effacing third person; the addition of his mother's name
characterizes the form in which a name appears in a prayer seeking
divine compassion.

this for the sake of His Name, and for the sake of His servant, our Rebbe (*May he be blessed with good health!*)."

21.

[My grandfather, the Rebbe Maharash, resumes his recollections, as repeated to me by my father.]

As I contemplated these chassidim, the whole scene before me left a remarkably favorable impression. But then, when I was about to leave, I noticed that right next to their *kloiz* there was a well.

"Why did you have to bring the water from so far," I asked the old folk, "if you have water right here?"

The same old man answered me: "R. Baruch Yossl, one of our well-to-do chassidim, asked and promised that if we would now take water from his well — both today, in preparation for the Rebbe's arrival, and tomorrow, the first day of the Rebbe's visit — then in honor of the Rebbe he would prepare a big festive meal for all the chassidim, at his expense."

* * *

Having finished recounting this incident as he had heard it from his father, the Rebbe Maharash, my father now commented: "We may gauge the impression that this encounter made upon my father from the fact that he related it in all its details. Moreover, when he had completed his narration he said to me: 'Here we can plainly see what spiritual forces the Baal Shem Tov drew down in This World, both for the mentors, that is, the Rebbes, and for the taught, that is, the chassidim, so that both the recipients and their mentors should — and shall indeed — ready the world for the coming of *Mashiach,* speedily, and in our own days, Amen!'

For a long while now my father remained silent, deep in thought.

The mentors: In the original, *mashpi'im.*
The taught: In the original, *mekablim* (lit., "recipients").

Then he said: "The old man's answer, as to why they did
everything themselves instead of through hired workers,
was good. But when it comes to the question as to why they
did not let their young men take a turn, they gave no answer
— for such a *mesirus nefesh*, of setting oneself aside for the sake
of some young man, is the distinctive contribution of *Chabad
Chassidus*.

"Belief in *tzaddikim* is what stood the chassidim of Poland
firmly on their feet. As the verse says, בֶּאֱמוּנָתוֹ יִחְיֶה — 'He lives
with his faith'; they truly *live* with their faith.

"The sensitivity to the beauty of holiness that led that
chassid to promise that if the water would be taken from his
well he would provide a public feast at his expense — and this
entails not only money, but a commitment of physical exertion by himself and his whole family — *this* is the meaning of
'living with their faith,' for such faith actively permeates
one's whole life.

"However, the virtue of 'living by one's faith' properly
belongs to the period preceding the Giving of the Torah.
Thus, for example, the Exodus from Egypt took place by
virtue of faith, as our Sages teach, בִּזְכוּת הָאֱמוּנָה נִגְאֲלוּ אֲבוֹתֵינוּ מִמִּצְרַיִם
— 'By virtue of faith our forefathers were redeemed from
Egypt.' While in Egypt our forefathers transmuted their faith
into *chiyus*, vitality, and thus lived with faith. By virtue of this,
they — and all of us too — were redeemed from Egypt, and by
virtue of this faith great revelations took place; in the words
of the *Haggadah*, שֶׁנִּגְלָה עֲלֵיהֶם מֶלֶךְ מַלְכֵי הַמְּלָכִים הקב"ה — 'the supreme
King of kings revealed Himself to them,' as is explained in
Chassidus. For indeed there is nothing loftier than faith, especially when it is translated into vitality, so that one is made
alive by one's faith. And when we say 'alive' we mean life of
the kind that encompasses all the aspects of one's existence,

He lives with his faith: *Hab.* 2:4; the verse speaks of a *tzaddik*. See end
of Section 33, below, for the classic *derush* of R. Shlomo of Karlin on
these words.
By virtue of faith...from Egypt: A variation of the version appearing
in *Yalkut Shimoni* on *Hosea*, Section 519, and elsewhere.

so that one's spiritual affairs, one's material affairs, the way one guides one's family, — all of this is made alive by one's faith. And this, to be sure, is a praiseworthy level.

"All this, however, is true of the period prior to the Giving of the Torah. With the Giving of the Torah, Jews were given an order of conduct for their divine service, an order involving Torah and the commandments — so that they would be able to infuse *vitality* into their *faith*. For the faculty of faith is *makkif* [lit., 'encompassing', transcendent; being by definition superrational, it is not restricted by the bounds of mortal reason]. Faith can tolerate the coexistence of opposites. Hence, at the very same moment at which one believes in G-d and lives by one's faith, one can conceivably do something which is opposed to His Will.

"When the Alter Rebbe visited Minsk for the first time for the great disputation, and stayed for the following well-known *Shabbos* — during which time he showed the so-called scholarly world the meaning of scholarship, and refuted the arguments of all the opponents of the teachings of *Chassidus* — scores upon scores of really erudite young men were drawn towards him. His opponents, seeing that men of this caliber were on the verge of becoming chassidim, called meetings, and decreed that it was forbidden to study *Chassidus* because of *bittul* Torah [i.e., a waste of time that should be spent on the study of Torah]. When the Alter Rebbe heard that this was the reason given for the prohibition, he said: 'The Evil Inclination has tackled the opponents of *Chassidus* with the reasoning

---

Minsk...great disputation: Dramatic confrontation in the summer of 1783, in which the Alter Rebbe was challenged by the scholarly giants among the *misnagdim* of all the surrounding provinces to publicly defend the doctrines of the Baal Shem Tov — but only after he had proved his own Talmudic erudition to their satisfaction. See: R. Nissan Mindel, *Rabbi Schneur Zalman of Liadi*, pp. 68-74; R. Chanoch Glitzenstein, *Sefer HaToldos: HaRav Shneur Zalman MiLiadi* (expanded edition), Ch. 6.

The Evil Inclination: Identified by the Sages (Tractate *Bava Basra* 16a) with Satan. In our text, personified with euphemistic vagueness as דער בַּעַל דָּבָר ("the other party," "the opposite litigant").

of a clever thief: as soon as he is caught in the act he starts calling out to G-d. True, he invokes the Name of heaven, but there can indeed be a veritable thief who at the mouth of his tunnel calls out to G-d.'

"This paradox is clearly explained in *Chassidus*. Faith, as we said earlier, is by nature *makkif*. This thief believes that it is in fact G-d who 'provides nourishment and sustenance' — except that he considers that his means of sustenance is theft, and that is why he asks the Almighty to prosper his endeavors at making a livelihood. A person's task in *avodah*, however, is to *internalize* his faith; that is, to bring vitality into his faith. This is what we are taught by the verse, וְשֶׁמֶן עַל רֹאשְׁךָ אַל יֶחְסָר — 'Let there be no lack of oil above your head.' The oil and the wine in Torah, — these are the study of *Chassidus*, through which one's faith is internalized.

"And when one's faith is thus brought to the level of *pnimiyus*, the manner in which one conducts one's *avodah* is utterly changed. In this new order of conducting one's *avodah* each individual grows sensitive to the positive value of the other; it begins to dawn upon a person's understanding that for the sake of bringing another closer to divine service, one ought to set oneself aside. When this happens, a person discovers within himself the power to find *mesirus nefesh* worthwhile — for the sake of warmly guiding a younger

---

Thief...calls out to G-d: Tractate *Berachos* 63a, in the version of *Ein Yaakov*.

Provides nourishment and sustenance: From the first paragraph of the Blessing after a Meal (*Siddur*, p. 89).

To *internalize* his faith: In the original, *emunah areintrogn in a pnimi*; i.e., to integrate and digest it, as it were, as opposed to allowing it to remain at the level of *makkif*.

No lack of oil: *Eccles* 9:8.

The oil and the wine in Torah: Wine (יַיִן) signifies the mysteries of the Torah (רָזִין דְּאוֹרַיְיתָא); oil (שֶׁמֶן) signifies the innermost mysteries of the Torah (רָזִין דְּרָזִין דְּאוֹרַיְיתָא).

Bringing another closer to divine service: In the Heb./Yid. original, the verb is *mekarev-zein*.

Warmly guiding a younger colleague: As above.

colleague, and setting his feet firmly on the path of truth."

22.

My father now enlarged on this theme: "My grand-father* once told my father** that one ought to sacrifice oneself for the sake of guiding a young colleague in the ways of *Chassidus* just as one ought to do so for the sake of saving the community of Israel. On his way from Minsk after the well-known disputation, the Alter Rebbe stopped off at Semi-lian, a town known for its Torah study, and the home of many learned young men. In the course of the week that he stayed there he made chassidim of a *minyan* of them, all of them scholars with a reputation throughout the entire region. One of them was R. Avraham Beirach of Semilian.

"When R. Avraham Beirach visited the Alter Rebbe for the first time at Liozna and entered his study for *yechidus*, the Alter Rebbe said: 'It is written, כִּי הָאָדָם עֵץ הַשָּׂדֶה — "For a man is a tree of the field." When a tree does not yield fruit it becomes barren. It is possible to have mastered the whole *Talmud*, and yet to be (G-d forbid) barren. A Jew should yield fruit! What is the value of your Torah study and your *avodah* if you have not diffused blight, if you have not brought light into someone else's life? Rava taught: "He who loves Torah sages will have sons who are Torah sages." He who turns a person who knows Torah into a lover of G-d, and shows him a path in the

---

* The *Tzemach Tzedek*.
** The Rebbe Maharash.

For a man is a tree: *Deut.* 20:19. Though in the Torah this phrase appears in the form of a rhetorical question, for the purposes of *derush* it appears here — as in many other places too — as a positive statement.

To have mastered the whole *Talmud:* In the original, *zein a Shas-Yid* (lit., "to be a *Talmud*-Jew").

He who loves Torah sages: Tractate *Shabbos* 23b.

He who turns...into a lover: An interpretation of Rava's teaching on the non-literal level of *derush;* "he who loves sages" is here understood in a causative sense, and taken to mean "he who causes sages to love."

service of G-d, — such a man will have sons who are sages.'

"That visit of R. Avraham Beirach's in Liozna lasted several weeks. On his way home to Semilian he passed through Liepli, where he stayed for some time, and began to yield fruit. One of his first fruits was R. Mordechai of Liepli."

Having completed his story my father paused, deep in thought, and I could see that he was in a joyous frame of mind.

After a little while he said: "This story provides us with a profound explanation — an explanation in the terms of *haskalah* — of two statements of the *Midrash*. There is a verse involving Yaakov Avinu that says, וְשִׁמְעוּ אֶל יִשְׂרָאֵל אֲבִיכֶם — 'And listen to Yisrael your father.' The *Midrash* [by altering the vocalization of the second word from *segol* to *tzeireh*] expounds as follows: אֵ-ל הוּא יִשְׂרָאֵל אֲבִיכֶם — 'Your father Yisrael is a G-d. For just as the Holy One, Blessed be He, builds worlds, so too does your father build worlds; just as the Holy One, Blessed be He, apportions (מְחַלֵּק) worlds, so too does your father apportion worlds.' Another *Midrash* refers to the verse, כֹּה אָמַר ה' בֹּרַאֲךָ יַעֲקֹב וְיֹצֶרְךָ יִשְׂרָאֵל . In its plain meaning, the prophet — here addressing his people — is saying: 'Thus says G-d Who created you, O Yaakov, and Who formed you, O Yisrael.' The *Midrash*, however, on the non-literal level of *derush*, expounds and paraphrases this verse as follows: 'The Holy One, Blessed be He, said to His world: My world, My world! I shall tell you who created you, and who formed you; יַעֲקֹב בְּרָאֲךָ יַעֲקֹב יְצָרְךָ — Yaakov created you, Yaakov formed you.' This teaching

---

And listen to Yisrael: *Gen.* 49:2.

Your father Yisrael: *Bereishis Rabbah* 98:3.

Builds worlds... build worlds: The verb is translated as paraphrased here — בּוֹנֶה; in the *Midrash,* the verb is בּוֹרֵא ("creates...create"). The concept of בּוֹרֵא in fact comprises both concepts appearing here — בּוֹנֶה and מְחַלֵּק ("apportions"). It will be noted that Ch. 4 of *Shaar HaYichud VehaEmunah (Tanya,* pp. 297-300) discusses the two elements simultaneously present in the process of creation.

Another *Midrash*...Thus says G-d: *Vayikra Rabbah* 36:4.

Thus says G-d: *Isa.* 43:1.

appears in a different version in *Yalkut Shimoni:* 'The Holy One, Blessed be He, said to His world: My world, My world! Who created you? I shall tell you who created you, I shall tell you who formed you; יַעֲקֹב בְּרָאֲךָ יִשְׂרָאֵל יְצָרֶךָ — Yaakov created you, Yisrael formed you.'"

My father now proceeded to explain how the story he had just told of the Alter Rebbe threw light on the latter *Midrash:* "The Alter Rebbe built worlds and apportioned worlds; the Rebbes who followed him *formed* worlds. [As a stage in the creative process, the world of] *Beriah* ('creation') represents the first created matter which subsequently underwent *Yetzirah* ('formation').

"In the above-quoted *Midrash,* then, G-d asks: 'My world, My world! Who created you? I shall tell you who created you, I shall tell you who formed you.' The answer is given in two parts. Firstly, יַעֲקֹב בְּרָאֲךָ — 'Yaakov created you.' Now the name יַעֲקֹב comprises two elements, namely, י, עָקֵב. The letter *yud* [as the first of the Four Letters of the Name of G-d] signifies *chochmah,* while עָקֵב (lit., 'heel') signifies the lowest level of creation. Hence, in terms of *avodah,* יַעֲקֹב בְּרָאֲךָ signifies the drawing down of the loftiest insights of *chochmah* (י) into the lowliest levels (עָקֵב) of the world which is thereby created (בְּרָאֲךָ) out of the *beirurim.*

"The second part of the answer is יִשְׂרָאֵל יְצָרֶךָ — 'Yisrael

---

A different version: *Yalkut Shimoni* on *Isa.* 43:1.

Formed worlds: In the original, [they were] יוֹצְרֵי עוֹלָמוֹת.

Beriah... Yetzirah: For an exposition of the concept of "worlds", see Rabbi J. I. Schochet, *Mystical Concepts in Chassidism,* Ch. IV; in *Tanya,* p. 852ff.

The first created matter: In the original, חוֹמֶר הָרִאשׁוֹן.

The answer is given...out of the *beirurim:* In the succinct original, יַעֲקֹב בְּרָאֲךָ הַמְשָׁכַת הַיוּ"ד דְחָכְמָה בַּעֲקֵבַיִם שֶׁל הַבֵּרוּרִים.

Created...out of the *beirurim:* In this context, *beirurim* does not refer to a certain kind of *avodah,* but to a state of existence; viz., matter which — as a result of *Sheviras HaKeilim* — is awaiting *beirur.* (See Schochet, *op. cit.,* p. 866ff.) This *beirur* of *tohu* is creation (*Beriah;* בּוֹרֵא חוֹשֶׁךְ); it is effected through the *yud* of *chochmah* (בְּחָכְמָה אִתְבְּרִירוּ).

Yisrael...drawing down of divine light: Once *Beriah* has given the fallen matter (the above-mentioned "first created matter") its initial eleva-

formed you,' for Yisrael represents the drawing down of
divine light through one's *avodah*."

After another few minutes' silence my father said:
"Praised be the Almighty for the light of *Chassidus* which our
fathers, the Rebbes, have bequeathed us. For it is an inheritance without bounds or limits. With G-d's help, from one
chassidisher seed a tree can grow, with many branches and
abundant fruit — and each fruit in turn will contain the seed
of new growth.

"One must exert oneself to the utmost in guiding one's
students. May the Almighty grant that they grow to be
luminaries that radiate light, and 'moist enough to moisten.'
It was for this that the Rebbes of the respective generations
sacrificed themselves, and their *mesirus nefesh* is the strength
which is invested from Above in the individual who strives to
fulfill the divine command, וּבָחַרְתָּ בַּחַיִּים — 'Choose life!'"

23.

In Lubavitch there was a resemblance between the eves
of two festivals — *erev* Yom Kippur and *erev* Pesach — in the
striking difference of mood that prevailed in each case
between the first and the second half of the day. In fact the
noon of each day seemed to mark off two different seasons of
the year.

On *erev* Yom Kippur my father would rise no later than
1.30 a.m. The subjects he studied that day included Tractate

---

tion, its subsequent illumination is effected through *Yetzirah* (יוֹצֵר אוֹר).
This is the *avodah* of Yisrael.

Exert oneself...in guiding one's students: The Tomchei Temimim Yeshivah
in Lubavitch was only 12 years old at the time, and the Rebbe Rayatz,
to whom the whole talk recorded here was addressed, had been
entrusted by his father with its direction almost from its foundation.

Luminaries that radiate light: *Siddur*, p. 43.

Moist enough to moisten: Cf. Tractate *Berachos* 25b.

Choose life: Deut. 30:19. In chassidic tradition this phrase is more than
mere advice or even a command: it is a נְתִינַת כֹּחַ — a bestowal of the
requisite strength to fulfill the command.

Included Tractate *Yoma*: The Yom Kippur service in the *Beis HaMikdash*,
especially that of the *Kohen Gadol*, is discussed there at length.

Yoma, Rambam and *Pri Etz Chaim.* I would often join him in his study by 3:00, and remain there until 5:00 or 5:15; *kapparos* would take place no later than 5:30.* These couple of hours were spent in the study and discussion of the *avodah* of Yom Kippur in general, and the *avodah* of the *Kohen Gadol* in particular, all in a spirit of extraordinary joy and pleasure. We would *daven* early, and the blithesome and holy mood would continue until noon. The midday meal too, which on *erev* Yom Kippur would take place not later than 11:00, was marked by a certain degree of cheerfulness.

At this meal my father would always explain some theme in *Chassidus* and in *avodah.* This was usually a discussion of how the *avodah* of *erev* Yom Kippur will be carried out when *Mashiach* comes — speedily, and in our days, Amen.

On one such occasion my father explained how when *Mashiach* comes the divine light will be revealed here below, in the level of *Asiyah* within the world of *Asiyah* — that is to say, in this material world — in a manner of *Elokus begilui,* G-dliness revealed, just as it is now in the world of *Atzilus.* (Strictly speaking, my last phrase — "just as it is now in the world of *Atzilus*" — is not exactly apt, for the future revelation will in fact be loftier than the degree of revelation in the world of *Atzilus* now. It is only that from our present perspective the world of *Atzilus* is the highest level among the worlds; though there exist worlds of *Ein-Sof* above *Atzilus,* these are beyond our grasp. And my father went on to briefly point out the distinction between the Ten *Sefiros* of *Atzilus* and [the yet higher level of divine emanation known as] *Adam Kadmon.)*

Chassidim know that the world of *Atzilus* signifies the

---

* The details of my father's customary conduct on the eve of the festivals and Sabbaths throughout the year are set out elsewhere.

Pri Etz Chaim: The teachings of the *AriZal* on the Kabbalistic *kavanos* of the various prayers are recorded there by his disciple, R. Chaim Vital.

World of *Asiyah...Atzilus...Adam Kadmon:* On the concept of "worlds", see Rabbi J. I. Schochet, *Mystical Concepts in Chassidism,* Ch. IV; in *Tanya,* p. 852ff. See also Footnote (3) on p. 343, *op. cit.*

Ten *Sefiros:* See Schochet, *op. cit.,* Ch. III, p. 826ff.

world of unity, the world in which "He and His life-giving
emanations are one," and "He and His causations are one."
The Ten *Sefiros* of *Atzilus* [each] comprise *oros* and *keilim*
("lights" and "vessels") — and the *keilim* of *Atzilus* are actual
Elokus, Divinity. For the very beginning of *metzius* ("existence")
is the world of *Beriah*, and everyone who studies *Chassidus*
knows that this does not at all mean existence literally: it
refers only to *hiuli* ("prime, potential, unformed matter") —
and the way in which *Ramban* understands the word בָּרָא
("created") in the opening verse of *Bereishis* is known to all.

In the world of *Atzilus*, however, the *keilim* too are actual
Elokus. My father now expanded this point, explaining that in
the world of *Beriah* — which is "the world of the throne" (עוֹלָם
הַכִּסֵּא), and which is part of "the hidden world" (עָלְמָא דְאִתְכַּסְיָא) —
the *chiyus* ("life-force") of the *nivra'im* (i.e., the created beings
whose source is in the world of *Beriah)* is in itself their *metzius*,
their existence, as is illustrated by the well-known analogy of
the sea-creatures. All this obtains when [one speaks of a level

———————

Life-giving emanations...causations are one: *Tikkunei Zohar,* Intro-
    duction 3b, as paraphrased in *Iggeres HaKodesh,* Section 20. The Aram-
    aic word here translated "His causations" (גַּרְמוֹהִי) literally means "His
    organs."

Oros and *keilim*: See Schochet, *op. cit.,* Ch. V, p. 860ff.

Actual *Elokus*, Divinity: In the original, אֱלֹקוּת מַמָּשׁ. The Rebbe שליט"א points
    out that the word מַמָּשׁ (translatable as "actually, truly, literally")
    implies coming down into existence, hence: tangibility. (Cf. end of
    Rashi on *Ex.* 10:21, *s.v.* וְיָמֵשׁ חֹשֶׁךְ, based on *Shmos Rabbah* 14:1.)

The very beginning of *metzius* ("existence"): In the original, רֵאשִׁית הַתְחָלַת הַמְּצִיאוּת.

Hiuli: Although, as *Ramban* points out, the term *hyle* is originally Greek,
    it is the Hebrew version הַיּוּלִי *(hiuli)* that is used here.

Ramban understands the word בָּרָא: In his comment on *Gen.* 1:1, *Ramban*
    writes that ברא is the only root in the Holy Tongue that signifies *yesh
    me'ayin,* the creation of existence out of nothing.

Beriah...world of the throne...the hidden world: Note the relation be-
    tween the Heb. כִּסֵּא and the Aram. אִתְכַּסְיָא. (*Likkutei Torah* (Kehot, N.Y.,
    1965), *Parshas Haazinu,* p. 148, citing *Etz Chaim*.)

The *chiyus*...is in itself their *metzius*: Their *chiyus* is the medium in which
    they live. By analogy, the water in which fish live *is* their *metzius*.

of creation at which] that which exists, the *metzius*, is *Elokus* (by virtue of its being immersed in *Elokus* and permeated by it). When, however, one speaks in terms of the *keilim* of *Atzilus*, *Elokus* is the *metzius*, that which exists (i.e., "existence" is exclusively *Elokus*). And this my father illustrated by an analogy drawn from the *keilim* (i.e., the "vessels" or faculties) of the intellect.

When *Mashiach* comes, This World here below will accord exactly with the truth. Physical space will be actual *Elokus*, not clothed at all by any of the garments of physicality, for the true face of physicality will then be discernible — the fact that it is actual *Atzmus*.

Just as this will be true of *space*, so too will it be the case with *time*. Each day will be illuminated by the real revelation appropriate to that day. When *Mashiach* comes, the divine utterance בְּתִשְׁעָה לַחֹדֶשׁ ("on the ninth of the month," referring to the eve of Yom Kippur) will illuminate its day exactly as it did when it proceeded from the mouth of the Holy One, Blessed be He. Just as in relation to space and to one's own corporeality, one will be able to see the Word of G-d which constantly brings them into being and gives them life, so too will one be able to see the Word of G-d that brings *time* into being and gives it life.

The era of *Mashiach*, then, will be the time of the realization of the verse, וְנִגְלָה כְּבוֹד ה' וְרָאוּ כָל בָּשָׂר יַחְדָּו כִּי פִּי ה' דִּבֵּר — "And the glory of G-d shall be revealed, and together all flesh shall see that the mouth of G-d has spoken." That is to say, the Word of G-d will be *visible* in space and in time.

When *Mashiach* comes, everyone will possess true perception, and whatever one sees one will understand — and truly understand, with the truth of the soul. Hence everyone will

---

Analogy...*keilim*...of the intellect: Here, too, the very *keilim* of *seichel* are themselves *seichel*.

Ninth of the month: *Lev.* 23:32.

Brings...into being and gives...life: In the original, מְהַוֶּה וּמְחַיֶּה. See *Shaar HaYichud VehaEmunah*, Chs. 1-3.

And the glory...has spoken: *Isa.* 40:5.

perceive the divine utterance בְּתִשְׁעָה לַחֹדֶשׁ ("on the ninth of the month") as it exists in its absolute essence.

My father concluded: In that era, when *Mashiach* comes, people will start hankering after the bygone days of *Galus*. It is then that they will start feeling regret for not having devoted themselves to *avodah*; it is then that people will feel anguish over their lack of *avodah*. As for now, during the era of *Galus*, these are the days of *avodah* — to prepare oneself for the Coming of *Mashiach*.

* * *

Straight after the early midday meal the light and joyful mood would change, and a few minutes past twelve my father would start readying himself for *Minchah*. This preparation consisted of *Tehillim*, which he read in a voice of hushed entreaty that would grip the innermost depths of your heart. Standing outside his door and listening to how he read *Tehillim* you would soak in tears. Here, so it seemed, a *sheliach tzibbur* for the whole House of Israel was closeted in his sanctuary, begging for mercy for an entire people.

This reading of *Tehillim* would usually take about one-and-a-half or two hours, after which came the *avodah* of the *Minchah* prayers, which also took a couple of hours. All in all, the several hours from midday until after the *Kol Nidrei* service were marked by a spirit of stern self-scrutiny.

So it was, then, that the first half of the day of *erev* Yom Kippur was a time of *Yom-Tov* and joy, while the *avodah* of the second half of the day was marked by tense and visible awe.

24.

On the morning of *erev* Pesach my father would rise no later than three. After putting on his *tefillin*, before *Shacharis*,

---

Avodah of...Minchah: On the eve of Yom Kippur, the *Shemoneh Esreh* of *Minchah* is expanded to include *Vidui*, the confession (*Siddur*, p. 301-305).

Stern self-scrutiny: In the original, *merirus*.

he would hold a *siyyum* to mark the completion of the study of a tractate. He would *daven* no later than five-thirty, and the whole of the time that remained until *biur chametz* was over was occupied with supervising and directing the removal of all leavened products and the storage of the utensils used for *chametz*. At noon it was time to make preparations for the baking of *matzas mitzvah*.

After the reading — or rather, the study — of the Order of the Pesach Sacrifice, which would take from over an hour to an hour-and-a half, the house was aglow with a fresh radiance: such an otherworldly bliss that everything bespoke joy. Every object on which one's eye fell shone with its own distinctive grace.

On *erev* Pesach my father used to *daven Minchah* early. During the couple of hours between the above reading and the *Maariv* prayers he would usually discuss the *Korban* Pesach from the perspective of *Kabbalah* and *Chassidus*, indicating too what this implied in *avodah*. In addition, he would pass on and discuss interpretations on the *Haggadah* that he had heard from my grandfather.

The spirit of tranquil pleasure that pervaded the house on *erev* Pesach after the study of the Pesach Sacrifice was not only a preparation for a *Yom-Tov*; rather, it was in itself an actual *Yom-Tov*, for this was the kind of joy that proceeds from positive thinking about the greatest and best hopes for the Coming of *Mashiach*.

Mashiach is just around the corner! The *Beis HaMikdash* is being built, we are offering the *Korban* Pesach, and we are occupied with it with such delight!

The delight of *erev* Pesach was different to the spirit of Simchas Torah or *Yud-Tes* Kislev. The mood of *erev* Pesach was one of tranquil pleasure, delight, and good spirits.

The Night of Watching sprouted forth from every

Order of the Pesach Sacrifice: *Siddur*, p. 408.
My grandfather: The Rebbe Maharash.
Mashiach is just around the corner!: In the Yid. original, *Ot kumt Mashiach!*
Night of Watching: In the original, *leil shimurim* (*Ex.* 12:42).

corner; the aroma of redemption could be felt on all sides; there seemed to be something aristocratic about our present situation. Wait, wait! In just another little moment something is going to happen that only we Jews have, something that is ours alone.

Within an hour, within half an hour, the air will resonate with "the voice of G-d striking flames of fire," for it is "a night of watching unto G-d, ... of watching over all the Children of Israel throughout their generations," when all the Jews of the whole world will unite in one thought, word and deed — to fulfill in exultation the *mitzvah* of recounting the Exodus from Egypt.

Elated with joy and free from care, we would go to *Maariv*. It was a pleasure of the soul to see the packed crowd of worshipers. True, all faces were worn with toil from the strenuous preparations for the festival — but everyone was in high spirits and radiant, and everyone was dressed in clean clothes. The walls and ceiling, freshly whitewashed, sparkled. No one spoke: everyone was waiting for the buoyant melody of *Shir HaMaalos* that would open the *Maariv* prayers.

A little later, when the praises of *Hallel* began, the many-throated voices of that congregation broke forth in tempestuous joy, with a beauty all their own. And from one song of praise to the next, the voices of the worshipers gain in intensity and certainty. When we reach the verse that says, הוֹדוּ לַה' כִּי טוֹב — "Praise G-d for He is good," it is everyone's heart that speaks out. You heard such a *"Praise Him!"* that choirs of angels are put to shame.

Voices are now subdued for מִן הַמֵּצַר — "From out of

The voice...fire: Ps. 29:7.
Recounting the Exodus: The phrase is from the *Haggadah, s.v.* עֲבָדִים הָיִינוּ, based on Ex. 13:8.
Shir HaMaalos: Siddur, p. 134.
Hallel: Ps. 113-118; *Siddur,* p. 241-245.
Praise G-d...good: *Ps.* 118:1; *Siddur,* p. 243.
You heard such a *"Praise Him!"*: In the Yid. original, *es vert aza Hoidu* (lit., "such a *Hoidu* comes into being").
From out of distress: *Ps.* 118:5; *Siddur,* p. 244.

distress I called to G-d." But the stillness is soon shattered by
the thundering plea: אָנָּא ה' הוֹשִׁיעָה נָּא — "We implore You, G-d,
deliver us! We implore You, G-d, grant us success!"

And the prayers of noble awe are brought to a close with
greetings of *Gut Yom-Tov!* that spring from the warmth of
ahavas Yisrael.

How loving and cordial is that *Gut Yom-Tov* as it is heard
among our brethren — and how beautiful it was in years gone
by!

25.

The full delight of *Yom-Tov* was experienced at the *Sedarim*
— especially the *Seder* of the second night, when we were less
limited in time than on the first night.*

My greatgrandfather, the *Tzemach Tzedek,* once told my
grandmother** that one should set the *Seder* table with all of
one's silver and gold utensils, to commemorate the "great
treasure" with which our forefathers left Egypt, and that this
should be done openly, for *Seder* night is "a night of watching."

For a start there was the physical charm of the numerous
silver candlesticks with their candles that stood on the tables
together with various other vessels of silver and gold, and the
long table surrounded by family, relatives, and guests of
venerable visage. Then, on the spiritual side of physicality,
there were the ceremonial objects that had been handed
down in the family by the Rebbes, our forebears — the Alter
Rebbe, the Mitteler Rebbe, my greatgrandfather, and my
grandfather. Then, on the physical side of the spiritual world,

---

* At the first *Seder,* though not at the second, a point was made of eating the
Afikoman before midnight.
** His daughter-in-law, the saintly *Rebbitzin* Rivkah, wife of the Rebbe
Maharash.

We implore You: *Ps.* 118-25; *Siddur*, p. 244.
Great treasure: *Gen.* 15:14; *Ex.* 12:35-36.
The physical charm: In the original, דעם גַשְׁמִיות/דיגן חֵן.
On the spiritual side of physicality: In the original, די רוּחָנִיות שֶׁבַּגַּשְׁמִיות.
On the physical side of the spiritual world: In the original, די
גַשְׁמִיות שֶׁבָרוּחָנִיות

there was that beautiful face — a Holy of Holies, suffused
with wondrous joy — and that sweet voice that read out the
Haggadah. And transcending all, on the spiritual side of the
spiritual world, stood my father's explanations of the phrases
and verses of the *Haggadah.*

Of the 30 years in which I was privileged to be together
with my father in this world — I say 30, because I am counting
only from 5650 (תר"ן; 1890) — it was my privilege to spend
Pesach with him 28 times. (On two occasions, 5661 (תרס"א;
1901) and 5667 (תרס"ז; 1907), I was for various reasons alone.)
And in the course of those 28 years I heard a certain number
of *maamarim* and expositions relating to the *Haggadah.*

With my father everything followed a certain order, and
this was true too of the way in which he conducted the *Seder.*
Before arranging the three *matzos mitzvah,* and again before
arranging the *Seder* Plate and reading the *Haggadah,* he would
consult the *Siddur* of the *Arizal* which lay on the table. He
would read the *Haggadah* out of a *Siddur Torah Or* (Vilna, 5649 /
תרמ"ט; 1889), while on the table next to him lay the *Siddur* with
the *kavanos* of the *Arizal* (Korets, 5554 / תקנ"ד; 1794), out of
which my greatgrandfather used to *daven* throughout the
year.

The first *Seder* used to start at about eight, and the *Haggadah* would be read and discussed until 10:30. By eleven my
father was making haste to perform the *mitzvos* of eating the
kazayis of *matzah* and *maror,* and then *korech,* each item being an
avodah with a beauty of its own.

That beautiful face...that sweet voice: A reference to the writer's
   father, the Rebbe Rashab, who presided over the *Seder* table.
On the spiritual side of the spiritual world: In the original, די
   רוּחָנִיּוּת שֶׁבָּרוּחָנִיּוּת.
Together with my father: The Rebbe Rashab passed away on 2 Nissan
   5680 (תר"פ; 1920).
Counting only from...1890: The writer then turned ten.
Siddur Torah Or: See Rabbi Nissen Mangel's Introduction to the *Siddur,*
   p. IX-X.
My greatgrandfather: The *Tzemach Tzedek.*

Many paths in *avodah* could be learned by closely observing how my father drank the Four Cups, or ate the *kazayis* of *matzah* and *maror*. In all of these *avodos* one could see that the physicality of the body was of no account. The body was no more than an agent for executing the will of the soul. Moreover, everything was carried out with such a tranquil deliberateness that it cast a deference and awe over everyone around — and a deepseated love as well.

My father's holy and openly joyous countenance, and the droplets of tears meandering down his face as he ate the *maror*, both seemed to transcend the usual state of human nature. And in this was reflected the whole loftiness and beauty of the dominion of Form over Matter.

26.

The Alter Rebbe explains the statement that הָאָבוֹת הֵן הֵן הַמֶּרְכָּבָה — "The Patriarchs themselves constitute the Chariot," by saying that all their organs were holy and detached from mundane matters. A chariot is subjugated to its driver. Because the Patriarchs were separated from matters of This World, their body was subjugated to their *neshamah*, to their divine soul.

Being holy and detached from mundane matters entails relinquishing one's hold on This World — not desiring it, and taking such steps as will distance oneself from it. Such was the path in divine service of the fathers of the Tribes, who chose solitude for themselves so that worldly considerations should not distract them.

This path, to be sure, is a lofty one. The ability to resign oneself from This World and to make every endeavor to shake oneself loose from mundane affairs certainly indicates a high level of attainment. Those who practice this may accordingly be termed *baalei madregah*, and through this

---

Patriarchs...the Chariot: I.e., the celestial Chariot of *Ezek.*, Ch. 1; *Bereishis Rabbah* 47:6, as explained in *Tanya*, Ch.23.

Chose solitude: The sons of Yaakov Avinu were shepherds.

avodah they become *baalei tzurah,* i.e., *baalei nefesh* in a high degree.

Now everything in the world has its own way of being set up — the handles, so to speak, by which it may be approached. A vessel, for example, has a handle by which it can be grasped. So too a concept has its "handles," through which it too may be grasped. And solitude is one — and only one — of the several "handles" of intellect. These follow a certain order, and solitude, though not the first in importance, is chronologically the first, because it paves the way for the other — and more important — "handles" of intellect.

I once heard from a chassid called R. Yisrael Nachman HaKohen the *Meshares** that when he was a *zitzer* in the *yeshivah* of the *tzaddik* R. Hillel, the latter was asked a certain question at a *farbrengen* by an elder chassid whom he particularly respected, and who was known as R. Avraham Yosef the Silent.** The question was, why did R. Hillel use a dipper with three handles when washing his hands for *netilas yadayim,* and R. Hillel had answered: "As is known, the concept on which one should concentrate during *netilas yadayim* is the drawing down of the light of intellectual perception (*mochin*) into one's emotive attributes (*middos*). Water represents *chochmah,* and I once heard from the [Mitteler] Rebbe that grasping the initial flash (or consciousness) of intellect takes place by means of three "handles": הַתְבּוֹדְדוּת, עִיּוּן וְהִתְעַכְּבוּת — solitude, profound

---

* R. Yisrael Nachman Mariashin was born in Dubrovna and studied in the *yeshivah* there. At *yechidus* the *Tzemach Tzedek* sent him to study under the guidance of R. Hillel. In later years he was a devoted chassid of the Rebbe Maharash.

** By this stage an old man: he had studied in turn under the Alter Rebbe, the Mitteler Rebbe and the *Tzemach Tzedek.* He was an outstanding *maskil,* and had a remarkable manner of *avodah* in prayer. R. Hillel once said of him: "Any statement of R. Avraham Yosefke warrants many months' study."

The Silent: In the original, דער שׁוֹתֵק.

The concept upon which one should concentrate: In the original, די כַּוָנָה.

Grasping the initial flash... of intellect: In the original, תְּפִיסַת הַשֵּׂכֶל שֶׁבַּחָכְמָה.

contemplation, and deliberateness; and this flash is invested in the intellect in three stages: נְקוּדָה, אוֹר וְחִיּוּת — first it appears as a point, then it radiates light, and then it gives life."

Indeed, we see this in our own experience. In order to approach intellect and to grasp a concept, one requisite handle is solitude, for intellect by definition resides only in a domain that is exclusively its own. As to the vessel itself, however, the real vessel for intellect is *bittul,* self-effacement. And *bittul* entails not only forgoing things of This World, but in addition forgoing one's own *self* — attaining a level at which the *intellect* becomes one's self.

This, then, is the direction to be taken in *avodah,* even if one seeks to attain no more than the comprehension of a mortal concept. That is to say, that if one seeks to secure the comprehension of a mortal concept, this too is possible only if one surrenders oneself to it, for thinking demands complete possession, that all of one's faculties and senses be subject to it.

This utter devotion of the faculties and the senses to the grasping of a particular concept has two sides to it. On the one hand, those faculties that advance this goal each need to fulfill their function; on the other hand, those faculties and senses whose function is unconnected with the attainment of this goal need to be as dormant as if they were nonexistent, in order that they should not distract. And this is where solitude comes in, for it facilitates both the eclipse of the faculties that need to be absent, and the revelation of those faculties and senses that promote the comprehension of the desired concept.

27.

No matter how lofty the *avodah* of solitude may be, it has a notable disadvantage that outweighs all of its virtues, namely, that it causes one to be torn away from the world.

True indeed, through solitude one attains the highest levels of *haskalah.* One moves to a world that is all good, a world in which heaven and earth, mountains and rivers, trees

---

This flash is invested in the intellect: In the original, הַשְׁרָאַת הַחָכְמָה אֵין שֵׂכֶל.

and grass, birds of all kinds, and the varied works of the Creator, all proclaim in their own way, 'ה מַעֲשֶׂיךָ רַבּוּ מָה — "How manifold are Your works, O G-d!" to the point that one arrives at an understanding of the exclamation, מַעֲשֶׂיךָ גָּדְלוּ מַה — "How great are Your works!" And from this one begins to yearn for higher levels of perception, arriving too at a certain level of *klos hanefesh,* expiry of the soul out of sheer love for the Creator.

True it is, that the genuine seeker of solitude advances by this means to the highest levels of *haskalah,* his thoughts soaring unencumbered throughout the loftiest worlds. With his spiritual faculties and senses, with his whole being, with his entire self he is utterly devoted to the highest of things, to the point that he becomes completely drawn into the loftiness and the holiness in which his thoughts are occupied.

But all of this is not the divine intention underlying the descent of the soul to one's body, and the creation of the· world at large. No matter how lofty *hisbodedus* may be, it is not the intention underlying the descent of the soul to one's body.

Before this descent, when it was in the store-house of souls, the soul had already experienced solitude, and had seen sights more beautiful than one sees in This World. Here one sees creatures with bodies; there one sees Divinity. It follows that when the soul was sent down from that treasure-house to This World, this must have been for a specific purpose — and that purpose cannot be realized through living in solitude.

Now our Master the Baal Shem Tov lived in solitude for many years. He was in a world that was all good, all light. He studied under Achiyah HaShiloni, saw things from one end of the world to the other, heard the conversation of creatures and palm-trees, walked about in celestial worlds — and was

---

How manifold: *Ps.* 104:24.
How great: *Ps.* 92:6.   1,
Studied under Achiyah HaShiloni: See p. 72 above, and footnotes there.
Saw things...to the other: Cf: Tractate *Chagigah* 12a.

very loath to take his leave of the world of solitude.

From the letters that R. Adam Baal Shem wrote the Baal Shem Tov, in which he compelled him to reveal himself, two things are apparent — the virtue and the greatness of solitude, of being separate from the world, and the loftiness and the necessity of revelation, of living *in* the world.

We, who live in the seventh generation after the Baal Shem Tov, can see the palpable difference between solitude and revelation. Consider how many hidden *tzaddikim* and Masters of the Name there were until the time of the Baal Shem Tov. R. Yoel Baal Shem, R. Adam Baal Shem, R. Mordechai the *Nistar*, R. Kehas the *Nistar*, — each of them accomplished great things in his generation, both by bringing salvation and healing to individuals and by bringing salvation and blessing to communities. Likewise, before he was revealed, the Baal Shem Tov wrought mighty deeds unperceived. These, however, were all the revelations of a *tzaddik* in solitude, not the revelations of a *tzaddik* in a state of revelation. But when the Baal Shem Tov revealed himself there began a state of affairs in which light was revealed, its accompanying *avodah* characterized by order and leadership.

Among my notes of the year 5663 (תרס"ג; 1903) there is a record of a talk of my father's on *Shabbos Chazon*, which fell that year on the eve of Tishah BeAv,* at the last meal before the fast. The talk, addressed to myself and to R. Yitzchak Gershon the *Melamed*, was a long and wonderful discussion of the generation of the Baal Shem Tov. We'll talk about it one day, with G-d's help. It is a subject that deserves a special niche of its own, not the kind of thing to be mentioned in passing. It is a talk both profound and seminal, rich in *haskalah*, and amply instructive as to the ways in which *avodah* should be tackled.

---

* On that *Shabbos*, *Shacharis* began at seven a.m., the midday meal was at eleven, and the above-mentioned *seudah mafsekes* was held at five p.m.

Letters that R. Adam Baal Shem wrote: See summaries of them in *Kovetz HaTamim*, pp. 116-117.

28.

Solitude and revelation, then, are two distinct paths in *avodah*, each of which has a virtue and a drawback. The virtue of *hisbodedus* is that it serves as a handle for intellect; its drawback is that through such a kind of *avodah* the divine intention of sifting and refining the world is not realized. The virtue of *hisgalus* is that it causes light to be revealed in the world; its drawback is that the initial revelation sears and shatters the world.

הוֹדוּ לַה׳ כִּי טוֹב כִּי לְעוֹלָם חַסְדּוֹ — "Praise G-d for He is good, for His lovingkindness is everlasting!" For the Almighty had compassion on His holy people, His sons and His inheritance, and arranged circumstances in such a way that the Baal Shem Tov should become revealed; moreover, that a new path in *avodah* should thereby become revealed through him, a path that would combine the advantages both of *hisbodedus* and of *hisgalus*.

The roots of this subject go back to ancient times — to the respective generations of Avraham Avinu and Moshe Rabbeinu. Both were generations of light and of revelation, yet they are essentially different.

"Until Avraham the world was conducted in darkness; Avraham appeared, and light began to appear." Until the time of Avraham there had also been great *tzaddikim*,* but in general the light that was then revealed was above *hisyashvus;* that is to say, forces of a different order would have been needed if this light were to be drawn down and (so to speak) *settled* in the universe.

This we see in a statement of the *Gemara.* "It was taught in the school of Eliyahu: 'The world will last for six thousand years — two thousand years of *Tohu* ("chaos"), two thousand

---

* See *Sichah* of *Yud-Tes* Kislev 5692 (תרצ״ב; 1931).

Sifting and refining the world: In the original, בֵּרוּר וְזִכּוּךְ הָעוֹלָם.
Praise G-d...everlasting: *Ps.* 118:1.
Until Avraham: Cf. *Bereishis Rabbah* 2:3; *Shmos Rabbah* 15:26.
It was taught...The world will last: Tractate *Sanhedrin* 97a.

years of Torah, and two thousand years of the Days of *Ma-shiach.'"* Though during the two thousand years of *Tohu* there were revelations from on high to *tzaddikim* of stature, we see that these revelations are nevertheless classified as the light of *Tohu* — and in the world of *Tikkun,* the light of *Tohu* is called darkness.

Avraham Avinu lived at the beginning of the two thousand years of Torah, so light began to appear, for Torah is a radiating light. But this is the light of *hisbodedus,* a light without order — the outpouring of lovingkindness on *all* comers, turning *everyone* into servants of G-d — for this is a light that transcends vessels and that can have no relation with them.

The generation of Moshe Rabbeinu, however, is quite a different matter. Moshe Rabbeinu represents the *chochmah* of the world of *Atzilus. Chochmah* also transcends actual (i.e., independently existent) vessels, for they are at the level of *binah.* Nevertheless, though *chochmah* transcends *keilim,* it is a light that comes down and (so to speak) settles in the confines of vessels. Indeed, even the highest level of *chochmah* can be held in some way by a vessel.

We observe in our own experience that when someone beholds an exceedingly beautiful picture or hears a wise saying of rich profundity he can become so enthralled by the experience that he can lose his tongue, as it were. He can find no words nor means of expression. He is filled to overflowing — with light.

* * *

When one studies one's portion of *Chumash* day by day, and along comes the ordinary workaday Wednesday of *Parshas*

Tohu . . . Tikkun: See Schochet, *op. cit.,* Ch. 9, p. 876.

Beginning of the two thousand years: *Rashi* on Tractate *Sanhedrin* 97a.

Settles in the confines of vessels: In the original, שֶׁבָּא בְּהִתְיַשְּׁבוּת בְּכֵלִים. This is the תְּפִיסָה spoken of in Section 26, above.

Wednesday of *Parshas Shmos:* The passage studied on Wednesday is *Revi'i,* the portion to which the fourth person will be called up at the Reading of the Torah on the following *Shabbos.*

Shemos, and one studies the passage beginning וּמֹשֶׁה הָיָה רֹעֶה —
"And Moshe used to pasture..." and ending זֶה שְׁמִי לְעֹלָם וְזֶה זִכְרִי
לְדֹר דֹּר — "This is My Name forever, and this is My remembrance from generation to generation," and when with one's
mind's eye one examines closely the theme that underlies this
passage, — then one can have some inkling of the question at
issue in the spiritual tussle between the Baal Shem Tov and R.
Adam Baal Shem over the subject of *hisgalus,* self-revelation.

29.

The Baal Shem Tov, as we have seen, did not want to
reveal himself. In this we may discern two trends — a reluctance to bid farewell to the isolated world of *hisbodedus,* and a
reluctance to join in the world of revelation. For a long time
he wrestled with R. Adam Baal Shem and evaded acceding to
his demand — until his Rebbe, Achiyah HaShiloni, assured
him that only by revealing himself would he secure the wondrous advantage of solitude; in other words, that through his
revelation the virtue of *hisbodedus* and the virtue of *hisgalus*
would unite.

From the verse, וּמֹשֶׁה הָיָה רֹעֶה — "And Moshe used to
pasture," we see that Moshe Rabbeinu chose to be a shepherd
in order to be able to live a life of solitude. As we have seen,
the great advantage of solitude is that it serves as a "handle"
to contemplation, and in fact it was when he was in that state
that the divine light was revealed to him.

When he beheld this light he said to himself: אָסֻרָה נָּא וְאֶרְאֶה
אֶת הַמַּרְאֶה הַגָּדֹל הַזֶּה — "I shall turn aside and see this great sight,"
and *Rashi* comments, אָסוּרָה מִכַּאן לְהִתְקָרֵב שָׁם — "I shall turn aside
from here to come nearer there."

On this aspiration — to *turn aside from here to come nearer there*
— hangs the whole of humanity; in this aspiration lies the
whole of *avodah,* and most particularly the *avodah* of the *misboded,* of him who serves in solitude. For with this aspiration

---

And Moshe...This is My Name: *Ex.* 3:1-15.
I shall turn aside: *Ex.* 3:3.

he climbs ever higher, never satisfied with his present rung. This aspiration of his pours forth in two directions — in an urge to "turn aside from here" and in an urge to "come nearer there."

It is an all-encompassing aspiration — not the inner content of some particular situation, but the inner content of a universal situation: it expresses the highest level of humanity in general, and of *avodah* in particular. It signifies a yearning, opening up new sources that lend strength to one's faculties and senses, so that one becomes an ever-flowing wellspring, a river that never ceases.

This aspiration exists both in relation to *haskalah* and to *avodah*. It is the peak of each, enabling one to perfect the *haskalah* of the *avodah* in which he is presently laboring.

In *haskalah* this aspiration finds expression in intellectual sharpness. Thus we observe that one who is gifted in this way handles concepts by constantly climbing and clambering through them with the greatest acuity. No sooner has a proposition presented itself in his mind than it is thrust aside by a more closely-argued proposition — and in this manner such a person climbs higher and higher. All these propositions and concepts constitute the pure essence of *haskalah*. They are the flashes of כֹּחַ הַמַּשְׂכִּיל, the superconscious origin of intellect that pours forth perceptive ideas. These arguments are expressions of the intellective soul, and through the exercise of intellectual sharpness one arrives at the perfection of *haskalah*.

30.

Only a *misboded* can arrive at a level such as the perfection of *haskalah*. Only one who of his own accord forgoes mundane matters and harnesses his spiritual faculties and senses to intellectual activity can aspire to the highest perfection of *haskalah*.

When Moshe Rabbeinu was a shepherd he was at the

Intellective soul: In the original, נֶפֶשׁ הַשִּׂכְלִי.

highest level that a *misboded* can attain. And, as we have seen, as soon as he beheld the divine light he said: "I shall turn aside and see"; that is to say, "I shall turn aside from here to come nearer there" — this being the aspiration of a *misboded*.

To this he received a reply from Above: שַׁל נְעָלֶיךָ מֵעַל רַגְלֶיךָ — "Remove your shoes from your feet."

True enough, the *avodah* of a *misboded* is something lofty — but there is something higher than it. And that higher level of *avodah* also contains the kernel of the aspiration, "I shall turn aside from here to come nearer there." However, in order to arrive at this aspiration as it is experienced at the higher level of *avodah*, there is a prerequisite, namely, "Remove your shoes from your feet." This signifies the *avodah* of being able to divest oneself of the dictates of one's reason, and subjugating oneself to that which transcends reason.

In the above-mentioned passage concerning Moshe Rabbeinu we see his path in *avodah*. First there is a revelation from Above, in which the Almighty tells him that He is the G-d of Avraham, of Yitzchak, and of Yaakov. Until this point his path has followed the inner direction of *hisbodedus*; from this point on, a new path in *avodah* will have to begin. Moshe Rabbeinu does not want to take leave of the world of *hisbodedus*, nor does he want to encounter the world of *hisgalus*, of self-revelation. And then a certain amount of bargaining goes on, until the Almighty reveals to him the teaching hidden in the verse, זֶה שְׁמִי לְעֹלָם וְזֶה זִכְרִי לְדֹר דֹּר — "This is My Name forever, and this is My remembrance from generation to generation." In other words, G-d reveals to him the secret of *beirurim*, which is the divine intention underlying the creation of the world — that the tasks of *beirurim* can be realized only through the *avodah* of *hisgalus*, of self-revelation.

And indeed, through the self-revelation of Moshe Rab-

Remove your shoes: *Ex.* 3:5.

Remove your shoes...divest yourself...of one's reason: A shoe (נַעַל) is so called because its root means "enclosed" or "locked" — hence also "restricted", or "limited", and the classic instance of limitation is mortal intellect.

This is My Name: *Ex.* 3:15.

beinu we were privileged to be given the Torah — and through the Torah and its *mitzvos* one sifts and refines the world. Likewise, through the self-revelation of the Baal Shem Tov we were granted the revelation of the *pnimiyus* of the Torah, the innermost levels of the Torah.

That is to say, that through the study of the Torah and the fulfillment of the *mitzvos* one readies the world in such a way that materiality should become a vessel for G-dliness; and through the *pnimiyus* of the Torah — the study of *Chassidus*, and being occupied with *Chassidus* — one draws down the revelation of G-dliness in This World.

The teachings of the Baal Shem Tov thus combine both advantages — the virtue of *hisbodedus* and the virtue of *hisgalus*, for they are a "handle" making possible the revelation of the essential light of *hisgalus* in such a way that it should find expression in one's intellectual faculties.

31.

We lack the brain to understand — and the strength to give praise for — the mighty gift that the Almighty bestowed upon us, *Chabad* chassidim, with the revelation of our great mentor and Rebbe, that giant among giants, who raised up the yoke of the *avodah* of *Chassidus*.

Speaking of the diversity of Torah teachings, the Sages discuss the verse, נִתְּנוּ מֵרֹעֶה אֶחָד — "They were [all] given by one shepherd." All of the disciples received the teachings of the Maggid of Mezritch, but each of them opened a distinctive gate and paved a public road so that the simple multitudes of our people should be enabled to arrive at the gate of heaven.

In the years 5628 (תרכ״ח; 1868) to 5632 (תרל״ב; 1872) my teacher the Rashbatz was an emissary of the Rebbe Maharash in the towns of the Ukraine. It once happened that when he

---

Through the study of the Torah: In the original, "through the study of the *pnimiyus* of the Torah" — an obvious misprint, in view of the parallel symmetry of this paragraph and the preceding one.

Mentor and Rebbe: The Alter Rebbe.

Given by one shepherd: *Eccles.* 12:11; paraphrase of Tractate *Chagigah* 3b.

All of the disciples: I.e., the colleagues of the Alter Rebbe.

The Ukraine: In the original, "Little Russia" (Malorussia).

was in Kremenchug, one of the people who came to hear him repeating a *maamar* was a prominent and learned chassid of Volhynia called R. Aharon.

In honor of the *Kiddush* that was held at midday on *Shabbos* all the dignitaries of the chassidic community of the town assembled. Thus it was that at that *farbrengen* there sat some of the well-known *maskilim* among the *Chabad* chassidim, such as R. Dov Masayev and R. Chaim Dov Vilenski, as well as some notable chassidim of Volhynian stock. In the course of the table talk some of the latter chassidim commented that Volhynia and the surrounding regions was the home of the Baal Shem Tov, as well as of the Maggid and his outstanding disciples, while in Lithuania there was no Rebbe apart from the Alter Rebbe and his successors.

Now all those present were men deeply steeped in the teachings of *Chassidus,* and men who engaged earnestly in *avodah.* And though the two parties were divided in their views, and each was a zealous advocate of his own tradition, they were nevertheless faithful friends, each side standing in respectful awe of the other's Rebbe. Both the *Chabad* chassidim on the one hand, and the Volhynian and Polish chassidim on the other, were familiar with the *vort* of the well-known chassid R. Binyamin Kletzker, *"Pan to pan"* ("The master's a master — but he's not mine").

When the *tzaddik* R. Menachem Mendel of Vitebsk, author of *Pri HaAretz,* set out for *Eretz Yisrael,* the disciples of the Maggid chose the Alter Rebbe as their leader in the all-embracing question of how they should relate to those who opposed the teachings of the Baal Shem Tov and his disciple, the Maggid.

In the year 5542 (תקמ"ב; 1782) or 5543 (תקמ"ג; 1783), an assembly of the disciples, the *tzaddikim* of Volhynia, was called. There a certain resolution was decided upon, which proposed means of casting off the exceedingly harsh edicts that had

Men who engaged earnestly in *avodah:* In the original, *baalei avodah.*
Pan to pan: See p. 312 below.
Edicts...issued in Vilna: This was the home of the Gaon, and headquarters of the *misnagdim.*

been issued in Vilna. Since for a certain reason the Alter Rebbe was not present, the participants delegated two of their number to visit him and inform him of their resolution. Accordingly, the *tzaddik* R. Shlomo of Karlin and the *tzaddik* R. Wolf of Zhitomir made the journey to Liozna in order to ask the Alter Rebbe to add his name to the assembly's proposal.

That resolution, the prolonged disputation between the two emissaries in the Alter Rebbe's study, and the very severe expressions that R. Shlomo addressed to the Alter Rebbe, — together these constitute a matter of some importance, and certainly not a story to be told in passing. So we will leave these points for now, and resume with what concerns us.

32.

Following that visit R. Ze'ev Wolf of Zhitomir remained in Liozna for almost three months. A number of stories of his stay there, told by the Mitteler Rebbe, have been preserved. R. Shlomo, however, left at once.

When he was about to set out, the Alter Rebbe sent several of his scholarly chassidim who studied in *Cheder Beis* to see him on his way. One of them was R. Binyamin Kletzker. On the way he and his colleagues attended to R. Shlomo's every need with the greatest respect. R. Shlomo of course understood that they were motivated not only by their esteem for him, but more particularly by an explicit instruction from their Rebbe. As they travelled he discussed with them *divrei* Torah — the revealed Law, *Kabbalah*, philosophical speculation and *Chassidus* — and was most impressed with the depth of their scholarship.

R. Shlomo's destination was Beshenkovitz, and the party of young men intended to accompany him part of the way there, as far as Vitebsk. As they arrived there R. Shlomo turned to R. Binyamin and said that if he would agree to continue with him as far as Beshenkovitz, he would be most grateful. R. Binyamin, as is well known, was a man with a rich

---

Philosophical speculation: In the original, חֲקִירָה.

soul and a profound intellect. He spent a couple of days in Vitebsk and decided to accompany R. Shlomo to Beshenkovitz.

On their way there R. Shlomo asked the wagon-driver to draw rein in a certain field, for it was time for *Minchah*. He climbed down, but could find no water with which to wash his hands before praying. He climbed up again, and sat for a while in the wordless ecstasy of *dveikus*. Suddenly the horses began to gallop along some side track, and no one could stop them. Across fields and hills and valleys they galloped — until they reached a stream. R. Shlomo smiled, climbed down, washed his hands, and said the *Minchah* prayers.

Though R. Binyamin Kletzker felt himself overwhelmed by the fiery ardor and the ecstatic enthusiasm of R. Shlomo's *davenen*, he nevertheless found it appealing.

When the *tzaddik* took his seat again, the wagon-driver said that since this region was utterly unknown to him he had no idea which direction to take. R. Shlomo thereupon told him to allow the horses to choose their own direction. On they galloped until they reached a highway. Arriving at an inn R. Shlomo gave the order to stop, and they climbed down. There they prayed *Maariv*, and the midnight service of *Tikkun Chatzos*, and when morning came, the *Shacharis* prayers. Resuming their journey, they arrived in Beshenkovitz in time for *Minchah*.

33.

This was a Thursday, and by this stage it was quite out of the question for R. Binyamin to return to his Rebbe in Liozna in time for *Shabbos*. He therefore stayed in Beshenkovitz, where he encountered many fellow chassidim of the Alter Rebbe. When they saw how their Rebbe held R. Shlomo in such esteem that he had sent scholars of the standing of R. Binyamin, who was by now well known, to accompany him on his journey, they too began to like and honor the visiting *tzaddik* more than they had previously done.

In the days when R. Menachem Mendel of Vitebsk was still in Horodok, R. Shlomo of Karlin used to visit various towns in the Vitebsk region, such as Beshenkovitz, Tchashnik and Liepli, spending some time in each. At the meeting that was held before R. Menachem of Vitebsk and R. Avraham of Kalisk left Russia for *Eretz Yisrael*, the other disciples of the Maggid divided up amongst themselves their respective spheres of influence in the dissemination of the teachings of *Chassidus*. In the course of this discussion, the Alter Rebbe was allotted Lithuania and White Russia (including the regions of Mohilev and Vitebsk). The disciples, however, had allowed special permission to R. Shlomo of Karlin to visit the three above-mentioned towns in the Vitebsk region.

Some time later R. Shlomo wanted to reside in Beshenkovitz, but he first wanted the sanction of the Alter Rebbe for the move. The Alter Rebbe made his consent contingent on three conditions. Firstly, R. Shlomo was not to speak lightly of those who devoted themselves to the assiduous study of the *Talmud* and the *Halachah* — the revealed levels of the Torah; secondly, he was likewise not to speak disparagingly of those who were endowed by nature with the fear of G-d; thirdly, he would inculcate his own chassidim and disciples with a sense of obligation to do their own toil in the service of G-d — with an exertion of the flesh and of the spirit, with intellectual endeavor and with prayer, the service of the heart — as opposed to the approach which demands of the individual chassid only that he should have faith in his Rebbe's ability to elevate him spiritually.

This, after all, is the basic difference between the *Chassidus* of Volhynia and Poland — and *Chabad Chassidus*, for this school of thought founded by the Alter Rebbe demands of each individual chassid (in keeping with his ability) prolonged intellectual exertion directed at attaining some grasp of Divinity; and so intensely should he become united with the concept under contemplation that it should be felt in his heart, the emotive experience of the love and fear of G-d having been generated by intellectual effort.

Thus it was that though R. Shlomo was prepared to accept the first two conditions he could not agree to the third, for he taught that those who are bound up with a *tzaddik* are raised up by *his* efforts in divine service. The task of such chassidim, therefore, is only to be enthusiastic in the practical observance of the Torah and its *mitzvos*, and to maintain their bond with the *tzaddik*.

In support of his approach R. Shlomo was fond of quoting the verse, וְאֶל בִּינָתְךָ אַל תִּשָּׁעֵן — "And do not rely on your own understanding," which he saw as an admonition that one should not engage in that which cannot be grasped. His other favorite verse was, וְצַדִּיק בֶּאֱמוּנָתוֹ יִחְיֶה — "And a *tzaddik* lives with his faith." [This he interpreted on the non-literal level of *derush*, treating the verb (יִחְיֶה) as if it were in the causative mood (יְחַיֶּה). Hence:] For R. Shlomo this verse came to mean that through his faith, and by cleaving to G-d, the *tzaddik* indeed *gives life* to all those who are bound to him.

34.

For two whole days after *Shabbos* R. Binyamin walked around like one in a daze, from all that he had seen and heard and sensed in R. Shlomo's divine service. It even occurred to him that he should stay on and spend some time in his company. When he finally entered his study in order to take his leave, R. Shlomo spoke to him for a few hours, entreating him to stay with him. He promised that he would reveal to him the most wondrous mysteries of the universe, and finally even told him that through his staying on his host would come closer to the Alter Rebbe's teachings. Moreover, he promised that he would gather around him a circle of disciples who would be worthy of his teaching.

R. Binyamin listened quietly to everything he said. When it came to giving his reply, he did so by quoting a Ukrainian

---

And do not rely: *Prov.* 3:5.
And a *tzaddik* lives: *Hab.* 2:4.
The *tzaddik* indeed *gives life*: See above, Section 21.
Ukrainian folk-rhyme: In the hybrid original,
> *Pan to pan, no nie moi,*
> *Khlopietz to khlopietz, no nie tvoi.*
Sharing fences with uninhibited Russian and Polish neighbors, the Ukrainian dialect borrows freely from both.

folk-rhyme (for R. Shlomo too would often flavor his conversation with folk adages in Ukrainian):

"The master's a master — but he's not mine;
The servant's a servant — but he's not thine!"

And he returned to his Rebbe in Liozna.

* * *

R. Binyamin's reply became a guidepost for real chassidim. Every chassid who was bound to his Rebbe knew that his friend's Rebbe was a master — but not his. And this approach strengthened chassidic conduct as a whole.

* * *

In the course of the above-mentioned *farbrengen* in Kremenchug, when the elder chassid called R. Aharon began to hand out points for aristocracy, boasting that Volhynia had many more *tzaddikim* to its credit than Lithuania, my teacher the Rashbatz replied: "Linen is made out of flax, and flax grows in fields — in whatever fields Divine Providence ordains that it should grow. Without flax one cannot produce linen, but there are various ways of doing this. The best work comes from abroad — from Holland, because there they have the advanced machines that brush all the impurities out of the flax, which they then spin into the finest linen. Over there, where the big machines are, there are people who know the real worth of flax, and can tell which fibers can produce the finest, cleanest, strongest linen."

My teacher the Rashbatz did not like spelling out the moral of every story. For every topic he would produce a parable that was so subtly and precisely apt that the moral was self-evident.

The above-mentioned *farbrengen*: See above, Section 31.
To hand out points for aristocracy: In the Yid./Heb. original, טײלען יחוס.
Linen is made: A variant version of this exchange appears in *Igros Kodesh*
    (Letters of the Rebbe Rayatz), Vol. II, p. 370.

35.

About a hundred years passed from the year in which the Alter Rebbe began to reveal his teachings in *Chassidus* until the year in which my father began to study *Chassidus* — 5633 (תרל״ג; 1873). And in the course of that century the teachings of *Chabad Chassidus* were further revealed by the Rebbes of the successive generations in an orderly progression.

For ten years during the lifetime of my grandfather the Rebbe Maharash — from 5633 (תרל״ג; 1873) to 5643 (תרמ״ג; 1883) — my father studied *Chassidus* and labored in its *avodah*. Manuscripts in his own hand are extant from the year 5635 (תרל״ה; 1875), when he was 14 years old, onwards — notes of *maamarim* that he had heard from my grandfather. Beginning in the following year, quite a number of *maamarim* bear notes of his own explanations, as well as lists of questions that he had asked my grandfather together with their respective answers, and notes of sessions of *yechidus*.

There is a distinctive flavor of vitality in my father's own *maamarim* of the early years, 5636 (תרל״ו; 1876) and 5637 (תרל״ז; 1877). Their theme is *avodah*. Every topic touched upon is seeped with a feel for the awe of heaven; in every word there is an echo of the service of the heart.

Once when I was strolling with my father in Marienbad, in the summer of 5668 (תרס״ח; 1908), he told me that about a year before his *bar-mitzvah* he asked my grandfather how one should go about one's studies if one seeks to ensure that they will find practical application in one's life.

When my grandfather had answered his question, he resolved to study all those laws of *Orach Chaim* that entail actual activity and to thoroughly accustom his body to them, so that of itself his body would be habituated to observing

---

Began to study...1873: In this year he became *bar-mitzvah*.
Find practical application in one's life: In the original, הֲלָכָה לְמַעֲשֶׂה.
Orach Chaim: The first of the four parts of the *Shulchan Aruch*, the Code of Jewish Law, covering the laws that apply daily, and on *Shabbos* and *Yom-Tov*.

them; as it is written concerning the prayer of *Modim*, הוּא כָּרַע מְגַרְמֵיהּ — "It (the head) bowed spontaneously."

On that occasion my father devoted a profound and scholarly talk to explaining the difference between the subjugation of the spiritual faculties (כּוֹחוֹת) and the subjugation of the senses (חוּשִׁים). This led him to a differentiation between the essential nature of the faculties and of the senses.

Though in general terms there are ten faculties of the soul, three of them intellective *(seichel)* and seven emotive *(middos)*, these are in fact ten categories comprising several branches, each of them in turn further and further subdivided. Likewise, though there are five senses, these too are comprehensive categories. And so it was that in the course of a four-hour stroll my father discussed the essential differences between the faculties and the senses.

At that time too my father explained in general terms the difference between כֹּחַ ("potential") and יְכוֹלֶת ("ability"). He said that philosophers, using intellectual speculation, do not know where lies the demarcation between the two. In the mind of *Chassidus,* however, this becomes clear, for *Chassidus* speaks of the concept of the ability (יְכוֹלֶת) of *Atzmus,* which is higher than the ability (יְכוֹלֶת) of *Seder Hishtalshelus.* And this enables one to attain a limited understanding of the distinction between כֹּחַ and יְכוֹלֶת.

After his clarification of the difference between the faculties and the senses, my father explained that the discussion thus far had referred to their essential nature, where the term used for each is a descriptive name (שֵׁם הַתּוֹאָר). However, one sometimes finds in the literature of *Chassidus* that the term כֹּחַ or חוּשׁ is no more than a borrowed name (שֵׁם הַמּוּשְׁאָל), each of them borrowing the name of the other. And some-

---

Prayer of *Modim*: At this point *(Siddur,* p. 51) the worshiper bows.

It...bowed spontaneously: *Talmud Yerushalmi,* Tractate *Berachos* 2:4, paraphrased in our text.

Ten faculties of the soul: *Tanya,* Ch. 3.

Philosophers: In the original, חוֹקְרִים, a term that includes Jewish thinkers.

times the term כֹּחַ or חוּשׁ is used as no more than a label (שֵׁם הַכִּנּוּי).

I spent about ten days at Marienbad at that time, and at every stroll there was a talk, the first few strolls being devoted to defining and exemplifying the distinction between the latter two kinds of names.

36.

These walks, which occupied almost twelve hours, served only as an introduction to the idea that the core and goal of *avodah* is setting oneself aside with *kabbalas ol*, the acceptance of the yoke of heaven. This *kabbalas ol*, however, ought to be an outgrowth of one's grasp of the divine concept that קִרְבַת אֱלֹקִים טוֹב — "The nearness of G-d is good"; not merely the sensation that לִי טוֹב — lit., "The nearness of G-d is good *for me*," meaning that *I find it pleasurable*. For this is a sensation of self, even though the source of the pleasure is *Elokus*, Divinity. And though this too is a worthy level of attainment, it contains nevertheless a sensation of self. There should be only an awareness of *Elokus*, the sensation that *it* is good.

And it is this awareness that should be the product of intellectual comprehension, and explained in the terms of mortal intellect — even though the proposition that G-d is good is axiomatic, for whomever one asks, so long as he has some degree of understanding, will immediately affirm that *Elokus* is good.

"True," said my father, "one must not build on mortal intellect, for to a certain degree it is an acquired faculty, comparable to the kind of knowledge referred to in the verse, יָדַע שׁוֹר קֹנֵהוּ וַחֲמוֹר אֵבוּס בְּעָלָיו — 'An ox knows its master, and the donkey knows its master's trough.' With beasts, to be sure, this knowledge is acquired through a trough, whereas with man, the creature gifted with the power of speech, his knowl-

---

The nearness of G-d is good: This initial paraphrase of *Ps.* 73:28 deliberately omits the word לִי.
An ox knows its master: *Isa.* 1:3.

edge is acquired through means that reflect his higher status. Nevertheless, his understanding too is only acquired. One must not build, then, on mortal intellect. Instead, *mortal intellect must be turned into a vessel fit to contain the divine intellect.*"

My father now devoted an entire profound explanation to the necessity of doing this. He discussed at length the essential natures of mortal intellect and divine intellect respectively, pointing out how distant they are from each other, how opposite they are to each other — and how they can unite, explaining in clear terms how the one can be turned into the finest vessel to contain the other.

It is at this stage, when mortal intellect becomes a vessel for divine intellect — and in this there are dozens of ways and levels — that the mortal intellect perceives that *Elokus* is good. And as a direct result of this understanding a person comes to setting his own self aside, out of a spirit of *kabbalas ol* which is directed to harnessing his spiritual faculties and senses to the service of G-d.

"The harnessing of one's faculties," said my father, "may be counted as a certain degree of a life of tranquillity. When with the Almighty's help one gets out of the Stagnant Vale of *gashmiyus,* of materiality; when one has come out victorious from the bodily battle, and has arrived at the point of harnessing the faculties of one's soul; — *then* begins the life of tranquillity. But even this is incomparable to the level at which one harnesses one's senses, for here there is not only a life of tranquillity, but a life of actual delight."

37.

If one does not count the year of mourning, ten years elapsed from the passing of my grandfather the Rebbe Maharash, on 13 Tishrei 5643 (תרמ״ג; 1882), and my father's as-

---

A life of tranquillity: In the original, חַיֵּי מְנוּחָה.

The Stagnant Vale: In the original, עֵמֶק עָכוֹר. See *Jos.* 7:24-26 for the origin of this place-name, here used metaphorically.

A life of actual delight: In the original חַיֵּי עֹנֶג מַמָּשׁ.

sumption of the leadership as Rebbe, on Rosh HaShanah 5654 (תרנ"ד; 1893). Throughout this period my father could be termed a *misboded*, one living in solitude. It is true that he taught *Chassidus* publicly, and from the year 5650 (תר"ן; 1890) received chassidim at *yechidus* — but he was still behind closed doors, alone. In the course of the ten years there were varying periods, as has been recorded in various jottings, but generally speaking this was a time during which my father followed the path of *hisbodedus*, working on himself and within himself.

From Rosh HaShanah 5654 (תרנ"ד; 1893) a new order begins, the path in *avodah* characterizing *hisgalus*, revelation — which has, as we have said above, the advantages of both paths. Now is not the time to relate the details of how my father conducted his *avodah* at that time — during Rosh Ha-Shanah, the Ten Days of Penitence, Yom Kippur and Sukkos — except for a few isolated points that are relevant to our present subject.

On the first day of Sukkos my father delivered a *maamar* that opened with the verse, וּשְׁאַבְתֶּם מַיִם בְּשָׂשׂוֹן — "And you shall draw water in joy." It began after *Minchah* and went on for a long time. Apart from the family, a number of guests from out of town joined in the festive evening meal, which turned spontaneously into a *chassidisher farbrengen* that lasted until daybreak. This happened several times during the nights of Chol HaMoed, as we celebrated *Simchas Beis HaShoevah*.

On Shemini Atzeres my father delivered a *maamar* that began with the words, תּוֹרָה צִוָּה לָנוּ מֹשֶׁה — "The Torah which Moshe commanded us." Again there was a *farbrengen* that went on right through the night. On this occasion my father spoke of the difference between repentance that stems from *merirus* (lit., "bitterness," i.e., earnest contriteness), and repentance that springs from joy. At the festive midday meal of Simchas Torah the joy of those present was indescribable, as my father delivered the well-known *maamar* on the words, אֵין

And you shall draw water: *Isa.* 12:3.
The Torah which Moshe commanded us: *Deut.* 33:4.

עֲרוֹךְ — "There is none comparable." Indeed, this *farbrengen* lasted from three p.m. until midnight.

Every *Shabbos* that year, from *Shabbos Bereishis* to the month of Tammuz,* there was a *maamar*, and most of these discourses were also issued in writing. Besides this, the year 5654 (תרנ"ד; 1894) was one of the happiest years for the *avodah* of *Chassidus*. There was a considerable number of *yoshvim* who engaged in the study of *Chassidus* and in "the service of the heart," and for me personally this was the first year of inner vitality.

At the festive meal of Simchas Torah in 5665 (תרס"ה; 1904), my father delivered a *maamar* which opens with the verse, וְלֹא יָדַע אִישׁ אֶת קְבֻרָתוֹ — "And no man knew his burial place," and which proceeds to quote the statement of the Sages that "it seemed to those on high that it was below, while it seemed to those who were below that it was on high." This was one of the many *maamarim* hearing which one beheld light; during its delivery one breathed quite a different atmosphere.

At that *farbrengen* my father said: "Our Sages teach us that אֵין הקב"ה מְקַפֵּחַ שְׂכַר כָּל בְּרִיָּה — 'The Almighty does not deprive any creature of its reward.' Just as one may not delude oneself concerning one's own failings (*chisronos*), so may one not delude oneself concerning own positive points (*maalos*). Apart from the fact that a well-ordered person ought to know what virtues he has, just as he ought to know what are his weaknesses, *this knowledge affects his labors* — for just as a *chisaron* needs to be rectified, so should a *maalah* bring about a benefit.

"A *maalah* is a step leading upwards [for *maalah* means both a virtue, and one step of a staircase]. If one stays put with

---

* At this point my father left for a health spa at Liman, near Odessa.

There is none comparable: *Siddur*, p. 204.
The first year of inner vitality: In the original, חַיּוּת פְּנִימִי. The writer turned 14 during this year.
And no man knew: *Deut.* 34:6.
It seemed to those on high: Tractate *Sotah* 14a.
The Almighty does not deprive: Tractate *Bava Kama* 38b.

one's *maalah*, it becomes a *chisaron*, a drawback. When is a *maalah* truly a *maalah*? — When it leads one upwards. And apart from all that, one may not 'deprive any creature of its reward': every person should know that he has a *maalah*.

"The years of toil have nurtured a deep-seated appreciation and a close identification with the *vort* of R. Shimshon Ostropolier: 'Praiseworthy is isolation with people, and solitude in the midst of one's fellows.'"

When one follows this path, and is steeped in the *haskalah* and *avodah* of *Chassidus*, one realizes the real intention that the Alter Rebbe and all the succeeding Rebbes had in mind; one realizes the destiny that *Chassidus* ought to fulfill, both in the individual and in the whole community of Israel.

R. Shimshon Ostropolier: Kabbalist, martyred during the Chmielnicki massacres of 1648 in the synagogue of Polonnoye, Ukraine.

Founders of Chassidism
and Leaders of Chabad-Lubavitch

Baal Shem Tov (בַּעַל שֵׁם טוֹב; lit., "Master of the Good Name"): R. Yisrael ben R. Eliezer (1698-1760), founder of Chassidism.

The Maggid of Mezritch (lit., "the preacher of Mezritch"): R. Dov Ber (d. 1772), disciple of the Baal Shem Tov, and mentor of the Alter Rebbe.

The Alter Rebbe (דער אלטער רבי; lit., "the Old Rebbe"; Yid.): R. Shneur Zalman of Liadi (1745-1812), also known as "the Rav" and as *Baal HaTanya;* founder of the *Chabad*-Lubavitch trend within the chassidic movement; disciple of the Maggid of Mezritch, and father of the Mitteler Rebbe.

The Mitteler Rebbe (דער מיטעלער רבי; lit., "the Middle Rebbe"; Yid.): R. Dov Ber of Lubavitch (1773-1827), son and successor of the Alter Rebbe, and uncle and father-in-law of the *Tzemach Tzedek.*

The *Tzemach Tzedek* (צֶמַח צֶדֶק): R. Menachem Mendel Schneersohn (1789-1866), the third Lubavitcher Rebbe; known by the title of his halachic responsa as "the *Tzemach Tzedek";* nephew and son-in-law of the Mitteler Rebbe, and father of the Rebbe Maharash.

The Rebbe Maharash (מַהַר"שׁ; acronym for *Moreinu* ("our teacher") *HaRav* Shmuel): R. Shmuel Schneersohn of Lubavitch (1834-1882), the fourth Lubavitcher Rebbe; youngest son of the *Tzemach Tzedek,* and father of the Rebbe Rashab.

The Rebbe Rashab (רַשַׁ"בּ; acronym for Rabbi Shalom Ber): R. Shalom Dov Ber Schneersohn of Lubavitch (1860-1920), the fifth Lubavitcher Rebbe; second son of the Rebbe Maharash, and father of the Rebbe Rayatz.

The Rebbe Rayatz (רייַ"צ; acronym for Rabbi Yosef Yitzchak), also known (in Yiddish) as *"der frierdiker* Rebbe" (i.e., "the Previous Rebbe"): R. Yosef Yitzchak Schneersohn (1880-1950), the sixth Lubavitcher Rebbe; only son of the Rebbe Rashab, and father-in-law of the Rebbe.

The Rebbe: Rabbi Menachem Mendel Schneerson, the seventh Lubavitcher Rebbe; eldest son of the saintly Kabbalist, Rabbi Levi Yitzchak, *rav* of Yekaterinoslav; fifth in direct paternal line from the *Tzemach Tzedek;* son-in-law of the Rebbe Rayatz.

Glossary

An asterisk indicates a cross-reference within this Glossary.

All non-English entries are Hebrew unless otherwise indicated.

For further definition of the terminology of *Chassidus*, see Rabbi Nissan Mindel, *Glossary*, in the Bi-Lingual Edition of *Likutei Amarim — Tanya* (Kehot Publication Society; London, 1973), p. 774ff.; and Rabbi Jacob I. Schochet, *Mystical Concepts in Chassidism, op. cit.*, p. 802ff.

achdus (אַחְדוּת): the Unity [of *Hashem*]

adamah (אֲדָמָה): soil; in *Chassidus*, signifies intellect

Adar Rishon (אֲדָר רִאשׁוֹן): the first of the two months of Adar in a leap year

Afikoman (אֲפִיקוֹמָן): last piece of *matzah* eaten at the *Seder*

Aggadah, Aggados (אַגָּדָה, אַגָּדוֹת): the non-halachic portions of the Talmud, composed mainly of ethical teachings based on the non-literal exposition of Biblical texts

Aha!: Vindictive expression of triumph upon winning an argument ("I *told* you so!"). In chassidic tradition, one such *Aha!* costs its brandisher his past six years of the painstaking labor of self-cultivation known as *avodah*. (In the Yiddish original, *"Mit ein Aha! geit arop zeks yohr avoideh."*)

ahavas Yisrael (אַהֲבַת יִשְׂרָאֵל): the love of a fellow Jew

Aleichem Shalom (עֲלֵיכֶם שָׁלוֹם; lit., "Upon you — peace!"): greeting used in response to *Shalom Aleichem*

aliyah (עֲלִיָּה) (a) ascent; (b) being called upon in synagogue to ascend the dais for the public reading of a portion of the Torah

aliyas haneshamah (עֲלִיַּת הַנְּשָׁמָה): lit., "ascent of the soul"

amora (אֲמוֹרָא; Aram.): authority of the 3rd-5th cents. quoted in the *Gemara*

Anash (אַנַ"שׁ; acronym for *anshei shlomeinu*, lit., "the men of our peace"; cf. *Jer.* 38:22, *Obad.* 1:7): cordial term used for the chassidic fraternity

anashim peshutim (אֲנָשִׁים פְּשׁוּטִים): pl. of *ish pashut* ·

Asiyah, the World of (עוֹלָם הָעֲשִׂיָּה; lit.,"the World of Action, or Making"): the lowest of the Four *Worlds

Atzilus, the World of (עוֹלָם הָאֲצִילוּת; lit., "the World of Emanation"): the highest of the Four *Worlds; as the one nearest (אֵצֶל — "near") the Source of creation, the *Ein-Sof*, it is still in a state of infinity

atzmi (עַצְמִי): one who is absolutely true to his true self, or *etzem;* sometimes implies independence

Atzmus (עַצְמוּת): the very Being of G-d

av (אָב): father

avodah (עֲבוֹדָה; lit., "work" or "service"): (in Torah usage) divine service, particularly through prayer and (in chassidic usage) through the labor of self-refinement

avodah shebalev (עֲבוֹדָה שֶׁבַּלֵּב; lit., "service of the heart"): prayer (and see also *davenen)

avodah zarah (עֲבוֹדָה זָרָה; lit., "alien worship"): idolatry

avodas halev (עֲבוֹדַת הַלֵּב): divine service stemming from the heart

avodas halev behispaalus (עֲבוֹדַת הַלֵּב בְּהִתְפַּעֲלוּת): ecstatic service of the heart

avodas hamo'ach, avodas hamochin (עֲבוֹדַת הַמּוֹחִין): divine service which is intellectually based

ayin hara (עַיִן הָרַע): the Evil Eye

baalei… (…בַּעֲלֵי; pl. of *baal*): people of [specified characteristics]

baalei avodah (בַּעֲלֵי עֲבוֹדָה): people who engage seriously in *avodah*

baalei batim (בַּעֲלֵי בָּתִּים): householders, as opposed to full-time scholars

baalei hassagah (בַּעֲלֵי הַשָּׂגָה): men of true understanding

baalei madregah (בַּעֲלֵי מַדְרֵגָה): lit., "men of [spiritual] rank"

baalei mochin (בַּעֲלֵי מוֹחִין): intellectuals

baalei nefesh (בַּעֲלֵי נֶפֶשׁ): lit., "men of [cultivated] soul"

baalei tzurah (בַּעֲלֵי צוּרָה): lit., "men of [refined and spiritual] visage"

Bamidbar (בְּמִדְבַּר): the Book of *Numbers*

bar daas (בַּר דַּעַת): person of sound understanding, level-headed

bar-mitzvah (בַּר מִצְוָה): religious coming of age at 13

batei midrash (בַּתֵּי מִדְרָשׁ): pl. of *beis midrash*

Bavli (בַּבְלִי; "Babylonian"): see *Talmud*

bedikas chametz (בְּדִיקַת חָמֵץ): the search for leaven on the evening before *Seder* night

beirurim (בֵּרוּרִים; lit., "sifting, refining"): the task of locating and extracting the sparks of holiness that are hidden in the universe as a result of *Sheviras HaKeilim,* and elevating them to their Source by the proper use of materiality

beis din (בֵּית דִּין): rabbinical court

Beis HaMikdash (בֵּית הַמִּקְדָּשׁ): the Temple (First or Second) in Jerusalem

beis midrash (בֵּית מִדְרָשׁ): communal House of Study

ben (בֵּן): son

ben-Torah (בֶּן תּוֹרָה): a Torah scholar

Bereishis (בְּרֵאשִׁית): the Book of *Genesis*

Beriah, the World of (עוֹלָם הַבְּרִיאָה; lit., "the World of Creation"): the second (in descending order) of the Four *Worlds. *Beriah* is called the "world of the throne." A throne is not only a support, but also a means of relating to a lower realm. *Beriah* likewise makes possible the descent of *Atzilus, enabling it to relate to the worlds below it

binah (בִּינָה): "understanding"; second of the ten *Sefiros*, or divine emanations; the second stage of the intellectual process *(see* *Chabad)*, developing the original concept (*chochmah)

bittul (בִּטוּל): self-effacement

bittul Torah (בִּטוּל תּוֹרָה): a waste of time that should have been spent in the study of Torah

biur chametz (בִּעוּר חָמֵץ): the disposal of *chametz before *Pesach

Chabad (חַבַּ"ד): acronym formed by the initial letters of the Hebrew words *chochmah, *binah and *daas, which are both (i) the first three of the Ten *Sefiros*, or divine emanations, and (ii) the corresponding stages that comprise the intellectual process (*seichel). *Chabad* also signifies: (a) the branch of the chassidic movement whose roots are in an intellectual approach to the service of G-d, and which was founded by R. Shneur Zalman of Liadi; a synonym for *Chabad* in this sense is *Lubavitch, originally the name of the township where the movement flourished 1813-1915; (b) the philosophy of this school of Chassidism

chadarim (חֲדָרִים; lit., "rooms"; pl. of *cheder)*: (a) Torah schools; (b) academy founded by the Alter Rebbe in Liozna for advanced students

Chai (ח"י; an acrostic): see *Naran...Chai

chakirah (חֲקִירָה): (in Torah usage) philosophical speculation on theological questions

chametz (חָמֵץ): leavened products forbidden for use on *Pesach

Chanukkah (חֲנוּכָּה): eight-day festival beginning 25 Kislev, commemorating the Maccabees' rededication of the *Beis HaMikdash* in the second century B.C.E., and marked by the kindling of lights

chassidish (with variable suffix; חסידיש; lit., "chassidic"): the Yiddish adjective means more than simply "chassidic": it embraces all the positive qualities of character that distinguish a person imbued with the teachings of *Chassidus*

Chassidus (חֲסִידוּת): Chassidism, i.e., (a) the movement founded in the eighteenth century by R. Yisrael, the Baal Shem Tov; (b) the philosophy or literature of this movement

Chassidus Chabad (חֲסִידוּת חַבַּ"ד): in this phrase, which follows the Heb. word-order, the second word is an adjective qualifying the first; hence, the philosophy or literature of the *Chabad branch of *Chassidus

chayah (חַיָּה): the fourth (in ascending order) of the five levels of the soul (see *Naran...Chai)

chayus: see chiyus

cheder (חֶדֶר; lit., "room"; pl., *chadarim): (a) Torah school; (b) a particular class within the school

chevrah kaddisha (חֶבְרָה קַדִּישָׁא; lit, "holy brotherhood"; Heb./Aram.): burial society, traditionally voluntary

Chillul HaShem (חִלּוּל הַשֵּׁם): desecration of the Divine Name

chitzon (חִצוֹן; lit., "one who is outward"): probably the most insulting epithet in the Chabad lexicon. Usually implies one whose avodah glistens from without more than it glows from within. Here its meaning is extended to include a subtler fault in his avodah

chitzoniyus (חִצוֹנִיּוּת): (a) the outward aspect of a person or thing (cf. *pnimiyus); (b) state of being a *chitzon

chiyus (חִיּוּת): (a) vitality, zest; (b) life-force

chochmah (חָכְמָה): "wisdom"; the first of the Ten Sefiros, or divine emanations; first of the intellectual powers of the soul which comprise *Chabad; reason in potentia

Chumash (חוּמָשׁ): the Five Books of Moses

chuppah (חוּפָּה): (a) the canopy under which the wedding ceremony is solemnized; (b) the wedding ceremony

daas (דַּעַת): "knowledge"; the third of the Ten Sefiros, or divine emanations; *chochmah, *binah and *daas together comprise *Chabad (or seichel), the intellectual process which daas completes; daas is not "knowledge" in the ordinary sense, but in the sense of concentration and attachment — the mental faculty where concepts mature into their corresponding·dispositions or attributes of character (middos)

daas elyon, daas tachton (דַּעַת עֶלְיוֹן, דַּעַת תַּחְתּוֹן; lit.,"higher understanding" and "lower understanding"): respectively, (a) the G-d-like perspective from which the spiritual world is perceived as reality, and This World a mere echo of it; (b) the opposite, earthbound perspective

daven, davenen (דאַווענען; Yid.): (a) praying, prayers; in Chabad usage also signifies (b) the *avodah of praying at length, the reading of passages in the *Siddur being interspersed with pauses for disciplined meditation from memory on related texts in Chassidus

derush (דְּרוּשׁ): (a) the non-literal or homiletical interpretation of Biblical words on a superrational or mystical level, as in aggadic exposition; (b) a *maamar

Devarim (דְּבָרִים): the Book of Deuteronomy

dibbur (דִּבּוּר): speech, one of the three *levushim of the soul

divrei Torah (דִּבְרֵי תוֹרָה; lit., "words of Torah"): formal or informal discussion of Torah subjects

dveikus (דְּבֵקוּת): the ecstatic state of cleaving to the Creator

eidim oif kest, an (אַן אײדים אױף קעסט; Yid.): a young scholar supported by his father-in-law

Ein-Sof (אֵין סוֹף; lit., "without end"): the Infinite One

Ein Yaakov (עֵין יַעֲקֹב): anthology of Talmudic *aggados for popular as well as scholarly use with commentary by R. Yaakov ibn Chaviv (15th cent.)

Elokim (אֱלֹקִים): one of the Names of G-d, signifying (variously) power, judgment and *tzimtzum (the latter attribute referring to His being concealed in nature)

Elokus (אֱלֹקוּת): Divinity

Elul (אֱלוּל): the month of stocktaking that precedes Rosh HaShanah, the New Year

eretz (אֶרֶץ): land; in *Chassidus, signifies the will

Eretz Yisrael (אֶרֶץ יִשְׂרָאֵל): the Land of Israel

erev (עֶרֶב): the eve of [a Sabbath or festival]

esrog (אֶתְרֹג): citron, used during the festival of *Sukkos for the mitzvah of the Four Species

etz chaim (עֵץ חַיִּים; lit.,"tree of life"): either of the two wooden rollers around which the parchment of a *Sefer Torah is wound

etzem haneshamah (עֶצֶם הַנְּשָׁמָה): the innermost point of the soul

farbrengen (פֿאַרברע‏נגען; Yid.): (a) an assemblage addressed by a Rebbe; (b) an informal gathering of chassidim for mutual edification and brotherly criticism

Four Cups (אַרְבַּע כּוֹסוֹת): the cups of wine drunk in the course of the *Seder

gabbai (גַּבַּאי): (a) person responsible for the proper functioning of synagogue or other communal body; (b) a kind of organizing secretary to a Rebbe

gabbai sheni (גַּבַּאי שֵׁנִי: lit., "second gabbai"): assistant *gabbai

Galus (גָּלוּת): (a) exile; (b) the Diaspora

Gan Eden (גַּן עֵדֶן): the Garden of Eden; Paradise

gaon (גָּאוֹן; pl., geonim; lit., "magnificent"): a Torah genius; especially, the head of one of the Babylonian Talmudic academies that illuminated the period that the world calls the "Dark Ages"

"garments", see *levushim

gartl (גאַרטל; Yid.): belt worn during prayer`

gashmiyus (גַּשְׁמִיּוּת): materiality; material reality (cf. *ruchniyus)

gefihl (געפיהל, Yid.): (a) spiritual sensitivity or perceptivity; (b) an intuitive spiritual insight

Gehinnom (גֵּהִינֹם): Purgatory

Gemara (גְּמָרָא; Aram.): (a) that part of the Talmud that discusses and explains the *mishnah; (b) loosely, the Talmud as a whole

geonim (גְּאוֹנִים): pl. of *gaon

gilui hamaor (גִּלּוּי הַמָּאוֹר): the revelation of the luminary

gilui or (גִּלּוּי אוֹר): the revelation of light

guf (גּוּף): body

guter Yid (גּוּטער ייד; lit.,"a good Jew"; Yid.): popular term for a chassidic Rebbe

Gut Yom-Tov! (גוט יום-טוב; Yid./Heb.): festival greeting

Haggadah (הַגָּדָה; lit.,"telling", from Ex. 13:8): book from which the *Seder service is conducted on *Pesach

Hakkafos (הַקָּפוֹת; lit., "circuits"): the sevenfold procession made with the Torah scrolls in the synagogue on *Simchas Torah, and accompanied by singing and dancing

Halachah (הֲלָכָה): (a) (upper case:) the entire body of Jewish law; (b) (lower case:) an individual law

Hallel (הַלֵּל): Psalms of praise and thanksgiving recited on certain festive days (Ps. 113-118, framed by appropriate blessings)

HaMotzi (הַמּוֹצִיא; lit.,"Who brings forth"[bread from the earth]): key word of blessing pronounced over bread

hamshachah (הַמְשָׁכָה): the drawing down [of divine light] from Above

HaShem (הַשֵּׁם; lit.,"the [divine] Name"): G-d

haskalah (הַשְׂכָּלָה; lit., "intellectualization"; unconnected except in etymology with the Haskalah, the so-called "Enlightenment" movement originating in the 18th cent.): the theoretical dimension of chassidic teachings, an exponent of which is called a maskil

havanah (הֲבָנָה): the fully-integrated understanding afforded by *binah

Havdalah (הַבְדָּלָה; lit., "separation"): benedictions pronounced over wine at nightfall at the conclusion of a Sabbath or festival to mark it off from the ordinary weekdays that follow; see Siddur, p. 234

he'arah (הֶאָרָה): illumination

hergesh (הֶרְגֵּשׁ): Heb. for *gefihl

hiddur (הִדּוּר; pl. *hiddurim;* lit., "embellishment"): enhancement or meticulous observance of a *mitzvah* beyond the demands of the letter of the law

hillula (הִלּוּלָא; Aram.): day of rejoicing; in the *Talmud* usually referring to a wedding celebration, and in chassidic circles applied to the anniversary of the passing of a *tzaddik,* because on that day every year his soul is granted an ascent (an *aliyah*) to ever-loftier levels in its perception of *Elokus

hisbodedus (הִתְבּוֹדְדוּת): solitude as a mode of divine service

hisbonenus (הִתְבּוֹנֲנוּת): profound contemplation

hisgalus (הִתְגַלּוּת): self-revelation

hiskashrus (הִתְקַשְּׁרוּת): the bond between chassid and Rebbe (see *mekushar)

hispaalus (הִתְפַּעֲלוּת): the excitation of emotions (i.e., of the emotive attributes of the divine soul)

hiuli (הַיּוּלִי, from Greek *hyle*): the prime, potential, unformed matter in which creation takes place

Iggeres HaKodesh (אִגֶּרֶת הַקֹּדֶשׁ; lit., "the sacred epistle"): a series of pastoral and expository letters circulated by the Alter Rebbe among his followers, and published as Part IV of his *Tanya

ish pashut (אִישׁ פָּשׁוּט; lit.,"a simple man"): an unscholarly person of simple faith

iyun (עִיּוּן): study (in the sense of contemplation)

Kabbalah (קַבָּלָה; lit.,"received tradition"): the body of classical Jewish mystical teachings

kabbalas ol (קַבָּלַת עוֹל; lit., "acceptance of the yoke"): subordination to the Will of G-d

Kaddish (קַדִּישׁ ; lit., "holy"; Aram.): brief prayer recited by mourner or by one leading communal prayer service; see *Siddur,* p. 77

kapparos (כַּפָּרוֹת): atonement ceremony on eve of *Yom Kippur

kashe (קוּשְׁיָא; Aram.): common Yid. mispronunciation of the word meaning a documented question querying the validity or consistency of an argument

kavanah (כַּוָנָה): devout concentration and intent, as in prayer and the observance of the *mitzvos

kavanos (כַּוָנוֹת; pl. of *kavanah*): mystical concepts on which the worshiper with a Kabbalistic training concentrates at specified points in the divine service of prayer and *mitzvos*

kazayis (כַּזַּיִת): the weight or mass equivalent of an olive

kedushah (קְדוּשָׁה): sanctity

kelippah (קְלִיפָּה; lit., "rind" or "shell"): used figuratively (on a personal or universal level) to signify an outer covering which conceals the light within; hence, the unholy side of the universe

Kerias Shema (קְרִיאַת שְׁמַע; lit., "the reading of *Shema*"): (a) the daily declaration of faith *(Siddur,* pp. 42-44); (b) the daily stocktaking that accompanies the reading of the *Shema* and certain other passages before retiring at night (pp. 141-147)

Keser (כֶּתֶר): as one of the faculties of the soul, represents the "super-conscious", whereas the other *Sefiros* from *chochmah* onwards correspond to the conscious powers of the soul

Kiddush (קִדּוּשׁ; lit.,"sanctification"): (a) blessing over wine expressing the sanctity of *Shabbos* or a festival; (b) the refreshments following the recital of *Kiddush,* the occasion usually being graced by *divrei* Torah and *niggunim*

kiruv (קֵרוּב; lit.,"bringing near"): the brotherly endeavor of familiarizing a fellow Jew with Torah and *mitzvos;* the verb (with Yid. suffix) is *mekarev-zein*

klafter (Rus./Yid.): pre-Revolutionary unit of linear measure equalling 3 *arshin,* or 1.80 meters

kloiz (קלויז; Yid.): see *shtibl*

klos hanefesh (כְּלוֹת הַנֶּפֶשׁ): expiry of the soul out of spiritual rapture

ko'ach hamaskil (כֹּחַ הַמַּשְׂכִּיל): the superconscious source of the intellect

kochos (כֹּחוֹת; pl. of *ko'ach;* lit., "powers"): faculties of the soul

Kohanim (כֹּהֲנִים; pl. of *Kohen*): "priests"; i.e., the descendants of Aharon

Kohen Gadol (כֹּהֵן גָּדוֹל): High Priest

Kol Nidrei (כָּל נִדְרֵי, lit.,"all vows"): solemn declaration opening the evening service of *Yom Kippur

kometz alef — oh (אָ): formation of the syllable which is traditionally the first lesson in reading Hebrew

kopek (Rus.): small coin

Korban Pesach (קָרְבַּן פֶּסַח): the sacrifice offered in Temple times on the eve of the festival

korech (כּוֹרֵךְ): sandwich of *matzah, *maror* and *charoses* eaten at the *Seder*

kotinke (קאָטינקע; Yid.): silk coat

kri and ksiv (קְרִי וּכְתִיב; Aram.): the way in which a word with variant readings in the Torah should be (respectively) read and written

kvass (Rus.): mild homemade beer

LeChaim! (לְחַיִּים; lit., "To life!"): greeting or blessing exchanged over strong drink

levushim (לְבוּשִׁים; pl. of *levush*: lit., "garments"): the instruments —
viz., thought, speech, and action — which "clothe" (i.e., give
expression to) the intellectual faculties and emotive attributes
of the soul

Likkutei Torah (לִקּוּטֵי תוֹרָה): basic compendium of **maamarim* of the Alter
Rebbe edited by the *Tzemach Tzedek*

limud zechus (לִמּוּד זְכוּת): seeking charitable ways of condoning another's wrongdoing

Lubavitch (lit., "town of love"; Rus.): townlet in Smolensk oblast,
Belorussia, which was the center of *Chabad* Chassidism from
1813, when the Mitteler Rebbe moved there from Liadi, until
1915, when his greatgrandson the Rebbe Rashab left it for
Rostov, after having established the Tomchei Temimim
Yeshivah there in 1897; the name of the township has
remained a synonym for the *Chabad* branch of Chassidism

lulav (לוּלָב): palm-branch, used during the festival of Sukkos for the
mitzvah of the Four Species

maamad (מַעֲמָד; lit., "support"): regular voluntary contribution made
by chassid for the maintenance of his Rebbe's household

maamar (מַאֲמָר; pl., *maamarim*; lit., "word" or [written] article"): in *Chabad*
circles means a formal chassidic discourse first delivered by a
Rebbe

Maariv (מַעֲרִיב): the evening prayer service

maaseh (מַעֲשֶׂה): deed, one of the three **levushim* of the soul

machshavah (מַחֲשָׁבָה): thought, one of the three **levushim* of the soul

maggid (מַגִּיד): preacher, often itinerant

makkif (מַקִּיף; i.e., or *makkif*): see **sovev*

makkifim (abbreviation for אוֹרוֹת מַקִּיפִים; lit., "encompassing lights"):
(a) supernatural revelations (see **sovev*); (b) the *makkifim* of the
soul are its superrational and transcendent faculties (see
*Naran...Chai)

maor (מָאוֹר): luminary; on the light-metaphor, see Schochet, *op. cit.*, p.
814-815

maror (מָרוֹר): the bitter herb eaten in the course of the **Seder*

mashgichim (מַשְׁגִּיחִים; pl. of *mashgiach*): supervisors of studies in a
*yeshivah

Mashiach (מָשִׁיחַ; lit., "the anointed one"): the Messiah

mashke (lit., "beverage"): in chassidic usage signifies sip of strong
drink over which **LeChaim* is said

mashpia (מַשְׁפִּיעַ): mentor of *Chassidus*

maskil (מַשְׂכִּיל; pl. *maskilim*): exponent of **haskalah* *massig* (מַשִׂיג): see *baalei hassagah

matzah (מַצָּה; pl., *matzos*): unleavened bread eaten on *Pesach

matzas mitzvah (מַצַּת מִצְוָה): the *matzah* with which one fulfills the obligation of eating *matzah* on the first night of *Pesach; usually
baked with especial punctiliousness

mayim shelanu (מַיִם שֶׁלָּנוּ; lit.,"water that spent the night"): water drawn
and allowed to cool overnight in preparation for the baking of
matzah

Mazel Tov (מַזָּל טוֹב; lit.,"good luck"): multipurpose expression of
congratulation

Megillah of Esther (מְגִלַּת אֶסְתֵּר): the Biblical Scroll of *Esther*, which
relates the story of Purim

Meir Baal HaNess Fund, Rabbi (קוּפַּת רַבִּי מֵאִיר בַּעַל הַנֵּס): roof organization
incorporating many individual funds for the support of needy
Torah scholars in *Eretz Yisrael*; here refers to Colel Chabad

mekabel (מְקַבֵּל): lit., "recipient"; disciple

mekushar (מְקוּשָׁר): (a) the adjectival form of *hiskashrus; (b) a chassid
who has developed a meaningful spiritual bond with his Rebbe

melamed (מְלַמֵּד; pl., *melamdim*): (a) teacher at Torah school; (b) private
tutor

memaleh (מְמַלֵּא; abbreviation of *or memaleh*, lit., "light that fills," i.e.,
permeates): the mode of divine influence or creative force
which is (as it were) bounded by the finitude of the recipient;
synonymous with *pnimi*, and *or pnimi*; in contrast to *or* *sovev

mensch (מענש; lit., "man"; Yid.): an upstanding person

meshares (מְשָׁרֵת): (a) domestic assistant; (b) beadle

mesirus nefesh (מְסִירוּת נֶפֶשׁ): (a) the power for self-sacrifice innate in
every Jew; (b) devotedness to the point of physical or spiritual
self-sacrifice

metzius (מְצִיאוּת): existence

middah tovah (מִדָּה טוֹבָה): a praiseworthy character trait

*middos*_ (מִדּוֹת; pl. of *middah*): (a) attributes of character; emotions;
mental states; (b) the Divine Attributes (e.g., Mercy)

Midrash (מִדְרָשׁ): (a) any one of the classical collections of the Sages'
homiletical teachings on the Torah; (b) a particular passage
therefrom

mikveh (מִקְוֶה; pl., *mikvaos*): pool for ritual immersion

Minchah (מִנְחָה): the afternoon prayer service

minhag (מִנְהָג; pl., *minhagim*): custom

minyan (מִנְיָן): (a) quorum of at least ten adult males assembled for
prayer or other *mitzvah*; (b) place of public prayer; *shul

misboded (מְתְבּוֹדֵד): one who practices **hisbodedus*

mishnah (מִשְׁנָה; pl., *mishnayos*): any one of the paragraphs collectively comprising the *Mishnah*, and containing seminal statements of law elucidated by the **Gemara*, which together with the *Mishnah* constitutes the *Talmud*

misnaged (מְתְנַגֵּד; pl., *misnagdim*): opponent of Chassidism

mitzvah (מִצְוָה; pl., *mitzvos*): a religious obligation; one of the 613 Commandments

mochin (מוֹחִין; lit., "brains"; Aram.): the intellectual component of divine service

Motzaei [*Shabbos*, etc.] (...מוֹצָאֵי): evening on which a **Shabbos* or **Yom-Tov* ends

Mussaf (מוּסָף): the additional prayer service of Sabbath and other festive days

Mussar (מוּסָר): books of ethical teaching

Naran (נר"ן; an acrostic): Cf. *Bereishis Rabbah* 14:9. *Naran* represents those levels of the soul which are a mere reflection (הֶאָרָה) of the root of the soul above, and which are consciously invested in the body. *Naran* comprises: **nefesh* — the natural, active faculties (*kochos;* lit., "powers") of the soul; **ruach* — the emotive faculties of the soul; and **neshamah* — the intellectual faculties of the soul. *Chai* (ח"י) represents those levels of the soul which reveal the root of the soul above, and when conscious are experienced as encompassing the entirety of the person, being unable to reside locally, as it were, in any particular organ of the body. *Chai* comprises: **chayah*, representing the superrational perception of the soul; and **yechidah*, representing **dveikus*, the cleaving of the soul to its absolute origin, viz., *Atzmus*, the very Being of G-d

nebbich (נעבעך; Yid.): poor fellow

nefesh (נֶפֶשׁ): (a) soul; (b) the lowest of the five levels of the soul (see **Naran...Chai*)

neshamah (נְשָׁמָה): (a) soul; (b) the third of the five levels of the soul (see **Naran...Chai*)

netilas yadayim (נְטִילַת יָדַיִם): ritual washing of the hands

niggun (נִגּוּן; pl., *niggunim*): melody, usually wordless, especially one figuring in divine service

nigleh (נִגְלֶה): the revealed levels of the Torah (e.g. *Talmud* and *Halachah*); in contrast to *nistar*

Nissan (נִיסָן): the month in which the festival of Pesach (Passover) occurs

Nistar (נִסְתָּר): hidden [*tzaddik*]

Nu (נו; Yid.): untranslatable multipurpose word used in conversation (cf., in English, "Well!...") to express a variety of reactions, varying with intonation

nussach (נוּסָח): the prayer rite traditionally followed by a particular group

ohel (אֹהֶל; lit.,"tent"): in chassidic usage means the structure built over the resting place of a *tzaddik*, and frequented by chassidim in prayer

oif kest (אוֹיף קעסט; Yid.): system whereby parents-in-law support young married Torah scholar

oneg (עֹנֶג): pleasure

or (אוֹר; pl., *oros*): light; on the light-metaphor, see Schochet, *op. cit.*, p. 814-815

Orach Chaim (אוֹרַח חַיִּים; lit.,"way of life"): title of the first of the four parts of the *Shulchan Aruch

or makkif (אוֹר מַקִּיף; lit.,"encompassing light"): divine light of a supernatural order (see *sovev)

or pnimi (אוֹר פְּנִימִי; lit.,"permeating light"): see *memaleh

Other Side, the: see *sitra achra

oved (עוֹבֵד): one deeply involved in *avodah

paritz (פְּרִיץ): local squire

parshah (פָּרָשָׁה): the portion of the Torah read publicly each week

Parshas... (...פָּרָשַׁת): the *parshah* of...

Pesach (פֶּסַח): Passover; seven-day festival beginning on 15 Nissan, commemorating the Exodus from Egypt

pesukei dezimrah (פְּסוּקֵי דְזִמְרָה; lit., "verses of praise"; Aram./Heb.): the bracket of Psalms and other passages in the daily Morning Prayer whose prelude is *Baruch She'amar* and whose finale is *Yishtabach*

pidyon [*nefesh*] (פִּדְיוֹן נֶפֶשׁ, abbreviated פ"נ; lit., "redemption of the soul"): note, accompanied by donation for charity, requesting Rebbe to intercede in prayer for the writer

Pirkei Avos (פִּרְקֵי אָבוֹת; lit., "the chapters of the fathers"): the Talmudic tractate *(Avos)* best known as "Ethics of the Fathers"

pitak (Rus.): coin worth five kopeks

Plishtim (פְּלִשְׁתִּים): Philistines

pnimi (פְּנִימִי; lit., "inward"): (a) (i.e., *or pnimi*): see *memaleh; (b) a man of inner integrity

pnimiyus (פְּנִימִיּוּת; lit.,"inwardness"): (a) the innermost levels of a person or thing (cf. *chitzoniyus); (b) inner integrity

Purim (פּוּרִים; lit., "lots"): one-day festival falling on 14 Adar and commemorating the miraculous salvation of the Jews of the Persian Empire in the 4th cent. B.C.E

rabbanim (רַבָּנִים): pl. of **rav*

rasha (רָשָׁע): a wicked person

rav (רַב; pl., *rabbanim*): rabbi; Torah teacher

ratzon (רָצוֹן): will

rebbitzin (רעביצין; Yid.): wife of *rav* or Rebbe

re'usa deliba (רְעוּתָא דְלִבָּא; lit., "the desire of the heart"; Aram.): the innate and unbounded longing for G-d always present and awake in the innermost point of the heart of every Jew

Rosh Chodesh (רֹאשׁ חֹדֶשׁ; lit., "the head of the month"): either one or two semi-festive days marking the beginning of the month

Rosh HaShanah (רֹאשׁ הַשָּׁנָה; lit., "the head of the year"): the New Year festival, falling on 1 and 2 Tishrei

ru'ach (רוּחַ): (a) soul; (b) the second (in ascending order) of the five levels of the soul (see **Naran...Chai*)

ruchniyus (רוּחָנִיּוּת): spirituality; spiritual reality (cf. **gashmiyus*)

Seder (סֵדֶר; pl., *Sedarim*; lit., "order"): the order of service observed at home on the first night of Pesach (and outside *Eretz Yisrael* on the first two nights)

Seder Hishtalshelus (סֵדֶר הִשְׁתַּלְשְׁלוּת): the scheme wherein the descent (so to speak) and progressive contraction of the divine light gives rise to the existence of increasingly material worlds

Sefer Torah (סֵפֶר תּוֹרָה): a Torah scroll

Sefiros (סְפִירוֹת): divine attributes or emanations which manifest themselves in each of the Four Worlds, and are the source of the ten faculties *(kochos)* of the soul

segulos (סְגוּלוֹת; pl. of *segulah*): spiritual remedies; talismans

seichel (שֵׂכֶל): the intellectual process, comprising **chochmah*, **binah* and **daas* (the acronym of which is *Chabad*); sometimes referred to as **mochin* (lit., "brains"), or as *immos* ("mothers"), being the source of the **middos*

Selichos (סְלִיחוֹת): penitential prayers read in the days preceding the Days of Awe

seudah (סְעוּדָה): meal, esp. a festive one

seudah mafsekes (סְעוּדָה מַפְסֶקֶת): last meal eaten before a fast

seudas (סְעוּדַת): *seudah* of..

Shabbos (שַׁבָּת): the Sabbath

Shabbos Chazon (שַׁבַּת חֲזוֹן): the *Shabbos* before **Tishah BeAv* (from the *Haftorah*, Isa. 1:1 ff.)

Shabbos HaGadol (שַׁבָּת הַגָּדוֹל): usually signifies the *Shabbos* preceding the festival of Pesach, but here borrowed in its literal sense — "a great *Shabbos* "

Shabbos Mevarchim (שַׁבָּת מְבָרְכִים; lit., "the *Shabbos* when one blesses"): the *Shabbos* preceding Rosh Chodesh (the New Moon), marked by a prayer for the forthcoming month

Shabbos Nachamu (שַׁבָּת נַחֲמוּ): the *Shabbos* following the fast of Tishah BeAv, when the passage beginning "*Nachamu*" (Isa. 40:1) is read as the *Haftorah*

Shacharis (שַׁחֲרִית): the morning prayer service

Shalom (שָׁלוֹם; lit., "Peace!"): greeting exchanged on meeting and parting

Shalom Aleichem (שָׁלוֹם עֲלֵיכֶם; lit., "Peace be upon you!"): greeting exchanged when meeting

shalom bayis (שְׁלוֹם בַּיִת): domestic harmony

shammes (שַׁמָּשׁ): synagogue caretaker

Shavuos (שָׁבֻעוֹת; lit., "weeks"): festival commemorating the Giving of the Torah at Sinai; in *Eretz Yisrael* falling on 6 Sivan, and in the Diaspora on 6-7 Sivan

shechitah (שְׁחִיטָה): the slaughtering of kosher meat

Shehecheyanu (שֶׁהֶחֱיָנוּ; lit., "Who has granted us life"): blessing pronounced on seasonal and other occasions for thanksgiving

sheliach tzibbur (שְׁלִיחַ צִבּוּר; lit., "emissary of the congregation"): worshiper leading a prayer service

Shema, the Reading of: see *Kerias Shema

Shemini Atzeres (שְׁמִינִי עֲצֶרֶת): festival immediately following Sukkos; in *Eretz Yisrael* observed for one day and coinciding with *Simchas Torah, and in the Diaspora extending into a second day which is known as Simchas Torah

shemurah (שְׁמוּרָה; lit., "guarded"; abbrev. for *shemurah matzah*, more grammatically *matzah shemurah*): *matzah* made from wheat or flour that has been guarded with especial care against dampness and consequent leavening

shidduch (שִׁדּוּךְ): matrimonial match

shiur (שִׁעוּר): Torah lesson or study session

Shivah-Asar BeTammuz (שִׁבְעָה עָשָׂר בְּתַמּוּז; lit., "the Seventeenth of Tammuz"): fast commemorating five calamities, including the breach of the walls of Jerusalem during the Roman siege

shluchei mitzvah (שְׁלוּחֵי מִצְוָה; pl. of *sheliach mitzvah*): persons on a mission to do a *mitzvah*

Shmos (שְׁמוֹת): the Book of *Exodus*

shochatim (שׁוֹחֲטִים; pl. of *shochet*): ritual slaughterers

shofar (שׁוֹפָר): ram's horn sounded on Rosh HaShanah

shtetl (שטעטל; pl., *shtetlach*; Yid.): East European township

shtibl (שטיבל; pl., *shtiblach*; lit., "little house"; Yid.): informal place of public worship

shul (שול; Yid.): synagogue

Shulchan Aruch (שֻׁלְחָן עָרוּךְ; lit., "a set table"): the standard Code of Jewish Law compiled by R. Yosef Caro in the mid-sixteenth century

Shulchan Aruch HaRav (שֻׁלְחָן עָרוּךְ הָרַב): the edition of the Code of Jewish Law which the Alter Rebbe began to compile in 5530 (תק"ל; 1770)

sichah (שִׂיחָה; pl., *sichos*): an informal Torah talk delivered by a Rebbe (cf. *maamar)

Siddur (סִדּוּר; lit., "order"): prayer book

simchah (שִׂמְחָה; lit., "joy"): an occasion for celebration

Simchas Beis HaShoevah (שִׂמְחַת בֵּית הַשּׁוֹאֵבָה; lit., "the rejoicing of the place of the water-drawing"): ceremony during *Sukkos in Temple times, recalled today by appropriate celebrations

Simchas Torah (שִׂמְחַת תּוֹרָה; lit., "the rejoicing of the Torah"): festival immediately following *Sukkos, on which the public reading of the Torah is annually concluded and recommenced; in *Eretz Yisrael* coincides with *Shemini Atzeres, and in the Diaspora falls on the following day

sitra achra (סְטְרָא אָחֳרָא; lit., "the other side"; Aram.): that aspect of the universe which is opposite to the aspect of holiness; the root of evil

siyyum (סִיּוּם; lit., "completion"): celebration marking one's completion of a Talmudic tractate

sovev (סוֹבֵב; abbreviation of *or sovev*, lit., "encompassing light"): the mode of divine influence or creative force which, being infinite, cannot be bounded by the finitude of the recipient, which it is therefore said to "encompass", i.e., transcend; synonymous with *makkif*, and *or makkif*; in contrast to *or* *memaleh

sukkah (סֻכָּה; lit., "booth"): temporary dwelling roofed with vegetation in which one lives during the festival of *Sukkos

Sukkos (סֻכּוֹת; lit., "Booths"): seven-day festival beginning on 15 Tishrei, taking its name from the temporary dwelling in which one lives during this period, and marked also by the *mitzvah* of the Four Species

tallis (טַלִּית): shawl worn during prayer and fringed with *tzitzis* (cf.

Num. 15:37-40)

tallis katan (טַלִית קָטָן; lit.,"small *tallis*"): four-cornered garment worn constantly by males, and fringed with *tzitzis* (cf. Num. 15:37-40)

Talmud (תַּלְמוּד): the basic compendium of Jewish law, thought, and Biblical commentary; when unspecified refers to the *Talmud Bavli*, the edition developed in Babylonia, and edited at end of the 5th century C.E.; the *Talmud Yerushalmi* is the edition compiled in *Eretz Yisrael* at end of the 4th century C.E.

tamim (תָּמִים): see **temimim*

Tanach (תַּנַ"ךְ): acronym for Torah (i.e., the Five Books of Moses), *Nevi'im* (the Prophets), and *Kesuvim* (the Writings; i.e., the Hagiographa)

tanna (תַּנָּא): authority of the 1st-2nd cents. quoted in the **Mishnah*

Tanya (תַּנְיָא): the Alter Rebbe's basic exposition of **Chabad *Chassidus;* "*Tanya*" is the initial word of the book, which is also called *Likutei Amarim* ("Collected Discourses") and *Sefer shel Beinonim* ("The Book of the Intermediates")

Targum (תַּרְגּוּם; lit., "translation"): the classic Aramaic translation and paraphrase of the *Tanach* by the second-century proselyte, Onkelos

tefillin (תְּפִלִּין): small black leather cubes containing parchment scrolls inscribed with *Shema Yisrael* and other Biblical passages, bound to the arm and forehead and worn by men at weekday morning prayers; "phylacteries"

Tehillim (תְּהִלִּים; lit., "praises"): the Book of *Psalms*

tekios (תְּקִיעוֹת): the blasts of the *shofar*

temimim (תְּמִימִים; pl. of *tamim*): students past or present of one of the senior *yeshivos* of the Lubavitch branch of Chassidism, which are known as **Tomchei Temimim*

tena'im (תְּנָאִים; lit., "conditions"): betrothal agreement

Ten Days of Penitence (עֲשֶׂרֶת יְמֵי תְּשׁוּבָה): the days that open with **Rosh HaShanah* and are climaxed by **Yom Kippur*

teshuvah (תְּשׁוּבָה; lit., "return"): repentance

teshuvah ila'ah (תְּשׁוּבָה עִילָאָה; Heb./Aram.): higher-level repentance

teshuvah tata'ah (תְּשׁוּבָה תַּתָּאָה; Heb./Aram.): lower-level repentance

tevilah (טְבִילָה): immersion in a **mikveh*

Tikkun (תִּקּוּן; lit., "correction, restitution, reformation"): for its meaning in *Chassidus*, see Schochet, *op cit.*, p. 876

Tikkun Chatzos (תִּקּוּן חֲצוֹת; lit., "midnight service"): an optional devotional exercise lamenting the Destruction of the *Beis HaMikdash* and the exile of the Divine Presence on a cosmic level

Tikkunim (תִּקּוּנִים): abbreviated title of the kabbalistic work whose full title is *Tikkunei Zohar*

Tishah BeAv (תִּשְׁעָה בְּאָב; lit., "the Ninth of Av"): fast commemorating the destruction of both Temples

Tohu (תֹּהוּ; lit., "chaos"): for its meaning in *Chassidus*, see Schochet, *op. cit.*, p. 876

Tohu vaVohu (תֹהוּ וָבֹהוּ; lit., "without form and empty"; cf. *Gen.* 1:2): as above

Tomchei Temimim (תּוֹמְכֵי תְמִימִים): (a) the *yeshivah* founded in Lubavitch in 1897 by the Rebbe Rashab; (b) one of its subsequent offshoots

Tosafos (תּוֹסָפוֹת; lit., "supplements"): classical commentaries on the *Talmud* beginning to appear in the mid-twelfth century

treifah (טְרֵפָה): non-kosher food

Turim (טוּרִים; abbrev. for *Arba'ah Turim*; lit., "rows"): monumental halachic code by R. Yaakov ben Asher (d. 1340), known as *Baal HaTurim*

tzaddik (צַדִּיק; pl., *tzaddikim*): (a) completely righteous individual; (b) Rebbe

tzimtzum (צִמְצוּם): the self-limitation of the infinite and emanating divine light by progressive degrees of contraction, condensation and concealment, and making possible the creation of finite and physical substances; see Schochet, *op. cit.*, p. 818-824

tzitzis (צִיצִת): see **tallis*

tzveier (צווייער; Yid.): Russian coin worth two kopeks

Vayikra (וַיִּקְרָא): the Book of *Leviticus*

viorst (Rus.): a unit of distance, of between 1 kilometer and 2/3 mile

vort (וָאָרט; lit., "word"; Yid.): a teaching which is brief, quotable and insightful

World of Truth (עוֹלָם הָאֱמֶת, Heb.; עָלְמָא דִקְשׁוֹט, Aram.): the Hereafter

Worlds (עוֹלָמוֹת), the Four: the main stages in the creative process resulting from **tzimtzum*; in descending order: **Atzilus, *Beriah, *Yetzirah* and **Asiyah*, often referred to by their acronym as אֲבִי"ע; see Schochet, *op. cit.*, p. 852ff.

yarmulke (יארמולקע; Yid.): skullcap

yechidah (יְחִידָה): the innermost of the five levels of the soul (see **Naran...Chai*)

yechidus (יְחִידוּת): private interview at which a chassid seeks guidance and enlightenment from his Rebbe

Yerushalmi (יְרוּשַׁלְמִי; lit., "Jerusalemite"): see **Talmud*

yeshivah (יְשִׁיבָה; pl., *yeshivos*): Torah academy for advanced students

Yetzirah, the World of (עוֹלָם הַיְצִירָה; lit., "the World of Formation"): the third (in descending order) of the Four *Worlds

Yevsektzia (lit., "the Jewish section"; Rus.): notoriously antireligious unit within the Communist Party

yichuda ila'a (יְחוּדָא עִילָּאָה; lit., "upper-level Unity"; Aram.): the state of reality transcending time and space. A perception (Yid.: *derher*) of this means the uplifting of reality into the Unity of *HaShem*

Yid (איד; Yid.): Jew

yom chinuch (יוֹם חִנּוּךְ; lit., "the day of training"): the day a boy wears *tefillin* for the first time

Yom Kippur (יוֹם כִּפּוּר): the Day of Atonement, fast day falling on 10 Tishrei and climaxing the Days of Awe

Yom-Tov (יוֹם טוֹב): festival

yoshvei ohel (יוֹשְׁבֵי אֹהֶל; lit., "dwellers in the tent [of Torah study]"): full-time scholars

yoshvim (יוֹשְׁבִים; pl. of *yoshev*): see *zitzers

yud (י): the tenth letter of the Hebrew alphabet

Yud-Beis Tammuz (י"ב תַּמּוּז; lit., "the twelfth of Tammuz"): chassidic festival marking the anniversary of the release from Stalinist incarceration (1927) of the Rebbe Rayatz, author of the present work, as well as his birthday (1880)

Yud-Tes Kislev (י"ט כִּסְלֵו; a date): chassidic festival celebrating the liberation of the Alter Rebbe from capital sentence and imprisonment in Petersburg (19-20 Kislev 5559/1798), after being slandered to the czarist authorities by his opponents, the *misnagdim*

yungelait (יונגעלייט; pl. of *yungerman*; lit., "young folk"; Yid.): in chassidic parlance signifies adult members of the brotherhood of any age whatever — on the confident assumption that in spirit, chassidim remain forever young

zeide (זיידע; Yid.): grandfather

zitzer (זיצער; pl., *zitzers*; lit., "sitter"; Yid.): full-time adult Torah student

Zohar (זֹהַר): basic work of the *Kabbalah*

הוצאת ספרים

קרני הוד תורה

קה

ליובאוויטש